Turnbull Jeffrey Partnership

Concepts of
# URBAN DESIGN

# Concepts of
# URBAN DESIGN

DAVID GOSLING BA DIP TP M ARCH (MIT) MCP (YALE) RIBA MRTPI ARIAS FRSA
BARRY MAITLAND BA (CANTAB) DIP ARCH MA PHD (SHEFFIELD) RIBA

ACADEMY EDITIONS · LONDON / ST. MARTIN'S PRESS · NEW YORK

First published in Great Britain in 1984 by
Academy Editions 7/8 Holland Street London W8

Copyright © 1984 David Gosling
and Barry Maitland
*All rights reserved*

Published in the United States of America in 1984
by St. Martin's Press
175 Fifth Avenue
New York NY 10010

Library of Congress Catalog Card Number 83-50703
ISBN 0-312-16121-2 (cloth)
ISBN 0-312-16122-0 (paper) USA only

Edited and designed by Frank Russell
with Richard Cheatle and Vicky Wilson

Printed and bound in Hong Kong

## PHOTOGRAPHIC CREDITS

Aerofilms Ltd., 74 top left; ALCAN, 49 top and right, 50 top and bottom; Peter Aldington, 111 top centre and right; Salman Al-Sadairy, 151; Emilio Ambasz, 121, 122, 131 top; Donald Appleyard, 45, 48 top right; Archigram (Ron Herron), 36 top, 63 bottom right; *Architectural Design* Magazine/Derek Walker, 39 top; Arrowstreet Inc., 72, 73; Arup Associates, 99; ASSIST (David Simister/Vernon Monaghan), 59 top; Associated Press, 123; Ian Athfield, 85; Leonardo Benevolo, *The History of the City*, Scolar Press, 12; Sefik Birkiye and Patrick Kelly, 104 bottom right; Blackpool Pleasure Beach Company, 113 right; V. Bogakas, 30; Alvin Boyarsky, 147 left top and bottom; Brecht-Einzig, 98 top, 111 top centre and right; Geoffrey Broadbent, 76; Neave Browne, 75; Building Design Partnership, 101 bottom; Martin Charles, 75; Cinco Por Infinitus Publishers, 44 top; Peter Cook, 62 left, 63 top left, centre and bottom right, 120; Lucio Costa, 22 top left; Christopher Cross, 146; Gordon Cullen, 6, 49, 50 top left, 51 left, 60, 132, 150; Cumbernauld Development Corporation, 56; Richard Dinsdale, 18, 22 right top and bottom, 79 top, 90 right, 97, 111 bottom right, 119 bottom left; Bob Dunlop, 41 top; EMBRATUR, 13 bottom, 16 top, 107 top left; Ralph Erskine, 68, 91 top left and right; John Ferguson, 50 bottom left, 113 bottom left, 148 bottom, 149 bottom, 150; Foster Associates, 98 bottom; Fotozenitale, 100 bottom left; Ulrich Franzen/Lionel Freedman, 66 top; Keither Gibson, 67 bottom left; Terry Gilliam/Eyre Methuen Ltd., 44 bottom; Michael Gold and Peter Baker, 90 left; David Gosling, 15, 16 top, 17, 20, 21, 23, 37 bottom, 40, 41 top, 43, 46, 47, 48 left, 57 right, 58 bottom left and right, 78, 79 bottom left, 82, 84 bottom, 109 top, 112, 113 right, 114 left, 115 top left, 126 centre and bottom, 148 top left, bottom, 149 bottom, 150 bottom; Miriam Gosling, 6; Michael Graves, 116; Cedric Green, 68; Vittorio Gregotti, 100 bottom left; Ara Guler, 28 top right; Nicholas Habraken, 38 top left; Rod Hackney, 59 bottom; Hall Photography, 57 centre and bottom left; Zvi Hecker, 119 bottom right; Herman Hertz berger 131 bottom Geoffrey Holland, 97; Irvine Development Corporation, 57 (with John Mills, 57, model; with Hall Photography, 57 centre and bottom left); Arata Isozaki, 36 bottom right; Italian Tourist Board, 29 top left; Allan B. Jacobs, 110; *Japan Architect*, 55 top right; Kikutake & Associates, 54, 55 bottom; Leon Krier, 103 centre and bottom right, 105, 135 left; Rob Krier, 103 top, 134; Lucien Kroll, 128; Brian Lawson/GABLE, 51 right; LDDC Design Team, 149 top right; LTV Aerospace Corporation, 66 bottom; Kevin Lynch, 48 top right; Richard MacCormac and Peter Jameison, 90; Mitsuo Matsuoka/Kikutake and Associates, 55 top right; Barry Maitland, 25, 28 top left and bottom, 29 top right, 31, 58 centre, 77 bottom, 108, 119 top, 149 top left, 154; Michael McKinnell, 100 top left and right; Richard Meier, 77 top; John Mills, 41 bottom, 57 (model); Mobil North Sea Ltd., 55 top left; Heinz Mohl, 124 bottom; Moira & Moira, 57 top left; Carlos Nelson dos Santos, 83; Wolf Pearlman, 119 bottom left; Cesar Pelli, 101 top; Colin Penn, 81; M.V. Posokhin, 125; Cedric Price, 38 bottom; Puschino New Town Corporation, 79; Richard Rogers, 62 top right, 98 top; RMJM/Crown Copyright, 67 bottom left; M.M.M. Roberto Associados, 84 top; Aldo Rossi, 106; Colin Rowe, 117, bottom; Runcorn Development Corporation/John Mils, 66 centre; L. Savioli, 102 top; Sheffield University Photo Lab (Architecture), 69 bottom, 148 top right; Paolo Soleri, 37 top; SPADEM (Design & Artists Copyright Society), 13 top, 19; Francois Spoerry, 124 top; Stadsingeniørens Direktorat, Copenhagen, 11; James Stirling Michael Wilford & Associates, 71, 87, 88, 89, 102 bottom, 111 left, 117 top, 135 right; Sundahl, 91 top right; Peter Szmuk, 102 top; Eva Szymanska, 80; Minoru Takeyama, 126 top left and right; Tivoli Ltd., 114 top and bottom right; Bernard Tschumi, 127, 133 right, 147 top right; Richard Turner, 115 top centre; O.M. Ungers, 104 top and bottom left; Derek Walker, 115 top right; Roger Walker, 129 bottom; James Wines/SITE, 129 top, 130.

*Front cover*

*Left:* Giambattista Nolli, plan of Rome, Italy, 1748 (see page 42);

*Right:* James Stirling, Michael Wilford and Associates, competition design for an administrative centre for Tuscany, Italy, 1977 (see page 102).

# CONTENTS

*Gordon Cullen, drawing
of Orléans, France, 1975.*

# INTRODUCTION

THERE IS A WIDELY HELD VIEW THAT PLANNING methods over the last three decades have failed to produce a satisfactory physical environment. These methods have resulted in a proliferation of land-use plans, traffic studies and economic and demographic surveys, while, more recently, sophisticated computer-modelling techniques have been used to optimize the land-use matrix. But all this has little to do with the way in which the city dweller actually perceives, uses and enjoys his environment. It has become apparent in recent years that the physical development of world cities has been going wrong and there seems to be considerable uncertainty as to what the logical priorities should now be.

The belief that, for all our investment in the complexity of individual buildings on the one hand and in elaborate engineering infrastructures on the other, we have failed to achieve a humane and coherent physical setting for social life at a time when the abstract setting of that life is increasingly bureaucratized and constrained, is not a new one. Camillo Sitte's critique in 1889 identified not a lack of planning controls, but the impoverished nature of urban design as the principal obstruction to progress: 'We are confused and disturbed because our cities fall so short of artistic merit. In seeking sensible solutions we are bewildered when, on every occasion, "block plans" are brought out for technical discussion as though the problem were purely mechanical in its nature.'[1] Although differing greatly in their judgement as to what would constitute 'artistic merit', a considerable number of writers and designers in the first half of this century developed Sitte's analysis of the design problem posed by public space, an investigation which culminated in the influential studies by Kevin Lynch in the United States and Gordon Cullen in Britain in the late 1950s.[2]

To this general background of concern with the form of the modern city, two developments in the 1960s brought a new urgency. The first of these related to changes in the training of the designers who would be concerned with the problem, and which threatened to aggravate the difficulties of achieving coherent solutions; for if earlier design attitudes had seemed crude and mechanistic, the possibility now arose that the design professions would be further fragmented by selection and training into mutually uncomprehending groups. Adopting policies which were also taken up in many other countries, both architectural and town planning professional institutes in Britain opted for separate full-time, science-based University courses for training students. This dissociation of two of the professions most immediately concerned with the design of the urban environment gave rise to misgivings, expressed by the architectural institution, the RIBA, in 1970 in the form of a report calling for people trained specifically in urban design, and incidentally offering a definition of the scope of that term as follows:

'Urban design is an integral part of the process of city and regional planning. It is primarily and essentially three-dimensional design but must also deal with the non-visual aspects of environment such as noise, smell or feelings of danger and safety, which contribute significantly to the character of an area. Its major characteristic is the arrangement of the physical objects and human activities which make up the environment; this space and the relationships of elements in it is essentially external, as distinct from internal space. Urban design includes a concern for the relationship of new development to existing city form as much as to the social, political and economic demands and resources available. It is equally concerned with the relationship of different forms of movement to urban development.'[3]

A somewhat more memorable definition was offered by Reyner Banham in his book *Megastructure*, where, having noted this growing recognition during the 1960s of an interdisciplinary gap between architecture and planning, he suggested that the intermediate field of urban design was concerned with 'urban situations about half a mile square'.[4]

Banham's book is relevant also in drawing attention to the second factor in the 1960s which gave a particular urgency to the need to find appropriate techniques and models of urban design. This was the unprecedented scale of urban redevelopment programmes which now took hold in the industrialized countries, which, together with an accelerating rate of urbanization in the developing countries, appeared to undermine the terms and patterns in which urban forms were conventionally understood. In the former case, a new scale of development agency, in both private and public sectors, made it possible to consider whole urban quarters as single design problems, undertaken by one developer, one design team and one contractor. The conventional distinction between the building and the city was thus called into question, along with assumptions about the ways in which change and growth are accommodated in the city fabric. Whether for economic or administrative reasons, the new mechanisms of development tended to exaggerate the tendency of city areas to functional specialization, and a picture thus emerged of large, single-use increments of development, of radically different form to the surrounding fabric which was blighted by the expectation of future extensions of the new pattern and by the road and parking provisions which supported it. The status of 'public' areas within the new precincts (whether shopping, office, residential, educational or whatever) was ambiguous, being often closed off at night and patrolled by private security organizations.

The need to reaffirm the primacy of a common, social pattern of spaces in the city to which these developments gave rise was no less great in those parts of the world where the massive immigration of rural populations to the city threatened its fabric in different ways. It might be argued that the priorities in a country like Brazil, for instance, should be concerned more with the solution of grave economic issues and social injustices than with the niceties of urban design, but this implies a narrow, cosmetic view of the subject belied by the experience of communities in the Third World. The traditional *favela* (shanty-town) system of Brazil, or the *barriadas* of Peru, have a coherent physical structure—for all their *ad hoc* construction and insanitary conditions—and perhaps more importantly a coherent social structure. Based upon principles of self-determination in terms of both physical and social development, they contrast markedly with the authoritarian government plans for their replacement by massive, inhuman multi-storey *conjuntos*. The documentation by John Turner[5] and others of the disruptive and alienating effects of these plans forms an indictment of their failure in urban design, as well as economic and social terms. There are general lessons to be learnt from the urban organization of the *favelas* and *barriadas* as there are from the examples of the urban structures of Florence and Boston analysed by Lynch, or the country market towns cited by Cullen.

Although the 1973 energy crisis, with its subsequent effect upon the scale of development programmes, has changed the terms in which the

problem is discussed and has suppressed some of its more exaggerated features, yet the need to devise valid design philosophies for 'urban situations about half a mile square', that is, at the immediately tangible scale of the quarter, remains as urgent as ever. This book is an attempt to examine the main responses to that need as they have emerged in recent years, to look at the problems and arguments which have generated them, and to

Favela, *Botafogo, Rio de Janeiro, Brazil.*

consider the directions which now seem open to us. It cannot stand as a complete survey of post-war urban design projects, since such a study would necessarily be monumental. Rather, it aims to provide a selection of relevant projects within the limitations imposed by availability of source material and its instructiveness in providing a framework of contrast. And where the authors' own works are illustrated, the intention is certainly

not to suggest that these are ideal solutions, but rather attempted applications of some of the original design theories.

Though a part of this book is devoted to urban problems, it is not intended that the discussion of critical social, economic or other issues should establish a pessimistic view of urban development. Rather, the intention is to set a realistic and technical background for the discussion of the varied and often opposing directions in urban design which follows and which forms the central objective of the book.

Despite a lack of clarity as to the function and status of the term 'urban design', there remains a widespread conviction that there exists a deep need arising out of a weakness, an omission at the boundaries of architecture and town planning. The recent resurgence of speculation and inquiry in the field, as exemplified by a spate of projects and competitions, and the renewal of interest in it by designers of a much wider range of sympathies than hitherto, are responses both to that weakness and also to the state of uncertainty in which those two disciplines now find themselves.

There is a hope that the heat now generated by activity at their common boundary might feed back into the parent disciplines as a source of new ideas and vitality. It is possible to envisage the regeneration of town planning through a new concern for its physical manifestations at the scale of the quarter. Similarly, for architecture, it is believed that the Modern Movement proposition that the internal logic of the programme is the primary source of building form might be modified by a complementary proposition regarding the integrity of its counterform, public space, and that this new dialectic might supply a significant element in a revitalized modern architecture. In the context of these hopes, this review of the varied directions and possibilities of urban design may provide a useful reference for future, and much needed, developments.

**NOTES**
1 Camillo Sitte, *The Art of Building Cities* (trans. Charles T. Stewart), Reinhold Publishing Corporation, New York 1945, p. 53.
2 Kevin Lynch, *The Image of the City*, MIT Press, Cambridge, Mass. 1960 and Gordon Cullen, *The Concise Townscape*, The Architectural Press, London 1961.
3 Royal Institute of British Architects, *Board of Education, Report of the Urban Design Diploma Working Group*, May 1970, p. 3.
4 Reyner Banham, *Megastructure: Urban Futures of the Recent Past*, Thames and Hudson, London 1976, p. 130.
5 John Turner, *RIBA Journal*, February 1974.

# PART ONE
# THE NATURE
# OF THE PROBLEM

BEFORE SETTING OUT TO REVIEW THE GREAT VARIETY of urban design theories and their applications which have emerged in recent years, it would seem desirable to establish just which problems lie within the scope of urban design, and which it may be expected to solve.

We have suggested that urban design is concerned with the physical form of the public realm over a limited physical area of the city and that it therefore lies between the two well-established design scales of architecture, which is concerned with the physical form of the private realm of the individual building, and town and regional planning, which is concerned with the organization of the public realm in its wider context. Inadequate as this delimitation is, it does at least indicate the difficulty of defining specifically 'urban design problems'. On the one hand, the material of urban design is the public aspect of private architecture, a notoriously diverse, multivalent thing, both art and science and as richly layered with social, economic and symbolic preoccupations as the personalities it serves. On the other hand, urban design is a particular issue within the context of the city and, as everyone now knows, the words 'city' and 'problem' are practically synonymous.

It has been suggested that the inevitable identification of urban problems is incorrect. Paul Davidoff has argued, for example, that: 'The concern with urbanism is misplaced. The real crisis of our times is not an urban crisis. Instead the crucial problem is a national problem, an international problem, a social problem. It is the fact of great social injustice.'[1] Nevertheless, in terms such as 'urban poverty', 'urban wasteland', or 'urban violence', the word 'urban' is widely taken to be not simply a description of the location of a problem, but a deeply implicated factor. Given the circumstances of urban development in recent history, this suspicion is natural enough. The spectacular growth and subsequent metamorphosis of cities which has universally accompanied the industrialization of countries forms a background of such extensive disruption and change that discussion of urban problems becomes meaningless without some recognition of it. The broad pattern of that background has been extensively studied and documented. The distinctive 'S-curve' of urbanization was first exhibited in Britain, where a period of gradual city growth in the late eighteenth century was followed in the nineteenth by dramatic increases, which, by the end of that century, subsided. This cycle was followed in turn by other industrializing countries. Thus in Britain the most rapid rise in the proportion of people living in cities of 100,000 or more lasted from 1811 to 1851, in the United States from 1820 to 1890 and in Greece from 1879 to 1921.[2] In general, the rate of this urbanization has increased as time has passed, so that the change from 10% to 30% of the population living in cities of 100,000 or more, which took 79 years in England and Wales, took only 66 in the United States, 48 in Germany, 36 in Japan and 26 in Australia.[3] At the same time, this proportional shift from country to city has been accompanied by a growing increase in the absolute numbers involved. It has been estimated, for example, that in Asia, Africa and Latin America some 200 million people made this move in the last ten years alone.[4]

The urbanization of a country is said to be completed when about 80% of its population is accommodated in its cities, a stage reached in Britain at the beginning of the twentieth century. Yet the period of dramatic growth was not then followed by stability. On the contrary, the cities of fully urbanized countries have continued to undergo violent transformations as they have attempted both to contain internal contradictions inherited from the first stage, and to accommodate new sources of instability.

If the city has thus come to be regarded as the focus of all the most intractable of society's problems, and itself as a collective problem of unprecedented complexity and scale, it would be convenient if we could in some way isolate urban design questions from this context. Two opposing views of the relevance of urban design do indeed offer such an escape. According to the first, the relationship between spatial and social order is so compelling that we may design an ideal society by designing an ideal city form for it, while according to the second, the relationship is so weak as to make architectural solutions irrelevant to the solution of social issues. Both of these positions allow a limited view of urban design as a largely formal activity which can be pursued independently of the problematic context of existing cities.

It is our view that the examples which follow illustrate the weakness of both these positions, which isolate one aspect of the city, the design of its built form, and attribute exaggeratedly high or low significance to it. The impossibility of isolating physical design in this way is suggested by observers in other fields. In particular, the epistemological positions of both Marx and Piaget emphasize the interdependence of subject and object in this sense, so that, as put by the latter: 'Whereas other animals cannot alter themselves except by changing their species, man can transform himself by transforming the world and can structure himself by constructing structures; and these structures are his own, for they are not entirely predestined either from within or without.'[5] Similarly Marx, in *Capital*, wrote: 'by acting on the external world and changing it, [man] at the same time changes his own nature'.[6]

Although a proper discussion of the many problems which beset the city cannot be given in this book, it is however necessary to give some outline of the main themes, since they form an inevitable context from which a valid urban design philosophy cannot isolate itself. From such an outline, the particular aspects of those problems which most concern the urban designer may emerge.

## 1.1  THE ECONOMIC BACKGROUND

THE ECONOMIST J.K. GALBRAITH HAS REMARKED THAT all of the problems of the city can be solved by the sufficient application of just one thing, and that thing is money. Such a view, of the city as a thing to be improved or cured by financial means, hides the fact that the city is itself a financial device, so important to the national economy that some authorities would regard the latter as little more than the sum of the urban economies it comprises. The economic functions of the city are so fundamental to its purposes that their symbolization in terms of land values forms a precise shorthand description of its differentiated structure. It is a commonplace that the form of the modern city tends towards a three-dimensional representation of land values, most graphically in the case of Manhattan, while a land value model, such as that constructed for the city of Copenhagen, is itself a caricature of contemporary urban form. Again, a general pattern of urban land values, such as that suggested by Brian Berry,[7] provides a vivid overall picture of urban structure, with ridges of higher value radiating from the centre, and punctuated with local peaks along their way. Such a pattern

draws attention to the tendency of high-value uses to cluster and to expose favoured positions within the circulation networks of the city. At a more detailed level, urban rent theory[8] provides a similarly graphic demonstration of the way in which central areas are used, offering a model closely related to both density of development and intensity of pedestrian flow.

Where the 'highest and best use' is shopping, the sensitivity of that use to subtle differentiations in pedestrian flow, influenced by visibility of attractions, shapes of streets, breaks in frontage and so on, produces a particularly intense interrelationship between urban form and land values which can express itself in the smallest details of the building design. This particular responsiveness of shopping uses to surrounding pressures makes their distribution another important indicator of urban structure. In nineteenth-century, working-class districts of English industrial towns, for example, small shop units proliferated freely through the pattern of terrace houses. Their location as 'corner shops' at all significant street corners, their clustering at more important cross-roads, and their grouping as continuous chains along the main roads, provides an eloquent representation of the patterns of movement through the community.

For the same reasons, shopping uses are often the first to reflect dynamic shifts in the pattern of the city economy, a potent source of urban problems. Many old cities display signs of such shifts, which may have occurred slowly and over a long period of time. The whole city centre, or CBD (Central Business District) may have migrated gradually across the city as in the case of Paris, or, as in London, the main shopping centre may have abandoned its original location to the highest land-value uses of offices in the City, and set off for the West End. In recent times, however, the pattern of change and response has become much more rapid and widespread. Agergard, Olsen and Allpass[9] have suggested that it adopts a spiral form, in which changes in economic conditions encourage the evolution of new trading patterns and shop types. These emerge first as low-cost operations, competing successfully against existing forms on cost grounds, and then against each other on increasingly sophisticated terms of assortment and service. This second competitive phase causes the operation to move up-market, leaving an opportunity at a later point in the spiral for a new low-cost form to evolve below it. The pattern of competition also has geographical significance, as new forms exploit newly advantageous locations in

relation to developing road networks and levels of car ownership. Thus the evolving shopping pattern inevitably induces changes in the urban hierarchy of main, district and local centres which may decline, change status or spring up in new locations according to changing circumstances.

The spiral theory depends upon the internal dynamic of changing technical factors within the retailing industry, coupled with a general expansion of the economy. The absence of the latter will undoubtedly modify the pattern, but the theory does provide a useful commentary on the great changes in urban patterns spearheaded by retail shopping developments which occurred during the 1960s in those countries which were already urbanized. Such changes were most dramatically illustrated in the case of the new out-of-town regional centres which effectively transferred large increments of the central-area shopping to peripheral sites, and, with the new focus thus created, in many cases banks, offices, medical centres, residential accommodation and other uses grew around them.[10]

David Harvey has drawn attention to the fact that adjustment to such dramatic changes is not uniform. Certain uses and certain social groups are more able to respond rapidly to new circumstances, while others react slowly. Thus, in the example of the out-of-town locations, first shopping, and then industrial and other commercial uses took advantage of the new low-cost, highly accessible locations, while more affluent and thus more mobile social groups benefited most from this relocation. As Harvey says: 'For this reason I believe it is very important to accept the notion that any urban system is in a permanent state of differential disequilibrium (by which I mean that different parts of it are approaching equilibrium at different rates).'[11]

It is this tendency of dynamic change in a city to discriminate against its weaker parts which has militated against allowing economic law to act unimpeded as the dominant urban structuring principle, as envisaged by Dunham when referring to 'the possibility that the price mechanism is a more adaptable and flexible method of land-use allocation than a flexible plan administered by an inflexible administrator'.[12] Yet the economic structure of the city is an extremely powerful determinant of urban form, diverted or restrained only with difficulty, and often with unexpected side effects. Marx's concept of surplus value identifies the birth of the city at just that point when surplus value first appeared, and specifies the city's functions from

*Land-value model of central Copenhagen, Denmark.*

tension'.[14] These contradictions became particularly visible in London during the 1960s and early 1970s, when property speculation met increasing opposition as a result of the huge fortunes made by a few developers, the destructive effect of development on existing communities, the absurdity, created by financial logic based on appreciating capital valuations rather than rental income, of buildings left unoccupied, and the overall change produced in the fabric and skyline of the capital. The story has been well documented in a number of studies,[15] as have the attempts by Central Government, through successive prohibitions and relaxations of office development controls, and by local authorities, through the exercise of planning restrictions and 'partnership' arrangements, to control the economic pressures of this 'secondary circuit', which only subsided in the mid-1970s when it succumbed, at least temporarily, to crisis.

Near the end of that cycle, in 1972, the radical, independent imprint Counter-Information Services produced a report on property speculation in central London[15] which took the development of Centre Point and the Euston Centre as particular illustrations of these events. In the case of the Euston Centre, the value of the development increased from £14,285,000 to £73,667,000 between the years 1964 and 1972. The Tolmers Square controversy resulting from this project drew attention to its impact upon the small houses, shops and work-shops which were being forced out of an area of central London already desperately short of such accommodation. Centre Point was even more remarkable in that the building was still not let in 1980 although the planning application dated back as far as August 1959. Despite this, the building had continued to increase dramatically in value, on a central site for which the ground rent was fixed in perpetuity. By 1972, the City of London had lost, according to Counter-Information Services, £12.9 million due to this fact alone.

Structured and logical as the patterns created by the price mechanism may appear to the external observer, its alarming indifference to their sometimes disastrous consequences has encouraged certain patterns of intervention by public authorities, of which the provision of major public engineering works has been among the earliest and most successful. Yet the very effectiveness of these devices in the recovery of key areas of public interest, such as health and freedom of movement, has paradoxically given rise to a further set of urban problems of which they themselves are the source.

that moment on as being concerned primarily with its circulation and control. Subsequently, Henri Lefebvre has suggested a distinction between two circuits in the circulation of surplus value in a modern city, the first being concerned with industrial activity and the conversion of raw materials into useful goods, and the second with subsequent speculation in property rights and returns on fixed capital investments. It is the second of these which has in recent years exposed some of the more problematic aspects of the 'price mechanism' in city development, for as Lefebvre argues: 'Whereas the proportion of global surplus value formed and realized in industry declines, the proportion realized in speculation and in construction and real estate development grows. The secondary circuit comes to supplant the principal circuit.'[13] This process, which some have argued is responsible for the relative decline in the industrial performance of the United Kingdom, also carries the implications suggested by Harvey: 'that the second circuit is far more crisis prone than the first, while contradiction between the two circuits is a constant source of

*Map of Paris, France, showing the extent of Haussmann's work. The black lines represent streets, the cross-hatched areas new districts, and the areas shaded with horizontal lines parks.*

## 1.2 ENGINEERING CONSIDERATIONS

THE CLASSIC EXAMPLE OF THE ENGINEERING approach to solving the problems of the city, which is repeatedly cited by both admirers and critics, is that of Georges Haussmann, whose implementation of a major programme of road building in Paris during his term as Prefect of the Seine between 1853 and 1870 combined precisely that mixture of motives and boldness of method which has characterized the approach.[16] Critics have emphasized the repressive purpose of Haussmann's boulevard network of 'strategic beautification', by which troops could be quickly moved from peripheral barracks to trouble spots in the city, and could be reinforced by the frontier armies through the new rail termini. Robert Goodman has indeed suggested[17] that Haussmann's system of public control was an architectural equivalent of what today is achieved chemically, with tear gas and Mace, and certainly, with barricades erected nine times in the streets of Paris in the 25 years before the Second Empire, this aspect of Haussmann's plan was significant. But the essential factor regarding motive was that it was not confined to one single problem, but rather aimed to dispel with a simple, decisive engineering solution, a whole complex array of intractable difficulties. Intended to control disease, and particularly the periodic cholera epidemics which occurred in the city, to relieve unemployment and stimulate the economy, and to reduce traffic congestion, the network of roads and accompanying sewers based on the 'great cross' of the principal north-south and east-west routes, was a multi-purpose mechanism to solve the problems created by unplanned urban growth, and at the same time to fulfil Napoleon III's ambition to make Paris 'the most beautiful city in the world'.[18]

In fact, new road construction was the only practical method available to attempt such radical reforms, since it was the only public activity in Paris at the time which carried substantial powers of compulsory acquisition. Haussmann's use of these powers, and method of implementation, was as remarkable as the plans themselves, and as typical of the engineering approach to the city's problems. Although his predecessors had framed extensive road improvement plans, they had generally attempted to implement them through piecemeal acquisition and enforcement of new building lines as properties came up for renewal. In addition, the high cost of public works had led Berger, the previous Prefect, to insist that they should be financed not through huge loans, but by an annual allocation from the city revenues. Louis-Napoleon and his Prefect, however, came to the opposite conclusion. Arguing that public works debts could be serviced and amortized by the revenue growth they would generate, they opted for the most rapid programme possible, in order that later phases would not be unduly penalized by the general rise in property values expected to result from the benefits flowing from the earlier works. Further, they set their road alignments wherever possible through the cheaper land in the centres of existing city blocks, rather than attempting to redevelop the old frontages, and bought additional land on either side of the new roads so as to benefit from the betterment created.

The interlocking of public works with economic forces which thus resulted, together with the multiple nature of the aims of this investment, which H.J. Dyos has similarly noted in the case of the growth of London,[19] distinguished the nineteenth-century engineer's approach and contributed to its successes. It provided perhaps the first and most convincing indication that the modern industrial city could indeed be planned in a manner closely analogous to that of building design, and that the new reach of the civil engineer could provide a decisive answer to the city's problems. The further suggestion that, beyond the elimination of congestion and disease, the perfection of urban engineering systems might participate in the reformation of society itself, is a theme which still holds conviction, as for example in Reyner Banham's account of Los Angeles, whose freeway system makes 'all parts of it . . . equal and equally accessible from all other parts at once', and in which 'the houses and automobiles are equal figments of a great dream, the dream of the urban homestead, the dream of the good life outside the squalors of the European sort of city.'[20]

Yet the approach also attracted early criticism. The scale and speed of operations in densely built-up areas provoked reactions familiar from modern urban motorway programmes: 'So many houses were torn down during the railway boom, which lasted down to 1875, that contemporaries likened the coming of the railways to the invasion of the Huns.'[21] The physical results were also challenged, notably by Camillo Sitte in respect of the Viennese highway engineers: 'Modern systems! That, indeed, is the appropriate term! We set up rigid *systems*, and then grow fearful of deviating from them by as much as a hair's breadth. Suppression, or sacrifice to system, of every ingenious touch that might give real expression to the joy of living, is truly the mark of our times.'[22]

This suspicion that the engineering approach, valid enough for certain problems, might be crudely inappropriate when carried beyond those limits, has been reiterated in recent years by a number of observers. Melvin Webber[23] has suggested that, in order to repair the shortcomings of the price mechanism, town planners use the methods of civil engineers rather than economists, evolving three basic techniques which are directly analogous to those in engineering—the technical standard, the masterplan and the land-use regulation. The spectacular success of those methods in some areas of city design disguised the fact that they were only appropriate for what Rittel and Webber[24] have described as 'tame' problems, with clear ends in sight. Most urban issues however are 'wicked' problems, which are impossible to formulate or to solve definitively, and are thus poor subjects for such methods.

Such difficulties have been particularly sharply exposed when the momentum of the simple engineering solution has brought it into conflict with its more complex context. Haussmann himself experienced the way in which a strong system, once formulated, becomes a fixed aim even when the circumstances it sought to resolve have changed. This self-generating characteristic has formed a major source of criticism of traffic engineering. Arguing that American urban renewal programmes have been distorted by automobile manufacturing and highway construction interests, Robert Goodman[25] cites a notorious diagram on the cover of the Asphalt Institute's publication *Asphalt*, for April 1966, entitled 'Asphalt's Magic Circle', in which increased road building is shown to stimulate travel, fuel use and hence tax revenues, which in turn become available for new road building.

Since the 1930s, the imposition of rigid traffic engineering standards in housing developments in Britain has resulted in lack of safety for pedestrians, undevelopable land, and undesirably low housing densities. The Mark I new towns which followed these standards created a bleakness of environment referred to in the technical press as 'prairie planning', often reinforced by a strict adherence to Radburn layouts in which pedestrian access and vehicular access were rigidly separated. The pedestrian greenways tended to be underused, whereas the garage courts became children's play areas. Agreements to relax these overtly beneficial standards have been achieved only slowly and with great difficulty, as in the early example of the Halton Brow Estate at Runcorn New Town.

Ivan Illich has similarly criticized inappropriate engineering standards in relation to the development of the highway network in Mexico to a point at which, he claims, it lost touch with the problem it aimed to solve and became paradoxically less efficient than before. During the 1930s, a network of dirt roads and tracks connecting towns and villages was established, serviced by rough trucks on which people, merchandise and animals could be moved cheaply across the country. Since 1945, however, new highways were built between the main centres and the old, all-purpose trucks abandoned. 'In most areas either the peasant must take a bus to go to the market to buy industrially packaged commodities, or he sells his pig to the trucker in the employ of the meat merchant. He can no longer go to town with his pig. He pays taxes for the roads which serve the owners of various specialized monopolies and does so under the illusion that the benefits will ultimately spread to him. In exchange for an occasional ride on an upholstered seat in an air-conditioned bus, the common man has lost much of the mobility the old system gave him, without gaining any new freedom.'[26]

The need for urban engineering systems to be centrally implemented, which automatically associated Haussmann's road improvements with Louis-Napoleon's political policies, has led, so Illich and others would argue, to the adoption of the engineering systems approach by central authority for all problems, 'tame' or 'wicked', regardless of its relevance. Thus, for example, the engineering logic of large-scale, simple layouts on flat sites for public services has led central authorities in some countries to clear squatter settlements which have sprung up on steep, awkward central sites, and relocate them in new, peripheral settlements which, in other terms, are more expensive and less satisfactory than the non-conforming patterns they replace. The inevitable entanglement of engineering methods with political issues has in turn given rise to new problems in the social sphere.

*Le Corbusier, proposal for Rio de Janeiro's 'second town', 1936. The single structure is carried on 120-feet high pilotis and the roof, 300 feet above ground-level, is a motorway linking all the hill tops to 'create order in the plan and townscape of Rio'.*

*Two-level expressway linking the southern suburbs of Rio de Janeiro with Barra de Tijuca, Lúcio Costa's new town for the city. By the mid-1970s, Le Corbusier's vision had been partially fulfilled.*

## 1.3 SOCIAL IMPLICATIONS

ACCOMPANYING THE DIFFERENTIATED ECONOMIC pattern of the city is a social pattern based upon a corresponding inequality of location and access to services and amenities. And if the former structure is most vividly revealed by the distribution of land values, so the latter has historically been articulated by that of population densities. As with the economic pattern, so the social pattern is a dynamic condition, constantly undergoing transformation in response to what Wolf has seen as the opposing tendencies of centralization and diffusion: 'Population redistribution in American metropolises can be interpreted as a dialectical process. The greater the attraction of population to the metropolis—centralization—the greater its repulsion towards the periphery of the metropolis —diffusion. Centralization and diffusion are therefore two sides of the same coin. This "unity of opposites" constitutes a dialectical process.'[27] Wolf likens the pattern of population growth rates which results from this process to the spread of a tidal wave whose peak progressively moves out across the suburbs from a hollow centre.

The precise form of social stratification which accompanies this shift varies from culture to culture, and stage to stage. Sutcliffe[28] has pointed out, for example, that a pattern of vertical social stratification in Paris in the early nineteenth century, with different classes living at different levels in the same building, was gradually replaced by a horizontal separation as the wealthier families moved out to new suburbs, leaving the poor to occupy the older core. And each of the distinctive conditions resulting from this stratification has been found to possess its own distinctive set of problems. In their classic study of an inner-city working-class community in Bethnal Green in London, Young and Willmott[29] described the disruptive effects upon families of the move to a new estate. In place of the interlocking kinship networks of the old, intimate neighbourhood, a more remote, even hostile set of relationships and a greater dependence on immediate family and home, is established. Nevertheless, even the comparatively featureless expanse of a huge modern estate can, over a period of time, support its own version of the kinship network so characteristic of the older, inner-city communities, as Willmott found with his survey of Dagenham's Becontree estate after 40 years of occupation.[30]

The invisibility of such social structures to outsiders, and the persistence of easy, stereotyped, but inaccurate, notions of what life is like in other people's sectors of the city, have been the themes

*Gustave Doré,* Over London by Rail, *1872.*

of several important studies. Jane Jacobs, for example, in her evocation of cosmopolitan life in the inner city,[31] castigates: 'The Boston planner who knew (against all the real life evidence he had) that the North End had to be a slum because the generalizations that made him an expert say it is.' Similarly Nicholas Taylor,[32] speaking this time on behalf of the virtues of the English suburb, notes that: 'To the planner, commuting to work from his own suburb, who sees other people's suburbs only from the top of the railway viaduct, such places may seem featureless and monotonous and sprawling and dull.' The resident, however, understands their essential qualities to be '... freedom, diversity and individuality—the ability of ordinary families to do their own thing.' By their observation of what Jacobs calls 'common, ordinary things', such authors have exposed some of the myths of city life, although it may be argued that they substituted alternative, selective idealizations of their own. If our perception of the social structure of the city is dangerously dependent upon such myths, this is nowhere more true than of its proverbially most problematic part, the inner city.

The characteristics of this area are described by Hauser: 'This is the area characterized by "blight" —the locus of the slums and disproportionate shares of the institutional and personal pathology of the metropolis. Physically, this is the oldest residential area of the city, which is still available for residential use—since the central business district, as it expanded in the growth of the city,

absorbed that which may have been older. It becomes an area of decay, partly because of the anticipated expansion of the central business district, which is evidenced by its anomalous relatively high land-values and low rents. The land is, in the main, held for speculative purposes frequently under circumstances which do not, on economic grounds, justify further improvement or even reasonable maintenance of the residential housing.'[33] The availability of work in the CBD drew new immigrants to this area, where the competition of high-rental, central-area uses forced them to live at high densities. This traditional function of the inner-city slums as the reception area for newcomers is set out by Richard Sennett in his description of 'the city of necessity' which 'broke apart the self-contained qualities of the various ethnic groups. The groups were not like little villages massed together in one spot on the map; rather they penetrated into each other, so that the daily life of an individual was a journey between various kinds of group life, each one different in its function and character from the others.'[34]

Since the period of the great European migrations to American cities however, the outward movement of Wolf's 'tidal wave' has undermined the employment basis at the centre. Harvey outlines the result: 'The urban system seems to have reacted very sluggishly indeed to the demand for low-income housing in suburban areas. The difficulty of expanding the supply in the inner city

Favela *near Gavea, Rio de Janeiro.*

*Affonso Reidy, Gavea Conjunto (housing project), Rio de Janeiro, 1954–82, with* favela *in the foreground (photographed 1961).*

(partly due to institutional constraints such as zoning regulations) means that poor-quality, low-income housing is relatively high priced and frequently more profitable for property owners than we would expect under true equilibrium conditions. Low-income families therefore have little option but to locate in the relatively high-priced inner city. In most American cities, of course, this condition has been exacerbated by the lack of an open housing market for the black population which, of course, just happens to constitute a large segment of the poor. Meanwhile most of the growth in new employment has been in the suburban ring and hence the low-income groups have gradually been cut off from new sources of employment.'[35]

Once again, however, it is all too easy to infer inaccurate myths from such general descriptions. In a paper whose title, 'Will the Inner City Problem Ever Go Away?',[36] reflected the exasperation of planners with the intransigence of the inner city, Ray Pahl pointed out that, in London at any rate, Government surveys showed that 'most of the poor are not low paid and most of the low paid are not poor', and that although the inner city represented the greatest concentration of poor families, numerically there were more such households elsewhere. This cast a doubtful light on purely area-based policies since: 'The more successful allocations are in channelling resources to particular categories in certain areas, the more attractive those areas then become.... Very radical activists who claim that something special is happening to the economic function of the inner city, as part of the inevitable profit-seeking expansion of State Monopoly Capitalism, provide a splendid argument for parties of the right. If capitalism inevitably leads to decay and poverty in certain limited areas then, it may be claimed, we only have to tidy up those limited areas and there need be no further trouble. It is evidently functional to preserve the ideology of area-based troubles as a cheap and convenient way of avoiding politically unpleasant alternatives.' Some of the most graphic illustrations of the dangers of basing public policy on such crude, if convenient formulations of social problems in the city have been provided by attempts to control the rapid growth of squatter settlements in the cities of the third world.

The *bandas de miseria* of Argentina, *bidonvilles* of Algeria, *gececondu* of Turkey, *barriadas* of Peru and *favelas* of Brazil, form an important part of the housing stock of their respective countries, accommodating by the late 1960s approximately 35% of the populations of Rio and Caracas, 45% of Mexico City and Ankara, 25% of Lima and Santiago, 15% of Singapore, 12% of Istanbul, and as much as 65% of Algiers.[37] The Official Bulletin of the Brazilian Secretariat of Social Services describes a *favela* as 'a group of dwellings with high density of occupation, the construction of which is carried out in a disorderly fashion with inadequate material, without zoning, without public services, and on land which is illegally being used without the consent of the owner'.[38] In fact, only the last characteristic can be applied with certainty, since *favelas* vary greatly among themselves and over time, often developing services and more substantial building construction as they mature. Their place in the cities of the industrializing countries is an important one, for they form, it has been argued, the means by which those cities 'respond far more readily to the demands of the poor majority than cities of the industrial or post-industrial world, like Chicago or New York, respond to their poor minorities'.[39] Nevertheless, their rapid and uncontrolled growth has often provoked in the host city hostility as great as that embodied in legislation passed by the medieval burghers of the City of London to exclude the immigrants camped in Southwark on the opposite bank of the Thames. Their alien character in terms of the conventional form of the city has made them the subject of myths which several researchers, notably Janice Perlman, John Turner and Carlos Nelson dos Santos, have tried to dispel.

In her study of *favelas* in Rio de Janeiro, *The Myth of Marginality*, Perlman describes the prevailing view held by officials, policy-makers, academics and large segments of the public: '... the favela is seen as a disorderly agglomeration of unemployed loafers, abandoned women and children, thieves, drunks, and prostitutes. These "marginal elements" live in "subhuman" conditions without piped water, sewage systems, garbage collection, and other basic urban services in an unclean and unhealthy atmosphere. In appearance an eyesore, the favela detracts from the picturesque panorama of the city. Economically and socially it is a drain, a parasite, demanding high expenditures for public services and offering little in return.... Considerations of health, economic efficiency, aesthetics, and political stability all point in the same direction: eradicate the favela.'[40] In contrast, Perlman and others have suggested that the *favelados* are in fact the most enterprising people of the rural communities who, having sought a better life in cities unable to cope with their arrival, have attempted to provide the facilities for themselves, with a remarkable degree of success, given their poverty, and in a way which, far from draining the city economy, leads to their full integration into it. The incompatibility of these two views has led to public policies for the clearing of *favelados* from inner-city sites in Rio and their relocation in official housing projects on the edges of the city, which Perlman regards as grotesquely inappropriate. Indeed, she saw that by the forcible removal of the *favelados* from sources of employment and the added burdens on them of rent and commuting costs, official ideology was perversely

*Partially occupied BNH housing project, 50 kilometres outside São Paulo, Brazil, built under licence with a French industrialized system. This project, completed in 1973 as part of the eradication of the inner-city* favelas, *is in marked contrast to Affonso Reidy's Corbusian projects of the 1950s.*

acting as self-fulfilling prophecy, creating precisely the marginalized population it was designed to eliminate.

The 1970 census in Brazil established that 26 million Brazilians obtained their water supply from a mains system, 12 million from artesian wells, 16 million had no means of supply at all (apart from carrying a water-can balanced on the head from the nearest stand pipe); 13 million were serviced by a public sewage disposal system, 32 million had earth closets or septic tanks and 8 million had no sanitary facilities whatsoever. In 1940, 30% of the population was urban. In 1980 it was approximately 80%. The 1970 census indicated that the number of persons earning up to 100cr/month (approximately £7 at that time) was 55% of all people employed. People from the rural communities, who were unqualified for urban activities, migrated to cities to work for virtually any salary.

According to Anthony and Elizabeth Leeds,[41] the population of *favelas* is due to four factors: marginality, stress, economics and taste. 'Marginality' is a situation in which people operate neither within the legal or illegal (criminal) economy of the city, but live by begging since there is no social security system. On the other hand, 'economics' refers to people with more or less stable but limited resources and choice, based upon a hierarchy of values. The *favela* is an urban squatters' community established on land of different ownership where sanitation, services and education are non-existent. In Brazil, *favelas* tended to be established in the centres of the metropolitan areas, close to sources of work and employment.

In 1964, the Brazilian Government established the BNH (National Housing Bank) in an attempt to solve the housing problem and to promote home ownership for millions. It is a financial institution consisting of funds deposited by employers for and on behalf of employees (similar to a pension fund) to be invested in public housing. But this housing is not offered at subsidized rents and has to make sufficient return to justify the fund. The scheme caters for families on one to three minimum salaries (£20–60 per month at 1974 levels) but people below that level—and there are many millions —do not qualify. BNH built 800,000 dwellings between 1964 and 1974. The main problem has been that BNH was merely the financial institution and the implementation of the housing projects was the responsibility of the State governments through COHAB. Neither organization employed physical planners until comparatively recently and consequently the sites selected were the cheapest —often some 50 kilometres from the metropolitan centres and place of work. The lower-income families who were moved out after the 'eradication' of the *favelas* (begun in Rio in the early 1960s by Carlos Lacerda, State Governor) could neither afford the time, transportation costs, or high repayment terms. Many have drifted back to establish new exurban *favelas* such as those described by Carlos Nelson in the northern part of the Bay of Guanabara. Income distribution in Brazil is worsening and so is the inability of cities to shelter adequately the large mass of rural immigrants.

*Copacabana, an affluent suburb, commenced its growth in the late 1930s. By 1960, due to a strict adherence to zoning and height regulations as well as a ban on advertisements, the completed suburb of one million people had a coherence unique in city development. Governmental and commercial pressures have destroyed this with the construction by French and American consortia of the two enormous hotels shown in the photograph.*

Similar problems of rural migration can be seen in their most extreme form in the Sudan with migration to the *only* major urban area of the three cities of Khartoum.[42] The introduction of system building exacerbated the problems in that many of the systems imported into Latin America were of European and particularly French origin. In one example in São Paulo, 50% of the houses are un-inhabitable because the system was incapable of adaptation to local climatic and site conditions.

Perlman's suspicion that official policies were sometimes based not on simple error, but on 'calculated misunderstandings', accords with observations made by other authors, describing different problems. Richard Sennett, for example, has suggested that the rich interpenetration of different activities and modes of life which used to characterize American cities, and was celebrated by Jane Jacobs, could only be maintained in 'the city of necessity', in which no area of activity 'was rich and centralized enough to wall itself off'.[43] With increased affluence however, 'those desires for coherence, for structured exclusion and internal sameness, can be played out. Whole urban regions can be divided geographically by class, by race, by ethnicity; "unsightly" activities like stores and entertainment can be hidden from home life, so that community identity through a brutal simplifying of human activities is achieved.'[44] In Sennett's analysis, 'community' becomes debased to a euphemism for sectional interest, and discord between groups is eliminated at a private level to reappear as the institutional and violent enforcement of those interests at a higher level.

Others have shared this pessimism regarding the ability of the city to resolve its social problems. Harvey's studies of the effective redistribution of real income resulting from the inequalities of the urban system lead him to conclude that they 'seem to be moving us towards a state of greater inequality and greater injustice. Unless this present trend can be reversed, I feel that almost certainly we are also headed for a period of intense conflict (which may be violent) within the urban system.'[45] One leading American theory of delinquency, according to James Patrick,[46] is that adolescent gang warfare is likely to arise in disorganized slums, characterized by high rates of mobility and populated in part by failures in the conventional world and outcasts of the criminal world. Adult crime in Maryhill, Glasgow, appeared to be unorganized and petty, but the neighbourhood was far more integrated and cohesive than this theory would lead one to suspect. Patrick, a social worker living

*Violent police suppression of the impoverished spectators of the Rio de Janeiro Carnaval procession who had been given free seats in stands along the processional route (photographed 1976). The spontaneity of city life, which often overcame some of the worst aspects of social stress, is now tending to disappear.*

incognito amongst the young Glasgow gangs, describes a visit to a local dance hall: 'On entry to the dance hall we were searched by the bouncers. Tim had surrendered a hatchet and Dave a bayonet for which they were given a cloak room ticket. One half of the ticket was licked and placed on the weapon—the attendant saying "I'll pit these in the corner un ye can get them when ye go oot".'

Violence, as the most explicit of urban social problems, is a theme which recurs in the writings of a number of urban theorists, notably Jane Jacobs, and more recently Oscar Newman. Despite, or perhaps because of, its long association with the city, it is the subject of more myths than any other social problem. Writing in 1969 in the wake of widespread rioting and violence in American cities, P. Lupsha reviewed the great variety of explanations of root causes of urban violence from Plutarch onwards.[47] He concluded that, in the case of the American race riots at any rate, the suggestion that violence was the result of 'the irrational rage of frustration' was quite wrong. On

the contrary: '... it is an anger arising from a rational evaluation of the situation. It is an anger directed at the inability and inadequacy of the political system and its institutions to live up to their promise. It is an anger directed at the inadequacy of the political system to process demands, and to make allocations in a responsive and responsible manner. It is the gap between the theory and the practice of government in the United States that is one of the root causes of urban violence.'

Harvey, however, would counter this with the suggestion that: 'We really do not have the kind of understanding of the total city system to be able to make wise policy decisions, even when motivated by the highest social objectives.'[48] This disturbing conclusion is based on Harvey's understanding of both social and ecological problems of the city and it is towards the latter, by which we are 'rolling out the carpet of opportunities in front of us while rolling it up even faster behind us'[49] that we now turn.

*'No-go' area in the Roman Catholic sector of Belfast, Northern Ireland showing the physical division of the city which has resulted from sectarian violence.*

## 1.4 THE THREAT TO ECOLOGY

THE IMAGE OF THE CITY AS AN UNCONTROLLABLE, vastly powerful force dominating man, suggests parallels with the forces of nature which phrases like the asphalt, or concrete jungle, tend to confirm. The metaphor also suggests that, in supplanting nature as man's customary habitat, the city's domination of man has been accompanied by a similar domination of nature itself, and it is the wider ecological consequences of that domination which form an important new source of problems for the urban designer.

To describe this as new may seem absurd. The epidemics of typhoid and cholera which followed the ecological failure of early European industrial cities with their inadequate sewage treatment, record the long-standing nature of these problems. Pollution of all kinds is an established fact of urban life, causing extensive damage to all living things within the city area, as well as eroding its fabric. In 1952, during the worst winter of London smogs, the deaths of 12,000 people were directly attributed to the combination of sulphur and smoke in the atmosphere. But while internal ecological disorders of the industrializing city continue to present major local difficulties, a number of observers have concluded in recent years that the increasing scale of urbanization threatens a larger and more catastrophic ecological failure. This arises in part from the sheer scale of contemporary global urbanization. The French philosopher Jerome Deshusses has vividly depicted this expansion by pointing out that each year new concrete covers an area of pasture equivalent to the size of the Netherlands.[50] Yet it is not so much the physical extent of the cities themselves which poses the most alarming threat, as the increasingly demanding burden which they place upon the hinterland. According to this view, the cities, through their ever-increasing demands for water, energy, raw materials and food, act as the visible *foci* of a global system of natural exploitation, from which the huge scale of ecological disruption is only beginning to become apparent. It then becomes impossible to divorce urban problems from, say, those arising from the deoxygenation and pollution of lakes such as the Great Lakes of North America, seas such as the Baltic and Mediterranean, and ultimately the oceans.

If such global concerns seem remote from the more immediate difficulties of urban design, it is as well to recall that some of the most far-reaching contemporary attempts to alter nature are being conducted with urban development as an incipient feature, and one expected to play a key role in the future exploitation. One of the most dramatic examples of this is in the Amazon basin, which contains one-third of the world's remaining forests and supplies one-fifth of the world's oxygen. Ecologists, and particularly Brazilian ecologists, have warned of the possibility of disaster following the Government decision in 1968 to create a network of highways criss-crossing Amazonas to develop the region. Though covered by dense forest, the subsoil is relatively thin and poor, and the ecological balance delicate. Experience in the drought-stricken north-east of Brazil in states like Ceará and Bahia, indicate that once the vegetation cover has been removed, the top soil is washed away in the heavy tropical rain-storms and desert is formed, which in turn lowers the rainfall. There are signs that linear strips of desert are already forming along these highways.

Much of the justification for this risk lies in the possibility of realising immense mineral wealth in the Amazon basin and creating huge cattle ranges in former forest areas. At the same time, the Government has justified its actions by arguing that they will create employment for the impoverished inhabitants of north-eastern Brazil, and to further this has proposed a settlement pattern to accompany the highways, taking the form of an hierarchically ordered chain of communities, of which the smallest unit is designated an *Agrovila*. This has a small rural district centre with basic communal services and 'urban plots' for up to 300 families, of which 40 or 50 would be admitted in the first instance to start a new community. In addition, each family has a small land parcel for producing cash crops. The *Agrovilas* are not built in isolation, but are related in groups of 8 or 12 to the *Agropolis*, 'a small urban agro-industrial cultural and administrative center meant to further social integration in rural areas',[51] which in turn lies within 70 to 120 kilometres of the third level of settlement, the *Ruropolis*, with a planned population of about 20,000.

Despite the reassuringly ordered framework, however, new settlers have found the remote jungle regions and relative infertility of the land hard to contend with. Particularly serious is the effect upon the native Indian peoples, many of whom face extinction through contact with western diseases and exploitation, despite the efforts of such men as the anthropologist brothers Villas-Boas.

The urbanization of Amazonas has been challenged on the grounds that an alternative tradi-

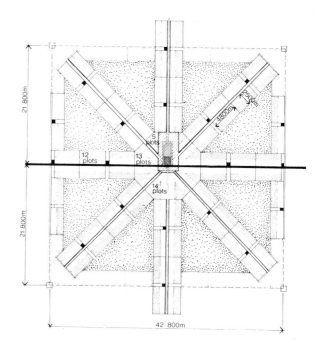

*Plan for an* agrovila, *Amazonas, Brazil.*

tional transportation system already existed in the great navigable rivers, and with the introduction of new forms of river craft such as hydrofoils and hovercraft, the existing urban settlements along the river banks could have flourished in preference to new and ecologically more dangerous patterns.[52] Whatever the validity of this argument, perhaps the most disturbing aspect of the whole debate is the impression that the implications of planning policies are simply not known; that, to repeat Harvey's words, 'we really do not have the kind of understanding of the total city system to be able to make wise policy decisions', and that, as in the past, sound planning policies only establish themselves after the worst implications of previous opportunist actions have become inescapable. The further possibility that well-intentioned, carefully constructed plans such as those prepared for the urbanization of Amazonas might actually create a catastrophe, or that man's oppression by the city might be increased rather than alleviated by incorrect or crude design concepts, introduces a further area of urban problems—those arising from the activities of the urban designer himself.

## 1.5 THE IMPOSITION OF DESIGN

THE PREVIOUS DISCUSSION SUGGESTS THAT THE CITY is an extremely complicated phenomenon whose problems interact in complex ways; that there is often fundamental disagreement about the nature of these problems; and that the whole picture is continually undergoing changes. If this description generally corresponds to the whole state of affairs which together constitute 'the problem' for the urban designer, we might observe a remarkable contrast between this and the many examples of what is offered as 'the solution', which is characteristically simple, ambiguous and static. Now it may be that these solutions do so clarify and resolve the conflicts of existing cities that a lucid and inevitable simplicity is achieved. Alternatively, it might be suggested that the simplicity is achieved in spite of the nature of the problem, and even that it represents a kind of exasperated impatience with the intractability of the city which, in an extreme form, provoked the extraordinary action of Pol Pot's Khmer Rouge army on 15 April 1975, in disurbanizing Cambodia, overnight forcibly evacuating the two million inhabitants of Pnom-Penh and leaving the deserted city to itself. Unjust as a comparison between this action and the efforts of urban planners to solve the economic, engineering, social and ecological problems of the city may be, some critics have suggested that the difficulty and urgency of urban problems have produced correspondingly exaggeratedly simple, sweeping, once-and-for-all responses, and that the attempts to implement these responses have in turn compounded the problems.

Sennett has described these planning responses as the pursuit of 'The "Urban Whole" as a myth of purity',[53] by which imponderables, and particularly those arising from unpredictable future growth and change, are transmuted into fixed, static objectives by the operation of techniques such as the statement of 'projective needs'. The dangers of applying what we have loosely called the 'engineering approach' to inappropriate 'wicked' problems is echoed in Sennett's analysis of the misleading use of the analogy of the city as a machine. Yet it must be said that the adoption of this analogy is a symptom rather than a cause of the 'myth of purity'. Its place, for example, in Le Corbusier's seminal urban projects is illuminated by Colin Rowe's observations on the differences between the designer's stance as an urbanist and as an architect: 'There is Le Corbusier, the architect, ... who sets up elaborately pretended Platonic structures only to riddle them with an equally elaborate

pretence of empirical detail, the Le Corbusier of multiple asides, cerebral references and complicated scherzi; and then there is Le Corbusier, the urbanist, the deadpan protagonist of completely different strategies who, at a large and public scale, has the minimum of use for all the dialectical tricks and spatial involutions which, invariably, he considered the appropriate adornment of a more private situation. The public world is simple, the private world is elaborate, and, if the private world affects a concern for contingency, the would-be public personality long maintained an almost too heroic disdain for any taint of the specific.'[54]

This curious reservation of the simplest solutions for the most complex problems is a long-standing characteristic of much urban planning, and forms one basis of contemporary criticism of its results. Among the earliest techniques used by planners to intervene in the development of the industrial city, it was zoning which laid the basis for such an

approach. For while the physical separation of land uses had undoubted environmental justifications, it also had the distinct advantage of achieving a radical simplification of the problem. Such concepts as land-use isolation and hierarchical community structures undoubtedly clarified the confusingly interdependent aspects of the problem to the point where a lucid design solution could be formulated, although critics have argued that such solutions were so sterile and so remote from the reality of the city that they were invalid. Attempts have thus been made to re-invest the end product with some of the functional and visual variety of pre-industrial or 'unplanned' cities, and a great many formulae for achieving this have been proposed. They have the disadvantage, however, that they appear only to make more acceptable the results of an initial faulty design decision, and thus substantiate Papanek's accusation that 'so far the action of the [design] profession has been compar-

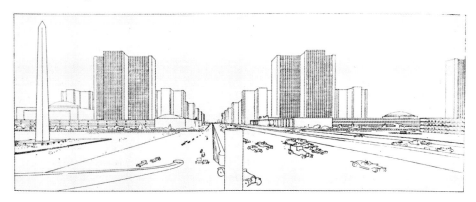

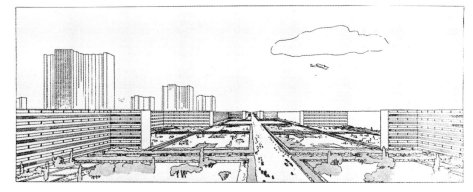

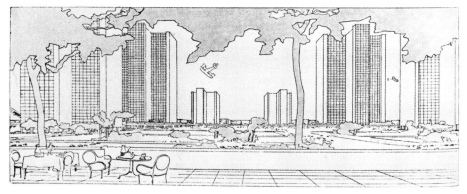

*Le Corbusier, proposal for a city of three million inhabitants, 1922.*

*Oscar Niemeyer, Museum in honour of President Juscelino Kubitschek, Praça dos Três Poderes, Brasília, Brazil.*

*Brasília, panoramic view along the east-west axis of the* plano pîloto *looking towards Oscar Niemeyer's Central Congress Buildings (1960), with Lúcio Costa's bus station interchange in the foreground.*

*Oscar Niemeyer, Foreign Office, Brasília, 1969.*

able to what would happen if all medical doctors were to forsake general practice and surgery, and concentrate exclusively on dermatology and cosmetics'.[55]

A more fundamental critique of attempts to simplify the problem has been offered by Christopher Alexander, notably in his essay 'A City is not a Tree',[56] in which he argued that such attempts were based upon a mistaken appreciation of the structural relationship of the city's elements which typically take the form of semi-lattices. The tree-like structure of most modern plans, from Clarence Stein's Greenbelt, Maryland, to Abercrombie's Greater London Plan and Tange's Tokyo Bay to Le Corbusier's Chandigarh, represents a 'trivially simple' case of the semi-lattice structure, and one in which 'life will be cut to pieces'.

We have noted the argument that the separation of interest groups in the modern city tends to occur with increasing affluence. If this social pattern does indeed arise, it reinforces the tendency to seek simplified design structures, which is often further abetted by development convenience, for very often the structure of development agencies and their preferred areas of interest follows a similar dissociated pattern. The simplified design approach therefore has the added merit that it can be more readily implemented. Robert Goodman has also suggested that the merit of explicability is also relevant, so that: 'the over-all design grows from the need of one professional, who doesn't live in the environment, to explain his design in simplistic terms, to groups of bureaucrats who also don't live in the environment (but control it through access to public funds). The need to *explain* the design thus becomes a prime motivation for what the design finally turns out to be.'[57]

Jane Jacobs found an equally jaundiced explanation for the interest of the planners in altering the scale of consideration of the problem of 'organized complexity' in the city: 'There is a widespread belief among many city experts today that city problems already beyond the comprehension and control of planners and other administrators can be solved better if only the territories involved and problems entailed are made larger still and can therefore be attacked more "broadly". This is escapism from intellectual helplessness. "A region", somebody has wryly said, "is an area safely larger than the last one to whose problems we found no solution".'[58] Such observations point to the tendency of designers when faced with a particularly confusing problem to think in terms which are calculated to lead to a coherent and realisable solution, even if those terms do not correspond as closely as they might to the actual conditions of the problem. An important factor in assessing how 'realistic' a solution is (that is, how readily it can be realized, not how closely it corresponds to reality) is the multiplicity of the design agencies themselves. As urbanism forms the focus of so many aspects of society, and is thus the valid territory of so many disciplines, Harvey has even suggested that 'we cannot promote an understanding of urbanism through interdisciplinary research, but we can promote an understanding of disciplinary contributions through a study of urbanism'.[59] An important task of an urban design solution would thus be to set down terms according to which different disciplines could effectively work together, and indeed one could view a number of projects in this way. In several schemes by the multi-disciplinary practice of Arup Associates, for example, the distinctive urban ordering system is established through the tartan-grid definition of specific zones within which structure, services, circulation and usable spaces can occur and, by implication, the specialist professions can operate.

Such design characteristics arising out of the nature of design itself may, of course, be beneficial, acting as a sort of 'third party' term of reference within which inherently unstable or irreconcilable elements of the urban designer's brief may be contained. However, urban design seems particularly prone to that condition which Illich describes as typical of 'manipulative' rather than 'convivial' tools, by which people's activities are arranged for the convenience of the institutional tool rather than the reverse. This case has been most powerfully expressed in relation to the issue of housing. Turner[60] defines two kinds of approach to the provision of adequate housing, which he characterizes as 'networks' and 'hierarchies'. The former provides for user control and is characterized by a multiplicity of routes to the same end, while the latter centralizes control in the hands of government or corporate producers. Although a choice between these methods is overtly a question of practical convenience or efficiency, Turner sees it as a deeper division between two ways of thinking about the problem—one 'convivial' and the other 'manipulative'—so fundamental indeed that he describes his conversion from the second approach, which he sees as the predominant philosophy of CIAM and most modern planning, to the first as 'the re-education of a professional'. The shift of design attitude alters the whole nature of the problem: 'When dwellers control the major de-

cisions and are free to make their own contributions in the design, construction, or management of their housing, both this process and the environment produced stimulate individual and social well-being. When people have no control over nor responsibility for key decisions in the housing process, on the other hand, dwelling environments may instead become a barrier to personal fulfilment and a burden on the economy.'[61]

A similar argument has been expressed by Colin Ward in his plea for an anarchic approach to housing, and again the attack upon institutional methods of solving a problem leads inevitably to a challenge to the planning professions, whose role may be seen either as superficial (as Papanek suggests) or sinister. Robert Goodman castigates them on both counts, arguing that the language of aesthetic ideology acts as a smokescreen, an elaborate euphemism for the imposition of political ideology, while planning tools such as zoning regulations are used to enforce the status quo.[62] Such criticisms have obliged urban designers to re-examine their relationship to the problems of the city and to admit the possibility that they are themselves an urban phenomenon and hence a part of 'the problem' as much as 'the solution'.

*Lúcio Costa, Oscar Niemeyer, Affonso Reidy and others, Ministry of Education Building, Rio de Janeiro, 1937, showing the profound influence of Le Corbusier on the development of modern Brazilian architecture and planning in the use of the brise-soleil, pilotis and the creation of public open spaces in densely developed downtown districts.*

*Lúcio Costa, bus station and transport interchange, Brasília, 1960.*

## 1.6 CONCLUSION: THE CITY IMAGE

IF IT WERE NECESSARY TO SUMMARIZE THE MULTIPLE problems of urban design in a single example, the case of Brasília could well serve—not because that city has more problems than most, but because its compressed history shows them in a particularly vivid light. The circumstances of its conception by a single man, Juscelino Kubitschek, to serve a combination of political, economic, social and symbolic ends, made it perhaps the most ambitious example ever of pure Haussmannism. The beginning was matched by the purity (or crudity, according to your point of view) of Lúcio Costa's cruciform plan, a plan of such elegant simplicity that its principles could readily be contained in a small freehand sketch, and which clearly articulated the principal functions of the new city.

Mistaken by many foreign observers and critics as a Beaux-Arts solution, Costa's plan was in fact an interesting proposal for a linear city. It proposed a linear development based on high-speed public and private transport using an urban expressway as its spine. Costa saw the city as one of mixed socio-economic groups and hoped that low-income workers would live in the *superquadras* (superblocks) of the *plano pîloto* (central zone) in the same way that other *superquadras* would house the higher-paid civil servants. Government policy determined that this was not to be, and the lower-paid groups were destined first to occupy squatter settlements near the *plano pîloto* and were then forcibly removed to the 'planned' *cidades satelites* (satellite towns).

The boldness of the plan was matched by that of its implementation. Determined by a political timetable, and lacking adequate road or rail communications, building materials were air-freighted 1,000 kilometres to the site in order to achieve the target population of 500,000 within ten years. The product of this very rapid growth was rigorously controlled in some areas, alarmingly anarchic in others. At the centre, along the ranks of Oscar Niemeyer's government buildings on the east-west axis, and among the residential *superquadras* of the curving north-south axis, the aesthetics of centralized authority were only perturbed by some imprecision in the commercial element of the city centre. Some discomforts resulted from this exacting architecture; the engineering approach to circulation provided traffic-free areas around each residential superblock but made pedestrian communication between them difficult, and residents who were used to life among the tangled mixture of uses in Rio or São Paulo objected to the fact that

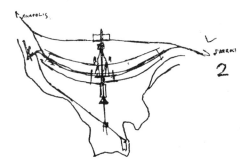

*Lúcio Costa, prize-winning entry for the national competition for the master plan of Brasília, 1957. Costa's submission was totally unlike the other entries in that it was presented merely as a small collection of outline sketches. The plan illustrated here shows the significant, but usually unrecognized, proposal for a linear city extending throughout the region.*

*Plan of the Federal District of Brasília, 1971, showing the location of satellite towns.*

Plano Pîloto, *Brasília (originally planned by Lúcio Costa in 1957), 1976 form.*

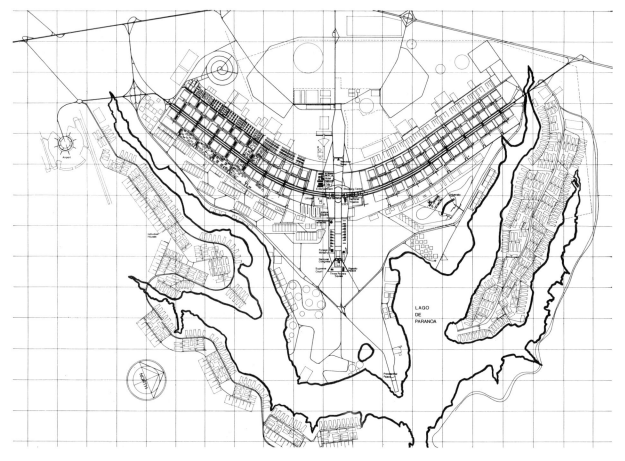

'Brasília não tem esquinas', (Brasília doesn't have any corners).[63] On the whole, however, the myth of purity was convincingly sustained.

A series of monographs published by the Department of Architecture at the University of Brasília in 1975–76, analysed residents' identification of planning failures. Maria Elaine Kohlsdorf suggested that the psychological effect caused by the physical environment depended on the perception of space in its totality—the spaces required external points of reference and orientability. She maintained that any person, whether a visitor, tourist, inhabitant or worker, would experience a sense of orientation or significance when viewing Brasília from without, but on penetrating the spaces within the city, the effects of meaning or orientation would diminish rapidly and progressively in intensity.

Outside the central zone, however, a different city took effect. On the south side of the lake (and killing it with their untreated sewage), a suburb of free-standing houses in an assortment of neo-colonial styles was built by the wealthiest citizens, while to the south-east the Cidade Livre (Free City), based on the camp established for construction workers, formed the first of a series of squatter settlements which grew up around the city. In 1970 official steps to eliminate the second of these aberrations took effect in the form of 'The Campaign for the Eradication of *Favelas*' (Campanha de Erradicacão das Invasoẽs). Rather than extend the linear, and potentially open-ended form of the residential axis of the *plano pîloto*, new satellite towns were constructed, of which the largest, Ceîlandia, with 120,000 inhabitants, was described by the highly respected newspaper *Estado de São Paulo* as 'the biggest official *favela*'. With the only sources of employment 30 kilometres away in the *plano pîloto*, it forms a dark counterform to that model, lacking a sewage disposal system, adequate water or electricity supply and paved streets.

Other injustices abound. The water tower in Ceîlandia which was to supply the population with a piped water supply did not function up to the end of 1976. Yet in the same year a bridge was built across the lake from the southern shore of the *plano pîloto* so that ministers could shorten their journey to work by three minutes. The cost of that bridge equalled the cost of completing the infrastructure for a piped water supply in Ceîlandia.

The physical appearance of Ceîlandia is remarkable, with exactly half of the town composed of shacks on separate lots which house the very poorest families, and monotonously identical houses erected by SHIS (a Brazilian public housing agency) stretching from horizon to horizon which house the slightly better off.

Brasília was a visionary experiment intended to open up the hinterland of Brazil. Costa's plan and Niemeyer's architecture had all the promise of a revolutionary idea which might have resolved some of the problems of social integration which remain in Brazil today. The change of policy in the development of Brasília in the 1960s, which eliminated that promise, was due to the shortsightedness of the administrators and not to the originators of the idea.

The attempt to solve the problems of unsatisfactory housing conditions in a central zone by transposing the inhabitants to a new residential township on the outskirts, which then proves to be unsatisfactory in its turn, is certainly not confined to Brasília. It forms a response which city authorities have made in many parts of the world. Johannesburg's version, the South Western Townships, or Soweto, has been described by a visitor as '. . . oceans of asbestos-roofed flimsy brick huts. They brim in the huge shallow valley, crest it, and then fill the next, and the one after that, and the one beyond, and others on both sides for 25 square miles. It is an astonishing vista, a munificence of bleakness, a prodigality of shoddy ugliness.'[64] Analogous policies have been followed in European cities too, and particularly in Glasgow, whose serious housing problems led to the establishment of zoned satellite estates situated in the south-west and east of the city and built in advance of supporting services. For years they consisted of nothing but houses with minimal shopping facilities and a total absence of commercial entertainment. A Town Council resolution of 1890 forbade the provision of licensed premises on municipal housing estates. It was one such housing area, Easterhouse, which achieved notoriety after the outbreak of widespread juvenile gang violence in 1968.

But it is perhaps Brasília which best expresses the dilemma which occurs when the crystalline planning idea is unable to absorb the dynamics of the city, creating an unplanned condition with which it cannot live. In such cases, the same authoritarian decisiveness which began the cycle is called into play again to dispel the nonconforming parts, but now creating a grotesque antithesis of the first solution.

If we can argue that this antipodal shadow was already contained in the impossible fixity of the pure planning concept, which failed to recognize the second half of Marx's conception of society 'as a totality of internally related parts with inner laws of transformation',[65] we should also acknowledge that it did attempt to address the first part of that description. Against the relentless internal transformations of urban society, some would argue that the greatest failure of urban design has been its inability to supply a convincing image of a stable totality—an image, that is, which, without sterilizing those internal transformations, shows the city as more than the haphazard outcome of economic competition for space, or semi-conscious and often malevolent social processes. The purpose of such a

*Housing project in a northern* superquadra, *Brasília.*

*Housing erected by the Government agency*
▽ *SHIS, Ceîlandia.*

*Ceîlandia, Brasília, self-build housing.*

*Cidade Livre, Brasília. The original construction camp was known as the*
▽ *Nucleo Bandeirante.*

city image is, in Mumford's terms, 'to further man's conscious participation in the cosmic and the historic process',[66] and if this sounds somewhat ethereal, the desired result is practical enough: 'Through its own complex and enduring structure, the city vastly augments man's ability to interpret these processes and take an active formative part in them ...'[67]

Such a view regards the city not as a passive vehicle of social forces, nor as a simultaneous expression of them, but as an intermediary, making society explicable to itself, reminding it of its sources, and perhaps protecting it against the worst effects of those future and increasingly rapid transformations which such authors as Alvin Toffler[68] have envisaged. Joseph Rykwert's account of the ancient city as a mnemonic and symbolic device in a wide range of ancient cultures, rather than, as in modern society, 'as an analogue of a pathological condition'[69] suggests this analysis, in which the urban designer's central problem, and perhaps the one which in the end makes the others soluble, is to re-establish the public realm, fragmented by private interest and hostile forces, in a built form which liberates rather than represses the life of the city.

## NOTES

1 Paul Davidoff, 'Normative Planning' from *Planning for Diversity and Choice* (ed. S. Anderson), MIT Press, Cambridge, Mass. 1968, pp. 173–79.

2 Kingsley Davis, 'The Urbanization of the Human Population' in *Scientific American* 213, September 1965, pp. 40–53.

3 *Ibid*.

4 Charles Abrams, *The City is the Frontier*, Harper Colophon Books, New York 1965, p. 3.

5 J. Piaget, *Structuralism*, New York 1970, p. 118, quoted in David Harvey, *Social Justice and the City*, Edward Arnold, London 1973, p. 297.

6 K. Marx, *Capital*, International Publishers Edition, New York 1967, Vol. 1, p. 175, cited by Harvey, *ibid*.

7 Brian J.L. Berry, 'General Features of Urban Commercial Structure' in *International Structure of the City* (ed. Larry S. Bourne), Oxford University Press, New York 1971, pp. 361–67.

8 See William Alonso, 'A Theory of the Urban Land Market' in Bourne, *ibid*., pp. 154–59.

9 E. Agergard, P.A. Olsen, J. Allpass, *The Interaction between Retailing and the Urban Centre Structure: A Theory of Spiral Movement*, Institute for Center-Planlaegning, Lyngby, Denmark 1968.

10 See D. Gosling and B. Maitland, *Design and Planning of Retail Systems*, The Architectural Press, London 1976.

11 D. Harvey, 'Social Processes, Spatial Form and the Redistribution of Real Income in an Urban System',

reprinted in *The City: Problems of Planning* (ed. Murray Stewart), Penguin Books, Harmondsworth 1972, p. 297.

12 A. Dunham, 'Property, City Planning and Liberty', reprinted in Stewart, *ibid*., p. 294.

13 H. Lefebvre, *La Révolution Urbaine*, Paris 1970, p. 212, cited in Harvey, *Social Justice and the City, op. cit.*, p. 312.

14 Harvey, *ibid*., p. 313.

15 See O. Marriott, *The Property Boom*, Pan Books, London 1969; P. Ambrose and R. Colenutt, *The Property Machine*, Penguin Books, Harmondsworth 1975; Counter-Information Services, *The Recurrent Crisis of London*, London.

16 See Anthony Sutcliffe, *The Autumn of Central Paris; The Defeat of Town Planning 1850–1970*, Edward Arnold, London 1970.

17 Robert Goodman, *After the Planners*, Pelican Books, Harmondsworth 1972, p. 142.

18 Persigny, *Memories*, p. 256, cited by Sutcliffe, *op. cit.*, p. 32.

19 H.J. Dyos, 'Urban Transformation: a note on the objects of street improvement in Regency and early Victorian London' in *International Review of Social History*, Vol. II, 1957, pt. 2, pp. 259–65.

20 Reyner Banham, *Los Angeles* 1971.

21 *The History of Working Class Housing* (ed. S.D. Chapman), David and Charles 1971, p. 18.

22 Camillo Sitte, *The Art of Building Cities* (trans. Charles T. Stewart), Reinhold Publishing Corporation, New York 1945, p. 59.

23 Melvin Webber, 'Permissive Planning' in *The Future of Cities* (ed. A. Blowers, C. Hamnet and P. Sarre), Hutchinson Educational in association with The Open University Press, London 1974, p. 223.

24 Horst W.J. Rittel and Melvin M. Webber, 'Wicked Problems' in *Man-made Futures* (ed. N. Goss, D. Elliott and R. Roy), Hutchinson Educational in association with The Open University Press, London 1974, p. 272.

25 Goodman, *op. cit.*, p. 115.

26 Ivan D. Illich, *Tools for Conviviality*, Calder and Boyars, London 1973.

27 L. Wolf, 'The Metropolitan Tidal Wave in Ohio, 1900–2000' in *Economic Geography* 45, 1969, p. 163.

28 Sutcliffe, *op. cit.*

29 M. Young and P. Willmott, *Family and Kinship in East London*, Routledge and Kegan Paul, London 1957.

30 P. Willmott, *The Evolution of a Community: a Study of Dagenham after Forty Years*, Routledge and Kegan Paul, London 1963.

31 Jane Jacobs, *The Death and Life of Great American Cities*, Penguin Books, Harmondsworth 1965 (first published 1961).

32 Nicholas Taylor, *The Village in the City*, London 1973.

33 P.M. Hauser, 'The Changing Population of the Modern City' in *Cities and Society: The Revised Reader in Urban Sociology* (ed. P.K. Hatt and A.J. Reiss), Collier-Macmillan, London 1957.

34 Richard Sennett, *The Uses of Disorder: Personal Identity and City Life*, Penguin Books, Harmondsworth 1970, p. 53.

35 Harvey, *Social Justice and the City, op. cit.*, pp. 61, 62.

36 Ray Pahl, 'Will the Inner City Problem Ever Go

Away?' from *Town and Country Planning Summer School 1978, Report of Proceedings*.

37 Janice E. Perlman, *The Myth of Marginality*, University of California Press, Berkeley 1976, p. 12.

38 Quoted in Perlman, *ibid*., p. 12.

39 John Turner, 'The Squatter Settlement: Architecture that Works', *Architectural Design*, August 1968, p. 357.

40 Perlman, *op. cit.*, p. 15.

41 A. & E. Leeds, 'Brazil and the Myth of Urban Rurality', in *City and Country in the 3rd World* (ed. A.J. Field), Schenkman 1970, Part IV(10), pp. 229–73.

42 Mustafa Hag, Bagi Ahmed, *Solutions to Low Income Housing Problems in the Sudan*, University of Sheffield, Ph.D. dissertation 1978.

43 Sennett, *op. cit.*, p. 46.

44 *Ibid.*, p. 47.

45 Harvey, *Social Justice and the City, op. cit.*, p. 94.

46 James Patrick, *A Glasgow Gang Observed*, Eyre Methuen, London 1973. See also Frank Allaun, *No Place Like Home (Britain's Housing Tragedy)*, Andre Deutsch, London 1972.

47 P. Lupsha, 'On Theories of Urban Violence', *Urban Affairs Quarterly*, Vol. 4, 1969, pp. 273–96.

48 Harvey, *Social Justice and the City, op. cit.*, p. 95.

49 *Ibid.*

50 Jerome Deshusses, *Délivrez Promethée*, Flammarion, Paris 1979.

51 Jose Geraldo da Cunha Camergo, *Rural Urbanization*, National Institute for Settlement and Land Reform, Brazil—INCRA 1971.

52 D. Gosling, *Report on the Development of Pioneer Zones in Amazonas*, Ministry of the Interior Brazil, University of Brasília 1976.

53 Sennett, *op. cit.*, p. 81.

54 Colin Rowe & Fred Koetter, 'Collage City', *Architectural Review*, August 1975, Vol. 158, No. 942, p. 81.

55 Victor Papanek, *Design for the Real World*, Thames and Hudson, London 1972.

56 Christopher Alexander, 'A City is not a Tree', *Architectural Forum*, April 1965, pp. 58–62, and May 1965, pp. 58–61.

57 Goodman, *op. cit.*, p. 163.

58 Jacobs, *op. cit.*, p. 422.

59 Harvey, *op. cit.*, p. 16.

60 *Freedom to Build*, (ed. John Turner and Robert Fichter) The Macmillan Company, New York 1972, p. 250.

61 *Ibid.*, p. 241.

62 Goodman, *op. cit.*

63 D. Gosling, 'Brasília', *Third World Planning Review*, Vol. 1, No. 1, Spring 1979, published by Liverpool University Press, pp. 41–56.

64 K. Allsop, 'Mr. Vorster's Showplace', *New Statesman*, 26 March, 1971, p. 424, quoted in Roger White, 'Town Planning in South Africa', *The Planner*, No. 7, Vol. 59, July/August 1973, pp. 311–16.

65 Harvey, *op. cit.*, p. 296.

66 Lewis Mumford, *The City in History*, Penguin Books, Harmondsworth 1966, p. 655.

67 *Ibid.*, p. 656.

68 Alvin Toffler, *Future Shock*, The Bodley Head, London 1970.

69 Joseph Rykwert, *The Idea of a Town*, Faber and Faber, London 1976, p. 190.

# PART TWO
# SOURCES
# AND THEORIES
# OF URBAN DESIGN

AN EMINENT ENGLISH JURIST HAS STATED THAT there are two distinct sources of laws—tradition and invention—and that they are judged by different criteria; the former must work and the latter must be intellectually rigorous. A similar claim can be made for the sources of urban design theories. History provides a large number of traditional urban forms which have survived the passage of time and which work to a greater or lesser degree. These constitute what we might call 'natural models' for further design, in contrast to those 'artificial models' whose virtues are hypothetical. The most complete version of the artificial model is the utopian resolution of all urban problems in a single new formulation of the city, but other more piecemeal analyses are possible, often elicited by contemporary developments in other disciplines. We might say, then, that urban design theorists have sought inspiration from idealizations of the past in natural models, from idealizations of the future in utopian models, and from study of the present in models drawn from the arts and sciences. These three sources form the background to our examination of urban design theories.

## 2.1 NATURAL MODELS

PERSISTING BEYOND THE LIFE-CYCLES OF THEIR component buildings, and metamorphosing beyond the intentions of their individual designers, towns possess a powerful sense of process which draws attention to their origins and raises the fundamental question, 'How did this process begin?'

Two types of answer can be offered. Firstly, many towns owe their foundation and underlying plan to a specific event, a 'big-bang' origin. Such towns were the result of a self-conscious design decision and existed as concepts before materializing in fact. Most of the settlements of the New World are of this type, while in Europe the bastides of France and Wales, and the Zähringer towns of Switzerland and South Germany, began in this way. Earlier still, the Roman colonial cities of Europe and North Africa offer very explicit examples of big-bang foundations, provided as they were with standard plans and carefully specified ritual to impose those plans upon the land, as in the cutting of a perimeter furrow, the digging of a central hole filled with offerings to the gods, and the symbolic transfer, by means of clods of earth, of the settlers' homes and ancestors to the new place.

The second type of beginning has no such precise definition. For such towns, it is no more profitable to pin down the moment of birth than to define that of the culture to which they belong. These 'steady-state' settlements seem to have grown organically with that culture and even where we can be fairly clear about the period of their beginnings, as with

*Djemila, Algeria. A fragment of urban order parked on the edge of the Saharan Atlas.*

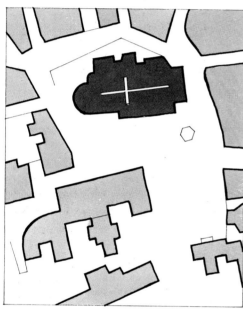

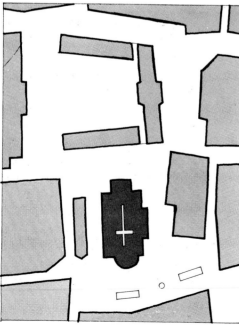

*Camillo Sitte, illustrations from* Der Städtebau, *1889.*

the many medieval towns of Europe which sprang up during the population expansion of the twelfth and thirteenth centuries, their lack of a master-plan and their irregular geometry suggests a different kind of origin from that of the planned foundations. While the latter are described as 'artificial', and often have the word 'new' persist in their names for hundreds of years after their establishment, the former are felt to be in some way 'natural' phenomena.

Now, of course, most towns are composites of these two types of formation. In Europe, big-bang Roman grids peek through the later steady-state medieval accretions, and 'artificial' sectors are added to 'natural' cores. However, the distinction between these two modes persists and the suspicion which arose in the nineteenth century, that with the Industrial Revolution the ability to effect the 'natural', 'organic' process had been altogether lost, created a recurring fascination with it. Ignoring the fact that 'artificial' grid-plans also have ancient origins, some critics have seen the irregular yet cohesive patterns of development as containing older values of human scale and social justice which industrial societies, with their orthogonal geometries, have lost and desperately need to recover.

One of the first, and most influential, of such critics was the Viennese architect Camillo Sitte, the publication of whose book *Der Städtebau* in 1889[1] played a crucial part in the development of a coherent appreciation of the qualities of 'natural' towns, and the lessons they had to offer to modern town planning. Sitte's critique was aimed against what he saw as the sterile results of planning from traffic considerations alone, and the isolation of that from the other factors involved in town design: 'We have three dominant systems for building cities, and a number of variations of them. They are: the rectangular system, the radial system, and the triangular system. Generally speaking the variations are bastard offspring of these three. From an artistic point of view the whole tribe is worthless, having exhausted the last drop of art's blood from its veins. These systems accomplish nothing except a standardization of street pattern. They are purely mechanical in conception. They reduce the street system to a mere traffic utility, never serving the purposes of art. They make no approach to the sense of perception, for we can see their features only on a map.'[2] To find an alterna-

tive to these 'systems', Sitte proposed to investigate the plans of old towns, but not 'as historian nor as critic. We wish to seek out, as technician and artist, the elements of composition which formerly produced such harmonious effects, and those which today produce only loose and dull results.'[3]

Confining his attention to public squares, Sitte considered a large number of Italian and German towns, analysing the relationship between buildings, spaces and monuments. The plans of 57 such squares were printed, all of them apparently random and irregular in arrangement, but all illustrating qualities of enclosure, grouping and effective composition from which he was able to distil certain principles of good design. Having drawn his lessons from the past, Sitte concluded by setting out a method of town design which effectively revised that of the 'systems'. It consisted first in formulating a programme for the town, and then in identifying the public buildings it would contain. These were grouped and located, and competitions were held to design the plazas, with their surrounding buildings, which would form the points of focus throughout the town. Principal routes could then be established between these points, and finally the intervening areas set out with 'worthwhile irregularities in the street pattern which are so greatly needed to overcome the banal and all-pervasive symmetry of the drawing board.'[4]

Sitte's work had enormous influence, first in Germany, where many designers abandoned 'French' axial layouts in favour of irregular plans, and then further afield as his work was translated and illustrated abroad. By 1909, when Raymond Unwin published *Town Planning in Practice*, he could already say that 'there are today two schools of town designers, the work of one being based on the conviction that the treatment should be formal and regular in character, while that of the other springs from an equally strong belief that informality is desirable.'[5] His book follows Sitte's in its organization, proceeding from an analysis of historical example, through the distillation of principles to their application in the design of towns, using case studies from his own work. It is clear that despite his insistence that both formal and informal methods are valid and might be brought together in some compromise arrangement, Unwin was strongly influenced by the German school, many examples of whose work are illustrated in his book.

Where Sitte considered his material as 'technician and artist', Unwin invited his readers to approach the question of the form of old towns in the spirit of tourists: 'Many Englishmen, as tourists, have become familiar with foreign towns as well as with those in their own country; but the tourist in examining town maps does not regard them as designs. Let any one so regard them and he will be astonished at the variety of types which he will find. It is only necessary to turn over the pages of Baedeker's or Baddeley's Guides to Great Britain to realise this.'[6] To Sitte's itinerary of mainly German and Italian towns, Unwin added English examples of medieval and vernacular building, so that evocative sketches of village streets, as of Dunster in Somersetshire and Kesey in Suffolk, join naturally with those of Rothenburg, Dinan and Bruges to broaden the sources of informal town planning. His use of drawings, which make proposals for the future indistinguishable from examples from the past, was particularly effective in communicating an atmosphere of timeless consistency and, in the case of his analysis of the centre of Buttstadt by means of a sequence of 'frames', anticipated later representations of serial vision. In addition, Unwin's analysis of the components of his selected old towns was much more detailed than Sitte's, and his book offered a convincing translation of both principles and detailed forms into modern usage, reinforced by their use in perimeter wall, gateway buildings, bridge buildings, corner buildings, and other examples, executed or proposed, for Hampstead Garden Suburb and Letchworth.

As the twentieth century continued, the Austrian's pencil and the Englishman's Baedeker were superseded by a new tool of perception. With the development of photography, and above all of aerial photography, the repertoire of 'natural' city forms available to the student of town design was enormously extended. No longer limited to the familiar products of European folk culture, he could marvel at the enormous diversity of patterns of settlement around the globe, much in the manner of a scientist studying the prolific forms of nature. This analogy, together with the excitement of the newly discovered view of the world, is apparent in the literature of the 1920s and 1930s, as in this passage by the French aviator Antoine de Saint-Exupéry: '... from the height of our rectilinear trajectories we discover the essential foundation, the fundament of rock and sand and salt in which here and there and from time to time life like a little moss in the crevices of ruins has risked its precarious existence.

'We to whom humble journeyings were once permitted have now been transformed into physi-

*Raymond Unwin, use of frames in an analysis of the centre of Buttestadt, from* Town Planning in Practice, *1909.*

cists, biologists, students of the civilizations that beautify the depths of valleys and now and again, by some miracle, bloom like gardens where the climate allows. We are able to judge man in cosmic terms, scrutinize him through our portholes as through instruments of the laboratory.'[7]

A more recent celebration of this scrutiny was provided by an exhibition of photographs mounted in the Museum of Modern Art in New York in 1964 by Bernard Rudofsky, which subsequently achieved wide circulation and influence through the publication of the book *Architecture without Architects*.[8] This contained a wide sample of folk structures, from China to Sweden, Zanzibar to New Guinea, the very arbitrariness of which emphasized the implication that *all* cultures possess such models of unselfconscious town building. Decrying the conventional concern only with the 'formal' architecture of 'a few select cultures', Rudofsky made a point similar to that developed in modern linguistics which recognizes no fundamental differences of relevance, structure or complexity between so-called 'civilized' and 'primitive' languages. The appeal of his argument was greatly strengthened by the fact that his examples of communal structures were able to generate, from

the most modest of individual parts, the most spectacular of results. His photographic survey, though by no means comprehensive, suggested the richness of solutions which have evolved through a close adaptation to a narrow range of circumstances and which might be found in any part of the earth where settlement dated back more than a few hundred years.

If we consider only the Mediterranean basin, for example, a region long regarded for its formal architecture, the parallel range of informal, 'natural' building which exists alongside is very great. It includes one of the few examples of town forms to which the term 'natural' can, in fact, be literally applied, at Göreme in Anatolia. There, in a valley of volcanic rock formations eroded into a strange landscape of conical towers, Anchorite Christian refugees in the seventh century (ironically a new community) tunnelled a town of multi-storey apartment towers and social rooms out of the soft rock. The fact that later residents abandoned these towers, which extended to as much as 16 floors in height, in favour of the small houses which now cluster around the lower slopes of the natural cones, reflects perhaps on the agility which was required to live in this extraordinary settlement.

Göreme, Anatolia, Turkey, natural conical towers.

Göreme, later houses cluster around the base of taller outcrops.

Ghorfas, southern Tunisia, one of many examples of 'architecture without architects'.

Elsewhere in the Mediterranean basin, the conical forms of Göreme are repeated by ancient building methods which still persist, as in the Trulli settlements of southern Italy. The suggestion they give of giant insect colonies, as of ants or termites, reinforces the impression of natural phenomena which is present in other works of folk architecture. The *ghorfas* of southern Tunisia recall the combs of bees, for example, both in their form as closely packed repeating cells and in their function as food stores for nomadic tribes of the Sahara.

The region also abounds in settlements which, though not as archaic as these examples nor as directly comparable to natural forms, still achieve a similar combination of simple repetitive components, complex and irregular internal arrangements and dramatic overall effect. These are the hill-towns, which occur in different variations in the Aegean, in Italy, in Spain and in North Africa and which achieve considerable articulation of their organizational structure and specialization of their component parts without losing their overall organic coherence. Indeed, in some cases, such as those of Umbria and Tuscany, this articulation and specialization enhances their identity over a range of town sizes from, say, 5,000 inhabitants to 50,000.[9] Typically, each such hill-town possesses a number of shared characteristics. Firstly, their presence is signalled over the surrounding countryside by their towers which rise up from the natural mound of the hill itself. Then their extent is defined by a hard edge, either a cliff as at Orvieto, or else a wall. This perimeter is breached at specific points of entry where arched gateways are built. Within the walls, the irregular pattern of building is penetrated by main routes which lead inwards from the gates. The climate of these routes forms a contrast with the hot, exposed spaces of the *campagna* in being cool, sheltered and enclosed, and, although rarely straight, they are structured in the sense that they rarely persist for more than about 200 metres before reaching a point of focus in the town. These nodes form the fifth common element, and are typically a square with accompanying church and fountain.

From these five elements a whole range of hill-towns is built up, each with a particular geometry suited to the topography. For example, both San Gimignano and Siena are built at the convergence of three ridges, and therefore both adopt a roughly triangular arrangement. Since the former is small, it comprises just one central node cluster of squares with the major public buildings facing onto them and then a single, 200-metre branch outward along each of the three ridges to the principal gateways. Siena, on the other hand, is large and builds out from its central node, the Campo, in a series of route lengths punctuated with nodes along its three ridges. Intermediate nodes along the main routes act as growth points for secondary routes branching off to the sides, and a triple hierarchy of nodes with adjacent buildings of ascending importance builds up to articulate the whole town mass. Similarly, Orvieto and Spello are based on linear spines, Urbino and Cortona on cruciforms and Gubbio and Assisi on stretched grids, all built up from the same urban elements in a pattern to suit their topography.

A somewhat different structure has been investigated by Raymond Gindroz[10] on the Island of Mýkonos. Gindroz points out that in many Greek towns, the form of connection between private family space and public corridor is extremely complex: 'A series of buffer areas, which are both part of the street and part of the house, protect the privacy of the house.' On the Island of Póros, the houses extend outside their walls and include the street as part of the living space. Gindroz says that the kitchen in the form of a porch may be on one side of the street and the living room on the other—and the public space is taken over by the inhabitants to accommodate a communal way of life. In this way, in a densely developed hill-town such as Mýkonos, the urban structure differs greatly from other Mediterranean hill-towns. The routes themselves decline in significance as an ordering system and the houses become one single agglomeration with qualities of unity and coherence.

In the case of Arab hill-towns, a repertoire similar to that of the five elements of the Italian examples is echoed in the form of the central mosque. First the location of the mosque is fixed by towers, which act as pointers to anyone within the narrow streets of the surrounding town. The reserved area is then protected by a high perimeter wall with elaborate entry gateways from which sheltered routes lead into and around the forecourt *sahn*, in the centre of which a ritual fountain and washing place is located. Thus the components of the informal folk language of the hill-town are acknowledged and repeated in its central building complex, but now in the formal language of high architecture.

Valuable as morphological analyses of these models of fine vernacular architecture and town planning may be, however, it must be admitted that they are not often considered in such a dis-

*San Gimignano, Tuscany, Italy, routes leading through the dense mass of building from the city gateways.*

*Village of Mýkonos, Island of Mýkonos, Greece.*

*The Campo, Siena, Tuscany, Italy. Here, routes lead into node spaces disposed throughout the town.*

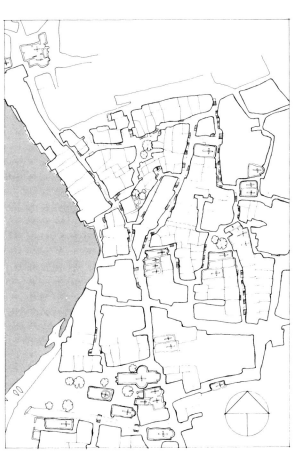

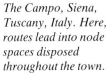

passionate way. The spirit of the technician or biologist commonly takes a second place to that of the propagandist, and all three of the books we have discussed use these models from the past to develop critiques of the present and propositions for the future, reinforcing their arguments with all the nostalgia and authority which this view of the past can provide.

Sitte's book begins: 'Memory of travel is the stuff of our fairest dreams. Splendid cities, plazas, monuments and landscapes thus pass before our eyes, and we enjoy again the charming and impressive spectacles that we have formerly experienced.'[11] And these spectacles may be argued to have a particular validity and authority where they seem to have been the product of the people as a whole, rather than of a few individuals: 'Little in ancient architecture was "designed". Things designed by a single line are mostly "sports", which must quickly perish. Only that which is in the line of development can persist.' And again: 'An expressive form of art is only reached by building out in one direction during a long time. No art that is only one man deep is worth much; it should be a thousand men deep.'[12] These quotations from W.R. Lethaby seem to have deeply influenced Unwin, and their deterministic tone, setting the weight of tradition against the triviality of individual 'sports', and 'natural' evolution against 'artificial' design, is echoed in Rudofsky's celebration of 'nonpedigreed architecture . . . we shall call it vernacular, anonymous, spontaneous, indigenous, rural . . .'[13] Not only is this architecture more valid in its forms, but its users are more healthy as a result: 'There is a good deal of irony in the fact that to stave off physical and mental deterioration, the urban dweller periodically escapes his splendidly appointed lair to seek bliss in what he thinks are primitive surroundings: a cabin, a tent, or, if he is less hidebound, a fishing village or hill town abroad. Despite his mania for mechanical comfort, his chances for finding relaxation hinge on its very absence.'[14] The natural town thus offers a critique of modern society and a study of it might provide us with a way forward: 'The wisdom to be derived goes beyond economic and aesthetic considerations, for it touches the far tougher and increasingly troublesome problem of how to live and let live, how to keep peace with one's neighbours, both in the parochial and universal sense.'[15] But Rudofsky's line of reasoning is not the only one which can be developed from a study of vernacular architecture, and other admirers of 'nonpedigreed' towns have used their example to develop quite different propositions.

*Village of Thíra, Island of Thíra, Greece.*

Le Corbusier, the poet of the right angle, might seem an unlikely member of this group. It was he, after all, who contrasted 'man's way' with 'the pack-donkey's way': 'Man walks in a straight line because he has a goal and knows where he is going. . . . The pack-donkey meanders along, meditates a little in his scatter-brained and distracted fashion, he zigzags in order to avoid the larger stones, or to ease the climb, or to gain a little shade; he takes the line of least resistance. . . . In the Middle Ages, men accepted the leading of the pack-donkey, and long generations endured it after.'[16] More recently, a fashion for this had recurred: 'The movement arose in Germany as a result of a book by Camille [*sic*] Sitte on town planning, a most wilful piece of work; a glorification of the curved line and a specious demonstration of its unrivalled beauties. Proof of this was advanced by the example of all the beautiful towns of the Middle Ages; the author confounded the picturesque with the conditions vital to the existence of the city. Quite recently whole quarters have been constructed in Germany based on the *aesthetic*. (For it was purely a question of aesthetics.) This was an appalling and paradoxical mis-

conception in an age of motor-cars.'[17] And, in contrast to this: 'Where the orthogonal is supreme, there we can read the height of a civilization. Cities can be seen emerging from the jumble of their streets, striving towards straight lines, and taking them as far as possible.'[18]

Despite this sharp attack on Sitte and apparent reversal of all his formal preferences, Le Corbusier was nevertheless a student and admirer of vernacular buildings and towns. In his map showing the route of the journey of self-education which he undertook in his youth through Europe and Asia Minor,[19] he marks the locations of points of study under the three categories of industry, culture and folklore, and his sketchbooks are full of observations of the third. His admiration for traditional town building continued throughout his life wherever he encountered it in his travels. While preparing a plan for Algiers, for example, he enthused about the Arab quarter: 'Pure and efficient stratification of the Casbah. Among these terraces which form the roof of the city, not an inch is wasted.'[20] This, in turn, was contrasted to the 'harmful stratification . . . of the civilized houses' of the European quarter which was encroaching upon it.'

Elsewhere using words which might have been written by Rudofsky, he writes: 'I look for primitive men, not for their barbarity but for their wisdom. America, Europe, farmers, fishermen.'[21] Like Rudofsky, he also distinguishes between formal, high architecture, and informal, folk architecture. Against photographs of the former he observes: 'Forms taken by culture in great cities, the other face of human destiny: "Oh man, live dangerously!" Those who can have always ventured into the lists of the great tournament: the spirit that uproots men from a life of quiet and spurs them on to higher destinies!' Then, against pictures of vernacular scenes: 'Forms taken by culture in scattered communities: "folk art". Perfect harmony achieved on a scale with *man*. Serenity of the pastoral life. Tools and equipment sufficient though precarious. . . . But the locomotive is either on its way or already there. . . . Death of "folk art", dawn of a new culture and accompanying distress.'[22]

Like Sitte, Le Corbusier was not averse to a selective borrowing of the forms of folk architecture, as in his projects for tourist villages at La Sainte Baume in 1948 and 'Roq' and 'Rob' at Cap Martin in 1949, which uncannily resemble the Tunisian *ghorfas* and, in the earlier project, adopt a similar anular layout.[23] But for Le Corbusier, always a devotee of the biological analogy, the essential lesson of 'natural' towns was precisely that they could be regarded as works of nature: 'All architectural products, all city neighbourhoods or cities ought to be *organisms*.'[24] Thus of an Arab settlement: 'an aerial view reveals sound biology, brilliant anatomy',[25] while a plan of Venice, with not a sign of the orthogonal emerging from the jumble of its streets, can nevertheless be admirable: 'This drawing is a revelation.... Doesn't it look like perfect biology?—the circulation of the blood in a living being? A functional city, Venice, extraordinarily functional.'[26] Like Nature, Venice is seen as hiding lucid order beneath apparent chaos: 'Nature presents itself to us as a chaos, ... But the spirit which animates Nature is a spirit of order.'[27] Therefore: 'Venice naturally forms an introduction to the urbanization plans for the new city of Antwerp....'[28]

Thus the same organic models which led Sitte and the German school to meandering plans for the suburbs of Augsburg and Cologne led Le Corbusier to a supergrid for 50,000 inhabitants on the left bank of the Scheldt. Similarly, others were able to draw from the same models as Rudofsky precisely the opposite conclusions. In the same year as his exhibition, for example, as Reyner Banham has pointed out,[29] Fumihiko Maki was defining the meaning of the term 'megastructure' in terms of the Italian hill-town while Peter Blake was suggesting that there was an essential similarity between that same model and the Archigram group's 'Plug-in City': 'Plug-In City's fundamental idea—the city considered as a single organic entity—is as old as Urbino. For here, too, the city was a skeleton of urban spaces (passages, steps, streets, piazzas) which held things together.'[30]

Built megastructures, like Geoffrey Copcutt's Cumbernauld Town Centre and Moshe Safdie's Habitat, seemed to suggest that the Italian hill-town had indeed contributed to the genre, and its components reappeared piecemeal in a number of the quintessential high-technology images of the 1960s. It was difficult to avoid seeing the towers of San Gimignano in Louis Kahn's development sketches for the Richards Medical Research Building, for example, while the big out-of-town shopping centres blandly took over the vocabulary of arcades, piazzas and fountains for their own purposes.

It may be felt from this that the vision of the 'natural', 'organic' town is more inspirational than factual in its message, less a model than a mirror of the preoccupations of the time. Yet it remains a particularly rich and fruitful source of ideas and perhaps for the reason that whereas the formal or 'artificial' towns can be regarded simply as designers' propositions about what might make a successful solution to a need, the evolved settlements are representations of the need itself, expressing itself through thousands of small decisions taken over a long period of time. Perhaps, then, they may contain, locked within their picturesque silhouettes, a potent and fundamental message for the urban designer, even if the interpretations of that message seem so much at variance.

*Al Azhar Mosque, Cairo, Egypt. The mosque is an analogue of the city—an architectural elaboration of a sequence of events.*

*Moulay Idriss, Morocco. The mosque forms an ordered focus within the dense texture of the North-African hill-town.*

## 2.2 UTOPIAN MODELS

DESPITE THE CONFUSING COUNTER-CLAIMS MADE upon it, the term 'organic' suggests an amoral development process, evolving naturally with the needs of society as it exists. In this, it contrasts sharply with another powerful tradition—the utopian or ideal—in which town design is closely allied to the design of society itself. And whereas the organic town can exist only in fact, as the physical result of a multitude of small forces and actions, the ideal town can exist only in theory, as one designer's formulation of a possible complete solution to the design problem 'town'.

The term 'Utopia' itself means both a place and a state of things, and it is often difficult to separate the two. Language and literature contain many references to this identification of the idealized society with the city, as in the New Jerusalem and the Heavenly City, and indeed the circumstances of the design method itself are often uncannily close. T.E. Lawrence described the established pattern for the lives of the social reformers and prophets of the Middle East as follows: 'Their birth set them in crowded places. An unintelligible passionate yearning drove them out into the desert. There they lived a greater or lesser time in meditation or physical abandonment; and thence they returned with their imagined message articulate, to preach it to their old, and now doubting associates.'[31]

So also Campanella, Bacon, Fourier, Le Corbusier, Wright and Howard all devised their utopian models during periods of either enforced or voluntary obscurity and isolation. Moreover, the relationship between the ideal society and its ideal city has not been the simple one of a programme and its delineation. As Fishman has pointed out,[32] the idea of the planner may precede even a statement of the problem, let alone a formulation of the plan, as in the case of Wright's early assertion that, 'The creative artist ... must dominate and transform this greatest of machines, the city, and give it A SOUL'.[33] Again, the persistence of certain utopian forms in city planning indicates how these may predate the social prospectus and be used again and again for quite different programmes. The family of centralized circular and polygonal plans deriving from Plato's vague description of his utopia, and from Vitruvius' preoccupation with the exposure of the ideal town to winds, is the most striking example of this. Whether coupled with a primary preoccupation with symbolic form, ventilation or deference to the central authority, these patterns became a recurring basis for a large number of utopian projects from Filarete's Sforzinda onwards.

The relevance to urban design of this perseverance of utopian forms is illustrated by the case of Freudenstadt in Southern Germany, a new town designed by Heinrich Schickhardt (1558–1634). The form is based upon a drawing of an ideal plan by Dürer on a square, rather than polygonal format. A large 200-metre wide open square forms the centre of concentric rings of housing terraces, with the main public and commercial uses located in or around the central square. This town was destroyed by fire in 1632, rebuilt and then again completely demolished in an air raid during the course of the Second World War, and again subsequently rebuilt. Although the detailed reproduction of the original buildings, as at Warsaw, was not attempted, the plan and those urban design features which reinforced it, were. Of these, the central square space, the location of public buildings in and around it, the provision of continuous arcades to buildings fronting onto it, and the maintenance of common scale and materials in the surrounding rings of terraces, were most important. Thus the memorable clarity of Dürer's ideal form has persisted through two major reconstructions and 400 years of continuous use.

Perhaps the most persuasive characteristic of these ideal patterns is the way in which they express the city as a singly conceived, complete design solution. This notion, a question of practical fact for the Romans and a great intellectual revelation to the men of the Renaissance, could be challenged as being highly undesirable. To the critiques offered by the advocates of 'organic' town design, we could add the profound philosophical objections of Karl Popper to utopianism, namely that it is historicist in nature, unscientific, oppressive, unable to learn from its mistakes and based upon a number of doubtful propositions, such as 'the colossal assumption that we need not question the fundamental benevolence of the planning Utopian engineer'.[34] As Popper observes, a wide range of utopian attitudes to man and his social organizations is possible, from the pessimism of Plato who 'believed that all change—or almost all change—is decay; this was his law of historical development. Accordingly, his Utopian blueprint aims at arresting all change'; to the optimism of Marx whose 'Utopian blueprint was one of a developing or "dynamic" rather than of an arrested society'.[35] All, however, must be condemned as 'holistic planning'.

Against this view could be set the argument that the purpose of utopian speculation is catalytic rather than prescriptive, clarifying the confused debates which occur in the real world by postulating alternative hypotheses in a pure and crystalline form: 'The great mission of the Utopia is to make room for the possible as opposed to a passive acquiescence in the present actual state of affairs. It is symbolic thought which overcomes the natural inertia of man and endows him with a new ability, the ability constantly to reshape his human universe.'[36]

Although most utopias aim to be comprehensive, we may identify a major group which is concerned primarily with the reformation of society, for which it then goes on to propose an appropriate city form. In contrast, a second group of ideal plans is primarily motivated by the technical difficulties of achieving a successful city form; in these cases the plan may well have little to say about the society which is to be accommodated except perhaps that it modify certain of its living patterns to suit the technical ideals. Finally, although by definition utopia can never be constructed, the widespread attempts in modern times to base real towns upon utopian models has produced a reaction against both social and technical centralized utopias which, paradoxically, could itself be described as utopian. The search for an ideal city which does not have to rely on 'the fundamental benevolence of the planning Utopian engineer' forms a third, more recent utopian tradition which we investigate here.

Although much utopian literature is concerned with moral, sexual and economic habits of society which have little direct bearing on urban design, its investigation of the relationships between people in a community, and the nature of work, raises fundamental questions concerning the size and structure of towns, and the relationship of town to country, which are central problems of urban design. Regarding the appropriate size of communities, for example, and of the groupings within them, the social utopias provide a fascinating variety of scenarios. Sir Thomas More's *Utopia* (a pun on the Greek words for 'no-place' and 'good place') written in 1515, envisaged a country of 100,000 square miles, supporting 54 similar towns each of 80,000 inhabitants. The basic economic and social unit of both town and country is the household, an extended family base of 10 to 16 adults in the former and 40 or more in the latter. In the town, groups of 30 households (i.e. up to 500 adults) assemble twice each day for communal meals in the house of a magistrate, each 10 of whom elect from their number a senior magistrate for the government of the town. The town is further broken down into four quarters, each of which supports a market. More's magisterial unit of 300–500 adults recurs in the ideal community size of 400 adult male citizens proposed by Johann Andreae in 1619. Here, however, they form a small independent town, Christianopolis, organized along the lines of a medieval guild, and planned within a 700-foot square, with different forms of work zoned to its four quarters.

The attempt of such ideal plans to define a scale of community for social, political and economic purposes somewhere between that of the individual family and that of the large town or city, received further attention from the utopian socialists of the nineteenth century. As Sir John Summerson has remarked in relation to the introduction and testing of new technology in the Victorian building industry, so also in the field of planning, much pioneering work was carried out on 'captive' users of one kind or another—the sick, the insane, the very poor and the imprisoned. Robert Owen's 'Villages of Cooperation', for example, were proposed to accommodate between 300 and 2,000—with an optimum of 800 to 1,200—poor people in a single quadrangular building form. Similarly, Jeremy Bentham's 'Panopticon', following the tradition of polygonal ideal forms, postulated an 'Industry-House Establishment' for 2,000 occupants to achieve 'Pauper Management Improved' in a single five-storey, multiple-use building.

The importance to modern planning theories of French utopian thinking of this period of the early nineteenth century, and in particular the remarkable parallels between the proposals of Charles Fourier and Victor Considérant and those one hundred years later of Le Corbusier, have been explored by Anthony Vidler.[37] Concerned by the somewhat arbitrary basis of such community groupings and planned associations, Fourier developed an elaborate theory of human personality from which he derived a population size of 1,620 as being ideal to sustain a balanced mixture of human types. As with Owen's and Bentham's communities, this association was to be housed in a single building, or building group, the 'Phalanstère', containing residential, social and work spaces, and would form 'the elementary cell in the great social beehive'. The affinity with Le Corbusier's Unité d'Habitation is made particularly vivid by his use of the nautical analogy deployed by Considérant in this argument put forward for the practicability of the idea: 'You have beneath your eyes, and very obvious to you, constructions housing 1,600 men,

not based on terrafirma, but very mobile, speeding at ten knots across the ocean, transporting their inhabitants from Toulon to the Cape, from the Cape to Calcutta, constructions for 1,600 inhabitants which navigate the winds of the great seas and the hurricanes of the Tropics. Now is it easier to lodge 1,600 men in the middle of the ocean, 600 leagues from every shore, to construct floating fortresses, than to accommodate 1,600 good country folk in a unitary construction in the middle of Champagne?'[38]

Vidler also indicates a second important source of Le Corbusier's themes in another utopian project by Fourier, for an 'Ideal City' which would become appropriate when civilization had advanced somewhat, to its next stage of development. The basic element now becomes a combined household of 100 family units grouped around an enclosed court, with the households linked together to provide covered circulation throughout the city. This has powerful similarities with Le Corbusier's project of 1922 for 'Une Ville Contemporaine', and with his plans for 'immeubles-villas'. The latter comprised 120 family apartments arranged in two parallel blocks with a central green court, and linked together by covered corridor streets. The whole ground floor of such units would be given over to 'an immense workshop for the household economy', and the cumulative effect of such a decentralization of service functions to local cooperative bases would be to make obsolete the large central markets of the city. Le Corbusier's explanation of his 'immeubles-villas' projects forms a lucid programme for all such utopian investigations into community size and form: 'Let us examine the needs of a household (a cell) and the needs of a certain number of cells in their necessary relationships, and let us estimate the number of cells that can usefully form a manageable group —manageable like a hotel or like a commune—a community which itself becomes a clear and defined organic element in the urban plan, having a well-defined function that allows strict needs to be recognized and the problem to be stated.'[39]

A second major theme explored by the social utopias, and one which became increasingly urgent as the Industrial Revolution developed, was the relation between the city and the country. The three alternative formulations of this relationship, expressed, in ascending order of urban density, by Wright's Broadacre City, Howard's Garden City and Le Corbusier's Ville Radieuse, are but the most famous of many such investigations. The problem is a central one for Marxist commentators,

dating back to the ninth of Marx's ten measures, set out in the 1848 *Manifesto of the Communist Party* as being necessary for the establishment of a communist society, which required 'Combination of agriculture with manufacturing industries, gradual abolition of the distinction between town and country, by a more equable distribution of the population over the country'.[40]

The difficulties inherent in trying to base a planning policy on this requirement have been set out in a fascinating account by Kenneth Frampton,[41] as they surfaced after the Revolution in Russia with two rival schools of Marxian urbanism competing for official recognition. For Sabsovitch and the 'Urbanists', the appropriate stategy lay in the dismemberment of existing large towns (being 'an expression of the capitalist regime') and their reassembly in 'agglomerations', each of about 50,000 inhabitants set in open country. Each agglomeration would be collectivized, its inhabitants housed in individual cells grouped into 'communes' of up to 4,000 persons, each sharing all domestic facilities. In contrast, Miliutin and the 'Disurbanists' proposed a Marxian development of the linear city concept proposed in 1882 by Soria y Mata for the 'Ciudad Lineal', Madrid, and comprising six continuous parallel linear zones for communications, industry, open space, dwellings and public buildings, parks and sports, and agriculture, extending to form a city of 100,000 to 200,000 inhabitants. Seductive as this second theoretical proposal was, both Miliutin and Ernst May, who was recruited with other German planners in 1930 to assist the Russian effort in planning the new town of Magnitogorsk, were unable to apply the ideal structure to a real topography with the rigour demanded by its inventor. Instead, 'agglomerations' became the official policy until, in 1931, the Central Committee renounced all utopian proposals, whether 'Urbanist' or 'Disurbanist', and all foreign planning theories from Broadacre City to the Ville Radieuse.[42]

It would perhaps be more correct to describe these Soviet theoretical formulations as 'idealist', rather than 'utopian', since, despite the faults which Popper sees as common to both utopianism and Marxism, there is a traditional antipathy between the two. Again this dates back to the *Manifesto of the Communist Party*, and Marx's analysis and rejection of the attempts of Saint-Simon, Fourier, Owen and others (a rejection, incidentally, not shared by the Parisian student revolutionaries of 1968, who re-erected Fourier's statue in the city) to devise clean-slate solutions:

'They still dream of experimental realization of their social utopias, of founding isolated "phalanstères", of establishing "home colonies", of setting up a "little Icaria"—duodecimo editions of the New Jerusalem—and to realize all these castles in the air, they are compelled to appeal to the feelings and purses of the bourgeois. By degrees they sink into the category of the reactionary conservative socialists depicted above, differing from these only by more systematic pedantry, and by their fanatical and superstitious belief in the miraculous effects of their social science.'[43]

In recent years in Europe, work has been done by Tafuri, Leon Krier and others to further relate contemporary Marxist theory to problems of architecture and planning. Again, the rejection of utopian solutions as irrelevant distractions is maintained. In his book *Architecture and Utopia: Design and Capitalist Development*, Tafuri analyses the development of utopian themes, first in the nineteenth century as a means of disguising the conflict between capital and labour, and then in the twentieth when: 'Utopia became of service to development as a reserve of tendentious models and as an arm for the extraction of consensus'.[44] Such criticism would presumably apply to those who have attempted to broaden and, perhaps, to neutralize the utopian tradition by developing it as a means for postulating and assessing possible alternative futures. Thus, in their influential postwar book *Communitas*,[45] Paul and Percival Goodman concluded their analysis of recent planning history by sketching design solutions for three possible ways forward, 'The city of efficient consumption', 'The new commune', and 'Planned security with minimum regulation', the purpose of which was 'a philosophical one: to ask what is socially implied in any such scheme as a way of life, and how each plan expresses some tendency of modern mankind'.[46]

For Tafuri, such speculation is largely irrelevant, and he concludes his book with the injunction that, on the contrary, 'Today, indeed, the principal task of ideological criticism is to do away with impotent and ineffectual myths, which so often serve as illusions that permit the survival of anachronistic "hopes in design".' Although criticized for its Marxism as much as its planning content,[47] Tafuri's work and that of Leon Krier opened an important debate on the place of theory in contemporary urbanism, and the need, as they assess it, for a 'Rational Architecture'.[48] According to their view, urban design cannot be regarded as a social panacea, but rather as part of a wider struggle against capitalism. In this struggle, the particular contribution of urban design will lie in its reintegration of the public realm and its expression in the rediscovered pre-industrial urban elements of the street, the square and the *quartier*.

Curiously enough, the development of an appropriate hardware for the public realm has also been a contributing preoccupation of that other utopian tradition, concerned with the perfection of the technical solutions required by the city. The compelling results which can follow from an obsessive attention to a single technical function are immediately demonstrated in one of the first such technical utopias which we have, that of Vitruvius as described in his *Ten Books on Architecture*.[49] Vitruvius' overriding preoccupation with the exposure of the town to winds, so as to give shelter but at the same time healthy ventilation, leads him by an unlikely piece of logic (itself contradicted by other Roman authorities[50]) to a polygonal form with 16 main radial streets, quite unlike our expectation of a Roman grid plan.

Although Vitruvius' strange obsession with problems of ventilation was not shared by subsequent planners, his iconic solution proved serviceable for other cases where a single functional requirement dominated the programme, as did defence in the numerous projects for fortress towns which were devised during the Renaissance. With these designs for the city as a strategic unit, we also see very clearly the expression of the public realm, not just in the imposition of an ordered pattern on the individual buildings, but in the development of major constructions which follow their own design logic, often quite independent of the pattern of elements they embrace. We might then trace the development of successive technical utopias as the increasingly ambitious attempt to envisage the city as a single piece of public hardware embedded with private components, and thus to advance the

*Etienne-Louis Boullée, project for the interior of the Metropole, Paris, France, c. 1781.*

*Friedrich Weinbrenner, Kaiserstrasse, Karlsruhe, West Germany, 1808.*

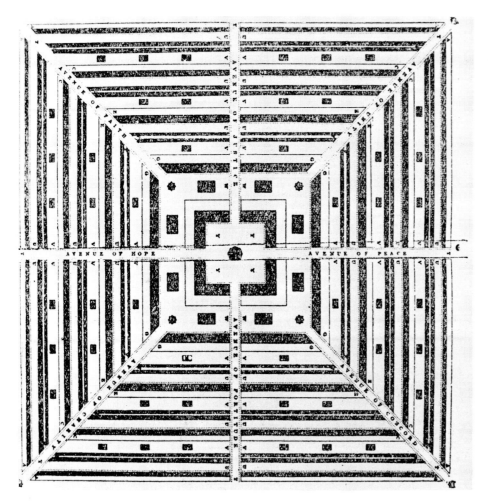

*J. S. Buckingham, plan for 'Victoria', 1849.*

design of its systems.

For the majority of such projects, the overt dominant technical problem has been that of circulation. Sixtus V's reconstruction of the circulation of Rome made explicit the Baroque idealization of the public realm in a network of avenues and node spaces of monumental scale. This ordering of external space was then reinforced by projects elaborating the public structures which might accompany and articulate it, as in Ledoux's plans for Chaux, or, as in the case of Boullée's designs for the Metropole and Newton Cenotaph, postulating public internal spaces of equally monumental scale. The connection of focal points by covered public routes was also demonstrated in such projects as that by Weinbrenner for the Lange Strasse in Karlsruhe, and this gradually came to be a plausible technical objective. As we have seen, Owen, Bentham and Fourier envisaged their ideal communities as having covered public circulation routes, and by 1849 James Silk Buckingham had extended this principle to a town for 10,000 shareholders.

Buckingham's plan for 'Victoria', similar in its pattern of concentric squares to that of Freudenstadt, envisaged covered galleries connecting the dwellings which, in their use of glass and iron, anticipated the technical innovations of the Crystal Palace. After 1851, the possibilities for the extensive enclosure of public space implicit in that building recur in a variety of both ideal projects and actual galleries and arcaded streets. Despite Howard's note added to the second edition of *Garden Cities of Tomorrow* that his ideal plan for a Garden City was a 'Diagram only. Plan cannot be drawn until site selected', his proposal shows a specific example of this in what he calls the 'Crystal Palace' which contains the town's shops in a circular glazed arcade, about one kilometre in diameter, which surrounds the central park.

In 1901, the year before Howard's second edition was published, Frank Lloyd Wright delivered his Hull House lecture, which included the reference to the 'greatest of machines, the city' which was cited earlier. Undoubtedly this analogy, extending the contemporary machine debate from the fields of architecture and product design to that of the city itself, was central to the technical utopias which followed. It suggested both a new conception of circulation and also the independence of the idealized city of its history and location. By 1914, both of these implications were incorpor-ated into the Futurist version of this utopia as set out by Sant' Elia in his famous drawings and in the *Messagio*: 'We must invent and rebuild *ex novo* our Modern City like an immense and tumultuous shipyard, active, mobile and everywhere dynamic, and the modern building like a gigantic machine. Lifts must no longer hide away like solitary worms in the stair-wells, but the stairs—now useless —must be abolished, and the lifts must swarm up the facades like serpents of glass and iron. The house of cement, iron and glass, without carved or painted ornament, rich only in the inherent beauty of its lines and modelling, extraordinarily brutish in its mechanical simplicity, as big as need dictates, and not merely as zoning rules permit, must rise from the brink of a tumultuous abyss; the street, which, itself, will no longer lie like a doormat at the level of the thresholds, but plunge storeys deep into the earth, gathering up the traffic of the metropolis connected for necessary transfers to metal cat-walks and high-speed conveyor belts . . . we must begin by overturning monuments, pavements, colonnades and flights of steps, by submerging streets and squares, by raising the level of the city, by altering the earth's crust to reduce it at last to serve our every need, our every whim.'[51]

The climax of Sant' Elia's fantasy is provided forty years later by Isaac Asimov: 'Gaal was not certain whether the sun shone, or, for that matter, whether it was day or night. He was ashamed to ask. All the planet seemed to live beneath metal. . . . He could not see the ground. It was lost in the ever-increasing complexities of man-made structures. He could see no horizon other than that of metal against sky, stretching out to almost uniform greyness, and he knew it was so over all the land-surface of the planet. . . . He was conscious only of the mightiest deed of man; the complete and almost contemptuously final conquest of a world.'[52] Asimov's description of the city-planet of Trantor, technologically overwhelming but fatally flawed in its dependence upon a galaxy-wide supply system to maintain its 40 billion inhabitants, provides an ironic background to subsequent projects updating the machine analogy, of which perhaps Archigram's 'Walking City' most wittily evoked the image of a Phalanstère for the twenty-first century.

Buckminster Fuller's analysis sees the 'One-Town World' as imminent: 'Within a few years we will be able to go in the morning to any part of the earth by public conveyance, do a day's work, and reach home again in the evening, and by the Treasury Department's income tax allowance for travelling expenses, we will not have been out of

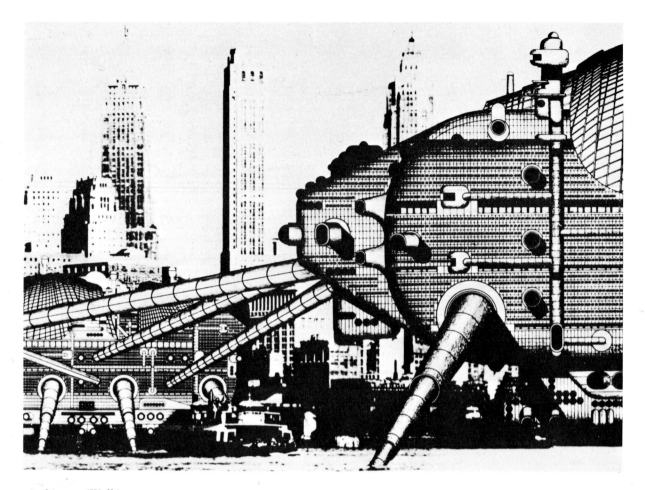

*Archigram, 'Walking City', 1964, drawn by Ron Herron.*

*Arata Isozaki, 'Space City', 1960.*

*Yona Friedman, 'Spatial Town', 1958.*

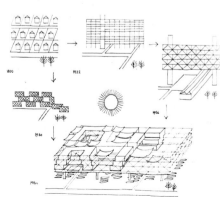

town. We will be realistically and legally in a one-town world for the first time in history.'[53] In view of this, the invention of utopias becomes not just desirable but essential. Raising the stakes of Le Corbusier's 'Architecture or Revolution' to a choice between 'Utopia or Oblivion', Fuller observes that: 'Cities, as we know them, are obsolete in respect to all of yesterday's functions.'[54] This massive technical failure requires startling, and utopian technological innovations, including sea-floating tetrahedronal cities, two miles to an edge and housing one million 'passengers' each, domed-over cities, air-deliverable skyscrapers and sky-floating, one-mile-diameter, geodesic sphere cloud structures, among others.

The fabulous character of these urban structures makes most contemporary technical utopias seem somewhat prosaic by comparison. Even Yona Friedman's diagnosis of 'the city as a machine', the earth 'a megalopolis composed of regions *in* the mesh of a continuous and unified network',[55] and apparent intention to Trantorize the lot by covering it with a suspended four-storey deep space-frame infrastructure, seems almost utilitarian. What practically all of these vast utopias of the 1960s share is a supreme optimism in the incorruptibility of 'the machine', untroubled by Asimov's earlier intimation that, even in the thirteenth millennium, its one dependable characteristic will be that it will go wrong. Among the monumental urban structures of the Japanese Metabolist group, for example, only Isozaki's strange sketches of crumbling megastructures collaged with gigantic ruined Doric temples, hint at the mortality of the machine. After the 1973 energy crisis, however, this theme haunts the work of the mega-utopians, as in Peter Cook's drawings for 'The Urban Mark' in which the nature which submissively lapped around Le Corbusier's crystal skyscrapers now consumes the uncompleted city.

This sense of the failure of technological utopia had already been evoked at the same time as its most confident assertions, and in the same region as its final flowering (for the time being), in the Southwestern USA, where Paolo Soleri stubbornly insisted on actually building one, called Arcosanti. There also, in 1965, Drop City appeared, ironically in the form of Fuller dome structures fabricated from cannibalized components from that automobile industry which he studied so intently as a model for the new industrialized urbanism. To describe Drop City and the similar communities which followed as utopian would no doubt be as incorrect as in the case of the Marxian idealizations, for it lacked a formal utopian programme. Indeed, its lack of an overt programme and its apparently casual and unstructured appearance were essential parts of its message. 'The unspoken Thing', as Tom Wolfe observed, was a central feature of the Open Commune: 'They made a point of not putting it into words. That in itself was one of the unspoken rules ... to define it was to limit it.' Nevertheless, this spontaneous flight of urban people to the land seemed to belong to a long-standing utopian tradition which acquired a new relevance as both the social and technical utopias became more all-embracing and, apparently, more nearly capable of implementation.

For this third tradition, which we might call that of the consumer utopias, a major concern becomes that of limiting the powers of the figure central to the other two—Popper's 'planning Utopian engineer'. Coupled with this concern, and related to it, is the question of density of urban development, since it is generally assumed that an increase in density tends to increase the need for, and powers of, centralized planning control. Thus, having abandoned his earlier enthusiasm for the Chicagoan machine-city, Frank Lloyd Wright sought to overcome its problems by the reduction of its density, to one acre per person, to the point where urban form, urban economics and urban control were dissolved away. Although he believed that new technology, in particular the motor car and telephone, favoured such a development in any case, it was the social implications of Broadacre City which were to be paramount. Through this decentralization, society would be freed of the insidious controls and exploitation which urban life imposed upon it, above all in the exaction of 'rent': 'The city itself is become a form of anxious rent, the citizen's own life rented, he and his family evicted if he is in arrears or the system goes to smash. Should this anxious lockstep of his fall out with the landlord, the moneylord, or the machinelord, he is a total loss.'[56] In contrast, however: 'When every man, woman, and child may be born to put his feet on his own acres, then democracy will have been realized.'[57] Some centralized control would still be necessary to maintain this Usonian ideal, which would depend upon the initial expropriation of landholdings larger than a single family would require, a step with which the Drop Communards of the 1960s, who were continually troubled by the American laws of trespass, would no doubt have had some sympathy. In addition, something of Wright's own autocratic personality may be glimpsed in the figure of the

*Paolo Soleri, Arcosanti, Arizona, US, 1965.*

*Drop City, Colorado, US, 1965.*

'County Architect', the most important official in Broadacre City who was responsible both for the design and maintenance of the public infrastructure and for a measure of building control over each individual homestead, to ensure that it was 'subject to his sense of the whole as organic architecture'.

Despite this element of enlightened control, Wright's utopia formed an important reference for those troubled by the increasingly authoritarian stance of centralized planning. For most European urbanists, however, the essential premise of Wright's solution—very low density of development—was seen as being unattainable. Was it then possible to give the consumer a corresponding degree of independence from the urban machine but at the same time maintain the high densities which, in a densely populated country like Holland, for example, were commonplace? The question of just what density is necessary in an ideally planned city region is one which has been addressed by a number of theorists influenced by Wright's model and notably by Leslie Martin and Lionel March,[58] whose studies have demonstrated the fallacies hidden in conventional thinking about the subject.

The assumption that it is essential in such a context to find a solution compatible with high densities does, however, underly the important contribution of Nicholas Habraken. His book *Supports: An Alternative to Mass Housing* sets out a powerful argument against the philosophy and techniques of centrally controlled attempts to solve the perennial housing problem. The result of these

attempts, 'mass housing', is seen as being essentially misconceived, itself exacerbating the problem it sets out to solve and in the process alienating the society which uses it and coarsening and corrupting the form of its cities. The root of the problem lies in the exclusion of the user from the process, resulting in a uniformity which is but a symptom of the wrongheadedness of the whole attempt:

'The greatest talents in the field of architecture and town planning have sought the liberating, all-providing design.... The ideal which has been pursued is not only unattainable because, like all ideals, it is subject to the imperfection of man's existence, but especially because the posing of the problem in itself excludes a solution.... That is to say: matter is not manipulated in harmony with society, but society is forced to conform to a method which pretends to perform this task.... A town is not a thing without people; a town is man

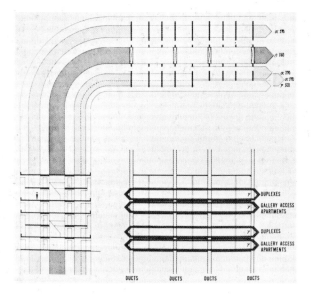

*Nicholas Habraken,
'Supports system' from
Variations, 1976.*

*Cedric Price, 'The
Generator', 1980.
Habraken's kit of parts
approach is developed
further by Price with a
scheme in Florida, US,
consisting of enclosures,
screens, services and
gangways based upon a
grid. A mobile crane
allows users to reorganize
the site as they wish with
the help of computer
facilities. It is described as
'a forest facility for
1–1,000 users.
Architecture is used as an
aid to the extension of
one's own interests. A
series of structures, fittings
and components that
respond to the appetites
that they themselves
generate. A "menu" of
items for individual and
group demands of space,
control, containment and
delight. A place to work,
create, think and store.'*

and matter together. . . . If a town is created before there is a population this fatal separation is implied. . . . But today we no longer think of a town as a unity with people, and when we should do all we can to stimulate a process, we spend our efforts in trying to reflect the form of the population in matter. We are very busy arranging in advance conformity of towns with their future populations because we do not understand that a town, a real town, can only emerge when this conformity already *exists*, and that it cannot be achieved by *making* a town, however beautifully or skilfully.'[59]

This powerful critique is followed by a proposal for 'a solution in principle', which relies heavily upon the assumption of high densities and is reminiscent of Le Corbusier's 1933 'Project A' for Algiers. Given high densities, the problem boils down to this: 'How do we pile up buildings without sacrificing their independence?'[60] The answer lies in the invention of the 'support structure', into which individual buildings can be freely constructed. This device separates out the realms of public and private interest, as also those of the architect and town planner. The latter would design the three-dimensional mass of the town through its support structures: 'By designing support-structure ribbons in a certain pattern, he can organize the town as a network of mutually-related building planes and lay down scale and extent, determine closed spaces, outline green areas, give context to free-standing buildings, and reach conclusions about main lines of development. Moreover, all this can take place without violence to the accidentals of life.'[61] A similar concept of a 'neutral' public infrastructure was present in Yona Friedman's suspended space-deck structures and was subsequently developed in his book *Toward a Scientific Architecture*[62] in which he described a mechanism, the 'Flatwriter', for the direct implementation of the user's requirements within the general framework without the need for an expert intermediary.

Whether such a substantial piece of public hardware as Habraken or Friedman envisage could actually separate the public and private realms as cleanly as they envisage, or free the individual to the extent anticipated, is debatable. More subtle is Christopher Alexander's concept of an infrastructure of ideas, a detailed network of agreed solution-types, consciously adopted by consumers to operate in both their own and the general interest. Although this approach requires none of the major engineering works of the previous two solutions, it does entail a far more comprehensive and pervasive shift of thought, for, rather than the demarcation of public and private interests, what is sought is their reintegration into a common, universal and interdependent network of preferred design solutions. Developing his earlier theoretical work on the structure of cities,[63] Alexander and his collaborators produced an encyclopaedic three-volume description of this 'Pattern Language', setting out the theory behind it, its method of use and an example of its application.[64]

The ambition of these books is certainly utopian in scale: 'The books are intended to provide a complete working alternative to our present ideas about architecture, building, and planning—an alternative which will, we hope, gradually replace current ideas and practices.' Ranging from the global arrangement of regions down to the minutiae of domestic construction, they set out a menu of preferred solutions to the main design problems encountered through all the scales of environmental design. These 253 'patterns' are interrelated, not as a fixed sequence, but rather as a network in which each is contained by or related to a number of larger-scale patterns 'up' the network, and in turn contains smaller-scale patterns 'below'. For example, pattern 31, 'Promenade', is related to the larger-scale patterns 8 'Mosaic of Subcultures', 12 'Community of 7000' and 30 'Activity Nodes'. The statement of the problem which makes pattern 31 necessary runs: 'Each subculture needs a center for its public life: a place where you can go to see people, and to be seen.' A discussion of the problem then follows,[65] concluding with a statement of the proposed instruction, pattern 31: 'Encourage the gradual formation of a promenade at the heart of every community, linking the main activity nodes, and placed centrally, so that each point in the community is within 10 minutes walk of it. Put main points of attraction at the two ends, to keep a constant movement up and down.' In turn, this pattern leads to others in the network, including 32 'Shopping Street', 33 'Night Life', 58 'Carnival', 63 'Dancing in the Street', 100 'Pedestrian Streets', 121 'Path Shape', and so on. Arbitrary or even quirky as some of the individual patterns might appear, the mosaic they create, of humane injunctions logically interrelated, forms perhaps the most comprehensive and appealing of consumer utopias to date, perhaps because 'These patterns can never be "designed" or "built" in one fell swoop—but patient piecemeal growth, designed in such a way that every individual act is always helping to create or generate these larger global patterns, will slowly and surely, over the years, make a community that has these global patterns in it.'[66]

The concept of EPCOT (the Experimental Prototype Community of Tomorrow) may be said to fall precisely into the category of urban utopias. But it remains, nevertheless, as a utopian concept rather than reality.

Walt Disney's original vision for EPCOT was that of an ideal community with parallels and analogies with many of the nineteenth-century utopias of Europe and North America. Disney's view was that 'People actually live a life they can't find anywhere else in the world today. EPCOT will be a "living blueprint" of the future ... a fully operating community with a population of more than 20,000. Here American free enterprise will constantly introduce, test and demonstrate new concepts and technologies years ahead of their

application elsewhere.'

But as Derek Walker has pointed out, the reality is sadly different. EPCOT never became the ideal community or the urban utopia. Instead it was developed by Disney's successors as a gigantic theme park or even a world trade fair. Construction commenced in 1976 and was nearing completion in 1982. Certainly the project perspectives and progress photographs show an uncanny similarity but neither reflect the utopian framework suggested in Disney's earlier statements. Perhaps the sponsorship by American industry did much to distort the original idealism and for all the advanced technology employed in the entertainment and movement systems the suggestion that EPCOT reflects an ideal world is somewhat far from the truth. Finance may or may not reflect the participation of such countries as Japan, West Germany,

*EPCOT concept drawings.*

Britain or Morocco—it certainly leaves a notable gap concerning views of eastern block or many third world countries. Similar to the current market-economy view of enterprise zones in England, EPCOT tends to turn its back on the world of reality. As a funfair such a disregard for reality can lead to enchantment; as an urban utopia such a view is unacceptable.

**Reference:**
*Architectural Design*, Vol. 52, Nos. 9–10, 1982, 'Epcot 82' by Derek Walker.

*EPCOT Center Construction, 1982.*

## 2.3  MODELS FROM THE ARTS AND SCIENCES

GIVEN THE COMPLEXITY AND INTRACTABILITY OF urban problems, it is not surprising that designers have found it helpful to borrow ideas from other fields in order to gain fresh insight. These references have taken two forms, analogy and translation, which together have constituted an important further source of urban design theory.

We have already noted the use of analogy in references made by the technical utopians to the machine, and this example illustrates well the way in which analogies tend to be used to suggest a completely new appreciation of the problem as a whole. Thus the suggestion that a city was like a large machine became a decisive insight for the Futurists and was subsequently pursued to the point where it could be imagined as a literal fact, as in Archigram's 'Walking City'. An equally pervasive analogy is that of the city as an organism, often a human one, so that the classic planning texts frequently sound like the reminiscences of pathologists over the corpses of particularly unfortunate victims. Ebenezer Howard regarded existing cities as 'ulcers on the very face of our beautiful island',[67] while their plans seemed to Frank Lloyd Wright like 'the cross-section of a fibrous tumour', and Le Corbusier, writing in *The City of Tomorrow* on the subject of Paris, devoted a chapter to the question of 'Physic or Surgery'.[68] In the case of Le Corbusier in particular, this was not simply a matter of vivid phraseology, since he used the metaphor in both building and town design to provide an analytical account of his subject in terms of its discrete but interdependent systems, as his regular use of such terms as 'cell', 'organism', 'artery' or 'lungs' continually reminds us. For Le Corbusier, the mechanical and biological analogies were almost interchangeable, the skeleton, organs and nervous system of the human body providing a complementary illustration to that of the chassis, engine and controls of the automobile, and the condition of the contemporary city alternating between that of a consumptive body or else 'like an engine which is seized'.[69]

Whereas such analogies offer novel holistic interpretations of the city, translations from one discipline to another tend to be more concerned with individual concepts or techniques. Since cities are formed of associations of quantifiable elements, we can borrow methods from set theory in the field of pure mathematics to help us manipulate them. Again, since the city is a cultural invention, imbued with meaning for its inhabitants, we can liken it to a

*Letter box and door bell, central Venice, Italy.*

language and seek insights from the discipline of linguistics, either in terms of syntactic structure or else, through the study of the meaning of signs, in semiotics.[70] This field, which is the subject of a major study by Geoffrey Broadbent and others, has been expressed by Gordon Cullen as the 'Language of Gestures'. He says: 'Communication between people and the towns they live in is primarily effected by signalization.... Rapport between ourselves and the environment, like conversation, brings continuing interest. Obviously this can only be achieved by signals or gestures that bring home to us the identity latent in environmental problems. Hence the need for a comprehensive language of gestures.'[71] This can arise either as the invention of a carefully structured system by the urban designer or else accidentally. An anonymously designed letter box and door bell in Venice, for instance, has similar impact and meaning in terms of orientation and imageability as the piece of sculpture laid carefully in the ground at the Louisiana Museum in Denmark.

Two other fields, anthropology and psychology, have seemed particularly promising, since their subject is man, and they have been keenly studied for directly applicable 'results'. In the case of the former, the concept of 'territoriality' seemed particularly relevant, since the whole city could be regarded as a physical representation of the operation of such a principle. 'Territoriality' has been studied in both animals and man, with some remarkable results. The scientist J.B. Calhoun, for

*Sculpture in the garden of Louisiana Museum, near Copenhagen, Denmark.*

example, has described the effects of increasing density and space restrictions upon laboratory populations of mice, tracing changes in fertility, physique, behaviour and susceptibility to disease which occur, and has extrapolated the theoretical results to human groupings, even postulating an optimum world population of nine billion.[72]

Suggestive as such results may be, the urban designer has another, more immediate, source of examples of territorial behaviour, most notably explored by Jane Jacobs: 'Cities are an immense laboratory of trial and error, failure and success, in city building and city design. This is the laboratory in which city planning should have been learning and forming and testing its theories. Instead the practitioners and teachers of this discipline (if such it can be called) have ignored the study of success and failure in real life, have been incurious about the reasons for unexpected success, and are guided instead by principles derived from the behaviour and appearance of towns, suburbs, tuberculosis sanatoria, fairs, and imaginary dream cities—from anything but cities themselves.'[73] By observing the way in which cities were actually used, Jacobs was led to question accepted prescriptions for the improvement of city environments: 'In orthodox city planning, neighbourhood open spaces are venerated in an amazingly uncritical fashion, much as savages venerate magical fetishes.... Walk with a planner through a dispirited neighbourhood and though it will be already scabby with deserted parks and tired landscaping festooned with old

Kleenex, he will envision a future of More Open Space. More Open Space for what? For muggings? For bleak vacuums between buildings?'[74] In place of these shibboleths, Jacobs proposed four 'conditions' which she believed to be essential for a successful district, and which read like prototypes for Alexander's later 'Patterns': 'The need for mixed primary uses'; 'The need for small blocks'; 'The need for aged buildings'; and 'The need for concentration'.

Eleven years later, another important study of the territorial behaviour of people in cities was published, which shared a number of features with Jacobs' work. Oscar Newman's *Defensible Space*[75] was similarly based upon observations made in New York City, and again took crime and violence to be the most urgent symptoms of urban design failure. Newman, however, was able to include large-scale post-war developments in his study, which concentrated on the way in which design features of buildings and neighbourhoods thoughtlessly undermine the checks and balances of social behaviour which, in traditional city forms, naturally accompany high-density life and make it possible. His development of the concept of 'defensible space' as a principle of allocation of responsibility for and supervision of territory in the highly artificial world of the city, implied a very strong connection between crime and poor design and drew attention to this fundamental character of city space. Some of Newman's theories, however, seem open to doubt. In a lecture at Sheffield, England in 1973, Newman suggested that developments such as St Francis Square, San Francisco, a medium-density low-rise ownership, would overcome many of the problems of social stress cited in his book. Each pedestrian square houses something in the order of 100 families (at 37 dwelling units per acre, total 299 houses). However, in Irvine New Town, in Scotland, the Pennyburn (1 and 2) development completed in the same year, 1969, was built to a lower density (12 dwelling units per acre) with 30 houses per square (total 240 houses). Again, houses were developed around pedestrian squares with vehicle entry only at the head of each square and pedestrian-only access at the rear of each house. Surveillance was possible from the living room at the front of each house so that children playing in the square could be seen. Yet the scheme failed in that there was lack of privacy, the density was considered too *high*, the private gardens too small and the lack of mobility of the Scottish families as opposed to their American counterparts meant that recreational opportunities

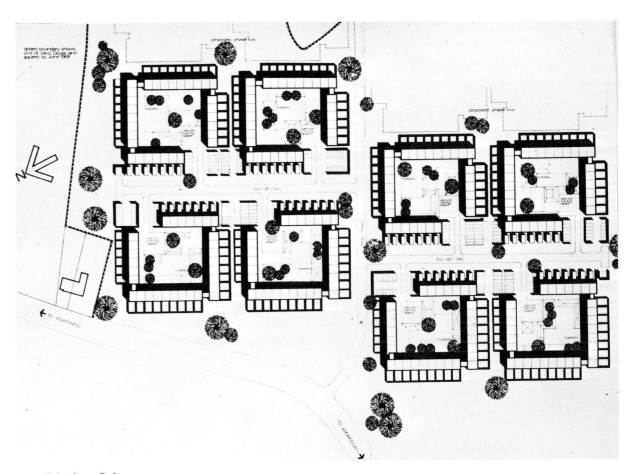

*David Gosling, Bob Dunlop and Jim Oswald, Pennyburn Housing, Irvine New Town, Scotland, phase one, 1969.*

*David Gosling, Bob Dunlop and Jim Oswald, Pennyburn Housing, Irvine New Town, phase two, 1971.*

were limited. Too many children played in each square, and landscaping deteriorated. It was thus fallacious on the part of the architect (who lived there) to assume that low-income families with lack of mobility could deal with an environment in which higher-income families with cars could live happily. Privacy should have had a higher priority.

If our instinctive appreciation of 'ownership' and 'occupation' of territory in the city is crucial to its success, the question of how we actually perceive and understand its complex spatial variations is obviously important, and has been one of the most active areas of interest for urban design theorists, bringing them into contact with a number of developments in the arts and sciences. The work of the Gestalt psychologists in the early part of this century was one of the first such developments which seemed to offer a firmer and more rational basis for the discussion of perception. Its essential message, that 'vision is not a mechanical recording of elements but the grasping of significant structural patterns',[76] accorded with the feelings of many engaged in visual design, and provided a description of the way in which such patterns are recognized.

Six 'conditions' were identified as playing an important, if not exclusive, role in producing visual forms: The Law of Proximity, by which objects close to one another tend to form groups; The Law of Similarity, where like objects are read as groups; The Law of Closed Forms, whereby lines enclosing a surface tend to be seen as a unit; The Law of 'Good' Contour, or Common Destiny, by which continuity of form is implied across interruptions; The Law of Common Movement, describing the ability of the eye to group elements which move simultaneously, and in a similar manner; The Law of Experience, which acknowledges the partial dependence of the comprehension of symbolic forms upon the circumstances under which they were learned.[77] These laws are reinforced by a fundamental law, described by Friedrich Wulf in 1922 as 'The Law of Prägnanz, according to which every Gestalt becomes as "good" as possible.... It is for this reason that memorable Gestalten tend towards unique forms.... Well known forms (structures) are themselves already stable.'[78] This visual bias in favour of simple regular forms seemed a particularly challenging discovery, as was also the Gestalt 'discovery' of the phenomenon of figure-ground. The latter was of particular interest to those concerned with the urban environment, since the inhabitants of cities are continually having to identify key signals against chaotic backgrounds,

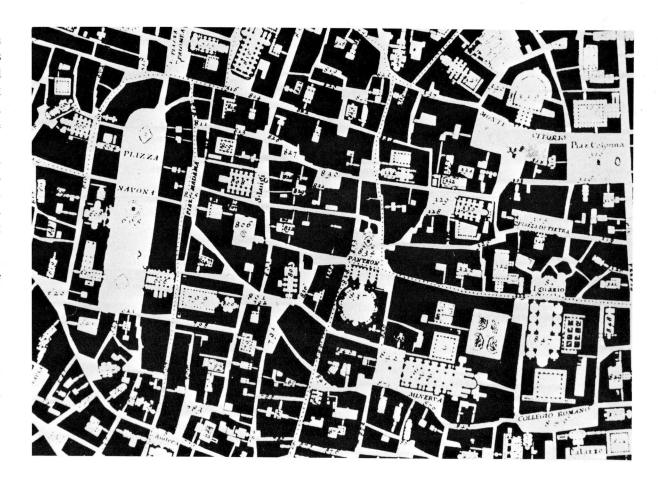

*Giambattista Nolli, plan of Rome, Italy, 1748.*

as a matter of course. Again, the whole concept of urban design relies upon a classic figure-ground reversal, in which what is normally regarded as figure (buildings) must be read as ground, and what is normally seen as ground (the surrounding spaces) becomes figure, a flip which was vividly demonstrated by the graphic technique employed by Nolli in drawing his 1748 plan of Rome.

Though subsequently superseded by the work of the Swiss child-psychologist Jean Piaget and the concept of 'schemata', or stereotyped responses to situations,[79] the theories of the Gestalt school of psychology were accepted into the thinking of many theorists in design in the inter-war years along with a second body of ideas on the question of perception, stemming this time from the arts. Concerned in particular with a redefinition of the notion of space, this set of ideas was propounded by Siegfried Giedion[80] and other theorists of the Modern Movement, and included two important concepts which came together in the 1920s and were relevant to urban designers. The first of these, with origins in De Stijl painting and the architecture of Frank Lloyd Wright, was the concept of space as a neutral continuum, with no

distinction between internal and external spaces. This was lucidly expressed by Mies van der Rohe's 1940 master plan for the IIT Campus in Chicago in which the structure of the buildings seemed simply a manifestation of an implicit Cartesian grid pervading the whole area. The second important concept was that of a freely moving observer, which introduced the possibility of simultaneous, fragmented and multiple vision as first postulated by the Cubist and Futurist painters and sculptors. These two ideas, nostalgically recalled by Superstudio's images of the 1960s, were invoked by Giedion in the term 'space-time', which though misleadingly seeming to suggest some connection with Einstein's Theory of Relativity, indicated the novelty of perception involved. Whether, as Giedion argued, a moving observer's experience of Rockefeller Center is different in kind from that of the towers of Bologna,[81] the emphasis upon motion and a variable point of observation had obvious relevance to questions of perception of urban phenomena, the implications of which, as with so many novelties of the Modern Movement, were first explored by painters.

Two artists of the Bauhaus in particular are

worth recalling in this connection. Paul Klee's work was notable not only for the numerous drawings and paintings of imaginary city forms which he made during the 1920s, but also for the attention he drew to the relationship between the techniques of drawing and the sequential recording of experiences. Thus, in his essay 'Creative Confession' of 1920: 'Klee proposes to his reader to accompany him on a walk, a little excursion into the country; wē shall see how the phenomena of nature are respresented by the graphic elements and their combinations. We start off from a point: that gives us a line. We stop once or twice; the line has been broken or articulated. We cross a river by boat —an undulatory movement. A ploughed field—a surface scored by lines. Mist in a valley—a spatial element. We meet people. Basketmakers coming home with their cart (a wheel). They have a child with them with funny curls (a corkscrew motion). Later the weather becomes sultry and lowering (spatial element). A flash of lightning on the horizon (a zigzag line). There are still stars overhead (scattered dots).... To sum up he writes: "All kinds of different lines. Blobs of colour. Stippling. Stippled and striped surfaces. Undulatory movement. Broken, articulated movement. Countermovement. Objects interlaced and interwoven. Masonry, peeling stone. Harmony with one voice. With several voices. Line losing itself, gaining strength (dynamic)." '[82]

This description of a shorthand graphic technique for recording a series of experiences foreshadowed a recurring preoccupation of later theorists, whose desire to treat perception as objectively as possible led them to the need for a precise notation, flexible enough to describe the great variety of events encountered in a city. Laszlo Moholy-Nagy, also a Bauhaus artist, was similarly concerned with finding techniques to record and communicate complex events, particularly through the use of new media. Following his notorious 'telephone paintings' (made by workmen in an enamelling workshop to instructions dictated over the telephone), he encouraged experimentation at the Bauhaus in new techniques, particularly in the use of film and collaged photography of the city. As with other artists, like Duchamp and Klee, Moholy-Nagy's pre-war work culminated in his own version of the machine, in the form of a kinetic light sculpture, the *Light-Space Modulator*, the variable lighting effects from which could be recorded on negative film. These interests were recorded by Moholy-Nagy after he had emigrated to the United States in his book *Vision in Motion*,[83]

a mixture of theory, Bauhaus Vorkurs exercises and demonstrations of experimental photographic and film techniques. These included his interpretation of the history of developing spatial concepts and a discussion of the problems of 'rendering motion (space-time) on the static plane', with an emphasis on the relevance of developments in the fields of the cinema, theatre and dance.

Both Giedion's 'space-time' and Moholy-Nagy's 'vision in motion' drew attention to a more dynamic approach to visual understanding which seemed to offer new insights into the processes of describing and analysing urban environments. The distinction between this appreciation based upon a mobile observer and the former perception from static, frontal viewpoints was subsequently developed by other commentators, such as Roger Hinks.[84] Similarly, Arata Isozaki has maintained that the Japanese do not recognise the Western serial concept of space and time.[85] Both are rather conceived in terms of intervals, as reflected in the use of the term 'Ma' in architecture, landscape design, music and drama, a concept which can signify the 'natural distance between two or more things existing in a continuity' or 'space delineated by posts and screens'.

The influence of the Bauhaus tradition upon American post-war urban designers was reinforced by Gyorgy Kepes, another former member who was a teacher at MIT in the 1950s when Lynch, Mumford and Appleyard were also there. His book *The New Landscape*[86] similarly emphasized the importance of photography as a technique for enlarging the scope of normal vision, as in the use of microphotography, telephotography and recorded effects on photosensitive film. In particular, he drew attention to the fifth Gestalt condition, regarding the perception of movement, in the way in which very extended, or very compressed, sequences could be made legible and continuous by the use of accelerated or decelerated film.

At this point, the efforts of several researchers in the United States became directed to translating these artistic experiments into practical and systematic methods of recording urban environments, narrowing the term 'space-time' from a grandiose abstract characteristic of the *Zeitgeist* to a literal description of experiencing the city, as necessarily a sequence of three-dimensional events in time, much as one might describe music as 'sound-time'. The differences between this sequence and that of music, or the film, or other controlled linear sequences, was analysed at this time by Philip Thiel, a graduate of MIT working at the University of

*Tramway, Corcovado, Brazil. Appleyard's analysis of movement through space along a predetermined route can also be experienced in the Corcovado mountain railway, in which a small tramway spirals its way up a steep, heavily wooded mountain with a gigantic statue of Christ at the summit. The line is used not only for tourists, but also as a link for small settlements at the base of the mountain. With the statue as a constant and growing reference point, appearing and disappearing from view and the roadway crossing sometimes above and sometimes below the tramway, the spatial experience is quite breathtaking.*

California at Berkeley.[87] Acknowledging the work of James Gibson[88] in classifying methods of representing space as viewed from a fixed point, Thiel suggested five techniques for extending these to indicate the experience of a moving observer, as:

1 Modification of linear perspective by the use of multiple vanishing points and horizon lines, in which a plurality of observation points is equivalent to movement in space. Saul Steinberg's drawings provide examples of this technique, as do scroll paintings and some of Leonardo da Vinci's work.
2 Transparency of overlapping forms to provide simultaneous representation of more than one point of view; examples can be drawn from X-rays, multiple exposure photography and primitive

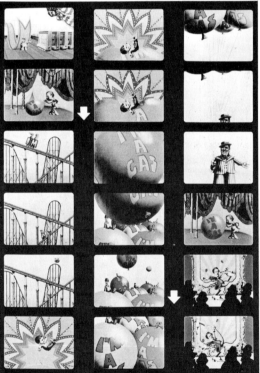

*Example from the comic* Cinco Por Infinitus, *Barcelona and Rio de Janeiro, 1969. The essence of the successful strip is the graphic portrayal of both movement and time combined with a deliberate distortion of scale.*

*Sequence from the British television programme* Monty Python's Flying Circus *using the comic strip to portray sequential events. In* Animations of Mortality, *Terry Gilliam uses this sequence to summarize the lessons expounded by graphics.*

drawings.

3 Reflections and mirroring, alone or in conjunction with transparency. Thiel himself experimented with this device, shooting a film in a Bay Area rapid transit train at a point where window reflections in an articulated two-car unit produced a multiple image of the views forward and to left and right. The Gestalt fifth condition operated to enable each to be read independently, and Thiel proposed extending the technique with the use of spherical and half-silvered mirrors.

4 Rotations of orthographic projections, used by geometers, primitives and Cubists. An early example of this technique for a purpose analogous to that of the urban designer is a book of maps published by Ogilby in 1698 in which, for example, the route from London to Folkestone was shown in a series of vertical strips, read from the bottom up and showing in isometric effect hills, forests and significant buildings along the road.

5 Simultaneous presentation of separate representations of successive events. Commonly used in medieval painting, this effect is reproduced by aircraft vapour trails and time-exposure photographs of automobile lights and similar moving objects. Undoubtedly, the most widely appreciated use of this method is provided by the comic strip, to the techniques of which two issues of the Swiss magazine *Graphis* were lovingly dedicated in 1972/73.[89] Tracing their development from the Bayeux Tapestry to the present day, the magazine concluded that: 'Comics produce a loom of image-language upon which they weave pictographic novels. They play with time, space and narrative progression in a way that no other art ever has, not even film.... The artist working in the narrative strip medium can extend the single instant backward or forward in time. Not only can he move slowly or suddenly or not at all, change his mind, hold his audience in suspense, sustain a mood, surprise or destroy; he can virtually wire his pictures for sound. By using balloons and captions, he can make his pictures talk. Finally, he can do something no painter before him could ever do: deal with the problems of beginnings and endings —and all in pictures.'[90]

Thiel investigated a number of parallel studies in other fields which offered clues for the urban designer, such as the technique devised by Sergei Eisenstein[91] to analyse film passages through a series of correlated horizontal strip sequences to show: 1 film frames (stills); 2 musical phrases; 3 musical score; 4 length (in measures); 5 diagram of pictorial composition; 6 linear diagram of 'move-

ment'. Thiel proposed a corresponding system of annotating urban sequences in a rolled or paged scroll form, although he acknowledged the difficulty created by the fundamental difference between comics, dance, music and cinema where the pace and direction of the sequences is controlled, and urban phenomena, where it is not.

There was, however, one type of urban experience, moreover a relatively recent one, where the variables of speed and sequence were much more closely controlled and thus where an almost metronomic sequence of visual 'stills' could hope to provide a reasonably precise description. This was 'The View from the Road', explored in Donald Appleyard's book of that name,[92] a kind of elaborate adaptation of Ogilby to the world of the freeway. By the use of picture sequences and linear diagrams indicating the pattern of events along the route, the experience of an existing highway, the Northeast Expressway in Boston, was analysed in a manner which made it possible to envisage the rigorous formulation and testing of a general 'highway esthetic'. Appleyard subsequently went on to develop his work on this important element of the city structure at the University of California at Berkeley, in particular through the use of TV and video systems in conjunction with large-scale models. As the conclusion of *The View from the Road* acknowledges: 'For the most part, we have considered highways on single linear sequences. We have not dealt with a network of highways, or, more properly, with a *system of movement* in a city.'[93] In this respect, Appleyard's work must be viewed in the context of the other studies being carried out at the Joint Center for Urban Studies of MIT and Harvard University in the late 1950s and early 1960s of which undoubtedly the most influential product was Kevin Lynch's *The Image of the City*.[94]

Having trained as an architect under Frank Lloyd Wright, Lynch came to MIT as an associate Professor of Planning. He was greatly influenced by Kepes, then an associate Professor of Architecture, with whom he worked on a number of joint urban design projects. One such research study was 'The Boston Image', carried out in 1958 by MIT graduate students, which proposed a modest restructuring of the downtown area of Boston to give it an identifiable image instead of the confused character experienced by most citizens. In addition to identifying certain desirable design measures, such as re-establishing the strong grain of 'Back Bay' on the north side of the peninsula, and introducing a series of squares and walkways in

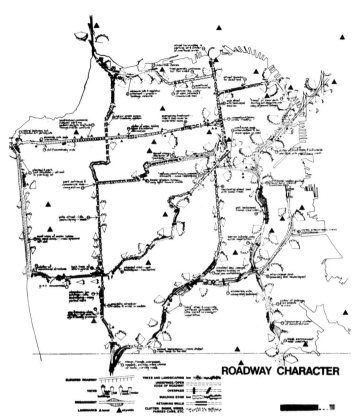

ROADWAY CHARACTER

Donald Appleyard, two-dimensional map using symbols to interpret roadway character.

Simulation Laboratory, University of California at Berkeley, US. Some of Appleyard's most interesting work has been carried out here during the last decade. Using sophisticated video systems and very large-scale models, it has been possible to simulate movement through space on the model and compare it directly with parallel video films taken on the existing highway route to be designed. Such techniques have obvious value in the physical planning process of urban environments but are surprisingly under-utilized.

Donald Appleyard, two-dimensional map using symbols to emphasize the characteristics of movement, enclosure, views, terrain, rivers, and urban development as they were experienced along a given route.

Donald Appleyard, results of video camera experiments using an optical probe at the University of California at Berkeley.

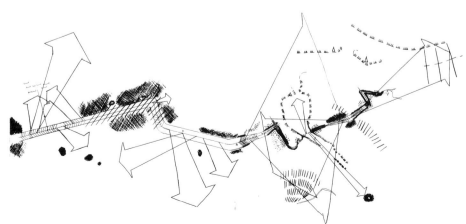

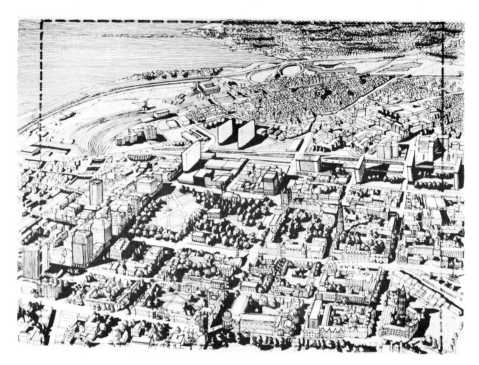

△ *David Gosling, Yale project, aerial perspective of New Haven city centre, 1958.*

▽ *David Gosling, Yale project, structural analysis of New Haven city centre, 1958.*

▽ *David Gosling, Yale project, route characteristics of the Wooster Square district, New Haven, 1959.*

△ *David Gosling, Yale project, aerial perspective of the Wooster Square district of New Haven, 1958.*

▽ *David Gosling, Yale project, spatial analysis of the Wooster Square district, New Haven, 1959.*

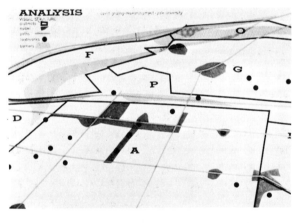

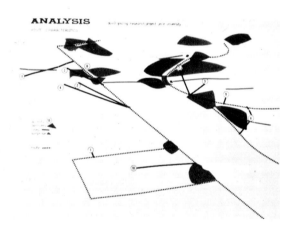

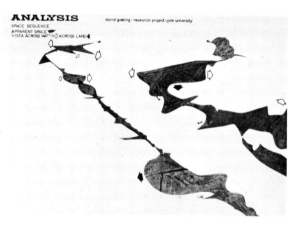

the South Boston/Roxbury black ghetto area, the study also used sequential illustrations to show the approach to the centre by different routes. One outcome of this technique was a proposal to clarify the subway routes by coloured lights and paints indicating place and direction, an idea rediscovered by the Boston Mass Transit Authority some 20 years later, in 1977. At the same time, Lynch was developing an important innovation in urban design technique through the use of interviews to establish how the city was in fact perceived by its inhabitants. These early studies, including the unpublished 'Go Take a Walk Round the Block' and 'The Unanimous Image' of 1957, laid the foundations for the 1960 publication of *The Image of the City*.

Co-author David Gosling's subsequent work with the late Christopher Tunnard at Yale, working on a Rockefeller Research project, was strongly influenced by Lynch's earlier studies as well as by the contemporary work carried out by Thiel at the University of California. Gyorgy Kepes too had provided a strong influence in evoking new graphic techniques of spatial representation. The MIT studies involved the recording of spatial sequences in an old environment (Beacon Hill, Boston) and a new environment (Shoppers' World, Boston). The three-dimensional sketches were supplemented by graphs, resembling a musical score. The horizontal scale was the time scale or actual measurement of progression through the sequence, and the vertical scale indicated the apparent expansion or contrac-

tion of space through the sequence. Both apparent space and intensity of space were recorded—similar to amplitude modulation and frequency modulation in sound recording. A second analysis of the two sequences was made of what Kepes termed the 'complexity factor'. This dealt with the psychological value of the visual character of the sequence. Both Gibson and Thiel have experimented in this field, although no really satisfactory graphic method has evolved. Gosling's analysis was based upon the relative dominance of experience character—confusion, bleakness, repose, intimacy bustle and so on. Each of these elements was indicated on the graph in a different transparent colour. The size of the colour area indicated the extent of that particular character. The method was

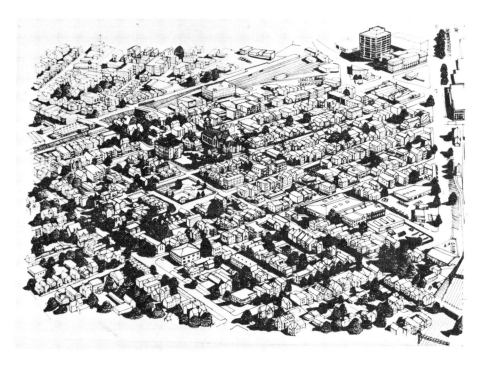

*Christopher Tunnard, James Skerritt, David Gosling, Yale project, Hill District analysis for the New Haven City Planning Commission, 1959.*

not successful in that there appeared to be confusion in people's minds as to the actual meaning of the terms used.

It is clear that the techniques described above have greater value if, as in the case of Thiel's experiments, they are carried out by a group, so that a comparative appraisal might be made. If the group is composed of lay people rather than professional planners, a consensus view might be obtained which could be translated by the planner into graphic analyses. The difficulty lies in establishing common terms which have the same meaning to all people of the group.

The Yale project, directed by Christopher Tunnard, was aimed towards the development of a comprehensive analysis or visual map of an entire city. New Haven was selected as the base of the study. Apart from consideration of the total envelope of the city and its structural form, the skyline hierarchies, approaches and gateways (drawing upon Lynch's techniques), the most significant part of the study was the series of district analyses. A visual analysis of the city was carried out through the survey of districts. Large aerial photographs were used as the basic tool from which aerial perspectives were drawn as a form of base 'map'. Aerial perspectives were considered a better tool than photographs since selected features could be stressed as opposed to the overall grain of a photograph. Redevelopment proposals were included in the perspective and transparent overlays used for the analysis of the city structure. One overlay indicated the visual structure of the district (nuclei, paths, landmarks, barriers). This method

of showing the visual structure was found to be more useful than merely indicating it on a two-dimensional map. The layman could associate himself with buildings in perspective and the analysis became more meaningful. A second analysis was a development of the MIT 'complexity factor' study. Areas of different character were delineated as well as buildings of symbolic significance. Again, the main drawback was the ambiguity of the terms.

A second district (Wooster Square) was also considered and the same techniques used, though the analyses were different, including a comparison between major routes through the district—the coastal expressway and the old Chapel Street thoroughfare. The first analysis was a space sequence study including vistas across land and water, while the second was of the route characteristics —accents (bridges, gas storage tanks, major buildings), lines or linear elements, and changes of vista or views.

Gosling also collaborated with the late James Skerritt and Christopher Tunnard on the Hill District project. This was a first tentative attempt at a visual design plan for a major urban renewal area which was subsequently presented to the New Haven City Planning Commission and developed as a live rehabilitation project. In 1959, this was one of the first major urban renewal plans with emphasis on both the retention of the existing social structure of the area and the improvement of the visual environment. The aim of the project was to prepare a prototype design plan for the area which could be used as a basis for other area studies. Residents' opinion surveys and aerial

visual analyses were prepared prior to the presentation of the final proposals in three-dimensional form. The most important factor in this work was that the final proposals should be a reflection of the inhabitants' visual image of the physical drawbacks and possible solutions, while the graphic techniques used were inexpensive and simple to understand in lay terms and did not require complicated equipment.

A subsequent attempt to translate a city centre design plan was carried out in Manchester, England in 1962 for the redevelopment of the central area on the line of the former 'processional-way' proposal of the post-war plan. Replacing a former scheme, it was suggested that a series of pedestrian networks become the basis of sequential spaces between the Town Hall and the Law Courts, based upon earlier studies by Ian Nairn and commented upon by Kenneth Browne in *The Architectural Review*.[95]

The novelty of Lynch's approach lay in his consideration of the visual character of the American city through study of the mental images of that city which are held in the minds of its citizens. Asserting that 'legibility' was a crucially important characteristic of a city environment, enabling inhabitants to place themselves in the general structure and establish a framework for individual action, he argued that such legibility depended upon the ability of the environment to communicate a clear 'image' of itself. This image would undoubtedly vary from individual to individual, but nevertheless certain strong common features would emerge to constitute a 'group image'. Thus the legibility of the city may be enhanced or diminished as this group image is reinforced or weakened. By interviews with citizens, including requests for descriptions of imaginary trips through the city, memorable features contributing to the overall imageability could be identified, as was demonstrated in *The Image of the City* in the cases of the central areas of three cities: Boston, Jersey City and Los Angeles. From these studies, Lynch concluded that although a variety of features contributed to the group images, they could be classified as belonging to one of five types of urban element, providing a list of key urban design categories or concepts—paths, edges, districts, nodes and landmarks—which has itself proved to be one of the most imageable features of subsequent urban design theory. In addition to the 'objective' method of approach, Lynch's study also owed its popularity to the fact that it provided, almost for the first time, an effective definition of precisely what it was that

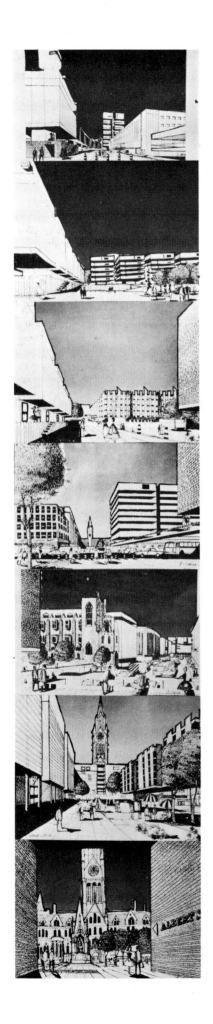

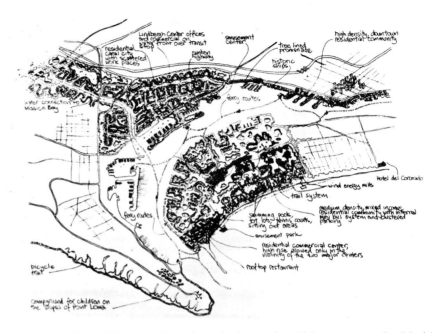

*Kevin Lynch and Donald Appleyard, San Diego regional study, Mission Valley, California, US, 1975.*

*David Gosling, sequential study for the redevelopment of Manchester city centre, England, published in* The Architectural Review, *August 1962.*

*Manchester city centre, partial development from the original plan, carried out between 1965 and 1968.*

the urban designer should be concerned with (the city image), and the method he might adopt to achieve his ends (the reinforcement of the five elements).

The effectiveness of defining the task of the urban designer in terms of these essential distillations of the city character is attested by subsequent attempts to improve on the menu, including, as we have seen, Jane Jacobs' 'Four Conditions' and Christopher Alexander's 253 'Patterns'. Charles Moore provides his version in *Body, Memory and Architecture* (without referring to Lynch's work): 'The inhabited world within boundaries then, can usefully be ascribed a syntax of *place, path, pattern* and *edge*. Within each of these four, architectural ordering arrangements can be considered which are made to respond to the natural landscape as well as to human bodies and memories.'[96] Norberg-Schulz (who does acknowledge Lynch) suggests: 'Place and Node; Path and Axis; Domain and District'.[97]

These classifications of essential concepts contrast markedly with that adopted in another seminal work, which was written in the same year as *The Image of the City* and published in 1961 in England as *Townscape*.[98] Indeed, the methods and approach of its author, Gordon Cullen, form an interesting comparison with those of Lynch and the American school. As Art Editor of *The Architectural Review* from 1947 until late in the 1950s, Cullen developed a number of studies on the subject of 'townscape', a term which he coined and which was to suffer almost as great a devaluation as Lynch's 'image'. A painter by talent and romantic by instinct, Cullen's investigations of the desirable qualities of good urban environments differed con-

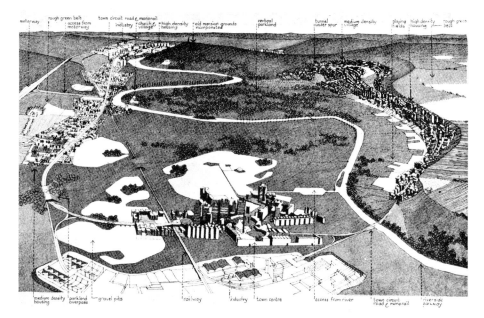

siderably from the academic analyses of Lynch. Ironically, the personal vision and graphic fluency which Cullen brought to the explanation of his ideas was to some extent a handicap, arousing suspicion in the minds of those for whom a more 'objective' explanation of the urban designer's purpose was necessary. Cullen reinforced the impression of an 'unscientific' approach by a similarly evocative and poetic use of language to accompany the visual images, in an attempt to communicate the great variety and subtlety of overlapping qualities which urban elements can have. Thus his list of essential concepts, as set out in the pages of *Townscape*, was a mixture of the architectural ('silhouette', 'division of space', 'looking out of enclosure'), the painterly ('distortion', 'black and white', 'texture'), the poetic ('the white peacock', 'the tell-tale', 'taming with tact') and the practical ('lettering', 'railways', 'multiple use') qualities which the urban designer should respect. Nevertheless, Cullen's method included a rather systematic framework for these sometimes elusive qualities, through the idea of 'serial vision'. This paralleled the efforts at MIT to devise a way of handling the temporal in urban design, and, like them, was a tool of both analysis and design, as Cullen illustrated in a number of examples, coupling a plan of a town with a series of photographs or drawings representing the sequence of key events on the route through it.

In 1964, Cullen published the first of four studies commissioned from him by Alcan Industries during the 1960s,[99] in which he developed this work further. Interestingly, *A Town Called Alcan* demonstrated the hidden but implicit connection between the use of serial or sequential images as a

*Gordon Cullen, 'A Town Called Alcan', 1964, general view of the city.*

*Gordon Cullen, 'A Town Called Alcan', 1964, sequential studies.*

*Gordon Cullen, sequential study for the proposed New Town of Llantrisant, Wales. Here Cullen suggests that the existing urban nucleus on top of a small ridge be further dramatized by approaches via bridges from surrounding hillsides and the development of steep streets and pedestrian routes to the New Town at the base of the ridge.*

# INDICATORS

**CONNECTORS**

    pedestrian access

    essential sight line

**POINT OF REFERENCE**

**SPACE ENTITY**

**AMBIENCE**
(using typical building as example)

**LINKED SPACE**

**SPACE BARRIER**

    access

    vision

**VISTAS**

    panorama

    vista

    glimpse

**SERIAL VISION SEQUENCE**

**INFINITY**

**WATER**

**GROUPS**

    random

    architectural

**GROWTH**

**PROPORTION**
cross section    P/1.2.1

**LEVELS**

    spot      + 250

    building      ⊕ 60

    height

    storeys      ⊕ IV

    towers etc.      △ 150

**FACING DIRECTION**
(statue etc.)

# VISUAL SURVEY

| Symbol | Label | Symbol | Label |
|---|---|---|---|
| | GATES | | DISTRICT |
| | LANDMARKS | _N | NEGATIVE AREA |
| | VIEWS | P | POSITIVE AREA |
| | FOOTPATH | | NODES |
| | HARD EDGE | | |
| | SOFT EDGE | | |

*Gordon Cullen, final study carried out for Alcan in an attempt to create his own system of urban analysis which he referred to as 'Notation'.*

*David Gosling, Gordon Cullen, John Ferguson, Church Village project, Bridgetown, Barbados, 1978, analysis study of the central area.*

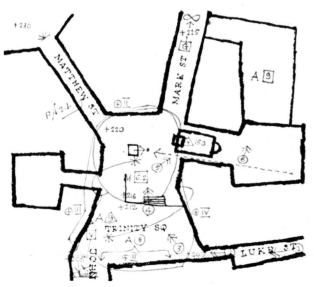

### Footnotes

**1** Scales and Indicators are only to be used where the interpretation of a plan could reasonably be in doubt. This obviously depends to some extent on the type of person who is going to read the plan.

**2** The Notation assumes the continued existence of standard planning symbols and that is why they are not duplicated.

**3** The author reserves the right to add, alter, rescind any Notations or pattern of Notations as the series progresses.

**4** You may say that all this information could be gained more simply by a photograph or a visit. But the purpose of the Code is mainly to explain what is *not* built—what is intended.

*Gordon Cullen, sequential study for the Church Village project, Bridgetown, 1978.*

*Computer-generated perspectives. During the last few years, computer-generated graphics have become more sophisticated, and Brian Lawson, of Sheffield University, has developed a programme to allow the generation of sequential perspectives for urban design purposes.*

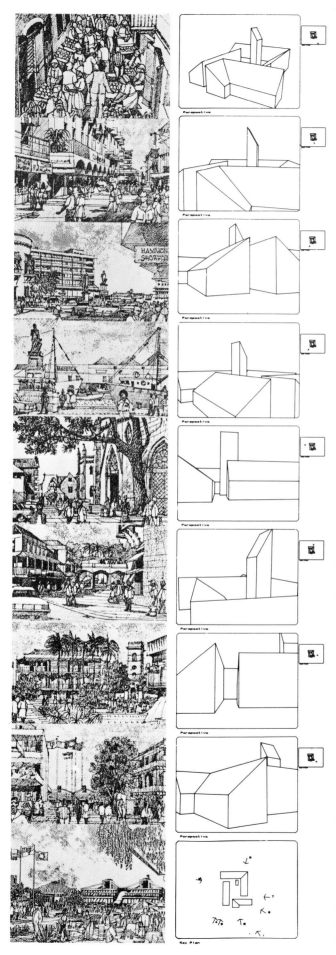

recording or analytical notation and as a creative design tool. While its circuit linear form had undoubted merits in circulation planning terms (and indeed was also taken up in Arthur Ling's contemporaneous master plan for Runcorn New Town), the linear organization of Cullen's plan for Alcan also happened to be ideal for representation in serial form, as Appleyard demonstrated that year with regard to highway design. Cullen in fact gave a summary of his proposals in the form of 12 successive sketch views, drawn as if they were stills from a movie, with notes for a script alongside. The town is not just being filmed—it *is* a film, and the urban designer a narrator.

In the later Alcan studies, Cullen wrestled with the problem of establishing a common vocabulary and shorthand notation for urban designers, which again paralleled similar efforts by the American researchers. *The Scanner* proposed a table of human and physical factors which the designer must satisfy, while *Notation* developed a method of annotating plans so that the essential characteristics of place could be recorded in an accurate, expressive and commonly understood form.

The work done in the 1950s and 1960s to understand and represent the way in which the city is perceived laid the foundations for further important studies. In 1969, Appleyard published the results of an application of Lynch's methods in the Venezuelan new town of Cuidad Guayana, which investigated the wide differences between the planners' view of the developing city and the inhabitants' actual perception of it.[100] Lynch himself produced a series of books which extended his thesis, notably *What Time is this Place?*,[101] which considered the perception of ageing towns, and *Managing the Sense of a Region*[102] which enlarged the scale of his investigation. Others have probed the psychology of the perception of the city, or 'cognitive mapping'.[103] Other analytical techniques of sequential representation can be seen in the 1978 drawings of Gordon Cullen for the redevelopment of Central Bridgetown, Barbados.[104] Finally, in a neatly subversive adaptation of the techniques devised at MIT, Venturi, Scott Brown and Izenour with a team from Yale managed to turn the whole argument on its head. Selecting that most 'imageable' but least 'architectural' of American cities, Las Vegas, they used sequence illustrations and notated plans recording such environmental factors as neon lighting levels and frequency of wedding chapels, to argue *against* the intentions of the planning authorities to cultivate a 'coherent image' for the Strip by such methods as trying 'to persuade

the gasoline stations to imitate the architecture of the casinos, in the interests of architectural unity'. Sadly, however, they found the techniques available still inadequate for their urban anti-design purposes: 'How do you represent the Strip as perceived by Mr. A. rather than as a piece of geometry? How do you show quality of light—or qualities of form—in plan at one inch to 100 feet? How do you show fluxes and flows or seasonal variation, or change with time?'[105]

**NOTES**

1 Camillo Sitte, *Der Städtebau nach seinen künstlerischen Grundsätzen* 1889, translated into English in 1945 by Charles T. Stewart as *The Art of Building Cities*, Reinhold Publishing Corporation, New York.
2 Camillo Sitte, *ibid.*, p. 59.
3 *Ibid.*, p. 2.
4 *Ibid.*, p. 94.
5 Raymond Unwin, *Town Planning in Practice*, T. Fisher Unwin Ltd., London 1919, p. 115.
6 *Ibid.*, p. 15.
7 Antoine de Saint-Exupéry, *Wind, Sand and Stars*, Heinemann 1939, translated from the French *Terre des hommes*. Penguin Books edition 1966, p. 57.
8 Bernard Rudofsky, *Architecture Without Architects*, Doubleday & Co. Inc., New York and Academy Editions, London 1964.
9 See Josiah Cox Russell, *Medieval Regions and their Cities*, David and Charles, Newton Abbot, for an assessment of the size of towns in central Italy in the Middle Ages.
10 Raymond Gindroa, 'Studies in Visual Structure for Urban Environments: Monumental v. Popular' in *Urban Structure* (ed. David Lewis), Elek Books (*Architects' Year Book* XII, 1968).
11 Camillo Sitte, *op. cit.*, p. 1.
12 Cited by Walter L. Creese in *The Legacy of Raymond Unwin: A Human Pattern for Planning*, MIT Press, Cambridge, Mass. 1967, p. 39.
13 Bernard Rudofsky, *op. cit.*
14 *Ibid.*
15 *Ibid.*
16 Le Corbusier, *The City of Tomorrow*, The Architectural Press, London 1971, p. 11, translated by Frederick Etchells from *Urbanisme*, Editions Cres., Paris 1924.
17 *Ibid.*, p. 14.
18 *Ibid.*, p. 43.
19 Le Corbusier, *L'Art Décoratif d'Aujourd'hui*, Editions Vincent, Fréal et Cie, Paris 1925, reprinted 1959, p. 216.
20 Le Corbusier, *The Radiant City*, Faber and Faber, London 1967, p. 230. Translation of *La Ville Radieuse*, Vincent, Fréal et Cie, Paris 1933.
21 *Ibid.*, p. 6.
22 *Ibid.*, pp. 136, 137.

23 Le Corbusier, *Oeuvre Complète 1946–1952*, W. Boesiger aux Editions Guisberger, Zürich 1955.

24 Le Corbusier, *The Radiant City*, *op. cit.*, p. 147.

25 *Ibid.*, p. 231.

26 *Ibid.*, p. 269.

27 Le Corbusier, *The City of Tomorrow*, *op. cit.*, p. 24.

28 Le Corbusier, *The Radiant City*, *op. cit.*, p. 269.

29 Reyner Banham, *Megastructure—Urban Futures of the Recent Past*, Thames and Hudson, London 1976, p. 8.

30 *Architectural Forum*, New York, August/September 1964, p. 114.

31 T.E. Lawrence, *Seven Pillars of Wisdom*, Penguin Books, Harmondsworth 1964, p. 37.

32 Robert Fishman, *Urban Utopias in the Twentieth Century*, Basic Books Inc., New York 1977.

33 Fishman, *ibid.*, p. 109.

34 Karl R. Popper, *The Poverty of Historicism*, Routledge & Kegan Paul, London 1963, p. 91.

35 Popper, *ibid.*, p. 73.

36 Ernst Cassirer, *An Essay on Man*, Yale University Press, New Haven & London 1963, p. 62.

37 Anthony Vidler, 'The Idea of Unity and Le Corbusier's Urban Form', essay in *Architects' Year Book* XII, Elek Books, London 1968, pp. 225–37.

38 Victor Considérant, cited by Vidler, *ibid.*, p. 231.

39 Le Corbusier, cited by Vidler, *ibid.*, p. 230.

40 Karl Marx, *The Revolution of 1848: Political Writings, Volume I* (ed. David Fernbach), Penguin Books, Harmondsworth 1978, p. 87.

41 Kenneth Frampton, 'Notes on Soviet Urbanism, 1917–32', essay in *Architects' Year Book* XII, Elek Books, London 1968, pp. 238–52.

42 Frampton, *ibid.*, p. 252.

43 Marx, *op. cit.*, p. 96.

44 Manfredo Tafuri, *Architecture and Utopia: Design and Capitalist Development* (trans. Barbara Luigia La Penta), MIT Press, Cambridge, Mass. 1976, p. 72.

45 Paul and Percival Goodman, *Communitas: Means of Livelihood and Ways of Life*, Vintage Books, New York 1960.

46 Goodman, *ibid.*, p. 20.

47 Peter Dickens, *Marxism and Architectural Theory: A Critique of Recent Work*, paper presented to the British Society of Aesthetics Colloquium, University of Sheffield, April 1979.

48 Leon Krier *et al.*, *Rational Architecture*, Archives d'Architecture Moderne, Brussels 1978.

49 Vitruvius, *The Ten Books on Architecture* (trans. Morris Hickey Morgan), Dover Publications Inc., New York 1960.

50 See Joseph Rykwert, *The Idea of a Town*, Faber and Faber, London 1976, p. 42.

51 Antonio Sant' Elia, *The New City*, 1914, Nuove Tendenze, exhibition catalogue, Famiglia Artistica, Milan, May-June 1914. English translation in Reyner Banham, *Theory and Design in the First Machine Age*, The Architectural Press, London 1960.

52 Isaac Asimov, *Foundation*, Panther Books, Granada Publishing Ltd., London 1979, p. 12 (first published 1951).

53 R. Buckminster Fuller, 'The Comprehensive Man', 1959, from *The Buckminster Fuller Reader* (ed. James Meller), Penguin Books, Harmondsworth 1972, p. 335.

54 R. Buckminster Fuller, *Utopia or Oblivion: The Prospects for Humanity*, Allen Lane, The Penguin Press, London 1970, p. 395.

55 Yona Friedman, 'Toward a Coherent System of Planning', essay in *Architects' Year Book* XII, Elek Books, London 1968, p. 57.

56 Frank Lloyd Wright, *The Disappearing City*, New York 1932, cited by Fishman, *op. cit.*, p. 125.

57 Frank Lloyd Wright, *The Living City*, New York 1958, p. 119.

58 Leslie Martin and Lionel March (eds), *Urban Space and Structures*, Cambridge University Press, London 1972. See also L. March, 'Homes Beyond the Fringe', *RIBA Journal*, August 1967.

59 N.J. Habraken, *Supports: An Alternative to Mass Housing* (trans. B. Valkenburg), The Architectural Press, London 1972 (first published in Holland 1961), excerpts from pp. 10–29.

60 Habraken, *ibid.*, p. 59.

61 Habraken, *ibid.*, p. 69.

62 Yona Friedman, *Toward a Scientific Architecture* (trans. Cynthia Lang), MIT Press, Cambridge, Mass. 1975.

63 For example, Christopher Alexander, 'A City is not a Tree', article in *Architectural Forum*, April/May 1965.

64 Christopher Alexander *et al.*, Vol. 1 *The Timeless Way of Building*; Vol. 2 *A Pattern Language*; Vol. 3 *The Oregon Experiment*, Oxford University Press, New York 1977.

65 Alexander *et al.*, *A Pattern Language*, *ibid.*, pp. 168–73.

66 *Ibid.*, p. XIX.

67 Ebenezer Howard, *Garden Cities of Tomorrow* (ed. F.J. Osborn), Cambridge, Mass. 1965, p. 131.

68 Le Corbusier, *The City of Tomorrow*, *op. cit.*

69 *Ibid.*, p. 96.

70 For a more substantial discussion of the relevance of semiotics to design, as also Gestalt psychology, see Christian Norberg-Schulz, *Intentions in Architecture*, Universitetsforlaget, Allen & Unwin Ltd. 1963.

71 Gordon Cullen, *Language of Gestures* 1974 and *Signs, Symbols and Architecture* (eds G. Broadbent, R. Bunt, C. Jencks) J. Wiley 1980.

72 J.B. Calhoun, 'Space and the Strategy of Life', from *Behaviour and Environment* (ed. A.H. Esser), Plenum Press, New York 1971.

73 Jane Jacobs, *The Death and Life of Great American Cities: The Failure of Town Planning*, Penguin Books Ltd., Harmondsworth 1972, p. 16 (first published 1961).

74 Jacobs, *ibid.*, pp. 99–100.

75 Oscar Newman, *Defensible Space: People and Design in the Violent City*, The Architectural Press, London 1972.

76 Rudolf Arnheim, *Art and Visual Perception: A Psychology of the Creative Eye*, Faber and Faber Ltd., London 1956, p. viii.

77 David Katz, *Gestalt Psychology* (trans. Robert Tyson), Methuen & Co. Ltd., London 1951, pp. 24–29.

78 Friedrich Wulf, 'Uber die Veränderung von Verstellungen (Gedächtnis und Gestalt)' 1922, from W.D. Ellis, *A Source Book of Gestalt Psychology*, Routledge & Kegan Paul Ltd., London 1938, p. 148.

79 J. Piaget & B. Inhelder, *The Child's Conception of Space*, London 1956.

80 S. Giedion, *Space, Time and Architecture: The Growth of a New Tradition*, Harvard University Press, Cambridge, Mass. 1959 (first published 1941).

81 Giedion, *ibid.*, p. 753.

82 G. di San Lazzaro, *Klee* (trans. S. Hood), Thames and Hudson, London 1957, p. 107.

83 L. Moholy-Nagy, *Vision in Motion*, Paul Theobald, Chicago 1956.

84 R. Hinks, 'Peepshow and the Roving Eye' in *The Architectural Review*, August 1955.

85 See *Japan Architect*, February 1979.

86 G. Kepes, *The New Landscape*, Paul Theobald & Co., Chicago 1956.

87 P. Thiel, 'A Study of the Visual Representation of Architectural and Urban Space-Time Sequences', unpublished paper 1958.

88 James Gibson, *The Perception of the Visual World*, Houghton Mufflin & Co., Boston 1950.

89 *Graphis*, Special Issue 'The Art of the Comic Strip', No. 159, Vol. 28, 1972/73 and No. 160, Vol. 28, 1972/73.

90 *Ibid.*, p. 6 and p. 89.

91 S. Eisenstein, *The Film Sense*, Meridian Books, New York 1957.

92 D. Appleyard, K. Lynch and J.R. Myer, *The View from the Road*, MIT Press, Cambridge, Mass. 1964.

93 *Ibid.*, p. 63.

94 K. Lynch, *The Image of the City*, The Technological Press and Harvard University Press, Cambridge, Mass. 1960.

95 I. Nairn, *The Architectural Review*, August 1960, p. 117 and K. Browne, 'Manchester Re-United', *The Architectural Review*, Vol. 132, No. 786, August 1962, pp. 116–20.

96 K.C. Bloomer and C.W. Moore, *Body, Memory, and Architecture*, Yale University Press, New Haven & London 1977, p. 79.

97 C. Norberg-Schulz, *Existence, Space & Architecture*, Studio Vista, London 1971.

98 G. Cullen, *Townscape*, The Architectural Press, London 1961.

99 G. Cullen, *A Town Called Alcan* 1964; *4 Circuit Linear Towns* 1965; *The Scanner* 1966; and *Notation* 1968, Alcan Industries Ltd., London.

100 D. Appleyard, 'City Designers and the Pluralistic City', in L. Rodwin (ed.), *Planning Urban Growth and Regional Development: The Experience of the Guayana Program of Venezuela*, MIT Press, Cambridge, Mass. 1969.

101 K. Lynch, *What Time is This Place?*, MIT Press, Cambridge, Mass. 1972.

102 K. Lynch, *Managing the Sense of a Region*, MIT Press, Cambridge, Mass. 1976.

103 See R.M. Downs and D. Stea, *Maps in Minds: Reflections on Cognitive Mapping*, Harper and Row, New York 1977. Also D. Canter, *The Psychology of Place*, St. Martin's Press, New York 1977.

104 D. Gosling, G. Cullen, J. Ferguson, *Church Village: Redevelopment Proposals for Central Bridgetown Barbados*, Central Bank of Barbados, Government of Barbados and Commonwealth Fund for Technical Cooperation, 1978.

105 R. Venturi, D. Scott Brown and S. Izenour, *Learning from Las Vegas*, MIT Press, Cambridge, Mass. 1972.

# PART THREE
# APPLICATIONS AND SOLUTIONS: INTERNATIONAL CASE STUDIES IN URBAN DESIGN

FROM THE PRECEDING DISCUSSION OF THE NATURE OF the problems addressed by urban designers, and of the sources of models and theories invoked for their solution, we might hope to develop a systematic approach, if not a precise taxonomy, for considering the huge range of projects which have relevance to the field of urban design. And indeed, an initial broad classification based on a perception of the nature of the *problem* does seem possible. Although all projects no doubt hope to supply a well-rounded and balanced solution, in almost all cases it is possible, without too much violence to the designer's intentions, to identify just one aspect of the problem—economic, technical, social, professional or formal—which seems to have been given primacy. Most urban design projects seem to be based on, or at least to illustrate the possibility of, an underlying premise of the type: 'The city is essentially a social phenomenon, and an urban design project is above all concerned with finding an appropriate physical form for the social organization.' We suggest these five strategic groupings (economic, engineering, social, professional and formal) into which most projects may be seen to fall, although further headings (ecological, for example) are certainly possible.

Within this broad classification a further, more specific subdivision can be made according to a functional definition of the programme. While the design of a central-area redevelopment project may illustrate general issues concerning the city perceived as a technological product, it also invites comparison with other similar central-area programmes. The diversity of such programmes, all assumed in this study to fall within the scope of urban design, is so great that some such functional classification seems inevitable, and would include: city planning frameworks; central-area development projects; new towns; villages; high, medium and low-density residential neighbourhoods; squatter settlements; conservation programmes; rehabilitation projects; pedestrianization schemes. Such a list of programme types might be further extended to include use types, such as universities or fun fairs, for which solutions of general relevance to urban designers have been developed. In addition, we might include a number of particular issues, like alternative transportation modes, energy efficiency, or design guides, which cut across use classifications but nevertheless embrace families of solution types.

Although the number of such programme types could certainly be increased from those suggested here, the 16 indicated above could, with the five basic problem subdivisions, provide us with a matrix of some 80 classifications of urban design approach based upon an analysis of the problem to be solved. Within each, a whole range of solution types could then be considered, depending upon the attitudes and beliefs of the designer and his sources of ideas from among those investigated in Part Two. We could, for example, find within the classification of, say, village projects exhibiting a preoccupation with formal cohesion, one deriving its formal vocabulary from organic models, another from mathematical analyses of land use and built form, and a third from theories of perception and serial vision.

No doubt, other ways of organizing the wealth of material offered by the subject of urban design are possible. A morphological analysis, for example, might be attempted. However, the approach adopted here is not intended as a universal classification system so much as a framework to help identify and relate attitudes contained within a wide range of recent applications. Since it is not possible to explore case studies exhaustively for all possible theories applied to all combinations of problem types within the confines of a book such as this, this section is restricted to a selection of some hundred or so projects which illustrate the most persistent themes. Apart from this criterion of relevance, the projects have been selected on the basis of their quality, their influence on other designers, or simply their availability and familiarity to the authors.

The applications investigated here are thus grouped firstly under the five broad areas of preoccupation—economic, technical, social, professional and formal—which were earlier discussed as problems. Within each group, certain programme types illustrate particularly sharply the issues raised by the group as a whole, and these form subheadings within which some three or four specific projects can be compared. Thus the programme type 'high-density neighbourhoods', while by no means oblivious to technical, economic and other issues, has nevertheless provided a focus for ideas relating to the general premise of the primacy of the social parameter stated earlier. 'High-density neighbourhoods' is therefore discussed within the general context of 'social' solutions, through the examination of several important projects. Each main group is introduced with a study of the work of one designer, which is felt to raise issues of principle in a useful way, and is concluded with a brief review of a relevant design competition. As Sir John Summerson has shown in his study of a number of famous Victorian architectural competitions, and as subsequent history has continued to demonstrate, for example with the Chicago Tribune and League of Nations competitions of the 1920s, these events cast a peculiarly revealing light upon contemporary ideas. Combining the speculative idealist's freedom from more mundane professional restraints with the vital complexities of a real brief, the competition first encloses the designer in an intense private communion with his programme and then finally exposes the result as just one of a series of parallel possibilities. For our purposes, the various solutions offered in each of the urban design competitions discussed provide a particularly lively commentary on the changing attitudes of designers to the problems they face.

## 3.1 ECONOMIC SOLUTIONS: THE CITY AS PROCESS

ALL REALIZABLE URBAN DESIGN PROPOSALS ARE obliged to recognize the power of economic forces to shape what can be achieved. Most starkly in the case of the squatter settlements of the Third World, but also for the most sophisticated proposal for a developed metropolis, the economic context provides a crucial parameter. For most projects this fact simply entails a restriction in resources available to realize ends defined by other considerations. For a few, however, the operation of economic forces itself seems to provide a model for the form of development. Unlike social, engineering or formal models, for example, which can suggest some fixed goal to be realized, this particular source inspires no physical end state, but rather a sense of the city as, above all, a dynamic process. Individual urban design proposals which are then seen as containers or channels for a flux of economic activity thus tend to be preoccupied with change, with the patterns which future growth may adopt and with stimulating activity in preferred configurations.

The designers whose work has been chosen to introduce these themes are the members of the Metabolist group of Japan, significantly perhaps

from the most dynamic post-war economy, whose projects are dominated by a sense of analogy with biological, and particularly botanical, processes. A group of New Town centres will then be examined for their varying responses to the problem of accommodating future growth, this time within the less sanguine economic climate of Scotland. The attempt to manipulate economic patterns in order to revitalize existing urban areas will then be considered in two further groups of projects, the first concerned with pedestrianization and the second with rehabilitation. Finally, the 1976 competition for a new master plan for the central area of Telford New Town in England's West Midlands provides an opportunity to examine alternative approaches to the common difficulty of reconciling the need to allow unpredictable patterns of future choice with the desire for a clear and stable image of the city.

### Designers: The Metabolists

To the idea of the city as a process, the Japanese Metabolist group added the notion of differential rates of change, and thus the possibility that change itself could act as an ordering principle for the urban designer. We may say, for example, that an individual dwelling has a shorter life-cycle than the supporting structure and services which sustain it, and that they in turn have shorter life-cycles than the city of which they form a part. Thus the relationship of parts is akin to that of the leaf to the tree, and the tree to the forest, and indeed the botanical analogy was used by the Metabolists both to explain their ideas and as a source of form. Noriaki Kurokawa, for example, proposed 'bamboo-type communities', in which a hollow 'stem' of circular plan form supported living cell units over its outer surface, and 'plant-type communities' where a vast Christmas-tree-like structure would provide platforms in the sky for housing, education and other functions.

Pursuing the same theme, Kiyonori Kikutake proposed a cylindrical community form similar to the bamboo-type, but with the added refinement that the whole construction would 'grow' and generate itself. A central shaft would first be formed as the core of the tower, and once formed would act as a production area for the individual units for 1,250 or so people to be attached around its outside. Once the first process of generation was complete, the core would then be converted into a laboratory for research and improvement of these cells, which would be changed with the needs and tastes of each generation. Kikutake further pro-

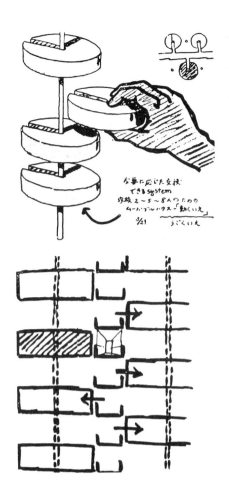

Kiyonori Kikutake,
Cylindrical Communities,
1964, sketches.

Kiyonori Kikutake,
Cylindrical Communities,
1964, model.

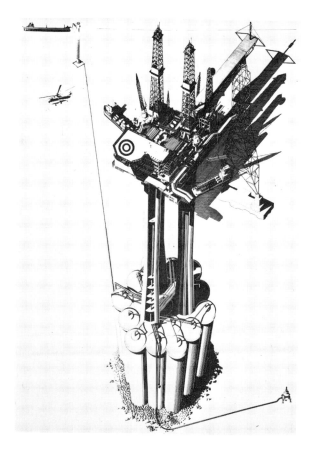

posed that such towers be grouped into 'Ocean Cities' which, discarding their used parts into the sea, would be free to move and would together constitute a new 'Marine Civilization' running along the coast of Japan.

The fantastical character of these speculations tended perhaps to obscure the real possibilities inherent in an acceptance and display of the process of change which, though present in all cities, is absent from most conceptions of city form, which tend to deal in images of a final, stable state. It was Kenzo Tange who demonstrated that the idea of 'the city as process' could be carried through into a powerful urban and architectural language. In his Yamanishi Communications building at Kofu of 1967, he offered a heroic metaphor of process, in which circular cores of variable height were slung with a partial set of trays of accommodation, and articulated with an array of brackets forming a complete vocabulary of the metopes, triglyphs and puttae appropriate to an imaginary (for their purpose was symbolic rather than practical) technology of change.

*Advertisement by Mobil Oil of a North Sea rig in the Beryl field, 1979. Although many of the urban design opportunities had been seen almost a decade earlier by Kikutake and the Japanese Metabolists, the North Sea challenge was never taken by architects.*

*Kiyonori Kikutake, Floating City for the Osaka Expo', Japan, 1970.*

*Kiyonori Kikutake, Floating City project, Hawaii, 1971.*

**References:**

*Architectural Design*, Vol. 34, No. 10, October 1964, pp. 479–524.

*Architectural Design*, Vol. 37, No. 5, May 1967, pp. 207–16.

## New Towns: Scotland

Three Scottish New Towns provide examples of the use of different urban design concepts to weld together the various components of a town centre, seen in these cases as a single building complex, within a context in which growth—its artificial inception, its stimulation and its daily side effects—is a major preoccupation.

Geoffrey Copcutt's design for Cumbernauld Town Centre offered one of the most convincing images of the possibility of a new form of urban core in which the forces acting to erode the quality of traditional centres—traffic, commercial shopping patterns, impermanence and change—could be triumphantly re-assembled into a pattern in which the values of the traditional centres would be realized in a new and strengthened form. When the project was first published, the critic Robert Jeffrey described it as projecting 'a new insight into the nature of urban architecture in our time' through 'an architecture of layers meshed together by vertical shafts of circulation' to provide 'an experience of a city centre as an incredible interlocking of uses and values'. Perhaps it was inevitable that the slow unfolding of Copcutt's original concept of 'a single citadel-like structure nearly half-a-mile long, 200 yards wide and up to eight storeys high' would disappoint those high expectations, but it is worth pointing to one particular issue on which the original design took a brave stand which was to be undermined by subsequent events.

Copcutt's explanation of his ideas placed particular stress on the problem of flexibility and change in both retailing and entertainment patterns, and on his decision to opt for 'a permanent structure with demountable enclosures rather than to provide short-term buildings creating at any one time an indifferent environment or to accept the normal time-cycle of growth and decay with consequent social and economic disruption'. But the designers reckoned without the 'time-cycle of growth and decay' in ideas, which would occur within the construction time of the permanent structure itself. The result is a town centre in which the first phase was modelled on the original concept, with pedestrian circulation decks above car parking and service levels; a second phase, comprising a Woolco store as a major part, in which open car parking was now brought up to the shopping level to allow easy trolley access; and finally a third phase in which parking is provided on the roof of the shopping areas. Thus in the course of a 15-year development cycle, the original sectional organization—a fundamental part of the concept—was

*Geoffrey Copcutt, Cumbernauld Town Centre project, Scotland, 1961, cross section through the town centre.*

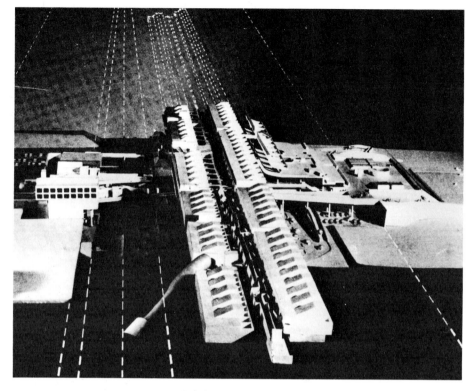

*Geoffrey Copcutt, Cumbernauld Town Centre project, view of the model.*

turned on its head.

The problem of devising a controlling urban design concept for a new centre, which nevertheless could stand piecemeal implementation over a period of years, was faced by the other two Scottish projects which, unlike Cumbernauld Centre, were to be constructed in areas of former settlement which were to be integrated into a larger New Town pattern. Although not formally designated a New Town, the burgh of Rutherglen in South Glasgow prepared, through its consultants Moira and Moira, a set of proposals in 1965 and 1966 for the reconstruction of the burgh which were comparable in scope. In particular, the central area project designer, Ian Beck, proposed a completely new town centre form to be constructed on the site of the existing. Its principal element was a meandering wall of nine storeys of housing extending along the northern edge of the centre, facing south over it and shielding it from an urban motorway and rail lines running along that boundary. At its lower levels, the decks of this wall extended routes out across the central area to generate shopping malls and ribbons of low-rise housing. Although obviously designed with the completed pattern in mind, the nature of the existing uses on

the site made it necessary to envisage the design as a linking together of self-sufficient armatures in what might prove to be an unpredictable order. The plans of anticipated phasing development thus resemble the growth of extended crystals from a number of points, eventually coming together in a completed lattice.

The idea of an urban design plan being as much concerned with controlling the pattern of growth as with supplying a city 'image', was important also at Irvine New Town, on the Ayrshire coast, 25 miles south-west of Glasgow. There, the New Town centre was envisaged as one of a pair of major centres located at either end of a sub-regional development combining both Irvine and Kilmarnock. The Irvine centre was to be integrated with the existing burgh centre, and was to exploit the largely unrealized potential of its coastal location. Thus the new centre, with all the infrastructure and investment it would entail, was seen as a means of overcoming thresholds—a river crossing, railway line, and belt of declining industrial uses—which over a period of 200 years had gradually separated Irvine centre from the harbour and foreshore areas which had originally supported the town and now formed a major recreational asset for it. The

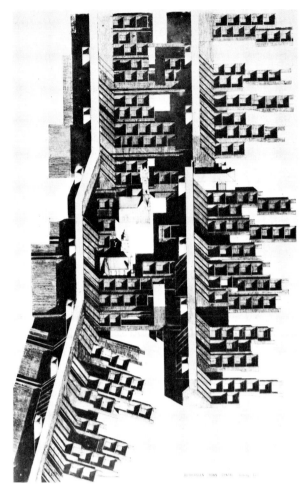

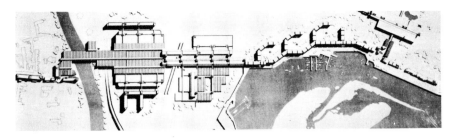

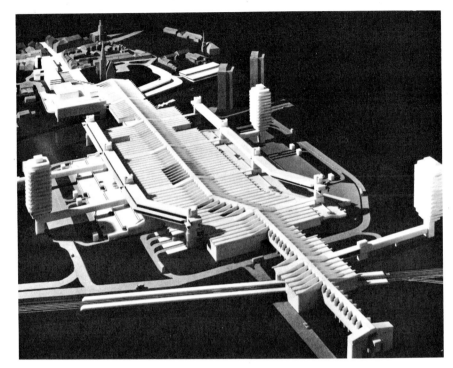

concept of the new centre as a linear structure growing out from the burgh centre to cross each of the development barriers in turn thus derived from this analysis. The key to achieving this pattern lay with the commercial core of the new centre which was to be financed by private capital in partnership with the Development Corporation, and a design was therefore prepared by the town centre project team, under Barry Maitland, setting out development principles. Developers, concerned primarily with the pattern of the shopping element, expressed a surprising variety of preferences for the form that the commercial core should take, and the company with whom partnership was eventually effected was that whose commercial preferences most closely matched the urban design priorities of the Development Corporation, resulting in the developed linear design for the centre.

**References:**

*Architectural Design*, Vol. 33, No. 5, May 1963, pp. 209–225, 'Cumbernauld New Town Central Area'.
Moira and Moira, *Royal Burgh of Rutherglen, Quinquennial Review, 1968*.
Irvine Development Corporation, *Irvine New Town Plan*, 1971.

*Ian Beck for Moira and Moira, Rutherglen town centre, Scotland, 1967.*

*Barry Maitland, David Gosling, Brian Lowe, Irvine New Town, Scotland, central-area project, 1970, plan.*

*Barry Maitland, Irvine New Town, central-area project, 1970, model.*

*Irvine New Town centre, sequential perspectives drawn by David Gosling.*

*Irvine New Town centre, 1976, aerial view.*

*Irvine New Town centre, 1976, Bridgegate entrance.*

### Pedestrianization Projects

One effect of the radical attempts of such New Town projects to channel patterns of economic growth to form integrated central-area structures, has been to encourage existing towns, with whom they may be in competition, to reconsider their own central areas. The numerous pedestrianization projects of the past decade may be seen in this way—as attempts to reconstitute sections of the downtown area, to form cohesive urban units, in both management and visual terms, which can stimulate economic activity. The degree to which the clarity of the urban image and the perception of urban structure can be enhanced by comparatively minor adjustments to the treatment of public spaces has been amply demonstrated by these projects. With relatively few material changes, the physical and economic benefits of these schemes for excluding traffic from selected streets seem in almost all cases to have been substantial, despite the initial misgivings of residents and traders.

The motives and aims of such undertakings are summarized by the case of Munich, where the pedestrianization of the main shopping area on Kaufingerstraße and Neuhauserstraße was completed in time for the 1972 Olympic Games. The post-war growth of the city was accompanied during the 1960s by a decline in the inner-city population, and progressively worsening traffic congestion in the commercial core, coupled with the growth of new competing suburban centres and hypermarkets around the edges of the city. The pedestrianization of the city centre was thus seen as part of a wider strategy to balance potentially disruptive changes in traffic and shopping patterns, a strategy which included an improved inner ring-road and extensive improvements to the public transport network, including a new U-Bahn system. A competition was held for the detailed design of the pedestrian area, which was to run east-west across the core of the old city, with future extensions along its main north-south street. The first phase thus established a unified public space, about 700 metres in length with an average width of 22 metres, including several squares, and spanning the width of the old city core, from the medieval Karlstor to Rathaus gates. Undoubtedly successful in commercial terms in providing a convenient and compact shopping centre, the project also added a new element to the life of the city, as attested by the great numbers of people who crowd into it and the variety of events and entertainments which occur along its length.

Many other cities have carried out programmes similar to that of Munich, often as part of a wider plan to restore the commercial and environmental integrity of the central area. In all cases, an important corollary has been the clarification and enhancement of the form of these urban spaces, which can now be read as coherent and related sequences.

In many cases, the pedestrianization of city centres has begun with a single major street, as in Munich, and then been gradually extended into the surrounding areas. Perhaps the longest established and most extensive of all such projects is that of Copenhagen, which began with the Strøget—a continuous linear route 1.6 kilometres in length—and then progressively enlarged along Fiolstraede and Kobmagergade until it became possible to envisage the pedestrianization network spread out across the whole city centre. The unification of the city centre which resulted from this can be seen in similar cases where the initial experimental road closures have been developed into a proper network, as in the English example of Leeds, where the pedestrianization of Victorian streets has been carried on in parallel with redevelopment projects based on enclosed shopping malls, to build up an extensive mesh of foot streets.

In a few cases, the process of 'reclaiming' a street, which begins with the exclusion of traffic and then moves into repaving, landscaping and the provision of shelters, fountains, seats and other such facilities, has gone as far as to emulate the enclosed precincts by covering the route. This transformation of the street into what is effectively a building entails a much more elaborate and expensive operation, involving questions of ventilation, smoke-logging and emergency vehicle access. Nevertheless, in the case, for example, of the 600-metre-long St Joseph Street in Quebec City, whose metamorphosis into the St Roche Mall was completed in 1974, considerable success in revitalizing an area by this method has been claimed.

References:
R. Brambella and G. Longo, *For Pedestrians Only*, Whitney Library of Design, New York 1977.
*Pedestrianized Streets*, report of GLC Study Tour of Europe and America.
J.G. Gray, *Pedestrianized Shopping Streets in Europe*, publication of the Pedestrians' Association for Road Safety, Edinburgh and District Branch.
*Leeds: Pedestrian Streets*, report prepared by the Project Planning Section, Planning and Property Department, Civic Hall, Leeds 1972.

*Van den Broek and Bakema, new pedestrian precinct, Lijnbaan, Rotterdam, Holland, 1953–.*

*Pedestrianization of the main shopping area, Munich, West Germany, 1979.*

*The Strøget, Copenhagen, Denmark, pedestrianization of existing streets, 1963–.*

## Rehabilitation Projects

As a counterpart to those urban design solutions which have been inspired by the patterns of economic growth and expansion, are those for which the central problems arise rather from disinvestment and decline. In these cases, the question of urban design becomes inseparable from that of the revitalization of both the local economy and its physical fabric. For such areas of our cities, the most appropriate action may involve no major new design at all, but rather the renewal and refurbishment of buildings and the retention of the well-established communities they house. Although the urban design content of such projects is thus limited in physical terms, they have been at the forefront of the debate concerning the relationship between the designer and the designed-for. By confronting the designer directly with his clients, with their existing patterns of life and needs for limited and piecemeal assistance, these projects have encouraged reinterpretations of the designer-client relationship which are the antithesis of that described by Habraken as typifying the 'Mass Housing' process. The work of three pioneering groups in the United Kingdom may be taken to illustrate variations of this approach.

In 1970, Raymond Young, a final-year student of architecture at Strathclyde University, Glasgow, completed a thesis on public participation in planning and design. To test his theories, Young started to work with local people in Govan, helping them to try to rehabilitate their 80-year-old tenement flats with the aid of improvement grants available under the 1969 Housing (Scotland) Act. This led to the formation of a grant-assisted architectural service, ASSIST, under the directorship of Young's tutor, Jim Johnson, which opened an office in Govan in 1972. Over the next six years, the office organized the installation of bathrooms and basic facilities in 185 flats and focused attention on the possibility of rehabilitating what was one of the most depressed areas of Glasgow, as opposed to the wholesale clearance and redevelopment which had already occurred in the Gorbals area. Although initially concerned only with helping each occupant carry out internal improvements, ASSIST gradually became involved in environmental improvement work, and in particular in the transformation of the inner courts of the tenement blocks from frightening derelict yards into the centres of the surrounding community.

The notion of an architect's office as a corner shop, operating in the middle of the community it serves and open to citizens for advice, was derived from legal-aid centres and was present also as a feature of the Black Road General Improvement Area (GIA) in Macclesfield, the first privately-run, self-help GIA in England. The resident architect of this project, Rod Hackney, initiated in 1972, on discovering his own house to be part of a local-authority clearance plan, what was to become a model form of community action to rehabilitate an area of nineteenth-century industrial terrace housing, including an environmental structure plan for the common areas between the dwellings.

The rapid growth of Housing Associations' involvement in rehabilitation work in England since the 1974 Housing Act has produced a variety of working methods and philosophies, of which the example of Solon in London is one of the most radical. Set up by a mixed group of professionals in 1970 as a charitable Housing Association, Solon adopted a 'worker cooperative' organization, in which tenants of the properties bought and improved were invited to become share-holders. Architects worked directly with their client-tenants, and all formal hierarchies within the association were avoided. By 1978, Solon had grown to include groups operating in three London boroughs and had carried out an impressive amount of permanent and short-life rehabilitation, as well as offering a genuine attempt to give some meaning to such conventional phrases of housing policy as 'tenant participation', 'user control' and 'responsiveness to special community housing needs'.

### References:

'Interim Report 2: ASSIST in Govan 1972/75', *The Architects' Journal*, No. 40, Vol. 166, 5 October 1977, pp. 630–36.
*The Architects' Journal*, No. 35, Vol. 168, 30 August 1978, pp. 377–89.

*Young, Johnson, Thornley, Simister, Monaghan, ASSIST scheme, Govanhill, Glasgow, Scotland, 1970–80.*

*Black Road, Macclesfield, England, before improvement.*

*Rod Hackney, rehabilitation scheme, Black Road, Macclesfield, 1972–.*

**Competition: Telford**

The case of the 1976 competition for a new town-centre plan for Telford New Town, in England's West Midlands, provides an appropriate conclusion to this selection of projects moulded by the economic parameter. Located near Coalbrookdale in Staffordshire, one of the first areas in the world to be disrupted by the Industrial Revolution during the eighteenth century, the whole New Town project was seen as an attempt to address the problems of economic growth and decline, and to induce a new cycle to repair the ravages of the first, with its destruction of a once fine landscape.

The fiction of spontaneous creation which has seemed to be a part of some New Town plans has been thrown back at planners in the phrase 'New Town Blues', which is said to afflict the inhabitants during the major growth period of the town. The difficulty of maintaining a balanced programme of new facilities to match the needs of the incoming population is serious enough when a steady growth rate can be assumed, but becomes acute when, as inevitably occurs during the 20 or 30-year development cycle of a new town, progress is subject to abrupt variations imposed from outside. For the urban designer, this poses a general problem in a particularly acute form. Any urban design intention raises the problem of how to sustain it over a period of time, and in the case of the New Town an initial unparalleled opportunity to devise a sweeping urban design solution is then followed by an obstacle course of changing economic circumstances, legislation, technology, social expectations and fashion, through which the original concept may or may not be sustained.

This was one problem faced by competitors in the Telford competition. Given a somewhat slower rate of growth than had been anticipated, coupled with the general economic repercussions of the energy crisis, the Development Corporation had decided in 1976 to re-assess its plans for the central area of the town, which at that point comprised a hypermarket and adjoining shopping mall with surrounding at-grade car parking in the centre of a road box served from a nearby motorway. In inviting an urban design strategy from competitors, the Development Corporation drew attention to the need for a plan which could survive the uncertainties which lay ahead, for an integrated landscape design to repair 200 years of industrial and mining dereliction in what had once been a 'garden of England', and finally for a concept which would be as appropriate a symbol of its time as nearby Ironbridge had been of the first phase of the

Industrial Revolution.

Three premiated submissions serve to illustrate the wide variety of responses which this brief produced. The winning project, submitted by A.G. Sheppard Fidler and Associates with Gordon Cullen, adopted a linear arrangement of single-use zones stretching the full length of the available central-area site from rail station to town park. Since each zone was confined largely to one use, its character was specific, so that the office area took the form of towers, the civic that of public buildings by a lake, and so on. The linear arrangement was ideally suited to that form of serial presentation devised by Cullen for his early *Townscape* studies, and the project was indeed presented in this narrative fashion, as a succession of contrasting or complementary events along a walk from one end to the other. Although the particular forms of buildings and spaces could only be suggested, the thematic relationship between them could constitute an overall plan. As one of the designers put it, 'We were writing the plot, not the story'.

For the second design team, Yarwood, Macdonald and Lees, the essential character of the urban design plan was not that of a narrative but of an image, so memorable that the individual and unforeseen future structures could be accommodated within it without loss of its identity. The image chosen was that of a citadel, involving the construction of a perimeter 'wall building' around a compact central area full of variety and incident, in which the existing, embarrassingly anti-urban structures could be buried. Citing such models as Rothenburg and Lhasa, the designers went on to illustrate the kind of building conditions which would reinforce the city image at key points, as of entry, changes in direction of the 'wall', internal squares, and so on.

It could be said that both of these solutions share the assumption that the job of the urban designer is to establish the maximum control over the appearance of subsequent built form compatible with the reality of change over an extended development period by laying down the most coherent and stable image of the end state possible, to act as a 'target' for all future actions. The third design begins with the opposite premise. Arguing that the only sure statement one could make about a central-area concept which could not be implemented fairly rapidly would be that it would be overtaken by events, this submission, by Design Teaching Practice, set out instead to define the minimum urban structure compatible with the desire for an explicit community form. It concluded that such a sense of

community would be best expressed through the limited and specific commitment of the Development Corporation to the establishment of a network of sheltered pedestrian routes throughout the central area. Taking the example of North American shopping centre practice, where the length of malls is limited to about 200 metres between 'magnet' stores to maintain pedestrian flows, the design proposed the structuring of the routes, and hence of the surrounding development, by nodes of activity at approximately those intervals. A tempered climate in the malls would be maintained using ambient energy sources, and the 100-metre radius of development around each node would constitute a balanced financial, as well as social, mix of uses, forming an increment of central-area growth. Although it was suggested that building heights be held to three or four storeys, no specific proposals for built form were included in the plan, which suggested indeed that an absence of overt symbolism, except perhaps in the form of markers at the node points, would be a more appropriate 'city image'. Instead, the first act of the Development Corporation would be the re-forestation of the whole central area, to establish a wooded landscape into which the covered routes and node packages of development would insinuate themselves as and when required.

These three schemes form an interesting commentary on the durability and scope of the urban design plan. The relevance of this question was underlined shortly after the competition winners were appointed to carry out their proposals, by the announcement that the Civic Centre, the climax of the prize-winners' 'plot', would no longer be included.

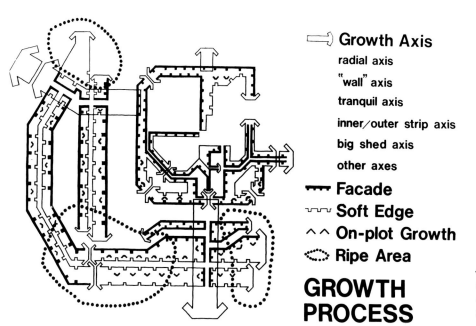

⇨ **Growth Axis**
   radial axis
   "wall" axis
   tranquil axis
   inner/outer strip axis
   big shed axis
   other axes
〜〜 **Facade**
〜〜 **Soft Edge**
∧∧ **On-plot Growth**
⬭ **Ripe Area**

# GROWTH PROCESS

*John Yarwood, Bob Macdonald and Dave Lees, Telford Town Centre Competition, 1976.*

*Barry Maitland and Design Teaching Practice, Telford Town Centre Competition, 1976.*

*Gordon Cullen with A. G. Shepherd Fidler Associates, Telford Town Centre Competition, England, 1976.*

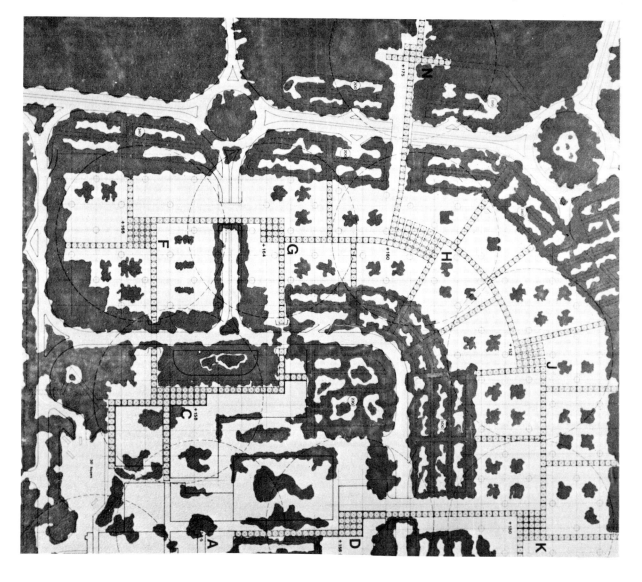

## 3.2 ENGINEERING SOLUTIONS: THE CITY AS A TECHNICAL DEVICE

THE MOST EXPLICIT GENERATORS OF PUBLIC SPACE IN the city have always been the patterns of circulation which have sustained its activities. As these became increasingly a 'problem' with the growing size of the industrial metropolis, and as more exotic mechanical systems were devised to sustain them, so these systems became more remote from that generative function. The work of the Archigram group serves here as an introduction to the work of a number of designers who have attempted to restore the circulation route system to its role as the central, integrating discipline of urban form, rather than the inconsequential and fragmenting collection of viaducts, fly-overs and sub-ways it has so often become.

Circulation, however, is by no means the only engineering problem presented by the city, and earlier fears of technical collapse due to atmospheric pollution or inadequate sanitation and fresh water supplies have now been joined by misgivings over the huge energy consumption of cities. Some projects have therefore been developed in which the urban design concepts arise from a consideration of the city as a device for absorbing and conserving energy.

The hidden implications of adopting large-scale engineering solutions, and their appropriate technology, for the 'wicked' problems of urban design will be considered by reference to an international competition for the design of a new community in Lima, which raised the issue in a particularly vivid way, and one which was to modify subsequent ideas.

### Designers: Archigram

Although 'short on theory', without a manifesto and with hardly a completed building to show, the half dozen young architects who formed Archigram in London in 1960 achieved a spectacular influence around the world, and the kind of testimonials ('... almost inconceivable effort'—Arata Isozaki; '... this evocative, provocative substance'—Hans Hollein; '... my world hasn't been the same since'—Peter Blake) which more conventional revolutionaries never receive. By means of vivid graphics and an updated version of the Corbusian game of machine/architecture associations, the group acted as a brilliant catalytic force through the 1960s and into the 1970s, offering a stream of impossible but seductively plausible visions of a glamorous machine urbanism.

At first, this urbanism had distinct references to

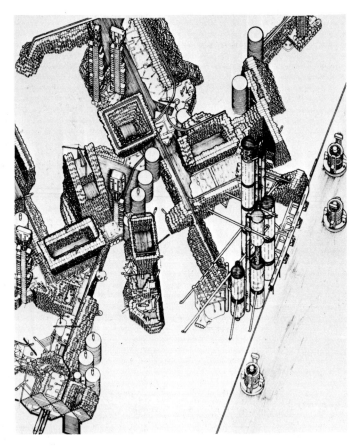

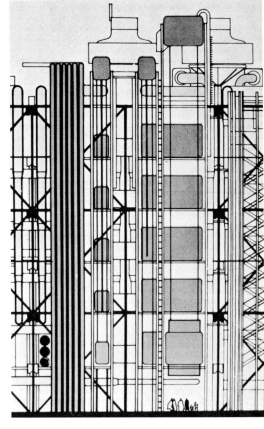

the earlier versions of the 1920s and 1930s. Peter Cook's 'Plug-in City', with its acknowledgement of that iconic Corbusian industrial image—the silo —and presentation, like Hannes Meyer's League of Nations project, in sharp axonometric projection against a totally abstracted site, renewed the authority of those images with a collage of new associations. It was not so much that the ordering ideas were new; the concepts of dwellings as cells slotted into a massive framework, of a circulation grid set at 45° to that of the fixed structures, and of stepped-back ziggurat building forms, all had respectable precedents by 1964. What distinguished 'Plug-in City' was the richness and vitality of what was devised from these principles: 'Craggy but directional. Mechanistic but scaleable ... whatever else it was to be, this city was not going to be a deadly piece of built mathematics.' It was this vitality, too, which saved it from the objection that the raw material being processed in this huge industrial complex was people. The machine had taken over, not to improve or enslave them, but simply because they so obviously enjoyed using and living in it, just as the thousands of visitors who crowd into the ducts of that final manifestation of Archigram fantasy, Piano and Rogers' Pompidou Centre, do so without any sense of being humiliated by the machine, but for the sheer fun of being processed.

Ron Herron's 'Walking City' similarly created a spectacular urban artefact out of recognizable antecedents from Cape Kennedy, the Thames Estuary and elsewhere. Gradually, however, from the mid-1960s onward, the images of monumental hardware gave way to recipes for responsive or interactive environments. 'The mechanical (problem-solving) assembly' began to be replaced by 'the really free-ranging set of parts that respond to personal needs'.

This shift away from traditional preoccupations with the form of the city was underlined by the central image of the citizen as a mobile, fully serviced nomad, emancipated from 'the determinism of the familiar city buildings' by the equipment on his back: 'Clothing for living in—or if it wasn't for my Suitaloon I would have to buy a house'. Curiously, this avoidance of anything that might suggest 'building' coincided with the introduction of actual sites in Archigram presentations. 'Instant City' made its most telling appearance when shown settling down into a real landscape, be it Los Angeles or Bournemouth, for the ephemerality of its balloon-suspended electronic projections was made all the more tantalizing by contrast with the static scene below.

In 1970–71 Archigram entered two competitions with real sites requiring substantial buildings, thus entailing a confrontation between two basic cat-

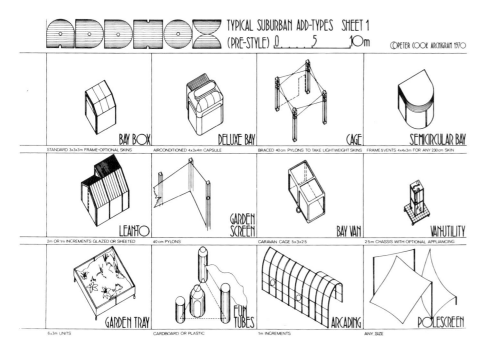

egories which, until then, seemed to have been carefully kept apart in Archigram's work. The solution for the Monte Carlo entertainments centre was to bury the building under the landscape, a move which seemed to confirm their mutual exclusiveness. However, with the Bournemouth 'Steps' project, planned to extend the shopping arcades of that town into a large new multi-use building complex, Archigram's architecture finally settled on the earth's crust, imitating its mound-like features and poking fun at its genteel seaside context, but undoubtedly an earthbound, buildable urban structure.

Since then Archigram has engaged the ground in a series of projects in which the natural landscape, or the existing fabric of towns, has played a major part. Peter Cook's 1971 'Addhox' project demonstrated the metamorphosis of urban scenes by the provision of a range of exotic do-it-yourself components, while 'Crater City' and 'Hedgerow Village' took on the exaggerated forms of natural features. All of them, as Banham said, were 'blessed with the power to create some of the most compelling images of our time'.

*Archigram, 'Plug-In City', 1964, proposal by Peter Cook.*

*Piano & Rogers, Pompidou Centre, Paris, France, 1971–77, design drawings.*

*Peter Cook, 'Addhox' project, 1971, component sets and suburban application.*

*Archigram, 'Walking City', 1964, drawn by Ron Herron.*

*Archigram, 'Instant City', 1969, drawn by Peter Cook.*

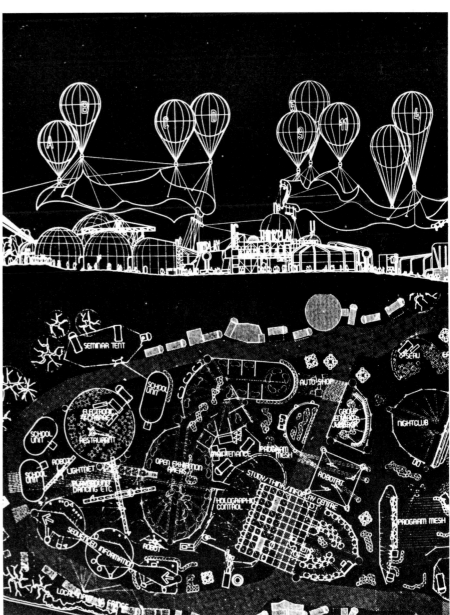

**References:**

*Archigram* (Peter Cook, Warren Chalk, Dennis Crompton, David Greene, Ron Herron, Michael Webb, eds), Praeger Publishers, New York 1973.

## City-Planning Frameworks

Archigram's early enthusiasm for heroically scaled engineering systems as the providers of urban form was part of a wider recognition of the growing scale of urban circulation infrastructure. This new order was invoked by the tall railway viaducts which stalk across Gustave Doré's scenes of Victorian London, and, with the addition of the mechanical elevator and the internal combustion engine, it became the essential inspiration for a whole series of visions of the modern city, from the Futurists onwards. For such plans, the key concept was the machine, and the machine meant circulation.

By the 1950s in North America, and the 1960s in Western Europe, the honeymoon period had come to an end as car-ownership levels had built up beyond the point (about one car per ten people) when serious and unexpected side effects had begun to become apparent, in particular the congestion of the downtown area coupled with the dispersal of some of its key elements to out-of-town sites made accessible by new regional highway systems. The construction during the 1950s of the first generation of huge out-of-town shopping centres in the United States (such as at Old Orchard, Skokie, Illinois, which provided 111,000m$^2$ of retail floor space on a 38 hectare site), together with the first proposals (as for example that by Victor Gruen Associates in 1956 for Fort Worth) for the major reconstruction of downtown areas to make them competitive with the suburban locations, mark the realization of the scale of the problem of circulation. It was not difficult to see the automobile as the major determinant of urban form, dictating where and in what manner usable space should be disposed, and its circulation system as the essential framework of a modern city. Three projects from this period, all unrealized, exemplified the attempt to come to terms with the urban design implications of that discovery.

All three projects accepted traffic as the generator of their designs, but it was Louis Kahn in his plans for Philadelphia of 1952-53 who first suggested that this might be more than a mechanical necessity. His analogy between the flow of traffic and the flow of rivers provided a novel analysis of the movement patterns of a large metropolitan area in almost Venetian terms, by which the city would not only function but would also become legible: 'Expressways are like Rivers. These Rivers frame the area to be served. Rivers have Harbors. Harbors are the municipal parking towers; from the Harbors branch a system of Canals that serve the interior; the Canals are the go streets; from the

Canals branch cul-de-sac Docks; the Docks serve as entrance halls to the buildings.' This poetic analogy, offering a new and symbolic urban design function to the banal structures serving traffic, was subsequently developed by Kahn in his designs for the elements. First there were the parking garage 'Harbors', each accommodating 1,500 cars off the Expressway and illuminated in different colours at night to identify the city sectors they served. Later, in his project for Market Street East, came a full repertoire of 'gateways', 'viaducts' and 'reservoirs'. Kahn also suggested that the tower entrances and parking terminals would provide a new stimulus for unity in urban design which would find expression from the new order of movement. At night, the towers would be recognized by their colour illuminations—yellow, red, green, blue or white—which would inform the motorist which sector of

the city he was entering. Along the approach, light would be used to regulate speed.

Nor was the formal resemblance of these designs to medieval defensive structures entirely coincidental: 'Carcassonne was designed for an order of defense. A modern city will renew itself from its order concept of movement which is a defense against its destruction by the automobile.' This emphasis on the renewal of an existing city by its assimilation of a new circulation infrastructure, just as a medieval town might have been renewed by the construction of a new set of defensive works in response to developments in the technology of warfare, distinguished Kahn's proposals of the 1950s and 1960s from his earlier 1941 plan for Philadelphia which involved, like Le Corbusier's Voisin plan of Paris, its complete demolition. It also separated his proposals from the other two

*Louis Kahn, proposals for central Philadelphia, US, 1952–53, traffic system diagram.*

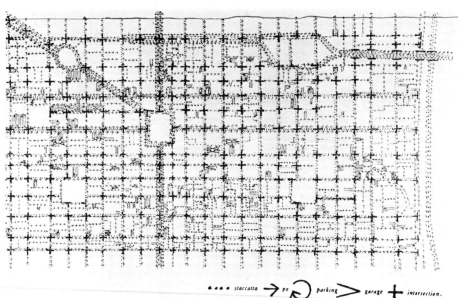

*Louis Kahn, proposals for central Philadelphia, traffic analysis.*

projects considered here, which, though also applied to existing cities, envisaged a much more drastic reordering of their parts.

The 1953 plan by Peter and Alison Smithson for Berlin rejected the possibility of reconciling the patterns of traffic and pedestrian circulation within a traditional street framework. Instead, the two systems were held to be so incompatible that they were made to adopt quite different geometries and to operate independently, the pedestrian network above the vehicular one, with the two levels spiked together by towers with points of vertical circulation between. This degree of articulation was necessary to limit the effect of the dominant vehicular system: 'It is the intention, by using the road-system as the town structure, to keep the apparent level of mechanization under control. We are no longer in the position of needing to play up

our devices, but rather to play them down, chanelling mechanical noise and excitement and creating "pools of calm" for family living and regeneration.' But although the intention might have been to 'play down' the mechanical devices, it is difficult to avoid the impression that, to use Kahn's analogy, the rivers had burst their banks and inundated the city, leaving pedestrians to move about on pier-like structures overhead.

The watery references which seemed to permeate the imagery of these projects were finally inverted in the third example, Kenzo Tange's 1960 plan for the expansion of downtown Tokyo across Tokyo Bay, in which, by projecting the infrastructure of his new city directly onto (real) water, the controlling framework of its highway system was revealed with a startling clarity. The great size of this project, which stretched 18 kilometres across

the bay, the perspicuity of its loop and branch road network, and the formal inventiveness of the extraordinary buildings which were clipped onto the highway skeleton, all combined to make this the most potent statement of a city form generated by automobiles.

**References:**
D. Gosling and B. Maitland, *Design and Planning of Retail Systems*, The Architectural Press, London 1976.
Vincent Scully Jr., *Louis I. Kahn*, George Braziller, New York 1962.
Team 10 Primer (ed. Alison Smithson), London 1965.
Kenzo Tange, 'Lineage of Urban Design', special issue of *Japan Architect*, September/October 1971.

*Kenzo Tange, Tokyo Bay plan, Japan, 1960, master plan.*

*Kenzo Tange, Tokyo Bay plan, megastructure system.*

*Ulrich Franzen, New
York City plan, US, 1975.*

*Runcorn Development
Corporation, busway in
operation at Castlefields
local centre, Runcorn New
Town, England, 1970.*

*LTV Aerospace
Corporation, Airtrans
system, Dallas/Fort Worth
regional airport, US,
1973.*

## New Transportation Systems

Following the energy crisis of 1973, the dominant role of automobiles in these circulation-generated city plans came under more careful scrutiny, as for example in Ulrich Franzen's 1975 plan for New York City. Emphasizing in his report the need for innovative attitudes towards improving the existing urban environment, his proposals included a linear support structure development along the East River, built in conjunction with the truckway and through-traffic by-pass and acting as an interchange system for different travel modes. Thus the conventional automobile would be stored in the interchange and small electric pod vehicles used on short travel distances across connecting bridges. Franzen noted that the entire eastern (Queens) edge of the East River was largely under-utilized industrial land and suggested that the service structure would promote 'dynamic growth'. Whilst not as visionary as Kahn's earlier plan, the utilization of small-scale transportation systems such as electric carts in caravan formation or pneumatic tubes for mail and goods services suggested an equally ambitious, if more energy conscious, circulation network.

Since mechanical transportation systems sustain our present cities in terms of their size and their distribution of uses and population, as well as determining much of their physical detail, any change in the form of such systems may be expected to have considerable implications for urban design. The recurrent scarcities and price increases of fuel for private cars have strengthened the argument in favour of alternatives to private transport in cities, whether of conventional or radically new types. A number of planners have called, for example, for the reintroduction of tramways in Britain such as have continued to be used effectively on the Continent. Again, the use of bus-only routes is advocated, as at Runcorn New Town, where a bus-only road loop links district and local centres and is given priority over the other roads it crosses by the traffic signalling system. Such methods, it is argued, would permit the reintroduction of a powerful public transportation network for the city without the major expense involved in developing new vehicles and routes, and with the minimum of environmental impact.

Others have argued that such conventional systems have already demonstrated their limitations in that they inevitably come into conflict with other forms of traffic, and particularly with pedestrians (a German expert has described how 'hundreds' of Germans are mown down each year by fast, silent 'street-railways'). By the early 1970s several companies in the United States and Western Europe were investigating systems which could overcome these difficulties and at the same time provide a more flexible movement pattern for passengers used to the door-to-door convenience of the automobile.

The solution proposed by most of them was a variation of 'Personal Rapid Transit', defined by Eino K. Latvala of Transportation Technology Inc.: 'In the completely automated, electrically powered, "Personal Rapid Transit" (PRT) system demonstrated by TTI at Transpo '72, people ride in air-conditioned, lightweight, low-profile, quiet-running cars, each able to carry 6–12 seated passengers and their luggage. The cars move on a controlled right-of-way, or guideway, unimpeded by street or highway traffic, and it is possible for an individual passenger or a family or other small group to have use of a car dedicated to a specific trip.'

Although few of the many systems of the type proposed in the early 1970s developed beyond the experimental track stage, LTV Aerospace Corporation's Airtrans System for Dallas/Fort Worth Airport demonstrated their possibilities. Using 68 rubber-tyred, steerable vehicles automatically controlled on a concrete U-shaped guideway, 21 kilometres in extent and running between 14 passenger stations, as well as additional pick-up points for baggage, mail and airport employees, the system was opened in 1973 to serve 10 discretely scheduled routes within the airport complex.

Although such a network could illustrate the technical implications of PRT, the special case of an airport context, in which for example the special track could run for 80% of its length at ground level, did not really show the impact of such an installation on an existing town. This was illustrated in some detail by two studies carried out by Robert Matthew, Johnson-Marshall and Partners on the application of PRT to Central London (1971) and Central Sheffield (1973). The first, using the Cabtrack system sponsored by the Transport Research Assessment Group of the Department of the Environment, with the Royal Aircraft Establishment at Farnborough, investigated a network of largely elevated trackway offering a maximum distance of 250 metres from any point in the area covered to the nearest cab stop. In both this and the second study, for Hawker Siddeley Dynamics' Minitram system on a 2.4 kilometre linear route through Sheffield's central area, the graphic use of photomontage and drawings to illustrate the impact of such a transport system upon an existing urban fabric caused much debate and controversy. Although questions of cost and effectiveness were raised, it was primarily the visual intrusion of the elevated trackways which disturbed critics, in response to which the consultants pointed to the piecemeal intrusion of existing traffic, finding 'this an image for the future preferable to an acquiescence in a steadily deteriorating environmental situation. And Cabtrack, or something like it, is the only instrument in prospect which might bring it about.'

If such systems are to be tailored to existing environments, then the great variety of the latter might be expected to foster a multiplicity of solutions. Certainly the argument raised against Cabtrack, that the centre of London was actually quite well served by public transport systems in comparison to the suburbs, which depended far more heavily than the centre upon private transport, was a relevant one. In the case of extensive areas of lower residential density, it has been argued that the solution lies not with elaborate new vehicles and trackways, but rather with a greater sophistication in the control and flexible routing of relatively conventional vehicles. Such an approach has been utilized at Milton Keynes, where the 'Dial-a-bus' service operates between local stops in response to telephoned requests by travellers, either from their homes or from telephones located at the stops.

Given the difficulties in inserting a tracked vehicle system into an existing town, it is in projects where system and town are planned together that the full possibilities of integration can be tested. Such was the case with Cullen's Alcan project, where the linear circuit was based on a monorail route, and again at Runcorn, where the figure-of-eight configuration of the bus-only route was instrumental in determining the plan form of the town. A further example of this type was provided by a plan by Gosling, Cullen and a team from Sheffield University for the Island of Porto Santo, in which an automated narrow-gauge tramway was to form the sole mechanical means of transportation along the inhabited coastal strip of the island. Again, Cullen's sequential views illustrated the connection between the system of movement and the plan of the town.

### References:

Ulrich Franzen, 'Urban Design for New York', *Architectural Record*, September 1975.

Eino K. Latvala, *The TTI Hovair PRT System*, Society of Automotive Engineers Inc. 1973.

LTV Aerospace Corporation *Fact Sheet: Airtrans System*.

*The Architects' Journal* No. 20, Vol. 153, 19 May 1971, 'Cabtrack', pp. 1112–23.

Robert Matthew, Johnson-Marshall & Partners, *Minitram in Sheffield*.

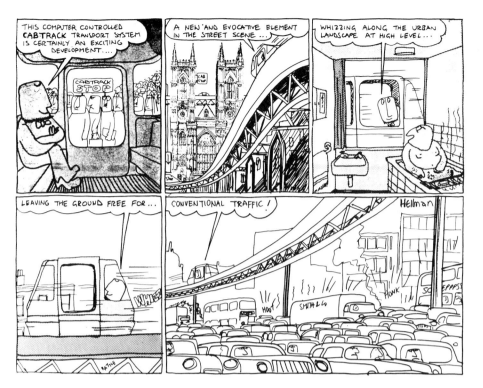

*Robert Matthew, Johnson-Marshall and Partners, Minitram project, Sheffield, England, 1974.*

*Louis Hellman, Architects' Journal cartoon of the Cabtrack proposals for central London, England, 1971.*

*Gordon Cullen, sequential sketches of the Porto Santo Island tramway proposal.*

## Energy Efficient Urban Design

In comparison to the amount of study which has been carried out on the energy performance of building designs, little has been said on the comparable performance of towns. And while analyses of the fuel usage resulting from alternative road networks for a town are relatively well established, methods to assess the energy implications of urban design effects upon built form are not. Yet our towns resemble nothing so much as giant radiators, displaying the maximum surface area for the minimum volume and orienting themselves with little regard to insolation and wind exposure. Perhaps it is time to recall Vitruvius' obsession with the wind effects on his ideal town plan.

One designer for whom this question has been a long-standing concern is Ralph Erskine, whose work above the Arctic circle has derived much of its strength from its response to the extreme climatic conditions. After completing his enclosed shopping centre project at Lulea in Northern Sweden in 1955, he developed a design for a whole Arctic town in 1958, setting out the principles of siting on a south-facing slope, compact planning within a shielding perimeter-wall building, and wedge-shaped forms for buildings in plan and section to reduce drag and turbulence in the Arctic gales. The seductive mixture of intuition and rationalism which characterizes so much of Erskine's work is present also in his descriptions of these and later Arctic projects, in which consideration of the psychological difficulties of living in the northern deserts figures as strongly as the physical needs for shelter and energy economy.

In 1973, Erskine was commissioned by the Government of the North-West Territories of Canada to design a New Town for up to about 1,000 Eskimo and immigrant settlers at Resolute Bay, which lies only a few miles away from the North Magnetic Pole. After a careful investigation to find the most favourable southerly slope in the area for the site, Erskine's design followed the principles established by the 1958 project, with central facilities, hotel rooms and apartments forming a horseshoe-shaped 'wall' building, enclosing a compound in which individual houses could be freely disposed. The design seemed to contain the very great difficulties with which it was faced, not only climatic but also social in the enforced cohabitation of two very different ethnic groups. More than this, however, it celebrated the resolution of these difficulties in powerful, but not overbearing, urban and architectural forms. Erskine has argued that: 'Cities in the north ... ought to, because of

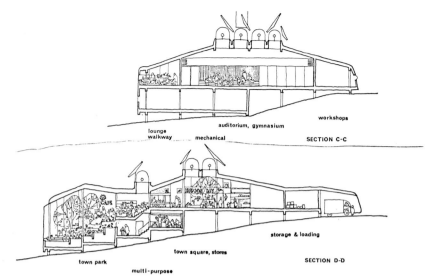

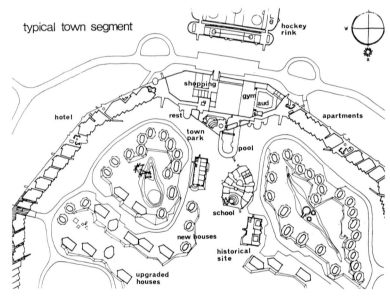

*Ralph Erskine, Resolute Bay project, Canada, 1973, sections through the town centre looking west.*

*Ralph Erskine, Resolute Bay project, typical town segment.*

their isolation, be done more attractive and pronounced than their counterparts in southern parts. They ought to be intensive communities with ample service and space for different interests. They ought to be gathered in a cluster to create a human environment in the desert.' This philosophy is apparent in Resolute Bay at both the large scale of design and the small, as in the rooftop polished-metal mirrors which reflect light both into the interior spaces of the buildings and out, so that: 'In the dark polar winter, the buildings should give off light, act as beacons, signalling human habitation in the wilderness.'

Although one would expect climatic factors to have the most dramatic effect upon urban form in the extreme conditions of the Arctic, they have traditionally influenced the design of cities at all latitudes, as can be seen, for example, in the general preference for establishing cities on the north (south facing) bank at river crossings on

Britain's east-west flowing rivers. With the disappearance of cheap energy to disguise this climatic factor in the design of towns at temperate latitudes, it must surely return, perhaps more powerfully than ever, since more elaborate expectations have to be sustained.

Since the early 1970s a number of energy-efficient projects have been proposed, extending experimental work on the use of solar and other ambient energy sources in individual buildings to their groupings in small communities. A design by Cedric Green and the Ecotecture Group at the University of Sheffield illustrates the implications for the urban designer. By passive means, using glazed conservatories on their south sides, heat stores under floors and in wall units and highly insulated surfaces elsewhere, the houses in this project achieve a high measure of energy conservation with uncomplicated technology and careful siting to give units adequate exposure to the sun.

Erskine's early project for an Arctic town suggested a heavy construction for buildings, with small windows, using the analogy of the opposite climatic factors operating for the Pueblo villages of Central America. Again, the rise in energy costs has brought a rediscovery of such passive means by which towns in hot climates have traditionally modified outdoor as well as indoor spaces, and a renewed interest in the possibility of devising new forms of both building and urban design to reduce dependence on high energy air-conditioning. A competition held by the International Union of Architects in Mexico in 1978 resulted in projects illustrating this concern. The competition was open to schools of architecture around the world, who were invited to submit designs for a local-government and village or town-centre development for a community of between 10,000 and 50,000 people in any chosen location. This open brief attracted some ingenious solutions, including one from a Russian school for a series of planned villages along a great river, served by a local-government centre in the form of a large hovercraft which visited each in turn. The entry from the Sheffield school selected a location at Cave Hill in Barbados, since this was a developing country with a system of open and democratic government, with a generally low level of income and with few natural resources. The continuous sunshine and, equally important, continuous though low-velocity breezes on an exposed site, suggested an architectural form which would also reflect open government. Local-government departments would be housed in corner shops along the covered walkways instead of in closed bureaucratic offices, and other community facilities scattered amongst the canopied structure. Barbados has an abundant supply of pure water, naturally filtered by the coral, and rotary windmills were proposed to pump the water up to troughs on the roof canopies to effect cooling by evaporation. The red canvas canopies, timber roof troughs and rotary windmills forming marker points would thus provide an articulated system of structures identifying the centre as a focal point in the community.

*Cedric Green, passive solar energy project for Sheffield, 1978 (prize-winner in the Misawa competition, Japan).*

*Pugsley, McHale, Johnson, Tsien (Sheffield University), self-sufficient energy project for Cave Hill, Barbados, winner of the French Government Prize in the International Union of Architects Competition for Schools of Architecture, 1978.*

References:

*Architectural Design*, Vol. 47, No. 11–12, 1977, 'Resolute Bay New Town, report by Ralph Erskine, Architect and Planner'.

*Solar Housing Experimental Design*, report by Ecotecture Group, University of Sheffield.

*I.U.A. Competition Mexico*, report by University of Sheffield, Department of Architecture 1978.

## Competition: Lima

In 1968 the Government of Peru sponsored a competition open to all Peruvian architects and 13 invited foreign architects for the design of a community of approximately 1,500 low-cost houses on a 40 hectare site in a new development area of Lima. The competition was supported by the United Nations Development Programme (UNDP) and was intended to stimulate the development of new concepts and techniques for the provision of flexible, low-cost housing. A housing mix was specified, with sizes of lots, and conditions laid down which required one or two-storey structures, capable of carrying a third floor in the future. Dwellings were to be regarded not as fixed units, but as 'a structure with a cycle of evolution', in which the initial contractor-built structure and fabric would gradually be extended and altered by the occupants. The community was to be planned with schools, sports centre, community centre, open space, and space for future car parking, although road construction, being unsubsidized and expensive, was to be kept to a minimum. Competitors were reminded of the Latin character of urban life in Peru, in which 'the traditional and compact open space elements to be found in Peruvian towns are the plaza, the atrium and the paseo'.

The solutions proposed by the 13 foreign competitors, all internationally regarded designers, formed an interesting commentary on both the preoccupations of the industrialized world (to which almost all belonged) at that time and on its view of what would be an appropriate solution for a developing country such as Peru. In particular, the choice of a relevant technology and the degree of imposition of a strong community form differentiated the entries. The jury awarded the three prizes to Atelier Five of Switzerland, Kikutake, Kurokawa and Maki of Japan, and Herbert Ohl of West Germany. However, a minority report strongly disagreed with this choice, castigating Ohl's solution as 'a personal regimented and expensive solution both as to dwelling units and site plan. It is inhuman.' Instead, the report advocated the entry by Christopher Alexander and the Center for Environmental Structure as being 'far above the level of all other projects and throwing a bright new light on a gloomy subject'.

The Atelier Five project established a middle ground between the two radical positions of Ohl and Alexander. An elegant and sensitive essay in the organization of patio housing forms, the regulation of pedestrian and vehicular routes and the use of a system of simple pre-cast concrete prefabri-

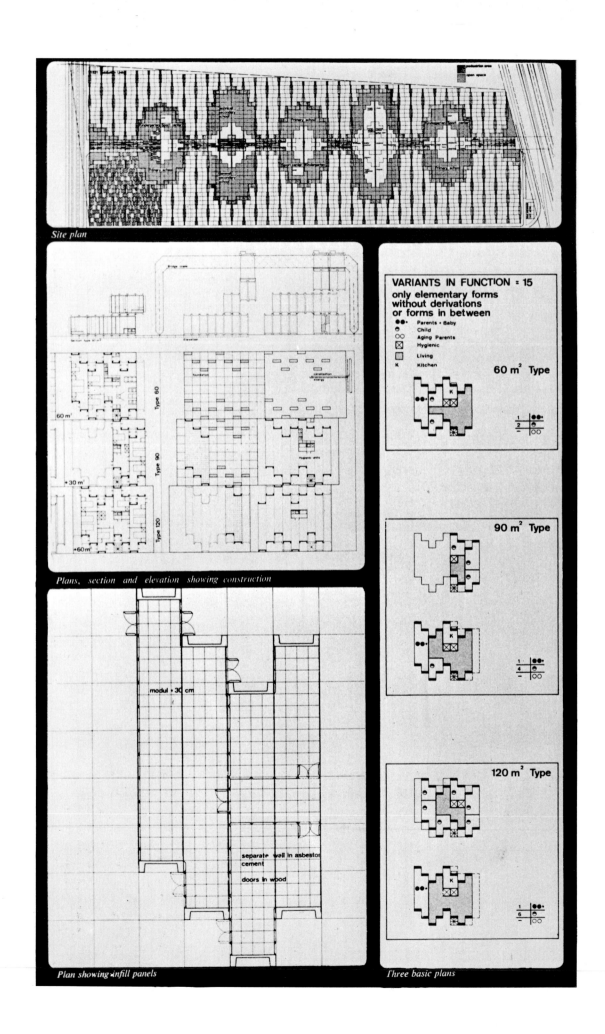

*Site plan*

*Plans, section and elevation showing construction*

*Plan showing infill panels*

VARIANTS IN FUNCTION = 15
only elementary forms
without derivations
or forms in between

- ●●● Parents + Baby
- ● Child
- ○○ Aging Parents
- ⊠ Hygienic
- ▣ Living
- K Kitchen

60 m² Type

90 m² Type

120 m² Type

*Three basic plans*

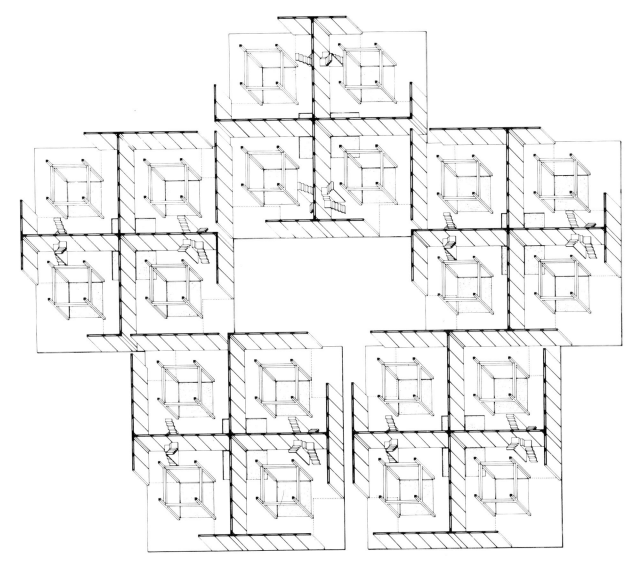

*James Stirling,
competition design for a
community of 1,500
low-cost houses, Lima,
Peru, 1968.*

*Herbert Ohl, competition
design for a community of
1,500 low-cost houses,
Lima, Peru, 1968.*

change between human and technological factors', a sentiment with which Alexander would no doubt have agreed, though with a somewhat different outcome.

No such domination of the whole solution by one single factor occurred in the case of Alexander's proposal. Rather, a series of design systems operated at different levels, meshing together to form the whole. At the technical level, for example, an elaborate and ingenious repertoire of low-key building technology was proposed, including mortarless block cavity walls, composite bamboo and urethane foam beams and floor planks, and the use of sulphur reinforcing and bonding agents. This proposal fitted the next level requirements, for the individual house plans, but did not impose itself on the scales above. Houses were to be grouped into 'cells' of between 30 and 70 dwellings, and these formed the basic social unit, which took the form of a pedestrian island surrounded by a sunken access road. At the next level, cells and circulation were organized about the long arc of the *paseo*, a central-spine pedestrian zone running down the length of the site and containing at intervals 'activity nuclei' with community facilities and shops.

It could be said that neither of these design solutions was hierarchical, the first being determined almost entirely at one level of organization, and the second, though operating at a number of different scales, doing so in largely independent patterns. It is therefore worth comparing them with one other entry in which the character of the design is primarily derived from neither the technological method nor the community structure, but rather from the architectural solution devised to meet those problems and from the strongly hierarchical formal nature which it adopted. James Stirling's solution was based on a square house plot, subdivided on a 3 × 3 basis to give a central open square courtyard around which the contractor 'first build' of pre-cast concrete wall and floor elements could then be expanded. Four such houses were then packed together with common party walls and services to form a larger square element, five of which were grouped around a common entrance patio, this unit then forming the basic cluster to make up a neighbourhood of about 400 houses. Four neighbourhoods, separated by public parks containing schools and other public buildings, made up the development.

**Reference:**

*Architectural Design*, April 1970, pp. 187–205.

cated components, it would have seemed, with some adjustment of car-parking provision, as valid a design for a new district in, say, Holland or Denmark, as in Peru. This is not so in the case of Ohl's and Alexander's projects, where the stringencies of the brief led to more radical solutions, although both of them could be said to be exploring general positions on the questions of technology and community within the context of the particular conditions of the competition.

Ohl opted for a centralized technology to overcome the problem of low-cost housing provision, and from this decision much of the character of the design, attractive to the main jury panel and oppressive to the minority group, arose. Standard pre-cast concrete structural units, 16,999 in all, formed the shells for all dwellings, and were to be brought to position on travelling bridge cranes, the routes for which had to be left clear and therefore provided the layout for footpaths within the site. Thus the pedestrian circulation routes, the layout of housing plots and the house forms were all fixed by the constructional method, while a comprehensive system of preferred dimensions coordinated infill elements. As Ohl put it: 'The basic order devised is intended to establish a democratic inter-

## 3.3 SOCIAL SOLUTIONS: THE CITY AS AN EXPRESSION OF SOCIAL ORDER

THE APPARENT IMPOSSIBILITY OF MAKING ANY technical decision about the city without thereby implying a corresponding social structure has persuaded many designers of the primacy of the social programme. Urban design is thus seen essentially as the attempt to find an appropriate form to sustain this programme or perhaps, more actively, to reinforce or even induce it.

A few examples have been chosen here from the great number possible, beginning with the work of a Massachusetts design group, Arrowstreet Inc., whose projects for relatively prosperous coastal communities in California and Aquitaine explore the possibilities for reconciling, through design, conflicts within the social programme, and for developing an appropriate formal vocabulary from it. Through a series of case studies, we then examine examples of particular social organization types: high-density, working-class housing projects sponsored by Western Socialist programmes, with their suggestion of the building group as a 'social condenser'; some medium-density, Social-Democratic schemes, less intensive than the first group, but nevertheless specific in their correspondence of community structure and built form; New Towns in the Soviet Union, arising from a centrally-directed programme; efforts to find a decentralized pattern of solutions in China; examples of social organization and resulting urban structure generated from within the community itself in the *favelas* of Brazil.

A competition held in 1976 to design a New Town to replace a squatter settlement outside Manila explored an issue raised by many of these projects: the degree to which design solutions may inhibit or distort the social patterns they aim to serve. This takes a stage further the debate opened eight years earlier by the Lima competition.

### Designers: Arrowstreet Inc.

Although the coastal suburbs of Los Angeles serve one of the most affluent communities we shall consider here, their development contains the same problems of resolving public and private interests into coherent and appropriate social patterns as we shall meet elsewhere. In 1972, a 220 hectare project at Laguna Niguel was halted by such a problem, arising from Proposition 20 and the establishment of the California Coastal Commission. This statement of public interest in preserving the integrity of the coastal strip, and public access to it, was in conflict with the estab-

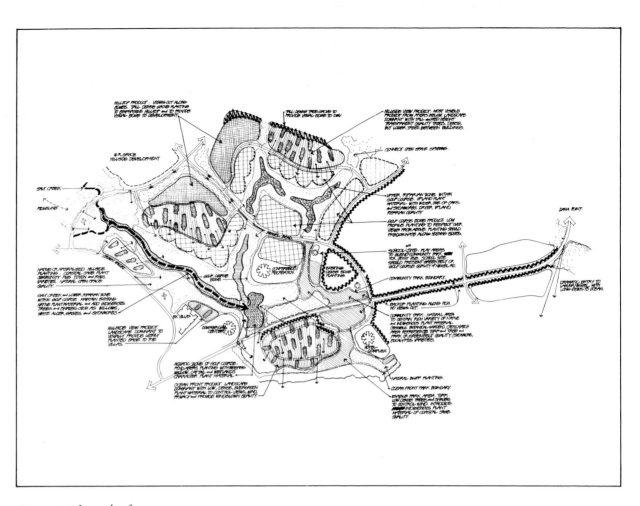

Arrowstreet Inc., plan for
Laguna Niguel,
California, US, 1979.

lished pattern of suburban sprawl, and in 1979 the State Commission accepted a new plan, prepared by John Myer, Richard Krauss and Robert Slattery of Arrowstreet, as a basis for reconciling the various demands upon the site.

Arrowstreet's plan adopted all the specific topographical and landscape features of the site, and used these to orchestrate the patterns of density of occupation and land use—including a commercial centre, school, golf course and beach-side hotel complex which were required in addition to the dominant residential use. Thus the housing increases in density as the land rises away from the beach, and follows corresponding changes in the character of the vegetation, from low, dense, evergreen material controlling wind and views along the ocean front to the tall, dense grove planting along the hilltops behind. Similarly, the destination resort hotel, associated with a public park route leading from the centre of the site down to the beach, is designed with a terraced form which

adapts itself to the natural bluffs which overlook the ocean.

The Laguna Niguel project thus uses landscape as a metaphor and prescription for social harmony, in which the civilized, unassertive accommodation of each private need, hidden under 'a green mantle of vines, trees and green tiled roofs' does not intrude upon the primary communion between each individual resident or visitor and the beach, framed by its 'natural' hinterland. The solution contrasts neatly with a second project by Arrowstreet, for Port d'Albret New Town on the Aquitaine coast of France, in which the metaphor is urban rather than natural and for which a more explicit statement of the rules governing development therefore became necessary.

In this master plan for a vacation community, designed for a consortium made up of the French government, a private developer and a tourism cooperative, acknowledgement of an existing context was again required, in this case the timber-

*Arrowstreet Inc., plan for
Port d'Albret New Town,
France, 1980.*

frame architectural tradition of the Landes region. The brief also placed emphasis on the expression and personalization of the individual units, a requirement which tended to clash both with the process of implementation, in relatively large contracts, and with the desire to emulate the visual cohesion of the traditional architecture of the region.

The balance between public order and private freedom, between community and privacy, takes on a particularly illuminating aspect in the case of holiday communities where, released from the normal captive relationship with their housing, people seek out peculiarly vivid versions of their preferred mix. Arrowstreet's intriguing solution to the contradictory requirements of the Port d'Albret version of that mix took the form of an open-ended rule system to guide both general and detailed design decisions to be taken by others. This was embodied in an *Architectural Notebook* which firstly defined a series of 'user needs', initi-

ally nine in number, summarized as follows:
'Regarding open spaces:
1 The hierarchy of spaces will be easily understandable.
2 Port d'Albret will function as a vacation place for the whole region.
3 Architecture should create a sense of neighbourhood and sharing spaces.
4 Residents and visitors can use outdoor spaces to express lifestyles and activities.
5 Access to cars should be convenient, but should not dominate spaces.
And regarding buildings:
6 References are made to traditions of the Landes.
7 The architecture should make Port d'Albret a special place.
8 Individual units in buildings should be identifiable.
9 Residents should be able to change their environments as their needs and inspiration dictate.'

Each such user need gives rise to an 'architec-

tural goal', which is then translated into a definition of the 'means' by which this will be achieved. Finally, a specific rule is framed as a 'measure' to satisfy the 'means'. As an example, the full statement of user need 8 runs as follows: 'The town should appear to be made up of individual families, not large-scale buildings. Expressing individual units will reinforce the sense that the town is made up of individual people.' The corresponding 'architectural goal' is in two parts:
'1 Buildings shall appear as aggregates of the units which form them.
2 Buildings should reflect different uses and locations.'
The 'means' is then defined in such terms as: 'Volume of each building—Each dwelling unit should have its own architectural identity within the larger structure. Buildings should appear as collections of such individual units.' This then leads to the appropriate 'measure', or rule: 'Each unit will have a unique place within a building. No grid shall be more than 3 units high or wide without a volumetric break in order to avoid non-unique locations. To give such identity, units or grids will have easily identifiable locations such as at corners, on top, or below or at the centre of a building. They shall have uniquely expressed volumes or be a special feature such as a bridge or tower.'

The reason for this elaborate explanation of the reasoning behind each rule is that the rules are seen as being open to variations and transgressions provided the user needs are still satisfied, rather in the spirit of the 'deemed-to-satisfy' clauses in the United Kingdom Building Regulations. Further, the user needs themselves are open to evolution as new participants and new needs emerge. The whole system thus forms not a finite master plan, but rather a 'Dynamic Accord' which would be continually revised by the participants in the development, including the administration, developers, architects, local officials and local residents. The architects' drawings which illustrate the *Architectural Notebook* are then seen as no more than postscripts, indicating the sort of possibilities which may follow.

In these two projects, Arrowstreet attempted to frame a precise and explicit set of urban design intentions, in tune with a particular social organization, which would still leave open the possibility of unexpected local-built solutions which would satisfy those intentions in novel ways. This contrasts with the assumption of a much more deterministic relationship between social programme and built form found in many of the examples which follow.

*Sheffield City Architects' Department (Lewis Womersley with Jack Lynn, Ivor Smith and Frederick Nicklin), Park Hill housing, Sheffield, England, 1961.*

*Ralph Erskine, Vernon Gracie and Associates, Byker Wall, Newcastle-upon-Tyne, England, 1973.*

## High-Density Neighbourhoods

Although the merits of different forms of high-density housing have been extensively discussed in terms of their performance as housing, the effects upon this performance of their parallel role as major urban elements is less clearly understood. Yet since the Modern Movement identified housing, and particularly high-density urban housing, as being a crucial area of design concern, the technical and social arguments have almost always been accompanied by some sense that a valid objective of housing design is to make urban design statements on a scale to match the social programmes which gave birth to them. Certainly many of the innovatory housing projects of the 1920s and 1930s did create imposing urban elements, as in the great walls formed by Hans Scharoun's blocks for Siemenstadt in Berlin, or define major spaces, as in Bruno Taut and Martin Wagner's Großsiedlung Britz at Neukölln. Perhaps the most notoriously memorable urban form was that created by Karl Ehn's Karl-Marx-Hof estate in Vienna, which was dubbed the 'Red Fortress' and became a symbol of the resistance of Communist workers in that city during the civil disturbances of 1934.

In England at that time, the familiar technical arguments in favour of new types of high-density housing, according to which the new technologies of prefabricated-frame construction and of mechanical services would overcome the traditional disadvantages of dense working-class housing forms, were similarly used to support designs with a strong sense of common form. R.A.H. Livett's Quarry Hill in Leeds was a good example of this, utilizing the very latest technology from the continent with French Mopin system steel frame and pre-cast concrete panel construction and Garchey system ducted waste disposal from each flat, as well as electric lifts at each staircase access point. At the same time the design formed the ranges of flats into very powerful formal elements; firstly a long continuous curved perimeter block which became progressively higher as the site fell away and was pierced by monumental arched gateways from the ouside, and then, within this boundary enclosure, a rectangular arrangement of blocks defining large public spaces. Quarry Hill thus evoked a strong identity of progressive ideas clothed in a powerful urban form, which suggested to some critics a democratized version of the crescents and squares of eighteenth-century aristocratic models. The analogy is an interesting one, since it was based not so much on the assumption that the residents of John Wood's Royal Crescent in Bath, or John

Nash's Regent's Park Terraces were actually better satisfied as a result of the part their homes played in such grand schemes, but rather that it would be historically appropriate for working-class housing now to take its place as a major generator of public statements on urban form. The effect of the powerful identity on the residents of Quarry Hill is difficult to determine. Despite the failure, as a result of the onset of war, to complete the facilities originally planned for the public open spaces, the estate was a popular and successful one in the early stages of its life. During the 1960s, however, corrosion was discovered in the steel frame and a number of only partially successful attempts were made to rectify it. The estate began to be used by the local authority as a 'decanting centre' for compulsorily evicted slum tenants and eventually in 1978 it was completely demolished. One final ironic comment on its strong physical identity was its reputed selection by the Germans during the Second World War as their future administrative centre for the North of England.

The connection between ambitious social programmes and bold urban form was reiterated by Reyner Banham with reference to a post-war housing development of similar scale and novelty to Quarry Hill: 'Ever since the war we have had the curious spectacle in Britain of social programmes that were grandiose in scale, being realised in penny packets of architecture.... But where, demanded a generation regarding with despair the coy scale of the New Towns, where is the building that is as big as the sociology?' The answer lay at Park Hill, in Sheffield, where the city architect Lewis Womersley, with Jack Lynn, Ivor Smith and Frederick Nicklin, completed in 1961 an urban structure to rival the pre-war superblocks of Berlin and Vienna. The street-deck access to the flats of Park Hill, as against the small and numerous staircase accesses at Quarry Hill, served to emphasize even more strongly the public nature of the form adopted by the housing, enclosing large polygonal courtyards and creating a dramatic wall back-cloth to the city centre across the valley of the River Sheaf.

Once again the success of this great urban design statement as housing has passed through an exaggerated cycle. Initially applauded by architects and planners, and popular among tenants, its standing among both groups has drastically declined. According to Jane and Roy Darke: 'Estates such as Park Hill, regarded as part of the Brutalist oeuvre, were also admired by the mainstream. At this time, the public were not asked for their opinion: research on the users concentrated on issues such as whether the current recommended minimum room sizes were acceptable.... Park Hill, applauded as the archetypical Brutalist council housing was the subject of a social survey by the resident social worker who acted as an arrivals officer, by helping households to settle in, and did this job successfully enough to get the design a massive endorsement from the occupiers. Eventually it became apparent that the Brutalist aesthetic was not really liked. By the late 1960s it had become so debased that it was difficult for anyone to defend.'

In contrast, and despite a general moratorium on high building for housing in Britain, a further project underway in Newcastle-upon-Tyne during the 1970s continued the tradition of making extended urban elements from housing, and in the process has achieved considerable acclaim. The precise differences between the perimeter block of Ralph Erskine, Vernon Gracie and Associates' Byker development and Park Hill seem marginal in comparison to their similarities of scale and operational principles. Over one kilometre in length, the sinuous Byker Wall carried its access decks only on the south facing side, broke them down into identifiable sections, and provided accommodation only for families without small children; undoubtedly sensible developments on the Park Hill arrangements. Again, the use of colour, of organic materials and an emphasis on landscaping created a more sympathetic vocabulary, while a sound relationship was established between the architects and the community they were building for through the operation of their site office which acted as an advice and consultation centre. Yet some ambivalence in the attitude of residents —particularly those in the small-scale housing shielded by the high block from the north wind and traffic noise—to the powerful imagery of the Byker Wall has been recorded by observers, despite the flair with which it had been carried through. Perhaps it is the case that such powerful public urban gestures entail a correspondingly vivid identification of the communities which occupy them, whether just or unjust, so that it requires a certain added confidence to be a resident of the 'Red Fortress' or the 'Byker Wall' or perhaps even the 'Royal Crescent'. Should that confidence diminish, the very boldness of the original gesture only exaggerates the inevitable cycle which results. Yet the curious instability in the appreciation of such large and apparently stable images cannot detract from the conviction they achieve when the urban form coincides with that of the community it serves.

*Neave Brown, Alexandra Road, Camden, London, England, 1978.*

Thus, in another recent example—Neave Brown's Alexandra Road development for the London Borough of Camden—the clarity of urban structure expressed in the long curving central pedestrian street, with its valley section and protecting wall against the railway tracks on the north side, implies a corresponding coherence in the community it houses. This suggests a conception of 'urban design' far removed from the empty gestures so often associated with high-rise housing which are dramatic, but essentially remote and inconsequential, gestures in an empty landscape.

**References:**
Tim Benton, 'The Rise and Fall of Quarry Hill', in *The Architect*, June 1975, pp. 25–28.
Reyner Banham, *The Age of the Masters*, The Architectural Press, London, 1975 edition, p. 140.
J. & R. Darke, *Public Housing: Policies and Architectural Styles*, March 1979.
*The Architectural Review*, Vol. 156, No. 934, December 1974, 'Byker by Erskine', pp. 346–62.
*The Architectural Review*, Vol. 166, No. 990, August 1979, 'Alexandra Road', pp. 76–92.

*Ricardo Bofill and Taller de Arquitectura, Kafka's Castle, Sitges, Spain, 1964–66.*

*Ricardo Bofill and Taller de Arquitectura, Walden Seven, near Barcelona, Spain, 1970–75.*

## Medium-Density Neighbourhoods

The idea that a continuity exists between the design of the individual dwelling and that of the whole city, and thus that the organization of the latter is already implicit in its cells and their smallest grouping, is present in the work of many thoughtful designers. In such work a small project can stand as a model or fragment of the larger solution, and the sense of compression which this creates intensifies its presence, perhaps to the point where it appears overworked. Such miniaturization is most readily realized through a powerful sense of formal order, for this provides an abstract vehicle by which the small, specific statement may be translated to the larger scale. Yet the relationship between formal order and social organization is not a simple one. If we accept that no deterministic relationship exists between them, we may feel compelled to dispense with strongly architectonic ordering in order to leave as much flexibility as possible for social patterns which we may not predict or wish to limit. Others, however, have argued that such a position misunderstands the dialectical relationship between form and use. Herman Hertzberger has demonstrated this position in a number of his buildings, as for example the Centraal Beheer offices at Apeldoorn in Holland, where a programme invoking a strongly participatory attitude to the building environment by its users is accompanied by a highly particularized and ordered architectural expression. The one, it is said, calls forth the other, and from the ensuing debate a true synthesis of form and function can arise. Some projects providing strongly ordered environments for relatively small, compact communities illustrate the directions this dialectic can take.

The work of the Barcelona Taller de Arquitectura of Ricardo Bofill is characterized both by powerfully geometric constructions and by a preoccupation with the forms of the city. The obsessive geometric symmetries which pervade the plans of this group's holiday community buildings on the Spanish coast—Xanadu, Kafka's Castle and La Manzanera—were already present in their first major work, the Barrio Gaudí, a low-cost development for 2,000 industrial workers' dwellings at Reus. Starting with topological arrangements of rooms about a basic kitchen/dining/living space, they built up dwelling plans of varying size using geometric transformations and groupings. This process was repeated on the basis of orthogonal and diagonal geometries, and from their interlocking the fundamental character of the Barrio Gaudí was established. Functional criteria of aspect, over-

looking, orientation and so on were used, not so much to generate form, as to exclude those particular variations thrown up by the form-generating process which could not meet the criteria. Paradoxically, and in line with Hertzberger's argument, the pervasive geometry and eccentric forms were offered as liberating qualities of the design, creating a variety of spaces and conditions which could be taken over and personalized by the inhabitants to engender a strong sense of specific plàce. The idiosyncratic methods and results of the Taller, which includes a literary critic, an economist and a poet, as well as architects, derive from their critique of the results of the Modern Movement:

'ARCHITECTURE NO LONGER EXISTS
Only impersonal cities, without description and without style which nobody has ever dreamed of, or desired.

Against these clear and facile modern towns, we launch monuments which single out space, destroying it and inventing it.

PLAN THE REVOLT

Against the thousands of identically repeated, stupid, lined-up houses.

Against the rational and schematic ordination of territory.

Against the importation of prefabricated, nordic cities.

AGAINST ARCHITECTURE ...'

'Architecture', at its highest level, might well be represented by a building such as Richard Meier's Bronx Developmental Center in New York, which, although a very specialized case of a medium-density neighbourhood, nevertheless provides an excellent illustration of the way in which a highly architectonic solution can be generated by the structure of the programme and its hierarchies of public and private space. Accommodating 350 resident physically and mentally handicapped children, as well as providing out-patient and extensive technical support facilities, the Center is situated in a blighted industrial area and is also concerned with the creation of a sense of place. Its success in doing so makes it a relevant source for the urban designer, and not least because it derived both its social and its architectural form precisely from 'the rational and schematic ordination of territory'.

The complex is organized in two parallel spines, with sheltered courtyard space between. The western spine block, containing support services, forms a neutral screen to the site approach and car parking areas. It is linked by bridges, one open and one glazed, across the courtyard to the parallel eastern block, from which 'L'-shaped residential groups grow out to the east in echelon formation, defining small, partially enclosed courtyards along the eastern edge of the complex. There is thus a layering of functions across the building, from west to east, from public to private, enlivened by the introduction of specialist elements along the way. The uses and organization of the building thus elegantly correspond, the functions made legible by a form derived from an analysis of the functions. The organizing principle of zones layered one on another is reflected in the detailed architectural treatment, and particularly in the anodized aluminium cladding panels which are set out in strata of fluctuating width up the face of the building and punctuated by integral window units varying in pattern according to the functions they serve. The sense of order, of unity, and yet of great formal richness and invention thus offers an unsentimental model for architecture as an ordering and yet liberating social framework.

If the Bronx Developmental Center demonstrates the ability of a clear social programme to evoke a correspondingly lucid architectural solution, the possibility of the reverse relationship is suggested by the history of the Danish community at Farum Midtpunkt. Occupying a 28 hectare site in the town of Farum, 20 kilometres north-west of Copenhagen, the development provided 1,625 flats in 27 four-storey parallel blocks running north-south down the site in a tightly packed array. In each, the ground floor, treated as a concrete podium for the flats above, contained vehicular routes and parking. In the centre of the plan at first-floor level an enclosed and heated access route ran the length of the block, serving the three storeys of flats which stepped back sharply to the west to provide terraces at each level, and which were dramatically clad in rusting panels of Cor-ten steel. Designed by Jørn Ole Sørensen with Professor Viggo Møller-Jansen and Tyge Arnfred, the development, which also included facilities for children and local services, was carried out by the Farum Building Company, a subsidiary of KAB, the largest publicly-owned building company in Denmark. Ownership was retained by the company, and in accordance with Danish law the residents were entitled to participate in the administration of the complex through the election by all residents of directors to a joint board. The number of directors would depend upon the size of the development, and in the case of Farum Midtpunkt would be 13 in all.

This structure was established by the new residents in 1972, but they soon decided that it did not

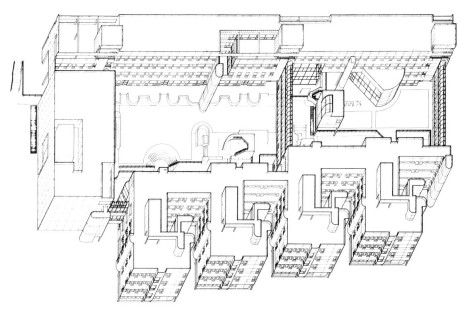

*Richard Meier, Bronx Developmental Center, New York City, US, 1975, axonometric.*

*Jørn Sørensen, Viggo Møller-Jansen and Tyge Arnfeld, Farum Midtpunkt, near Copenhagen, Denmark.*

correspond to their needs, and so a parallel participatory structure was established without legal status but tacitly accepted by all parties. Each of the 27 terrace rows which formed the development housed about 50 families and, with their common sheltered access and physical independence, these established a substantive subdivision of the community into effective groups. Each of these was run by its residents through its own 'building meetings' at which a chairman and secretary were elected, fixed monthly subscriptions collected, and two representatives elected by all residents, adults and children, to represent the building on the 'block committee'. The block committee, representing the whole community through its 56 representatives (one building was twice as big as the others and had four representatives) became accepted by all parties as being responsible in practice for the

running of the development, even though the Farum Building Company officially had that duty. The committee gradually came to adopt an active entrepreneurial role on behalf of the community, establishing a small supermarket, for example, when it became apparent that local shopping facilities were inadequate. An offset print shop for residents' use, and banking and insurance services were also provided. These service functions were organized through a limited-liability cooperative society established for the purpose and which grew to employ 30 full-time staff, drawn from the resident community and paid a uniform hourly wage. The committee also conducted two major campaigns on regional planning issues which affected the community—the establishment of effective public transport links with Copenhagen and the rejection of plans for a regional shopping centre in

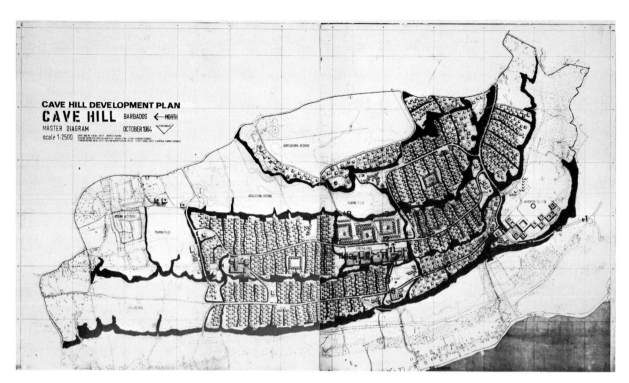

CAVE HILL DEVELOPMENT PLAN
CAVE HILL BARBADOS ← NORTH
MASTER DIAGRAM OCTOBER 1964
scale 1:2500

*David Gosling, Peter Stevens, Iain Morrison, Cave Hill, Barbados, development plan, 1964.*

*David Gosling, Iain Morrison, Cave Hill, Barbados, prototype houses, 1966.*

of the traditional chattel house but give a higher degree of privacy. It was assumed that this complex of interlocking courtyard dwellings would stimulate a social unity previously experienced in the rural villages but not in the urban areas. Though a small prototype scheme was built, land speculation pressures led to the abandonment of the original proposal and its replacement by upper-income housing constructed by a speculative development company from Britain.

Bridgetown, of which Cave Hill is an extension, can be best described as a linear town stretching from Oistins in the south-east to Speightstown in the north-west. Its shape is the natural outcome of a continuous coastal highway with the attractions of a fine sea coast and sandy beaches. Coastal cliff formations and the physical land pattern of rising terraces running parallel to the coast have emphasized this attenuated form. The logic of such an urban form under local conditions was recognized and the Island Development Plan was based upon this concept of the linear city. The Cave Hill area formed an important part of the plan and its physical characteristics (a series of terraces parallel to each other, to the coastline and to the main highway system) reflect the overall urban pattern and lend themselves to the design of a self-contained community in linear form. A primary consideration was the visual effect of movement, both by vehicle and on foot, bearing in mind that a district needed to be experienced from a state of mobility. The visual aesthetic experience is derived from passing through a series of interrelated spaces —the effect described by Cullen as serial vision. The design of the Cave Hill plan is the linear park, which permits people to traverse the whole area by way of a pleasant and interesting sequence of spaces, right from their patio door to shop, school or other local destination.

Farum—as well as setting up various social clubs and amenities (including the purchase of a 'second hand mare'). Thus in the 'shipyard' (for its resemblance to a dry-dock filled with rusting hulks), the 'millionaire colony' or the 'red people's commune', as it has been variously described, a determined social form has grown out of an equally powerfully expressed building form, and a match achieved which depended as much upon the ingenious post-construction design of a social organization as on the provision of a sympathetic prior framework.

A medium-density development plan was developed for Cave Hill, Barbados, by Gosling, Stevens, Morrison and others. The plan provided a skeleton and programme for the development of a

new urban framework housing 12,000 people from low-income families. The great majority of the population of this former British colony occupied timber 'chattel houses', capable in theory of being moved and re-erected on different sites. These were erected by the families themselves but to higher constructional and design standards than seen in the conventional squatter settlements. In the mid-1960s, the Government of Barbados decided to intervene in the housing market by financing owner-occupation for low to middle-income families—an unprecedented move since hitherto owner-occupation of permanent houses was confined to a minority of high-income families. The plan proposed a new form of courtyard housing which would meet the tropical climatic conditions

**References:**

*Architectural Design*, Vol. 45, No. 7, 1975, 'Bofill' by Geoffrey Broadbent, pp. 402–17.

*The Architectural Review*, Vol. 154, No. 929, November 1973, 'The Taller of Bofill' by Geoffrey Broadbent, pp. 289–97.

*Richard Meier, Architect, Buildings and Projects, 1966–1976* (introduced by Kenneth Frampton), Oxford University Press, New York 1976.

*Arkitektur* (Denmark) No. 1, 1976, 'Farum Midtpunkt', pp. 1–11.

*Cave Hill Plan*, Gosling, Stevens & Dyer, Government of Barbados, 1964.

## New Towns: Eastern Europe

The Soviet Union has provided one of the most extensive test beds of New Town planning, with New Towns amounting to about 60% of all urban settlements by 1974, and accommodating almost 40% of all the population increase (90 million people) which occurred in the previous 50 years. This huge investment in New Towns has occurred in the context of Marxist theory on the nature of the city, and its relationship to the countryside, embodied in a 'unified system of settlement'. According to the 1961 Central Committee draft of the Party programme, the 'elimination of the socio-economic and cultural everyday distinctions between town and country will be one of the greatest results of Communist construction'.

A direct result of this aim has been the policy of restricting the growth of cities to an optimum size, variously estimated at between 20,000 and 350,000 inhabitants, beyond which, it has been argued, costs of transportation and environmental hygiene reduce the efficiency of the town. Within a community of this size, a primary intention of the plan is to ensure equality of housing conditions, service provision and mobility for all citizens. In the absence of the operation of the market, a normative approach to the allocation of land uses has been adopted, with functional zoning of uses and a high level of investment in public transportation to try to achieve equal accessibility between zones. In practice, these policies have been relaxed to some degree, as the priorities of industrial development have led to urban expansion beyond planned limits, and as some light industries have been found to be compatible with a location in residential zones. However, the philosophical bias underlying the planning of the Soviet New Town has given it a form distinctly different from that of New Towns in, say, the United Kingdom. 'Equality of housing conditions' has been interpreted as a general equality of density of housing apartment blocks through the town, ending abruptly at its edge. The preferred subdivision of such residential areas is the 'microdistrict', of between 4,000 and 18,000 inhabitants, served by a district centre within about 400 metres of all homes. The concept of the microdistrict serves both ideological and practical purposes, as described by the eminent Soviet economist Strumilin in his ideal 'palace commune' in which intensive group associations based on shared facilities serve to engender collective life and 'eradicate extreme individualism and egotism'.

In contrast to Western towns, the centre of the Soviet New Town has virtually no commercial

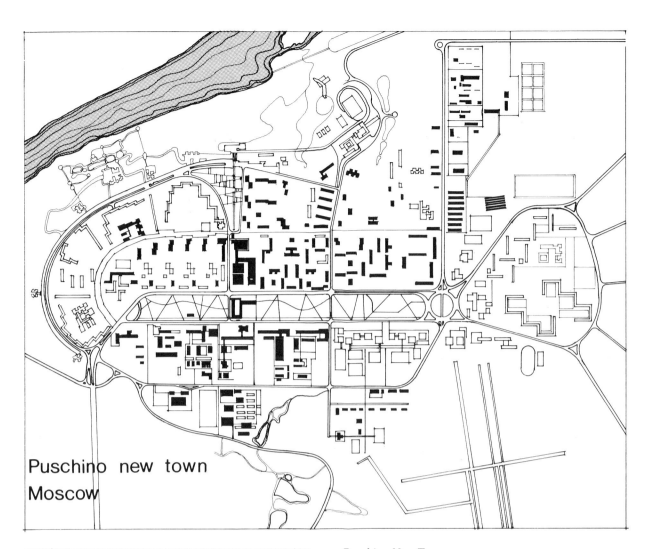

Puschino new town
Moscow

*Puschino New Town, south-west of Moscow, Soviet Union, 1963–80, master plan of the town, 1963.*

*Puschino New Town, 1963–80, children's playground.*

*Puschino New Town, 1963–80, view of completed riverside housing area.*

function, its role being instead primarily that of a 'politico-cultural-administrative' centre, and as at Nizhnevartovsk in the oil-producing Tyumen region of central Russia, for example, a setting for spaciously disposed public buildings and monuments.

Despite the differences in form, it has been argued that the Soviet planning process shares many of the characteristics of British planning between the 1947 Act and the 1960s, in that it is 'plan-oriented, physical, design-based, normative, unitary, scientific and technical and deterministic'. In support of this contention, the resemblance in both style and content of the 1971 General Plan for Moscow and Abercrombie's Greater London Plan has been remarked. One could also point to parallels between the elemental planning of central Nizhnevartovsk and, say, Le Corbusier's plan for St Dié and similar plans of that period.

The most remarkable planning, as opposed to architectural, concepts, however, are to be found in the eight New Towns which encircle Moscow. Each of these towns is based upon a single branch of scientific research and the research industry thus generated. The justification for these New Towns is rather hazy. One could assume that the decisions were taken for military defence and/or security reasons—but there does seem to be some justification in psychological terms in creating a quiet, campus-like atmosphere in the countryside where scientists can undertake their research free from bureaucratic or other pressures. Whether this psychological and intellectual tranquility is achieved at the expense of social isolation it is hard to say. In physical planning terms, the concept of a New Town based upon a single science or industry is perhaps disturbing to the Western planner since it would create an imbalance of services. On the other hand, the economic implications of this in a British New Town are irrelevant in the Soviet Union where all industry and research is state controlled and not subject to competition. In social planning terms it may be more disturbing, since this policy seems to create an elite within Soviet society.

The eight towns encircle Moscow at a distance of between 100 and 130 kilometres from the city centre. Populations vary—depending on whether it is a 'green-field' New Town like Puschino or one based upon an existing town like Dubna. Scientific bases vary but include the bio-medical sciences, bio-chemical sciences, physics and chemistry.

Puschino, to the south-west, was founded in 1963 and its population in 1979, supporting six bio-chemical research institutes, was relatively small at 17,000. The town is not a satellite town since it is entirely independent in employment and self-sufficient in social provision. The plan is interesting and imaginative and situated on a beautiful river escarpment. Social provision is lavish and includes a magnificent children's playground as well as a special music school.

Dubna, 130 kilometres to the north of Moscow, is based upon the Institute of Physics and includes the nuclear physics research laboratories. It is not constructed on a green field site but is an expansion of a small existing lakeside town. The 1979 population was approximately 44,000. Again, it has an imaginative plan, which is linear in form following the lakeside.

While other Soviet New Towns, such as the Volga car plant town of Togliatti, have tended to be developed along similar lines, not all urban projects have been of this type. One of the main aims of planning policy, effected through restrictions in the growth of existing towns coupled with a system of registration and internal passports for people wanting to move home, has been to channel growth towards newly-established towns in the underdeveloped areas of Soviet Asia. The severe climatic conditions faced by many of these settlements have periodically given rise to suggestions that radically new forms of urban development be adopted, and from time to time imaginative, and generally imaginary, projects have been published. Such for example is the case of the work of the NER group, which illustrated at the 1968 Milan Triennale that the contemporary preoccupation with megastructures was by no means confined to the West. This reaction against rigid functional zoning has occurred also among designers in other East European countries. In Poland it led Zbigniew Gadek to analyse a large number of multi-use building projects from which he proposed certain universal principles of organization and association which he set out as 'multi-use system', an antidote to 'zones and their characteristic specialization, [which] have lost or to a very large extent confined the communication amongst inhabitants which is what next destroyed communal life in cities'. An evocative illustration of the principle was provided by his colleague Ewa Szymanska in her 1971 project for a recreation complex in the Tatra Mountains, whose biomorphic forms recall the microphotography of Kepes' *The New Landscape*.

**References:**
Paul M. White, *Urban Planning in Britain and the Soviet Union: A Comparative Analysis*, University of Birmingham, Centre for Urban and Regional Studies, Research Memorandum 70.
The State Committee for Civil Construction and Architecture under the USSR GOSSTROY, *Urban Development in the USSR; Master Scheme of Residential Distribution on the Territory of the USSR* and *New Towns in the USSR*, 1970.
Zbigniew Gadek, *The Creation of Multi-Use Building*, Polytechnic of Cracow 1971 and *Multi-Use System*, School of Architecture, Kingston-upon-Hull 1974.

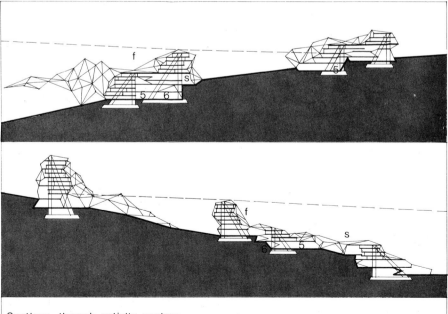

*Ewa Szymanska, project for a recreation complex in the Tatra Mountains, Poland, 1971.*

Sections through activity centres
f = flats , s = open spaces , 5 = passenger conveyor . 6 = goods transporter

## Chinese Communities

An essentially rural society, with 80% of its population living in rural areas, China nevertheless possesses a long tradition of town building peculiarly its own, which makes recent urban design projects in that country of particular interest.

Historically, the town as an isolated entity never gained the significance it did in Western countries. Instead, urban development was considered in a hierarchical sense, with space seen as a series of walled squares starting with the organization of the nation, with the capital at the centre, down to the organization of domestic space. The analogy which thus existed between the highly structured bureaucracy of traditional Imperialist China and this formation of urban and architectural space has been analysed by Sam Webb.

Today, the 'rural cities' are generally centres of administration, but also have local industry associated with agricultural production. Architectural design is traditional and rural housing construction not state-controlled in the conventional sense. Colin Penn has described the repertoire of traditional elements employed in the domestic architecture of Chekiang Province, for example, where the hot humid climate, with a yearly average temperature of between 16° and 19°C and a maximum reaching 32°C, necessitates the extensive use of small courtyards referred to as 'open-front halls'. Moveable partitions are used in the dwellings to allow a free flow of air currents through the structure. In the larger dwellings the hall is positioned in the centre of the building and provides space for a multiplicity of domestic activities. The hall is provided with removable doors and windows which are installed for climatic protection in winter. The verandah around the courtyards serve not only as the circulation system but as a domestic activity area as well. The use of full-length windows and removable doors between interior and exterior increases the flexibility of the house.

What is remarkable about the rural villages is that the adaptation of vernacular forms has given a

unity and coherence to the urban structure but at the same time has provided a visual variety which is lacking in other contemporary housing projects in socialist states.

Sawyers has also noted the contrast to Soviet and Western cities in a lack of focus on the city centre as the prime organizing core. Canton, for example, is seen as a continuous series of small towns, each area with its own shops, playgrounds and food stalls. Roof tops are of equal height, undulating with the curves of the land rather than projecting from it. Skyscrapers are unknown, and because of the spread of the city, a journey reveals only a gradual progression in visual character. It is true that some Chinese cities have large ceremonial squares similar to those of the Soviet Union, but it is suggested that these are more relics of a bygone age than of current ceremonial importance. If this description of Chinese cities is accurate, then their form has important lessons for urban design in the achievement of structural unity.

Nevertheless, the creation of mixed land-use neighbourhoods is open to question. A rolling stock plant is described as 'an essentially self-sufficient unit; it combines both industry and agriculture in productive work and has integrated housing, schools, factory, health centre and farming into one area.... The main factory is surrounded by a number of subsidiary factories and cottage-type industries.... The factory owns a large amount of farmland, also worked by residents of the complex.'

Sawyers also noted the development of self-reliant communes which combine industrial and agricultural production in the countryside. In contrast to the Soviet Union, where housing construction is the responsibility of the local Soviet or city authorities, in China the factory complex is run by a Revolutionary committee responsible for both the factory and the surrounding neighbourhoods, suggesting an analogy between such a community and that projected by Ebenezer Howard in his *Garden Cities of Tomorrow*. Chinese communities

are planned to foster a sense of community, of people working and living together as an integrated unit.

Robin Thompson has discussed the reappraisal of urban planning brought about by the Cultural Revolution in response to Mao's rejection of the Leninist theory that the benefits of developing heavy industry would eventually be diffused throughout society; rather he proposed to sacrifice rapid economic growth by building the economy from the bottom up. The Chinese view in 1973 was thus that the social costs of rapid industrial growth based on towns would be too heavy to justify economic gains which would advantage only the privileged city dwellers, although changes of policy since Mao's death have modified this position.

One of the most distinctive characteristics of Chinese urban planning described by Thompson is the employment of incremental means to achieve long-term principles or goals. The 'master plan', in the Western sense of the term, is rejected. Uncertainty over the future economic and demographic development of a country suggests that this rejection of the physical master plan may well be right and the Chinese concept of incrementation—'a methodology of achieving long-term goals by the accumulation of short-range anchors, each capable of quick and definite implementation'—a valid alternative.

References:
*L'Architecture d'Aujourd'hui*, No. 201, February 1979, pp. 1–89.
C. Penn, 'Chinese Vernacular Architecture', *RIBA Journal*, October 1965, p. 502.
L. Sawyers, 'Urban Planning in the Soviet Union and China', *Urban Planning*, March 1977, pp. 35–47.
Committee of Concerned Asian Scholars, *China: Inside the People's Republic*, Bantam, New York 1972, p. 107.
R. Thompson, 'City Planning in China', *World Development* 1974, pp. 595–605.

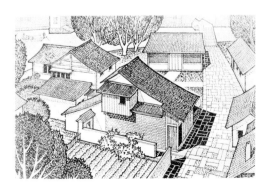

*Group of dwellings at Wuhsing (formerly Huchow), Chinese People's Republic.*

*Riverside dwellings, Wuhsing, Chinese People's Republic.*

*House in Upper Tienchu, Hangchow, Chinese People's Republic, sectional perspective.*

## Favelas

Despite, or perhaps because of, their subsistence economies, improvised forms of construction and lack of centrally provided facilities, the self-built squatter settlements which occur in most cities of the developing world provide particularly vivid examples of the mutually dependent relationships of public and private space within a community. A definition of 'urban design' which excludes these examples, concentrating instead exclusively on the elaboration of public visual statements which can only come with some measure of surplus public wealth, is itself surely an impoverished one. Three Latin American *favelas* may serve to illustrate here the relevance of these projects as examples of direct action by communities to establish their own built form, a process in which formally designated 'designers' may, as these examples show, participate to a varying degree.

In 1963 rumours spread that land in the Dom Bosco suburb of Belo Horizonte in Brazil was being given to the poor. Dozens of families staked the site and started to build huts. The landowner then authorized his representatives to eject the squatters by force, and although many families fled, the poorest, who had nothing to lose, decided to stay and fight. Finally, the *favelados* solved the problem themselves by moving onto adjacent land which belonged jointly to the Diocese and Municipality. Within a few months of existence, the settlement resembled the other 70 *favelas* in the city, with small huts two or three metres square made of corrugated iron and timber packed together on a site lacking environmental services

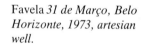
Favela *31 de Março, Belo Horizonte, 1973, artesian well.*

Favela *31 de Março, Belo Horizonte, Brazil, 1973, general view.*

and thus prone to the spread of vermin, gastro-enteritis and other diseases.

The first initiative was the formation of a cooperative, which was registered in the National Institute of Agrarian Development under the name Cooperativa de Prestação de Serviças de 31 de Março. Lacking a leader or executive committee, its objective was mutual help and community resolution of common problems, of which lack of sanitation and water were major examples. Nevertheless the inhabitants decided to start with the construction of a primary school which they considered fundamental to the development of both children and adults. Women and children worked on the site by day and men by night until the building was completed. Because it was not a recognized school, the State would not provide the teachers. The inhabitants started a common fund to pay for the training of their teacher, a girl from the *favela* itself. When she graduated she taught without pay until the State recognized the school and agreed to pay a rent for the use of the premises and provide additional teachers.

The *favelados* then tackled other basic problems. A doctor visited the *favela* at the weekends and gave free consultation and medicines, though the pharmacy was subsequently closed by the public health department. A community meeting concluded that the basic cause of ill-health was the *favela* itself and that sewage disposal and water supply networks were required to eliminate disease. The municipal water department said that it would take almost two years to construct, and after debate the community decided to build the artesian well themselves and within nine months every family had a piped water supply. Electric power and street widening followed within a year.

Many of the women in the *favela* are employed as washer-women, though some are servants in the nearby suburbs. The Cooperative formed a union and established a laundromat with automatic washing machines in 1968. The medical post was reinstated and in 1973 a technical school was established for the younger men. The girls were already receiving secretarial courses by that time. With the introduction of evening classes, nearly all the inhabitants can now read and write. The *favelados* only contribute to the Cooperative at a time of essential work and they do this spontaneously. An aid fund is devoted to assisting the poorer inhabitants and cases of illness or bereavement. The Cooperative is not hierarchical and there is no leader nor the vesting of power in a minority of the community. It genuinely acts in the interests of all. It is a commune in the true sense of the word with all major decisions decided by vote at mass meetings.

Visually, there is little to distinguish 31 de Março from the other *favelas*. What is noticeable is the lack of dirt, litter and disease and an air of tidiness and well-being. The presence of the artesian well tower and the primary school are of great symbolic importance in the community, which achieved its improvements without the help of architects or planners.

This was not the case, however, with the reconstruction of the Bras de Pinã *favela* in Rio de Janeiro in 1967 which was assisted by a small group of young architects led by Carlos Nelson dos Santos. The *favela* had existed for 30 years prior to 1967 and had, in that year, a population of 4,416 inhabitants and approximately 812 dwellings with a median density of 400 inhabitants per hectare. The land on which the *favela* was constructed was not the more usual mountainside site found in Botafogo and Ipenema at that time, but rather a flat and swampy area at the northern end of Guanabara Bay. 94% of the houses were constructed of wood and 77% of the population were economically active (70% of women were domestic servants and 14% of the men were in the building industry, 11% in transport, 17% in handywork). 92% of the population owned their own houses, though 83% of the total area lacked a sewage disposal system. An alley system served the pedestrian circulation in the interior of the *favela*.

When Bras de Pinã was one of the first six *favelas* selected to be moved to the COHAB townships, violence erupted. The Dwellers' Association decided that the only way to guarantee their permanence was to produce a plan proving to the authorities that 'urbanization' was possible—with legalization of land tenure, infrastructure construction and improvement in space standards. With the assistance of Carlos Nelson, a survey was prepared including topographic plans, housing location plans and availability of services. A preliminary redevelopment plan was produced in 1966–67 upon which basis the inhabitants could act on their own initiative, and which identified five scales of subdivision of the settlement, with corresponding requirements for each:

1 The total *favela*, requiring new infrastructure, street paving and community space programmes
2 The two halves of the *favela* on either side of the recognized streets
3 The three main housing sectors
4 The blocks in each sector

5 Each group of eight houses
The circulation pattern was to retain the original urban structure and preserve all pedestrian streets.

The construction work commenced in 1969 and was complete by mid-1971. Land reclamation, water supply and sewage disposal were the first priorities. The rehabilitation of the housing plots was more difficult. Existing houses were moved a maximum distance of 200 metres, and each house-owner was asked to prepare a plan of his housing requirements. These plans were interpreted by the architectural team, who, working with a kit of parts of prefabricated timber units, attempted to provide a house as close as possible to the requirements of the individual family. Successful in visual terms in their reflection of the vernacular architecture of the original *favela*, they were developed from some 300 requested plan variations translated into a typological study of 13 different models. Government finance was offered to the house-owner who purchased his own building materials from the kit of parts and often erected the house himself.

Bras de Pinã thus provided a new, low-income housing solution in Rio de Janeiro. Although they have some similarities with conventional urban tissue, the housing prototypes are unusual.

Our third example illustrates the somewhat different involvement of architects in the reconstruction of a settlement by means of a major planning competition launched in Brazil in the early 1970s for the 'urbanization' of the Alagados *favela* in Bahia, Salvador. In the 1940s, the population of Alagados had been about 1,000 people, but by 1972 it had grown to around 90,000 in the Cidade Baixa area, which constituted one of the largest *favelas* in Brazil. Constructed on mud flats in the Bay of Bahia, it was one of the unhealthiest and most insanitary of squatter settlements. Many of the inhabitants worked as fishermen in the Bay, though production was dropping because of industrial pollution.

The competition was won in 1972 by the architectural practice M.M.M. Roberto, which was originally founded by three brothers who were among the early pioneers of Modern architecture in Brazil. Their proposal was impressively simple. Since most of the houses were constructed on light timber jetties across the mud flats, the architects proposed that the lines of these jetties should also form the basis of a future infrastructure proposal, referred to as the 'Viela Sanitária', and providing a combined circulation and servicing system. Reconstructed houses were proposed as clusters around the Viela Sanitária and each house lot was designed

Former houses in the favela *Bras de Piña, Rio de Janeiro, Brazil, 1966.*

Proposed house plan drawn by a favelado, *Bras de Piña, Rio de Janeiro, 1967.*

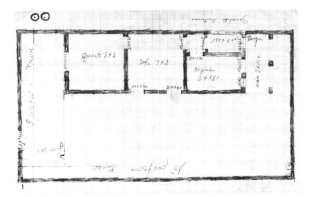

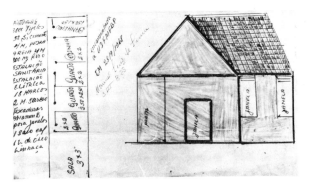

Proposed house plan drawn by a favelado, *Bras de Piña, Rio de Janeiro, 1967.*

New houses under construction, *Bras de Piña, 1967.*

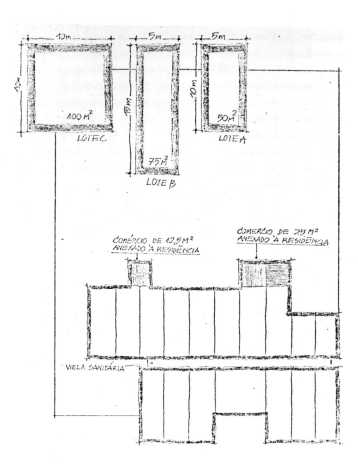

M. M. M. Roberto,
*Algados competition
proposals, Salvador,
1972.*

*House in existing squatter
settlement, Algados
favela, Salvador, Brazil
(photographed 1976).*

as a flexible unit in much the same way as the
*bariadas* of Peru described by John Turner. As the
family grew, so also would the house grow within
the limits of the plot. The new urban structure is
thus delineated as an infrastructure system with a
constantly changing housing pattern.

These three *favelas* represent a spectrum of
professional involvement, from the non-parti-
cipation of professionals in urban reconstruction at
31 de Março to a relatively sophisticated form of
new urban structure designed by architects at Alagados. All three, however, express a view that the
professional design of the houses forms a low social
priority and that the visual vitality of the community comes from the decisions of the inhabitants
themselves.

The experience of these Brazilian examples is
reflected in similar self-help communities around
the world. Geoffrey Payne has described instances
in Ankara, for example, where complete settlements have been planned by their occupants whose
resident groups have not only taken over control of
house building but also of settlement planning,
including designating sites for major buildings such
as schools and mosques, and leaving the municipality the responsibility for water supply. The plan of
such a settlement indicates a conscious urban design decision by the inhabitants to locate the school
at the top of the hill where it will be clearly visible,
with shops placed on the main paths which wind up
the hill, forming a village street. Payne argues that
such squatter settlements have important lessons
for 'developed' countries, in their demonstration
that the most viable way, both socially and economically, of improving housing is to increase local
control over it, so that people can participate
actively in making decisions which affect their daily
lives—a theme effectively developed by Colin
Ward in his book *Tenants Take Over.*

References:

D. Gosling, 'Housing Case Study in Brazil II',
*Architectural Design,* January 1975, pp. 38–41; also see
T. Braga, 'Uma Favela Modelo', *Opiniao* 2–8 July 1973,
p. 5.
Geoffrey Payne, 'Housing: Third World Solutions to
First World Problems', *Built Environment*, Vol. 5, No. 2,
1979, pp. 99–100.

## Competition: Manila

Eight years after the Lima competition, the United Nations Habitat Conference of 1976 provided the opportunity for a further international competition for the design of low-cost settlements to meet the problems of rapid and uncontrolled urbanization around the cities of many of the developing countries, this time based on a site in the Tondo foreshore area of Manila. From the competition conditions issued by the sponsoring body, the International Architectural Foundation (formed by the two architectural magazines *Architectural Record* and *L'Architecture d'Aujourd'hui*), and from subsequent events, it became apparent that the attitude of the international architectural community and of the proposed recipients of such designs had changed. As the sponsors noted: 'The world's urbanization problems are such that it is not possible to talk of an "architectural solution", or perhaps of any "solution", although it is possible for architects to make their contribution.'

Although the competition conditions were broadly similar, indicating low-rise, high-density, low-cost solutions for the planning of 500 dwellings on a five hectare site, greater emphasis than before was placed on the need for establishing the self-sufficiency of the community in terms of public services, employment and construction effort. Although the site was already occupied by a squatter settlement operating at a density over 50% higher than that of the competition brief, the plan was to involve the minimum relocation of residents, who were to be consulted on its implementation (though not on the choice of competition winner). As at Lima, the main design problems seemed to be those of appropriate building technology and community form, but in practice both sponsors and competitors seemed much more conscious of another problem underlying both of these: the degree to which any design could or should be imposed from outside. What precisely did 476 design teams from around the world have to offer their 3,500 user-clients in Manila? This question was asked by the squatters themselves when many of them were arrested for protesting at the refusal of the Philippine authorities to allow a group of their representatives to visit Habitat Forum in Vancouver, where the competition entries were displayed.

It was perhaps a sensitivity to this issue which principally distinguished the winning entry by the New Zealander Ian Athfield, since it comprised in essence a system of almost defensive enclosures within which community subdivisions of the whole

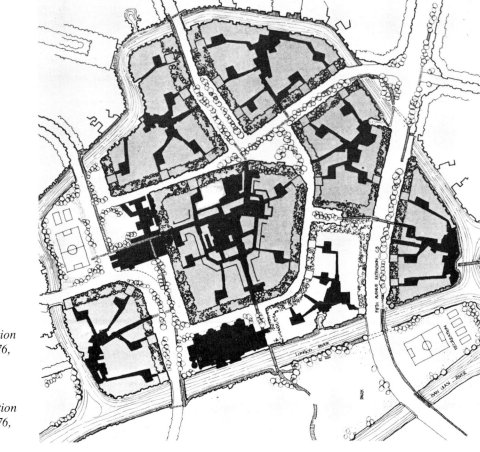

*Ian Athfield, prize-winning competition scheme for Manila, 1976, site plan.*

*Ian Athfield, prize-winning competition scheme for Manila, 1976, housing details.*

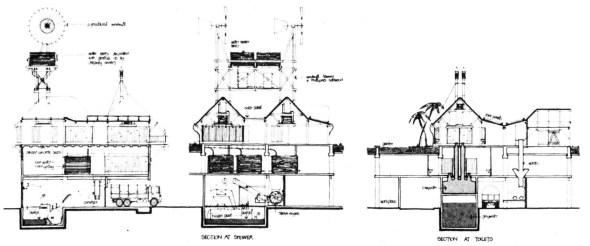

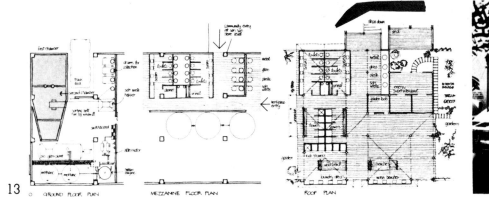

13

town could operate with a high degree of autonomy. Taking the community structure indicated by the brief of the New Town (15,000–20,000 families); the zone (1,500–2,500 families); the community or *barangay* (500–750 families); the neighbourhood or *purok* (100–150 families); and the family (15–10 persons), Athfield adopted the *barangay* as the most substantial physical subdivision of the town. All cars were excluded from this unit which was to have bounding access roads and be surrounded by a wall of workshops for light industry. The construction of the linear workshop building would be the first task of the community and in addition to providing the main location of future employment, it would also house the residents' cooperative which would control the supply, manufacture and use of building materials, as well as community 'energy centres', established to utilize waste products and ambient energy sources. Within the compound formed by the perimeter buildings, the housing layout would make space for local *purok* centres. Each family would receive financial assistance to build its own house, using timber and other by-products from the coconut palm, and it would be at the level of individual advice to each family that the design team would mainly operate.

There was considerable disagreement among the competitors about just how much of such planning was necessary for the community. The Californian team of Freebairn-Smith, Crane, Grundstein and Meier, for instance, while accepting the *barangay* subdivision of the town, and the idea of a focal centre for it, advocated as little further control as possible, and in particular disagreed with Athfield's control of building materials 'to give a visual unity to the *barangay*', advocating rather that, 'restricted only by lot configuration, every family would build according to its immediate needs and its resources'. Others, such as Eldred Evans and David Shalev of the United Kingdom, proposed a complete architectural solution in which individual families would act as their own building contractors to a predetermined design. This scheme, like Stirling's at Lima, also adopted an intermediate grouping of family units around a shared courtyard. This social unit, described by Evans and Shalev as the 'courthouse' in deference to the traditional institution of the 'long-house', was also present in some other projects, as in Kurokawa's 'Big House' grouping of similar (7–20 families) size, and introduced a much tighter social as well as architectural hierarchy to the planning of the *barangay*. Some of the logic and illogic applied to solving the problem of balancing

*Freebairn-Smith, Crane, Grundstein and Meier, competition scheme for Manila, 1976.*

*M. M. M. Roberto, competition scheme for Manila, 1976.*

*M. M. M. Roberto, competition scheme for Manila, 1976.*

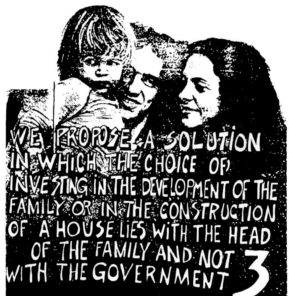

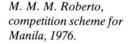

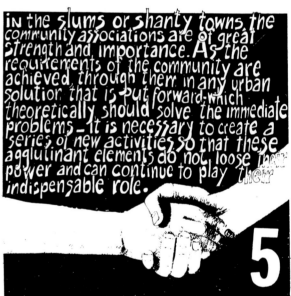

freedom and flexibility at the level of the individual family with a coherent community structure was exposed by the solution offered by Yona Friedman of France. 'Community structure' here literally materialized in the form of a three-layer 'low-cost' bamboo megastructure, offering support and umbrella roof to the private spaces defined within it by screens and, for personal valuables, 'treasure rooms'. Thus freedom for 'self-design' in which 'inhabitants of the settlement can and will do their design for themselves' was purchased by what, at least to sceptical observers, appeared to be a crippling social and financial discipline imposed by the enabling mechanism.

A final ironic comment on this interesting competition was provided by Mrs Imelda Marcos, first lady of the Philippines and Governor of metropolitan Manila, who, concurrently with the competition, ordered the construction of 500 housing units in the area of the site as a demonstration project. Too expensive for the Tondo squatters, and diametrically opposed in philosophy and approach to the intentions of the competition sponsors, it was attacked by confused critics of the competition who assumed that it was Athfield's prize-winning design.

**Reference:**

Michael Y. Seeling, *The Architecture of Self-Help Communities: The First International Design Competition for the Urban Environment of Developing Countries*, Architectural Record Books, New York 1978.

## 3.4 PROFESSIONAL SOLUTIONS: THE CITY AS A RESOLUTION OF DESIGN PROBLEMS

DESPITE THE CHALLENGE TO THE PROFESSIONAL designer contained in such projects as the Manila competition, it can be argued that wherever the source of design decisions happens to be, the process involved is inevitably one of design, requiring designers in whatever guise. Taken a little further, this argument points to those many architectural projects which offer solutions at the scale of urban design but which remain essentially design resolutions of all the economic, engineering, social or whatever components of the brief which happened to come together in that place at that time. Urban design may then be seen as an accommodation of highly articulate specific design solutions brought together by fortuitous, but carefully studied circumstances.

Such an approach, lacking any overall, imposed framework, depends above all upon the ability of individual designers to produce powerful and appropriate urban set-pieces. We have used some projects by James Stirling and Michael Wilford to illustrate this point, and to introduce a series of project groups in which the resolution of problems associated with particular building types generates urban form. The section concludes with some projects for one specific building type, the administrative centre, and in particular with the competition for UN City in Vienna, in which highly elaborate urban prototypes arise from the complexities of the brief.

### Designers: James Stirling and Michael Wilford

The consistent ability of James Stirling, with Michael Wilford and his other associates, to produce what Colin Rowe early recognized as 'the spectacle of intransigent and very memorable building' has given his work a special relevance in the field of urban design, where the spectacle of opportunist and unmemorable building is more common. His projects with a strong urban design content have been generally of two types, either large-scale building complexes on empty sites in which the solution has suggested an idealized urban form, or else smaller-scale interventions within the fabric of an existing city. The former category includes the 1958 competition design for Churchill College, Cambridge, which inspired Rowe's observation in his essay 'The Blenheim of the Welfare State'. The project radicalized the form of the medieval Cambridge college court in a way suggestive of a Roman fortress, and was referred to by its designer as 'this new urban complex'.

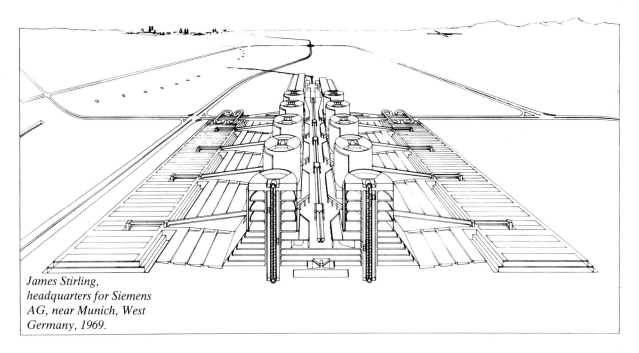

James Stirling, headquarters for Siemens AG, near Munich, West Germany, 1969.

Ten years later a similar urban reference was made for the design of central-area housing at Runcorn New Town, alternative studies for which investigated 'the English idea of using repetitive housing to create urban spaces as can be seen in Bath, Edinburgh, London, etc.' Again in the Siemens project of 1969, a number of features pointed to the design as a model of an urban structure. There was the elevation of a relatively minor element of the programme, the social facilities, to a major status in the design, as a grand, formal tree-lined boulevard, or 'social valley', down the axis of the complex. The project also incorporated a whole hierarchy of transportation systems including an axial public travelator. Again, it was suggested that the cylindrical office silos would have the character of 'clubland'. Finally, Stirling used as an untitled postscript to his presentation of the project a tiny illustration by Le Corbusier of his 1929 scheme for a new city centre for Buenos Aires, to be constructed out in the waters of the Rio de la Plata.

Memorable as these designs are, it is perhaps in the second category of projects that the quality of 'intransigence' provides the most interesting results, since it must be achieved without destroying the context in which it is placed. For whereas the relatively bleak fields of the Madingley Road in Cambridge, the southern central area of Runcorn and the fringes of Perlach all positively invited the powerful, large-scale and self-sufficient designs which were proposed, the same could not be said of the complicated and difficult sites tackled by the interventionist schemes. In these cases, the problem of creating a strong and coherent design which stands as a completely satisfying solution on its own (as demanded by 'intransigence') is compounded by the requirement that that scheme should also interlock with an existing situation, the outcome of a long historical sequence of fortuitous events, in such a way that the result be also entirely convincing.

Such was the case with the competition entry for Derby Civic Centre of 1970, in which the whole building programme was bent (literally) to an urban design purpose, the creation of a 'public space with as great a significance as has the Piazza del Campo to Siena, the Royal Crescent to Bath, or the Rockefeller Plaza to New York'. To achieve this purpose—the recomposition of an historic central place which had been fractured by traffic—the particularities of the Civic Centre accommodation were surprisingly muted. The auditorium, for example, an element dramatized in Stirling and Gowan's Leicester Engineering Building, and used by some other competitors as a feature of their designs, was buried in the block form along with all the other 'significant' civic components. Without compromising their functional interrelationships, their symbolic and plastic possibilities were suppressed, so that they became simply an 'urban material' to be moulded to the primary aim, the creation of major public spaces, in particular the 'arena' of the Market Square itself and its tall

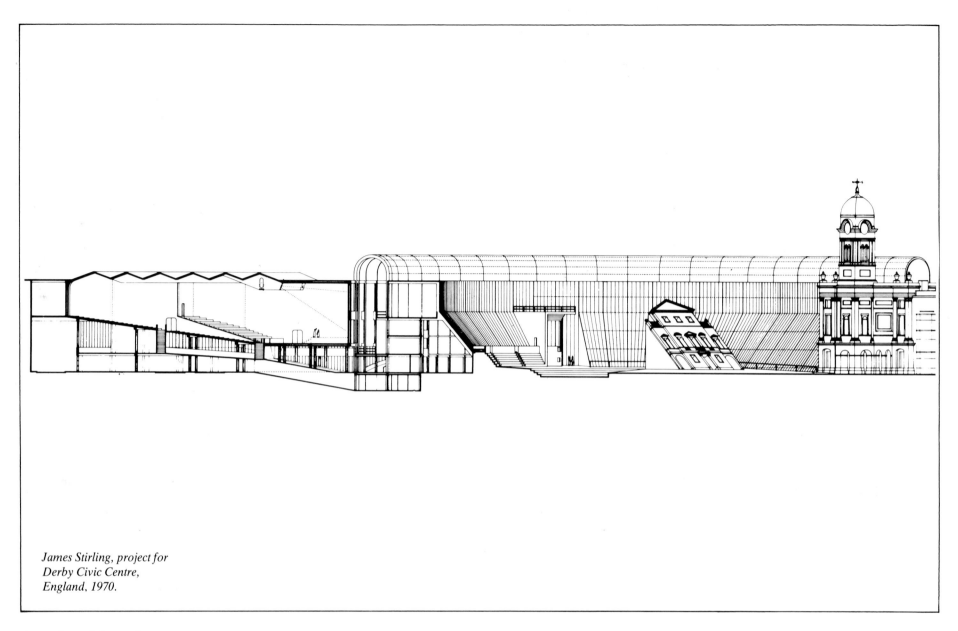

*James Stirling, project for
Derby Civic Centre,
England, 1970.*

circumferential arcade.

Decayed as was the Market Square of Derby, it did at least possess a clear urban purpose towards the re-establishment of which the new building could direct itself. This was not the case with that part of the centre of Cologne which lies above the Rhine at the bridgehead of the Hohenzollern-brücke, which formed the subject of a competition design by Stirling in 1975. The area is dominated by two huge and incompatible structures, the Cathedral and the railway station, whose tracks cross the bridge on the axis of the Cathedral before sweeping up to the skew alignment of the station. Add to these the roads, car parking areas and bus station associated with the station, the dual carriageway running along the Rhine, and the decks which emerge around the Cathedral and adjacent Römisch-Germanisches Museum as the indeterminate edge of Cologne's system of pedestrian

streets and squares, and a thoroughly confused picture emerges, described by the competition sponsors as 'an urban vacuum a quarter of a century after the end of the war'. Thus, although a prestigious building, for the Wallraf-Richartz Museum, formed the content of the brief, it was the urban design implications of the site which posed the major challenge.

Faced with a much more fragmented and complex set of conditions to resolve than at Derby, Stirling's solution was made up of a number of parts, each designed to respond to a particular problem. A pair of cube-like pavilions was placed to receive the railway bridge as it hit the bank and the tracks changed direction; another wing responded to the Cathedral and defined the southern edge of a piazza; a third element marked the beginning of a pedestrian route across to a second piazza, Breslauer Platz, on the north side of the

tracks; and so on. The external pressures on the site were thus resolved or received by a family of urban elements which simultaneously related to one another, primarily through their function in controlling and defining a route through the now ordered spaces of the site. This 'discovery' of a set of architectural events which, while uniquely responding to the specific conditions of its location, also forms a rigorous constitution in its own right, suggests a powerful and flexible method of urban design.

Particularly interesting is the internal relationship between the buildings and the route. The architects' treatment of external spaces as partially enclosed 'rooms' (even going so far as to treat a sunken sculpture court as a diminutive figure/ground reversal of the Cathedral above); their description of the architectural events in such terms as 'Gateway buildings (monumental) are posi-

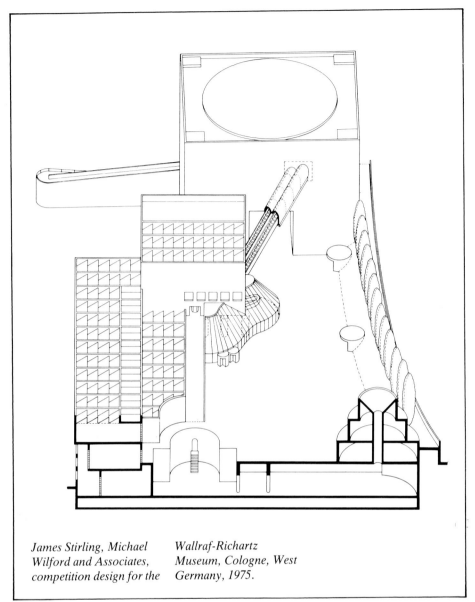

*James Stirling, Michael Wilford and Associates, competition design for the Wallraf-Richartz Museum, Cologne, West Germany, 1975.*

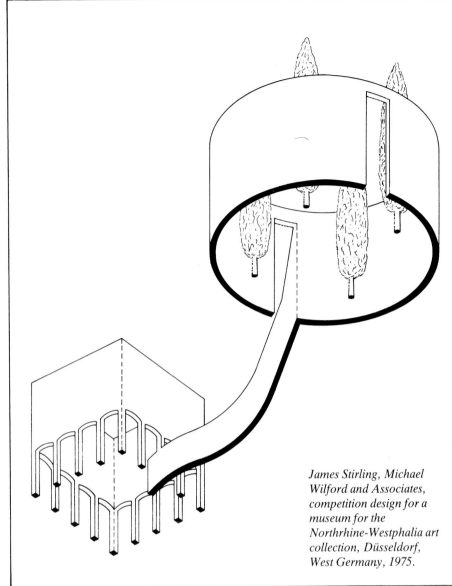

*James Stirling, Michael Wilford and Associates, competition design for a museum for the Northrhine-Westphalia art collection, Düsseldorf, West Germany, 1975.*

tioned either side of the bridge and semi-enclosed within these buildings are circular piazzas ...'; their use of primary geometric forms; and finally the elevation of the public *promenade architecturale* to an ordering principle all suggest, inevitably perhaps, references to a possible antecedent such as Le Corbusier's Cité de Refuge building in Paris. There a similar sequence of monumental primary forms, in part 'outdoor rooms', direct the approach from the street to the tall slab of the main building behind. In that case, the elements stand as foreground counterpoint to the neutral curtain wall backdrop of the dormitory accommodation which rises behind them. Indeed, one might speculate that while Modern architecture has tended to concentrate on the slab block of the latter as a preferred urban model, Stirling at Cologne did the opposite, taking the primary elements of the foreground, inflating them in scale, and setting them not against the grid of a curtain wall but against the grain of an existing city.

A third 'interventionist' project, dating from the same year as the Cologne design and also set in Germany, combined some of the characteristics of that scheme and the earlier one at Derby. The site for the proposed building for the Northrhine-Westphalia Art Collection on Grabbeplatz in central Düsseldorf had enough of the surrounding city fabric intact to suggest the Derby tactic of using the new building to complete the city block. At the same time, this block was pierced by a narrow lane along a line once occupied by the city wall, and the extension of this as a pedestrian route through the new building and out onto Grabbeplatz on its other side provided the opportunity for a route-sequence of urban rooms and events similar to that proposed for Cologne. Once again, the impression of an architectural spatial organization enlarged to an urban scale, the development of formal themes by figure/ground and circle/square inversions, and the inflexions in response to surrounding events, suggest the scalar transformation of the orthodox language of Modern architecture to solve problems of urban design in an unorthodox way.

**References:**

Colin Rowe, 'The Blenheim of the Welfare State', essay in *Cambridge Review*, 31 October 1959.

*James Stirling: Buldings and Projects, 1950–1974* (introduction by John Jacobs), Thames & Hudson, London 1975.

Le Corbusier, *Précisions*, Editions Vincent, Fréal et Cie, Paris 1929.

*Architectural Review*, Vol. 160, No. 957, November 1976, 'Stirling in Germany', pp. 289–96.

*Le Corbusier et Pierre Jeanneret, Oeuvre Complète, 1929–1934*, Les Editions Girsberger, Zürich 1957, pp. 97–109.

## Low-Density Neighbourhoods

The use by James Stirling and Michael Wilford of individual building programmes to reconstruct the city through a series of specific resolutions is not the only way in which a 'professional', designer-oriented solution can be achieved. At first sight, the examples of lower-density residential projects which follow might be held to belong to that range of housing-type solutions, of which we have already considered high-density and medium-density examples, in which the built form may be argued to be an attempt to acknowledge the social organization which underlies the brief. However, in these low-density examples, the strong building patterns arise from a variety of sources—considerations of traffic, of theoretical land-use studies and of patterns of pedestrian movement—any and all of which are refined and then elevated as geometric principles to give clarity and cohesion to the end result. We might say then that the solution arises from a selective understanding of the geometry of the problem, without any special weight being given to the social component of the brief, although the resulting correspondence, or lack of it, between geometric and social structures is an intriguing feature.

The first three projects illustrate some possible basic configurations. At one extreme, the solution to the problems of access, orientation and building form appropriate to the brief and location, having been identified and framed for one case, may be repeated in a uniform mat, with no intermediate grouping between the individual plot and the community as a whole. Although this principle often underlies much speculative housing, it is rarely applied with the rigour adopted in the design by Michael Gold and Peter Barker for housing at Coffee Hall, Milton Keynes, in 1972. In this case, the solution at the scale of the individual unit was a single-storey house occupying the full width of the plot and thus forming one slice of a continuous low terrace or ribbon of building. At the scale of the whole community, two models were adopted: firstly the simple rectangle, half a mile by a quarter, of 'an historical image of an integral settlement at traditional scale, set in countryside, designed and constructed as a unified architectural conception in the manner of, say, Montpazier'; and secondly a road pattern of long straight avenues without cross streets running the length of the rectangle, in accordance with a theory of optimum road layouts proposed by Christopher Alexander in a paper first published in 1966. Across the neutral mesh thus set down (aligned to give each dwelling a precise

east-west orientation), hedgerows, trees, banks and other features of the natural landscape were allowed to run, flipping from 'ground' to 'figure' as they crossed the boundary between the developed rectangle and the surrounding fields and providing a chain of open spaces through the community.

Precisely the opposite principle of development is illustrated in a variety of projects by Richard MacCormac and Peter Jamieson, whose work on housing has been strongly influenced by their theoretical studies of density and development patterns. Derived from investigations carried out in the Cambridge University School of Architecture in the early 1960s, including Colin Rowe's writings, Colin St John Wilson's modular studies and subsequently research by Sir Leslie Martin, Lionel March and Philip Steadman into the geometry of built form, MacCormac and Jamieson's approach combines a radical attitude to site planning with a concern for the social patterns implied. Of particular interest to them has been the property of land usage contained in the Fresnel Square, as indicated by Martin and March, which comprises a set of concentric squares of diminishing band width towards the outside in which the area contained in each band is identical. The property suggests that 'if housing is stretched around other land uses or in the interstices between them, problems of block spacing are avoided and residual land minimized so that densities may be achieved with two or three-storey construction which could only be met on constrained central sites by resorting to high buildings.' This principle of perimeter site planning is

*Michael Gold and Peter Barker, Coffee Hall housing, Milton Keynes, England, 1972.*

exemplified in MacCormac and Jamieson's scheme for private housing at Duffryn in which a continuous coiled terrace form of housing at a density of 175 persons per hectare occupies the perimeter zone of a 38.5 hectare site, leaving the original landscape untouched in the central area, in which woodland banks define three 'landscape rooms' of public open space, one of which contains a primary school. The hierarchy of spaces which this design provides ranges from the private garden of each house, through the 'greens' which are formed on the inward side of each coil of the terrace (as a counterform to the parking court formed on the outer side) to the large space in the centre. Yet although the loops in the terrace suggest some local grouping, the scheme essentially operates, as did Gold and Barker's, at the two primary scales of the individual family on the one hand, and the community of 977 homes on the other.

Standing in between these two geometric poles, and offering an intermediate scale of organization, Ralph Erskine's neighbourhood of 750 dwellings at Nya Bruket in Sandviken, Sweden, also adopted a clear formal structure. This was suggested by the site itself which lay in the inner area of an industrial town, and had been occupied by older houses which had had to be demolished. They had left behind a grid of mature sycamore trees based on the old property lines, and the retention of these trees (as well as the old service runs alongside) established, not a counterpoint to the grid as at Coffee Hall, but the grid itself. The new housing was thus formed into a regular pattern of two-

*Richard MacCormac and Peter Jamieson, housing at Duffryn, Wales, 1979.*

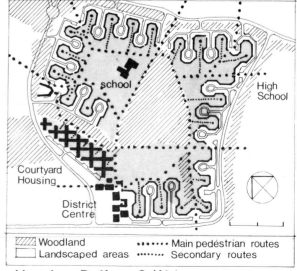

Housing , Duffryn , S.Wales

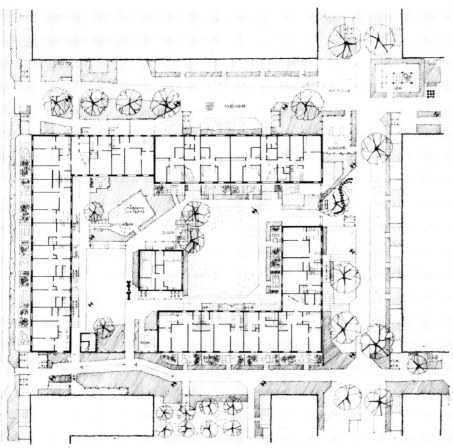

*Ralph Erskine, housing at Nya Bruket, Sandviken, Sweden, 1974–, plan.*

*David Gosling et al., community route concept for Western Gailes, Irvine New Town, Scotland, 1971.*

*Ralph Erskine, housing at Nya Bruket, 1974–.*

storey courtyard clusters, each containing about 35 gallery and staircase-access flats, and each with its own small common room or laundry building in the centre. As with the other two projects, the clarity of the original geometric choice was carried through rigorously in the built form, making a reading of the physical and social corollaries of that selection particularly vivid.

The strong geometric determinism shared by these three examples is not, however, an inevitable corollary of the desire for a clear and readily perceived urban framework for low-density communities. The use of a 'community route' principle at Bourtreehill and a new version of back-to-back terraces at Highgrove illustrate alternative possibilities.

The Annick Valley development at Irvine New Town is based upon a new approach to the integration of old villages, new communities and a new public transport system. Bourtreehill, designed by the Development Corporation, forms a major part of this development. An important innovation in the conceptual development was the 'community route' structure. Whereas some of the British New Towns like Runcorn incorporated a purpose-built transportation track at high cost, the community route idea utilizes existing roads and country lanes as public transport routes. This idea was developed

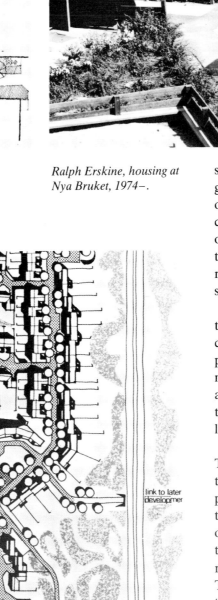

by the traffic engineers Jamieson and Mackay and published in the 1971 Irvine New Town Plan.

The advantage of the idea is the economic use of an existing infrastructure which, before the New Town commenced, linked community facilities in the villages and other settlements. This was to form the basis of the new public transport and pedestrian system. Community routes were seen as the focus of surrounding development with social, educational and other facilities located at public transport stops. The higher-density housing adjacent to the routes could provide a pedestrian system to allow residents to move from district to district with maximum weather protection. Distributor roads were developed in parallel to the community route as housing was built. Finally, the community route carried public transport vehicles and could be adapted to future transportation systems such as tracked air-cushion craft.

The primary school and local shop requiring a support population of around 4,000 were taken as the basic elements of the community structure with a maximum walking distance of 0.5 kilometres or five to seven minutes. The basic communities of

*Irvine Development Corporation (Peter Fauset, Al Mackay), community route housing with polychromatic cement render, Bourtreehill, Irvine New Town, 1973.*

*Irvine Development Corporation (Al Mackay, Peter Fauset, Vernon Monaghan, David and Mary Simister), internal cluster group with monochromatic cement render, Bourtreehill, Irvine New Town, 1973.*

1,100 dwellings were grouped on either side of the route and related to a comprehensive school and local centre.

The community route added strength to the form of the town. Owner-occupied housing areas where car ownership could be high were located near to the peripheral distributor roads, whilst housing areas of higher density were close to the community route and based more on pedestrian need and the availability of public transport. The build up in density and form towards the community route emphasized its significance and created a higher-density spine of development punctuated by centres containing social, educational and shopping facilities. Strong colours were used along the route to give it a village-street character, whereas the clusters of houses at the rear were monochromatic. Pedestrian/vehicle mix was allowed on the access roads in a manner similar to Halton Brow at Runcorn New Town.

Finally, Edward Cullinan's housing on a relatively constricted site at Highgrove in the London suburb of Hillingdon provided wide-frontage housing with a high degree of privacy and garden space which might have appeared impossible on the land available. He achieved this by using a system of back-to-back housing, each cluster having four dwellings. In attempting a new approach to low-density public housing which would permit a degree of flexibility and privacy hitherto unavailable in council housing without the constraints of cross walls and narrow frontages, the architects sought to find a new housing expression in a suburban setting. The coherence of the development is enhanced by the startling use of blue steel roof-sheeting which nevertheless does not diminish the essential 'cosiness' of the project. Despite the combination of traditional elements of street, yard and alley, the variety achieved within an apparently rigid grid structure is noteworthy.

**References:**
'Coffee Hall, 1972', *Architectural Design*, Vol. 47, No. 9–10, 1977, pp. 668–69.

Christopher Alexander, 'The Pattern of Streets', *Journal of the American Institute of Planners*, Vol. 32, No. 5, September 1966.

'MacCormac and Jamieson', *Architectural Design*, Vol. 47, No. 9–10, 1977, pp. 691–706.

*Roads in Housing Developments*, Conference Papers/Study team report by the Scottish Local Authorities Special Housing Group, March 1977, September 1977.

*The Architects' Journal*, Vol. 166, No. 30, 27 July 1977, pp. 159–67, article on Highgrove.

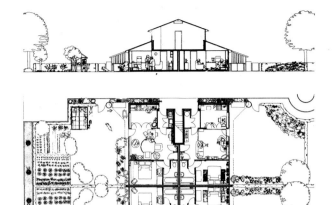

TYPE C    GROUND FLOOR

*Edward Cullinan, housing at Highgrove, Hillingdon, London, England, 1978, section and ground-floor plans.*

*Edward Cullinan, housing at Highgrove, Hillingdon, 1978.*

## New Towns: England

Although the rationale for building New Towns has generally been expressed in quite prosaic terms —to relieve pressure on metropolitan areas or provide a stimulus to local development—the act of literally 'breaking new ground' has usually been accompanied by a desire to do so in design terms also. This ambition, and the generally freer circumstances of development control which they enjoy, makes the New Towns vivid carriers of current urban design ideas, and worth examining in those terms. In particular, the design of New Town centres has indicated the ways in which the evolution of new urban components might lead to a reassessment of urban design as a whole.

Among the first New Towns to result from the 1947 New Towns Act, Sir Frederick Gibberd's Harlow New Town now stands as the quintessential image of that post-war liberal democracy envisaged by its founders. Though unmistakably of its own time, it incorporates the familiar images of an English, or perhaps Scandinavian, market place, to give, as Colin Rowe has remarked, 'modern architecture and planning leaning heavily on nostalgia'. Or, to use Sir Hugh Casson's terminology, it seems a masterpiece of the herbivores, before they were driven off by the carnivores of the New Brutalism.

Runcorn New Town Centre would undoubtedly rank among the products of the carnivores. Despite the loss of overdeck housing bridging between its towers, as originally envisaged by David Gosling and the town-centre design team, the imposition of a large-scale urban grid through shopping centre, offices and multi-storey car parks—subsequently reinforced by James Stirling and Michael Wilford's housing to the south—supplied a quite different version of what a New Town centre should be. This project brought together a number of current ideas —notably Ove Arup's tartan grid for structure and services developed at Loughborough University and Kenzo Tange's loop system of circulation roads devised for his Tokyo Bay scheme—in a design for a viable central area funded in large part by commercial developers. A later proposal by the design team in 1967 suggested that the megastructure concept could be extended into the surrounding housing districts with deck-access housing forming continuous all-weather routes from houses to shopping centre. Each access tower of these decks would also serve as a nodal point for cluster groups of single-storey housing. Only the Southgate development by James Stirling succeeded in reflecting this concept.

*Sir Frederick Gibberd and Partners, Harlow New Town, England, master plan, 1951.*

*Sir Frederick Gibberd and Partners, Harlow New Town, market square, 1956–57.*

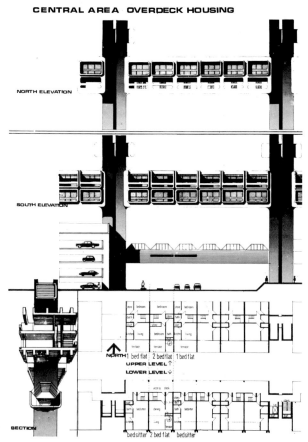

NORTH ELEVATION

SOUTH ELEVATION

SECTION

NORTH 1 bed flat | 2 bed flat | 1 bed flat
UPPER LEVEL ↑
LOWER LEVEL ↓

bedsitter | 2 bed flat | bedsitter

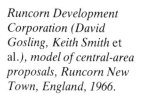

*Runcorn Development Corporation (David Gosling, Keith Smith et al.), model of central-area proposals, Runcorn New Town, England, 1966.*

*David Gosling, overdeck housing scheme for Runcorn New Town central area, 1966.*

*Runcorn Development Corporation, Shopping City, Runcorn New Town, aerial view of the completed phase one project, 1971. The housing in the background (under construction) is James Stirling's Southgate scheme.*

*David Gosling, sequential perspectives of Runcorn New Town central area, 1966.*

The shopping centre was seen as a highly serviced building accommodating change and as a generator of structural, services and circulation systems which would establish the urban megastructure for the central area as a whole. The proposed adjacent deck housing was intended to interlock visually with the overdeck housing spanning the shallow valley and the shopping centre itself. In unequivocably expressing the whole complex of town centre functions as a single unified concept, rather than as a historically accreted collection of buildings, Runcorn exposed the fact that 'urban design' could no longer be regarded as a matter of 'control' or 'coordination', but rather was, indeed, a question of design.

In a curious way, and shorne of its nostalgia, the third and latest English New Town example has more in common with Harlow than Runcorn. Adopting a pattern of single-use pavilions set in a well-landscaped grid of boulevards, Milton Keynes centre reinterpreted the low-density precinctual format of the early English and Scandinavian New Town centres on a larger scale, and in the cool Cartesian language of Mies' original IIT campus design. Thus combining the unlikely mixed economy philosophies of the idealized Socialist New Town with the entrepreneurial convenience of the out-of-town shopping centre in a highly-controlled and elegant architectural language, Milton Keynes, like its predecessors, managed to encapsulate more clearly perhaps than any contemporary urban design project in an existing town, the preoccupations of its makers.

*Keith Smith, John Randle, Law Courts, Runcorn New Town central area, phase two, 1974.*

*Derek Walker and Milton Keynes Development Corporation, Milton Keynes city centre, England, drawn by Helmut Jacoby, 1973.*

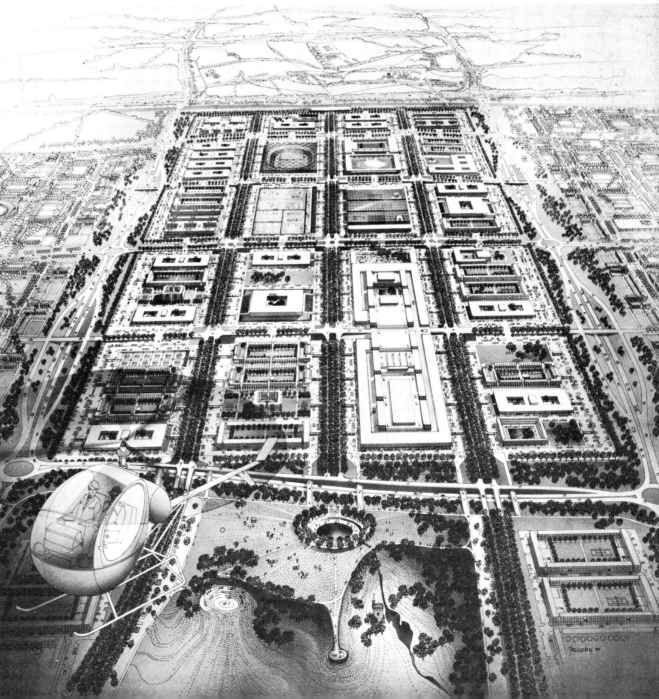

**References:**

Colin Rowe, 'Collage City', *The Architectural Review*, Vol. 158, No. 942, August 1975, p. 74.

Runcorn New Town centre is illustrated, with references, in David Gosling and Barry Maitland, *Design and Planning of Retail Systems*, The Architectural Press, London 1976.

'Milton Keynes Centre (Architect: Derek Walker and Milton Keynes Development Corporation)', *Architectural Design*, June 1973.

*Patrick Hodgkinson,*
*Brunswick Centre,*
*London, England, 1970.*

squares, accommodate mixed uses, be built in a variety of materials and withstand subsequent adaptation, the high-rise buildings of the post-war years were socially, technically and spatially rigid and unadaptable. They were unable to form a 'common building type' which would have the generality, the universal sufficiency of the former model. Thus, 'the Foundling Estate development stems from an attempt to search for a framework and to apply it to a particular locale and set of circumstances'.

The chosen framework was contained in the section of the development, which was linear, low rise and open-ended. Occupying the full width of a city block, the section located housing along both sides, in each case in double stepped-back ranges, so that housing access decks were contained in the sheltered void between the ranges which either looked inward to the central 'valley section' of the block, or out to the adjacent streets. Down the centre of the section ran a shopping mall, with public terraces on the roofs of the shops, and stores, car parking and a cinema incorporated into lower levels. Thus a mixture of commercial and residential uses could be brought together in a high-density development which nevertheless contained a major public space, 'a town room', down its centre which was flanked with housing on a scale to match its extent, while along its perimeter the outer ranges of housing could be kept to a lower scale appropriate to the streets they fronted.

The strength of this sectional idea was attested by its ability to survive numerous major changes in the housing mix and the range of other accommodation, although it was impoverished in detail in the process. Whether it achieved the same universality as the much simpler models invoked by Hodgkinson's original analysis was, however, more problematic. The powerful physical presence of a polemical statement, which has characterized so much Modern. architecture, was precisely that quality which Hodgkinson detected as being inimical to the development of a common, universal language of urbanism: '. . . but now, concerned more with image making and invention, [architects] have lost the thread of logic needed to find a common building type'. Although the centre formed 'an entity of urban scale which should not be extended in length', the section, unique, ingenious and dramatic, was unstoppable, and it is perhaps on the northern and southern edges of the site, where the section is sliced off against the street frontages which face it, that the nature of the dilemma exposed by Hodgkinson's analysis is most poign-

### Central-Area Projects

While all urban design can be said to be fundamentally concerned with establishing a balanced physical framework of public and private interests, of communality and privacy, the search for an appropriate urban design approach has nowhere been more intense, or more frustrated, than in the case of redevelopment projects for the central area of cities. The heightened costs and values of potential development in these locations, the intensification of uses and traffic generation they must contain, and the existing strongly established patterns of life which they must respect, have all made this the most testing, and therefore perhaps the most appropriate, case in which to demonstrate a truly modern urbanism. Examples of such demonstrations and of subsequent reaction to them could

be drawn from any of the countries which have engaged in large-scale urban reconstruction over the past 20 years, but a few projects from Britain serve to illustrate the general experience.

Proposals for the redevelopment of the Foundling Estate in Bloomsbury in London were first prepared in 1960, although eight years of changing clients and briefs were to elapse before construction began on the Brunswick Centre, as it was then christened. Patrick Hodgkinson, the architect for the project (following an initial period with Sir Leslie Martin) has described his design intentions in terms of a search for an urban form as flexible as the eighteenth- and nineteenth-century terraces among which it would be located. In contrast to the English townhouse of that period, which could be tailored to any pocket, could form streets or antly revealed.

The second redevelopment project we shall consider was also first conceived in the early 1960s, at a time when such questions were rarely framed. The 1961 Report prepared by the city planning department of Newcastle-upon-Tyne for the future of the city centre referred to the forthcoming redevelopment process as being 'almost of Central Area revolution rather than evolution', in which the largely Victorian centre would be swept away to 'permit the production of a virtually new centre within a short period'. An important section of this scheme would lie in a prime 4.5 hectare site around Eldon Square, which had been the first piece of formal urban planning to be carried out in Newcastle in 1824–26 by architect John Dobson and builder Richard Grainger.

Once again, the project went through an extended period of tangled negotiation and alterations to the brief, partly influenced in its early stages by the reluctance of the Minister of Housing and Local Government to approve the demolition of the square. By 1972 the architects, Chapman Taylor Partners, had produced some 32 schemes in response to alternative formulations of the brief which was negotiated between the developers, Capital and Counties, and the city authorities. In its final outcome, as completed in 1977, the scheme comprised principally shopping use, with a market, some offices, car parking, bus concourse and a recreation centre.

With retailing as the dominant use, the plan inevitably developed around its circulation pattern of enclosed shopping malls, running between main space users, and connecting to major points of generation of pedestrian traffic, either on adjoining shopping streets, or car parks and bus station. The introspective nature of the ideal double-banked shopping mall, which forms a major public route and yet is also a private, single-purpose space, is notoriously difficult to relate to a surrounding urban structure which it can, in terms of its internal functioning, largely ignore. Requiring no frontage to the outside edges of the development, but only to the central mall, the shopping use, when exposed, offers nothing to the surrounding city. The natural location for this form of development is thus to be embedded in an outward-facing use, either, as in the Brunswick Centre, in housing, or, as has been done elsewhere, behind existing street-fronting commercial uses. One of the difficulties faced by the architects of the Eldon Square project was that for much of the extent of their development, neither form of solution was to be used.

Adopting none of the generalized propositions of city form which Hodgkinson had advocated, they instead inserted their network of internalized routes into the irregular pattern of city blocks defined by the site boundary. And where their building faced out to the surrounding town, and particularly on the important new frontages to Eldon Square, they offered a dignified architectural statement in scale with the public spaces they encountered. Yet the absence of any need on the part of the new development for an organic connection of any sort to the outside along these frontages, and the abrupt transition from the urban order of the streets and squares outside, to that of the malls within, makes it difficult to avoid the analogy so often cited, of a heart transplant, and one in which the species of the donor and recipient are alarmingly different. What happens when rejection occurs is illustrated by our third example.

In 1966 government approval was given to plans to move London's central fruit and vegetable market from its 700-year-old site in Covent Garden to a new location across the river at Battersea. At the same time, a consortium of the Greater London Council, Westminster City Council and Camden was formed to plan the redevelopment, not only of the 5 hectare market site, but of a large surrounding area, amounting to 40 hectares of London's West End. A project team under Ralph Rookwood, and subsequently Geoffrey Holland, proceeded with surveys and appraisals of the area which in 1968 resulted in the publication of a Draft Plan. This was remarkable in being one of the few

attempts to apply the principles of Lynch's work to the evolution of a design. In addition to conventional analyses of land use, traffic studies and so on, the plan included an appraisal of the existing visual structure in terms of nodes, districts, paths, edges and landmarks, and went on to propose 'an overall three-dimensional concept for the area as a whole, dealing broadly with the heights, shapes and siting of major building groups'. The important historic buildings in the area would be retained, but large-scale redevelopment would occur, particularly in the form of two spines along the north and south boundaries, along the lines of major new roads, to accommodate substantial entertainment and cultural uses, as well as a large conference centre, hotels, shops, offices and housing.

The plan was extremely well received and the team moved forward to prepare for its implementation. By 1971, however, doubts were raised as to whether residents had been adequately consulted, and whether their interests would be protected as the pressures of development took hold. In particular, these questions were raised by a member of the planning team, Brian Anson, whose subsequent dismissal from the project, coupled with allegations that the GLC had tried to suppress debate, led to widespread media coverage of the issue, the formation of a Covent Garden Community Association and the gradual spread of opposition to the wholesale redevelopment of the Covent Garden area. This dramatic reversal, which Holland subsequently described as 'what must go down as one of the most extraordinary sequences of events in

*Draft plan for Covent Garden, London, 1968, urban visual analysis.*

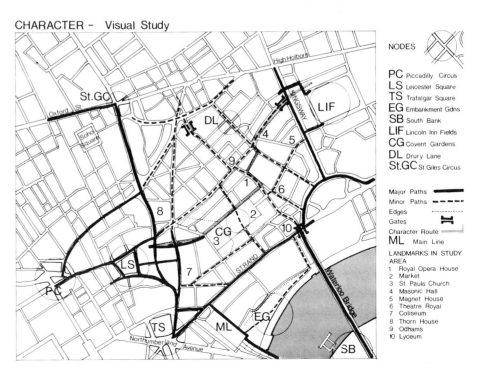

CHARACTER – Visual Study

NODES

PC Piccadilly Circus
LS Leicester Square
TS Trafalgar Square
EG Embankment Gdns
SB South Bank
LIF Lincoln Inn Fields
CG Covent Gardens
DL Drury Lane
St.GC St Giles Circus

Major Paths
Minor Paths
Edges
Gates
Character Route
ML Main Line
LANDMARKS IN STUDY AREA
1 Royal Opera House
2 Market
3 St. Pauls Church
4 Masonic Hall
5 Magnet House
6 Theatre Royal
7 Coliseum
8 Thorn House
9 Odhams
10 Lyceum

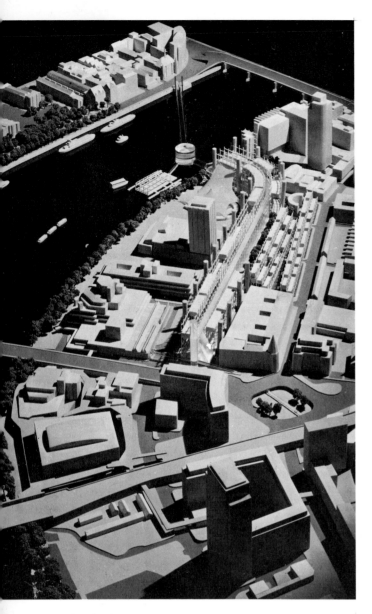

planning history', culminated in 1973 in the outright rejection by the Secretary of State of the GLC plan, the listing of 300 buildings within the area for retention, and the requirement to draw up a new plan with full public participation.

As a result of these events, all proposals for redevelopment in the area, apart from some piecemeal sites, were abandoned and a major programme of rehabilitation by a wide variety of agencies was undertaken. The GLC itself acquired the bulk of the former market authority buildings, and implemented an extensive project to restore and adapt them to new uses, and this pattern was taken up elsewhere with a stream of projects for the imaginative conversion and re-use of old buildings on a scale which would never have been contemplated a few years earlier.

Two further London projects from the late 1970s illustrate the continuing sensitivity of central urban areas to large-scale redevelopment and the way in which the internal requirements of such projects can throw up important new forms of urban development. In 1979 a controversial public enquiry concerning the redevelopment of an area of London's South Bank, known as the Coin Street development, produced a number of opposing schemes. The most notable and most imaginative was that produced by Richard Rogers who was drawn into the controversy, somewhat unwillingly, as architect to one of the developers. He proposed a linear development of mixed uses, with blocks of between nine and twelve storeys ranged along a central spine. Though the proposal contained a high proportion of office space, the plan also included housing and shopping as well as leisure and recreation buildings, and extended into the Thames with the construction of a new pier, funfair and a footbridge across the river. Rogers' proposal

was violently opposed by local pressure groups who claimed that 'London needs more offices like it needs another plague', although it could be argued that Rogers was likely to be one architect with the imagination to revitalize the decayed environment in an appropriate manner. The Beaubourg centre in Paris, designed by Rogers and Piano, was sufficient indication that imaginative twentieth-century urban development could become a major tourist attraction in itself and a distinctive addition to the urban fabric of the city, generating all manner of subsidiary activities.

Earlier in 1979, an equally novel urban component proposed by Norman Foster for Hammersmith was abandoned in the course of controversy between pressure groups and the developer. Foster's plan for a major transport interchange created a new central plaza on land previously occupied by a road intersection. Surrounded by a fortress-like wall of buildings, the roofed central space promised, nevertheless, to provide a lively and much needed public nucleus in west London.

References:

'Brunswick Centre', *The Architectural Review*, Vol. 152, No. 908, October 1972, pp. 196–218.
'Market Values at Eldon Square', *The Architectural Review,* Vol. 161, No. 962, April 1977, pp. 212–26.
*Covent Garden's Moving: Covent Garden Area Draft Plan*, Consortium of Greater London Council, City of Westminster, London Borough of Camden, 1968.
*The Architects' Journal*, Vol. 170, No. 32, 8th August 1979, Richard Rogers' Scheme for Coin Street, London pp. 270–71.
*The Architects' Journal*, Vol. 168, No. 31, 2nd August 1978, Norman Foster's proposals for Hammersmith, London pp. 202–03.

*Richard Rogers, Coin Street development proposals, London, 1979.*

*Foster Associates, Hammersmith development proposals, London, 1979.*

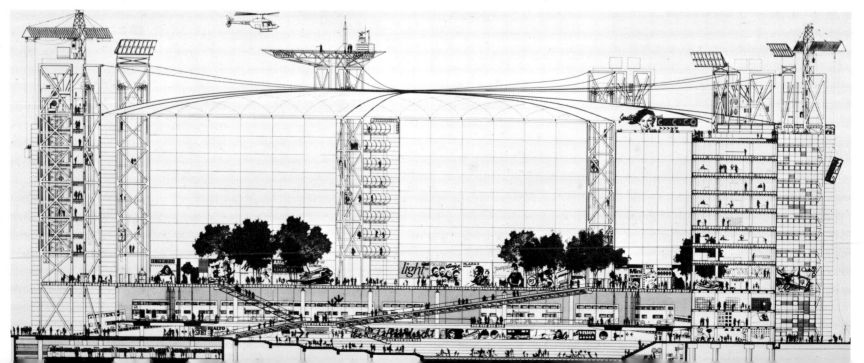

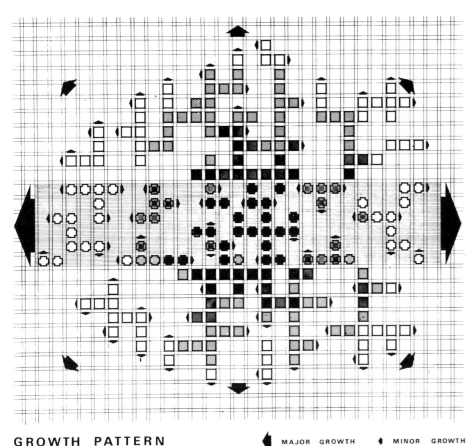

**GROWTH PATTERN**   ◀ MAJOR GROWTH   ◀ MINOR GROWTH

*Arup Associates,
Loughborough
University, England,
master plan, 1966.*

### Universities

The worldwide expansion of university facilities during the 1960s created opportunities for the design of new communities under carefully controlled conditions which were often regarded by their designers as models for more general urban application. Ranging from the great megastructures of Oscar Niemeyer's Brasília University and John Andrews' Scarborough College in Toronto, Canada to the more idiosyncratic designs of Basil Spence at the University of Sussex in England, these ambitious programmes formed an interesting test bed for urban design as well as for academic ideas.

From the wide range of examples available, three projects, one British, one American and one Italian, clearly illustrate the major preoccupations during this period of growth, among which the indeterminate growth of variable functions, the integration of engineering services into building design, and the discipline of systems of circulation in large building complexes, played a major part.

The 1966 Master Plan for Loughborough University by Arup Associates was one of the most influential megastructure concepts of that decade. The basic theme of a tartan-grid dimensional discipline extending across an entire district and accommodating diverse building types within an inte-

grated circulation/services/structural system, was one which had a general relevance, as evidenced by its subsequent use in other quite different situations, such as Shopping City at Runcorn New Town. In particular, Arup's design represented the most lucid attempt to date to come to terms with the needs of both growth and change. An apparent lack of a well-defined initial brief, resulting from the client committee's inability to predict with certainty future developments in teaching disciplines, convinced the architects that such an approach was essential.

The proposals comprised a series of dimensional relationships realized as grids, providing a discipline within which the various parts could be related to each other and to the whole, and made up of four networks:

1 A master grid, defining the structural space unit of growth of building types and with a 'gridline thickness' (or narrow bay width) determined by the space required at the vertical circulation points.

2 A planning grid defining the smallest increment of space common to all *predictable* sizes of rooms and spaces, with a gridline thickness determined by the thickness of partitions and walls.

3 A structure grid defined by the horizontal structural elements, the thickness of which established the grid thickness.

4 The services network defined by the main paths of service runs. This was seen by the designers as space left over between structural grids, coincident with the planning grid to allow services to avoid structural elements and utilize hollow partitions to provide services to rooms.

This attempt to establish a universal solution received a mixed reception from the academic body of the University. Many heads of department took the traditionalist view that purpose-designed laboratories were far more acceptable than rationalized design on such a massive scale, and only the first phases of Arup's plan were constructed. The subsequent, rather chaotic development of the campus forms a sad rejoinder to that decision.

Kallmann and McKinnell's 1972 plan for Athletic Facilities at Harvard owed much to the Loughborough theories, and placed particular emphasis on 'movement systems as generators of built form'. A contemporary article in *Architectural Record* recognized the influence of the Loughborough plan, and also drew attention to the wider urban design implications of the use of the circulation systems to generate the plan: '... as building complexes become larger, and their programs more and more indeterminate, they tend increasingly towards neutral configurations.... However, if generated solely by its own autonomous system, the built form can become alienated from the context and present to the immediate environment only the manifestation of an internal logic.... An architecture organized by an infrastructure of movement systems is able to reinforce the urban structure that is itself generated by patterns of mobility. Not only can the movement system of the building extend to that of the city, but the linear organizations that result from such a morphology can adjust themselves to and reinforce existing or embryonic street patterns and the enclosure of the built form can become also the walls of the street.'

The plan proposed a single spine system with a linear aggregation of sports halls. Besides accommodating an integrated service system of locker rooms, showers, mechanical equipment and storage, the spine allowed for the segregated movement of spectators at an upper level and athletes at ground level as required in this building type. Growth and permutation becomes possible by linear extension or infill between the sports halls. A similar planning device was used in 1970 proposals for a Leisure Centre at Irvine New Town in Scotland, completed in 1976, and has provided the basis for a number of similar building projects in which clearly articulated circulation and services distribution systems must be reconciled with an unpredictable accretion of variable spaces, as in the British 'HARNESS' hospital system, which drew attention to the analogy with the wiring harness principle adopted for the electrical systems of mass produced cars.

The 1972 prize-winning competition entry for the development of Florence University, designed by Vittorio Gregotti and Associates, suggested a more formalistic and less flexible approach than either Harvard or Loughborough. Nevertheless, like Loughborough, it is seen as a development of urban scale. The scheme is ranged as a series of massive walled decks, with road traffic circulation at ground level and a proposed metro as an overhead system with stopping points within the complex and a downward distribution of pedestrian traffic. The five main longitudinal 'walled' units contain the academic facilities, whereas a much looser arrangement of latitudinal buildings accommodates a variety of purposes including sports stadia, cafeterias, and service buildings. Three squat tower units in the centre of the complex, which are not clearly integrated in the general scheme, contain the administration.

In morphological terms, the proposals have been described as 'conceived as an articulated portion of the city which compares territorially with the historic centres of Florence and Prato—the foundation of large parallel blocks measures and reduces to an urban dimension the territorial interval between Florence and Prato.' It may be argued that such a massive visual intrusion in the Florentine landscape is of dubious value. Nevertheless, it provides one of the last and most powerful architectural statements of megastructure theory, carried to an abstract form quite unlike other major academic developments.

**References:**
Loughborough University of Technology, *Arup Associates Master Plan Development*, Interim Report 1967, p. 3.
*Architectural Record*, November 1975.
*Casabella*, No. 361/1972, p. 25.

*Kallmann and McKinnell, Athletics Facilities, Harvard University, 1972, interior.*

*Kallmann and McKinnell, Athletics Facilities, Harvard University, Cambridge, Massachusetts, US, 1972, linear development plan.*

*Vittorio Gregotti and Associates, prize-winning competition design for the University of Florence, Italy, 1972.*

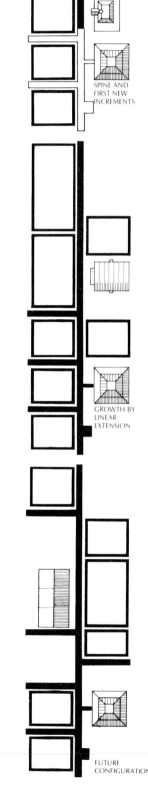

SPINE AND FIRST NEW INCREMENTS

GROWTH BY LINEAR EXTENSION

FUTURE CONFIGURATION

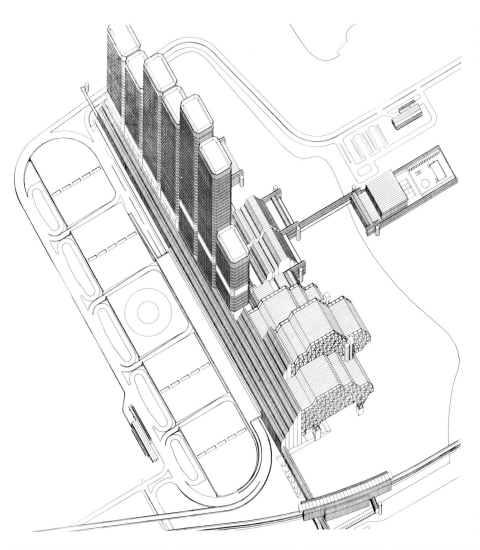

*Cesar Pelli, competition design for UN City, Vienna, Austria, 1969.*

*Building Design Partnership, competition design for UN City, 1969, sectional model.*

## Competition: UN City

This selection of projects which draw ordering principles of general urban design relevance from the specific resolution of their individual programmes, concludes with one further building type, the large-scale administrative complex and in particular with a competition for a major project of this sort.

Among competition projects for individual buildings, some are, by their size, by the variety of their functions and by their need to take account of growth and change, inevitably seen as models of city form. Such was the case with the competition held in 1969 for UN City in Vienna. The brief called for office and support accommodation for the UN agencies together with a large conference centre for the city, and envisaged a working population in the complex of some 30,000 people with 5,000 cars. The site was in the Donaupark, a flat area of land between the old and new channels of the Danube on the east side of the city centre.

The first prize-winning design for the first stage of the competition was submitted by an American team from Gruen Associates led by Cesar Pelli. This took two ordering principles from the field of urban commercial architecture and combined them in an original way. The first of these was the tower and podium arrangement of office and supporting functions familiar from the Lever Building and a host of subsequent projects, and the second the use of a spine mall as an ordering element for a series of irregular horizontal elements. The latter theme has been used by Pelli in a number of his projects, such as that for the Santa Anita Fashion Park shopping centre in Arcadia, California, where the conventional shopping mall, which normally forms a subservient link between major department stores, emerged out of the building mass to become a large, extruded, open-ended and asymmetric glazed section into the sides of which the one-off elements plugged. At the much larger scale of the Vienna project, this major circulation spine was supplemented by secondary spurs running off at 48 metre intervals between blocks occupied by conference centre auditoria, restaurants and other support functions. Against the horizontal extension of these elements were set the offices in, not one tower, but a whole series of abutting towers of varying height. The two ordering ideas were then welded together by locating the range of towers directly over the mall, like the spinal plates of a Stegosaurus, so that the central route became the generator also of the spurs of vertical circulation rising up through the offices.

Like the Pelli design, that submitted by the British firm Building Design Partnership (which was placed second in the first stage competition) offered a particularly coherent urban image. Indeed, its authors saw this as an important reference for the design, '... in effect a linear city ... a microcosm of life and movement ... a truly urban environment ... the heart of the building, being a series of interlocking streets, becomes an extension of the city centre, establishing a new, self-contained district with shops and restaurants; and all the necessities of a thriving urban community. Its internal and external communications systems ensure convenience of travel within, and to and from the city centre. Like all the best towns it gives shelter from the elements but is closely linked to the outdoors.' This emphasis on the public circulation as the focus of the design paralleled the Gruen scheme, but here the concourse was not an independent design element on to which other functions were locked, but rather it was a central route formed by the A-frame configuration of the functions. This section, again with recognizable precedents such as Tange's Tokyo Bay and Boston Harbor projects, was here developed as an ordering principle of urban form which could accept a multiplicity of uses, maintain future options for growth, and yet create integral public spaces of great scale and richness.

Sadly, neither of these two projects was built, despite the selection of the BDP design in the second stage of the competition by eight of the nine judges. Instead, in a decision which caused widespread controversy, the Austrian government commissioned an Austrian architect, Johan Staber, to build the design which now stands in the Donaupark.

An interesting postscript to the UN City project is provided by a series of subsequent governmental centre projects around the world—of which Savioli's 1973 project for Cannes and 1977 proposal for Florence are examples—which built upon the design ideas expressed by BDP in the earlier Vienna competition. Savioli's proposal for a variable or flexible centre for Cannes had a fluidity in its design which was lacking in many of the contemporary megastructure schemes. More interesting, however, was the 1977 competition scheme for a regional administrative centre for Florence. Comparatively unknown, this project epitomized the megastructure idea with a design lyricism quite unlike any comparable scheme.

James Stirling and Michael Wilford's 1977 competition entry for an administrative centre for

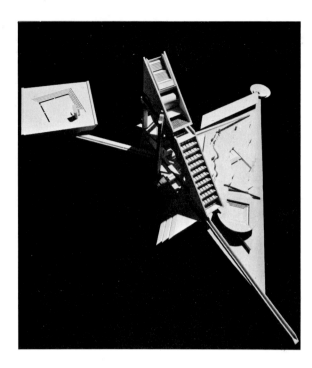

L. Savioli, competition design for a regional administrative centre for Florence, Italy, 1977.

James Stirling, Michael Wilford and Associates, competition design for an administrative centre for Tuscany, Italy, 1977.

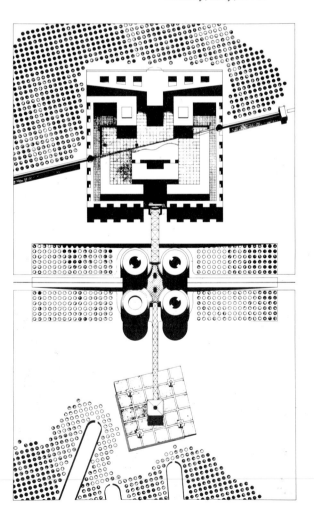

Tuscany showed a totally different approach, described by its authors thus: '... the need to preserve as much of the valley as a green zone for Florence ... suggested a compact and protected group of buildings for the new Regional Headquarters of Tuscany.... The new complex was positioned a little distant from Castello to allow a pole of urbanism to develop that was not entangled with the outbuildings of Castello. Nevertheless very strong connections were developed between Castello and the new centre. The "stone garden" element which was nearest Castello was a threshold, a front door step, for the sequence of buildings which make up the complex—"garden/gateway/island". From this threshold there were sheltered walkways through the woods connecting with the new railway station and important streets in Castello.... The area round the site had been laid out in the 1st century BC and the Roman grid superimposed on the valley has influenced the subsequent development of fields, dykes, roads, etc., this still being visible today. A Roman grid line runs through the central plaza and this antique sign was utilized to position and shape the new buildings. Walkways out of the island into the adjoining fields and woods are along "Roman Walls" that correspond with this Roman grid.'

Stirling and Wilford also designed in 1978 a competition entry for the government centre at Doha, Qatar, in the Arabian Gulf. This scheme, like Stirling's German projects, showed a marked change of direction in design philosophy from earlier work. The serried ranks of Ministry buildings along the coast, linked by monorail, have similarities to Niemeyer's earlier work on the ministry blocks in Brasília in terms of their highly formal composition.

References:

Gruen Associates, *U.N. City*, report 1969.

Building Design Partnership, *International Organizations Headquarters and Conference Centre in Vienna*, report 1970.

Leonardo Savioli, 'Concurso Nazionale Aniacap', *Domus*, October 1973.

## 3.5 FORMAL SOLUTIONS: THE CITY AS COHERENT EXPERIENCE

ALTHOUGH THE PRECEDING CASE STUDIES HAVE BEEN presented as drawing their particular characteristics in each case from a concentration on just one aspect of the collection of problems faced by the urban designer, we might suspect that in most cases the original impetus to consider the question of urban design at all lay elsewhere. For it is the unresolved and unsatisfactory visual or formal quality of our urban environment which seems to act as the starting point for many investigations of alternative possibilities. And while economic, social and other underlying causes of urban disorganization may be acknowledged, most urban designers seem to retain some conviction that they can make a specific contribution to the reduction of visual squalor, monotony or illegibility in our cities. In the projects which follow, a great variety of alternative models of coherent urban form are offered as an alternative to that existing state.

### Designers: The Rationalists

Most fundamental attempts to design solutions for urban problems have claimed, at least, to proceed in an inductive manner, progressing logically from an analysis of the technical, social, economic and other manifestations of the problem, without pre-judging the formal outcome, to arrive finally at a proposition, in a design form, of a resolution of these difficulties. Whether such a method can or should be applied to a design problem like the city may be debated, but it certainly seems to have been a common accompaniment to the mechanical analogy, by which the city may be regarded as a gigantic machine with certain clear functions to perform. According to this view, traditional city forms have no specific validity except in so far as they perform their necessary functions, and when problems arise we may, indeed should, set these forms aside and redesign the machine from scratch. In fact we should be constantly searching for improved models, so that a New Town or utopian project may be considered as an opportunity to formulate a new possibility (the use in Britain of the engineering jargon of Mark I, Mark II and Mark III for New Towns confirms this), a Whittle or Wankel engine for the next generation of urban models. The rejection of this approach has tended to lie with the equally polarized conservationist or neo-vernacular view that whatever expedient steps must be taken to solve the functional difficulties, the appearance and texture of preferred historical models must be sustained.

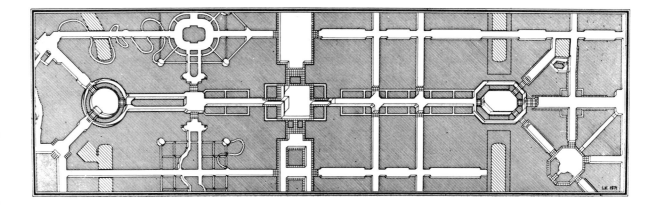

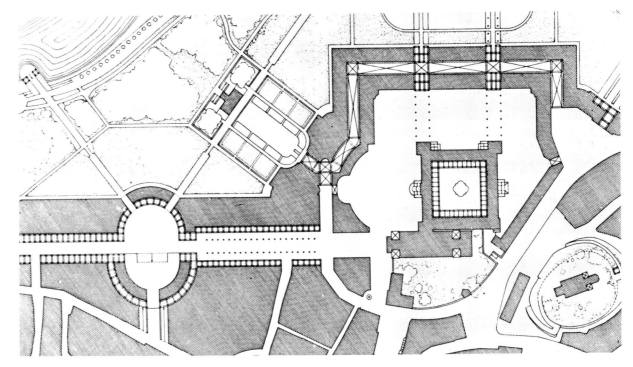

*Rob Krier, project for the centre of Leinfelden, West Germany, 1971.*

*Leon Krier, project for Echternach, Luxembourg, 1970, plan of the central area.*

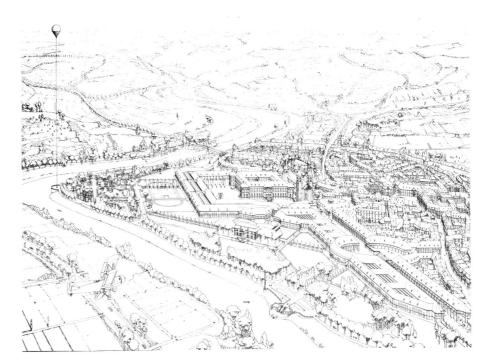

*Leon Krier, project for Echternach, Luxembourg, 1970, perspective.*

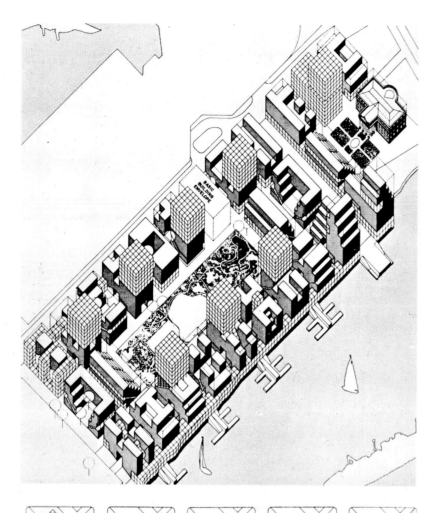

*O. M. Ungers, competition design for Welfare Island, New York City, US, 1975, axonometric.*

*O. M. Ungers, competition design for Welfare Island, New York City, 1975, detailed axonometrics.*

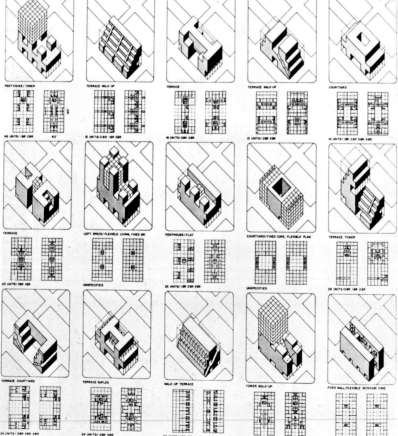

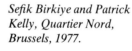

*Sefik Birkiye and Patrick Kelly, Quartier Nord, Brussels, 1977.*

While these crude descriptions of extreme positions may be no more than caricatures, it would be true to say that for all the painstaking surveys and analyses of existing city environments, they tend to omit, between the considerations of the city as functional systems and as historic or pictorial ambience, any appreciation, except in the vaguest terms, of how existing cities work in architectural or urban design terms. A group of designers, such as the Rationalists, who concern themselves with the morphology and structure of towns in this sense, is therefore offering something of importance. However, as Albert Einstein put it: 'Without an anticipatory world view we don't know how to approach the data'. Before looking at how the Rationalists have used the 'data' offered by the conventional forms and patterns of cities, we should therefore say something of their 'anticipatory world view'. As set out in Leon Krier's essay 'The Reconstruction of the City', this view includes a number of themes relating to architectural, planning, technical and political issues. Firstly, Modern architecture has been an unqualified disaster, responsible for 'a cultural tragedy to which there is no precedent in history' and by its servitude to speculators an instrument in a greater destruction of European cities 'both physically and socially than in any other period of their history, including the two world wars'. Coupled with the sterility of Modern architecture (exemplified by the 'obsessive emptiness' of the Plaza of the Three Powers in Brasília) is the bureaucratization of planning into a meaningless obsession with 'endless reports and regulations on isolated technical problems—real

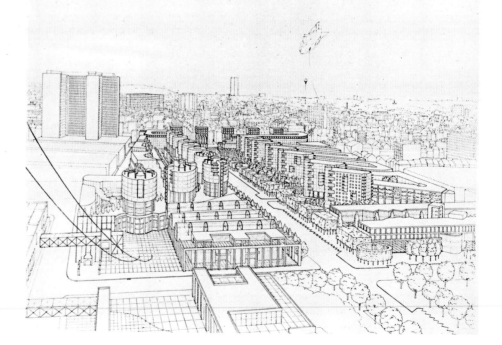

orgies of quantitative thinking....' These catastrophes have been accompanied by a third, the decimation of 'an artisanal building culture' by the pursuit of the ephemeral benefits of industrialization. And finally, the solution to these ills, 'a rationalist theory of the city and of its architecture', if it is not to become 'reduced to a style', must be 'part of an integral vision of society, it has to be part of a political struggle.'

Equipped with this cataclysmic view of recent history, familiar enough from the polemics of the Modern Movement itself (the essay even refers, as did Le Corbusier 50 years before, to 'a new spirit' which can be felt, appeals to 'precise facts' and speaks of the 'rediscovery of the primary elements of architecture ...') the Rationalists, a group whose work was first shown at the 15th Milan Triennale organized by Aldo Rossi, with a catalogue entitled *Architettura Razionale*, set about studying the data. Arguing that historical city centres form 'desirable models of collective life', they studied the elements presented by the traditional city, 'the street, the square, the quartier' in terms of their use of 'urban space as the primary organizing element of the urban morphology'. This study was directed to seek out generic 'types', again a familiar pursuit and again, as in Le Corbusier's *objets-type*, to be revealed, not by 'high art', but by anonymous products, in this case of the city. These types are not function types but form- and space-types, typical configurations of the public realm as carved out of the urban material available, of whatever use. Idealized and purified of their contextual associations they could then be reapplied to specific conditions. Rob Krier's project for the centre of Leinfelden and Leon Krier's for Echternach, for example, both propose monumental systems of public spaces of this kind across the fabric of existing towns.

In the work of O.M. Ungers, such as the Welfare Island Competition of 1975 and project for housing at Lichterfelde, Berlin of 1976, the urban block was investigated as the 'fixed typological unit', again in a series of standard variants of a generic theme. Leon Krier's studies of Luxembourg investigated the city 'as a federation of quarters' (studies of historic cities having established that urban quarters never exceed 33 hectares), and the notion of the quarter as a valid increment of urban design was taken up in other projects, such as Sefik Birkiye and Patrick Kelly's 1977 scheme for Quartier Nord in Brussels. These large-scale type-studies were also accompanied by more local, but no less generic, manifestations of the public realm.

*Leon Krier, St Peter's Square and a projected new piazza at the junction of the via Condotti and the via Corso, part of Krier's 'Roma Interrotta' proposals, 1979. The drawings illustrate Krier's idea for* rione *or* centri rionali *(social centres) of a new kind. Both urban monuments and social facilities, these would replace the now defunct 'sclerosed institutions'.*

In particular, Leon Krier's projects for a new public building type, a social centre typically comprising a roofed square with cafés, workshops, small libraries and other sympathetic functions housed in the supporting columns, proposed a focus for the social life of the new quarter which would 'soon replace the decadent institutions of church and State, the cathedrals, the schools, the "case popolare".'

Though sometimes pursued with as ruthless a disregard for the surrounding urban fabric as the redevelopment projects they condemned, the obsessive concern for the character, shape and organization of public space exhibited in these projects gave their vision of the meaning of the term 'urban design' a particular urgency. The fact that it was expressed in terms familiar enough to those who, having developed doubts about the efficacy of the Modern Movement nevertheless felt unable to abandon its rigorous climate in favour of the more soporific alternatives of conservation, townscape and the rest, could only make it more acceptable.

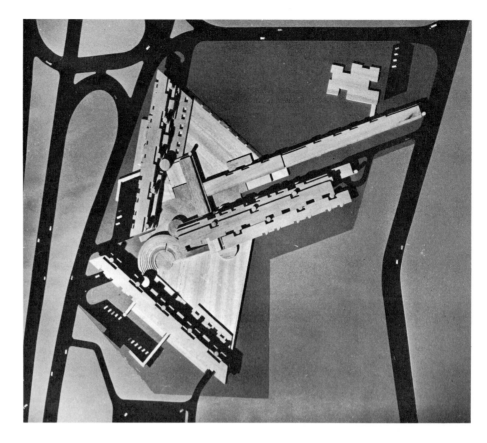

*Carlo Aymonino and Aldo Rossi, Gallaratese Housing, Milan, Italy, 1967–72, aerial view of the model.*

*Carlo Aymonino and Aldo Rossi, Gallaratese Housing, Milan, 1967–72.*

**References:**

Leon Krier, 'The Reconstruction of the City' in *Rational Architecture*, Archives d'Architecture Moderne, 1978.

Alan Colquhoun, 'Rational Architecture', in *Architectural Design*, June 1975, pp. 365–70.

*Architectural Design*, March 1977, 'Tafuri/Culot/Krier: The Role of Ideology', pp. 187–213.

*Architectural Design*, April 1978, 'Urban Transformations', pp. 218–66.

*Architectural Design*, January 1979, 'Typological and Morphological Elements of the Concept of Urban Space' by Rob Krier, pp. 2–17 and 'The Cities Within a City' by Leon Krier, pp. 18–32.

Rob Krier, *Urban Space* (foreword by Colin Rowe), Academy Editions, London 1979 (first published in Germany as *Stadtraum* in 1975).

*Aldo Rossi, Gallaratese Housing, Milan, 1969–73, elevations.*

## Historic City Conservation

For those cities where a sizeable area of homogeneous older construction may have survived, the Rationalists' contention that the city itself provides models for its own restitution may be translated into a demand that all further investment be channelled into the precise and authentic restoration of that former model. The dynamic of the modern city, and its corresponding ability to aggravate natural processes of decay, have made it necessary to adopt a calculated attitude towards the conservation of its older parts. So long as building methods remained fairly stable over long periods of time, and development cycles reasonably long, the survival of large sections of a city's history alongside its newer parts could be expected. Just as eighteenth-century cities began to adopt and preserve areas of nature within their boundaries, so now self-conscious decisions about older quarters of the city itself must be made, if their survival in anything like authentic condition is to be effected. These decisions involve questions of funding, viability, technique and control as rigorous in their way as those applied to the instigation of new development.

An excellent example of this, and perhaps the most successful in Latin America, is that offered by the continuing efforts to conserve the city of Ouro Preto over the last 50 years. A regional colonial capital of Brazil, Ouro Preto was founded by Portuguese settlers in 1674 and grew in the eighteenth century with the mining of gold and precious stones in the state of Minas Gerais. Its architecture included some of the best examples of Brazilian Baroque, including work by the sculptor/master mason Aleijudinho ('the little cripple'). Unlike the neighbouring town of Sabarà for instance, where examples of florid Plateresque are as ornate as corresponding late Baroque in the Iberian Peninsula, its architecture is dramatically simplified, leading some observers to draw parallels between it and the work of modern Brazilian architects like Niemeyer.

In the nineteenth century, the state capital was moved and Ouro Preto declined in importance, preserving its original form intact. However, the outstanding quality of the town was recognized by the state government in Belo Horizonte and attempts were begun in 1925 to restore individual buildings. In 1933 the national government designated it a national monument and commissioned a plan for its restoration, as a result of which a government Department for Historic and Artistic Conservation (Servico do Patrimônio Histórico e Artistico Nacional) was established in 1937.

The work was given additional impetus by financial support from UNESCO in 1968, and in 1970 a major survey and planning study was initiated, covering not only building conditions but also landscape conservation and an appraisal of the whole urban structure of Ouro Preto and nearby Mariana. This report, prepared by the autonomous government physical planning agency Fundaçao João Pinheiro, constituted one of the most thorough studies of its kind, ranging from proposals to consolidate the natural setting of the city—a central square and town hall set on a mountain ridge with alleyways and streets cascading down the hillsides and various churches built on natural rock platforms below—to detailed surveys of traditional building elements. The gradual and continuing work at Ouro Preto—to remove overhead power lines and manage traffic for example—has been made all the more urgent by plans for the construction of large-scale industrial developments in the surrounding areas, which will entail the protection, both visually and ecologically, of the whole Ouro Preto–Mariana district.

The importance of involving the whole community affected by conservation on this scale in the processes of that effort is demonstrated by the case of the New Town area of Edinburgh in Scotland. The area comprises one of the most extensive and coherent examples of Georgian city building in Europe, and concern at its worsening condition during the 1960s culminated in 1970 in a conference entitled 'The Conservation of Georgian Edinburgh' which was supported by the Scottish Georgian Society, the Cockburn Association (Edinburgh Civic Trust) and the residents' associations. A voluntary survey of the external fabric of all 11,000 properties in the 310 hectare central area, carried out by the Edinburgh Architectural Association, was presented to the conference, as a

*Ouro Preto, Brazil, general view of the city which was part of a major conservation plan by the Fundação João Pinheiro.*

*Aleijudinho, Baroque church, Ouro Preto.*

*Oscar Niemeyer, Hotel, Ouro Preto. One of the few modern developments.*

*Ouro Preto, view of the central square which has now become totally pedestrian.*

result of which central and local government together agreed to set up the New Town Conservation Committee on which both they and the voluntary bodies which had organized the conference, including the residents, would be represented. This committee then acted as a channel for advice and grants to a large number of individual conservation projects which were initiated within the area, either by individual property owners or the 50 street associations and larger amenity groups. The overall priorities for repair and restoration were implemented through a grant system inversely related to the value of property, so that the highest grants were given to owners of property on the 'tattered fringes' of the area, and were reinforced by financial incentives to adjoining owners to undertake 'mutual' repairs. Above all, the committee appointed a full-time executive Director, Desmond Hodges, to implement this policy and to run a conservation centre in a shop in the New Town. This provided an exhibition of the committee's work, a central library of architectural details in the New Town, and information on the proper maintenance and repair of features such as cast-iron railings, glazing bars, slate and lead roof coverings, and especially the sandstone walling from which the greater part of the city is made, as well as acting as a central clearing-house for the collection and re-use of salvaged stone and other materials.

If examples like Ouro Preto and Edinburgh New Town illustrate the determination and professionalism required to sustain a conservation programme for an area undergoing gradual deterioration, it is perhaps the examples of abrupt and catastrophic destruction of older cities which bring out most vividly the motives which lie behind efforts at restoration. The powerful attachment of people to urban areas of particular character indicates the inadequacy of any analysis of urban design which treats it as the provision of a simple commodity. The explicit identification by the German people of their culture with the urban forms of Nuremberg, for example, made that city a target for destruction by allied bombers. Similarly, the punishment of the citizens of Warsaw for the 1944 rising was the systematic destruction of their city by the German army, and its subsequent reconstruction was an act of more than utilitarian significance.

To describe the reconstruction of the old quarter of Warsaw as 'conservation' could hardly be less accurate, since in 1945 hardly a stone was left standing, and yet in a sense it is the most complete and perfect example of the preservation of an historical area of a city. Painstakingly rebuilt from architectural students' measured drawings, Canaletto paintings and old photographs, the reproduction is entirely authentic and forms perhaps the most disturbing of all war memorials. Without making any overt monumental gesture, it impresses simply through the knowledge that it is now as it used to be, but for a time was not there at all. Extreme as this example is, the layering of new symbolic or associational values onto existing structures by the decision to conserve and restore them is a phenomenon shared perhaps inevitably by all rehabilitation projects.

*James Gillespie, Moray Place, Edinburgh New Town, Scotland, 1820–.*

*Warsaw, Poland, post-1945 reconstruction.*

**References:**

Fundação João Pinheiro *Plano de Conservação, Valorização e Desenvolvimento de Ouro Preto e Mariana* 1975.

Colin McWilliam, *New Town Guide: The Story of Edinburgh's Georgian New Town*, 1978.

B.S. Maitland, 'When the Duck Speaks for the State', *Architectural Design*, Vol. 49, No. 3–4, 1979, pp. 96–97.

## Design Guides

The conservation of unique historical areas of cities provides a highly specialized case of the general problem of achieving unity and coherence of urban form. In such cases, history itself provides the model, complete in every detail. Where no such given model exists, however, attempts have been made to devise and impose one, through development control and in particular through its instrument, the design guide.

The idea of urban design as a form of development control has a long history. One of the earliest recorded building laws is a statute of 1262 regulating the form of houses fronting the Piazza del Campo in Siena, and in the following century a further regulation enforcing compatibility of window design with that of the Palazzo Pubblico was adopted. Unlike, say, the Piazza Ducale in Vigevano which was designed and constructed as a single development, or the Piazza di SS. Annunziata in Florence, whose sides each formed one project, related by its architect to what had gone before and as it were forming the next phase of a 200-year programme, the Piazza del Campo was thus largely formed by the imposition of a public idea upon a large number of private actions. Control of this kind was also exerted informally in the past by powerful individuals; the story is told in Chester of a nineteenth-century Duke of Westminster, the important local landowner, who stopped his carriage in front of a newly completed building on the Rows, clad in white faience, and gave orders for it to be immediately covered in half-timbering to make it match its mediaeval neighbours. On the whole, however, legislation governing the height, form and details of buildings has until recently been concerned more with matters of public health and safety than of appearance (although the effect of such legislation on the appearance of towns has been enormous).

The notion of the town as a single conception which unavoidably had to be delegated in some measure to others, gave rise in this century to a reconsideration of controlling legislation as an instrument for achieving the grand design. This at any rate would seem to be the underlying assumption of the design control practised in the early years of Brasília to ensure uniformity of approach with Oscar Niemeyer's central-area buildings among other architects practising in that part of the city. The magazine *Módulo*, founded and directed by Niemeyer, set out the reasoning behind this rigid policy in a leading article in 1959, entitled

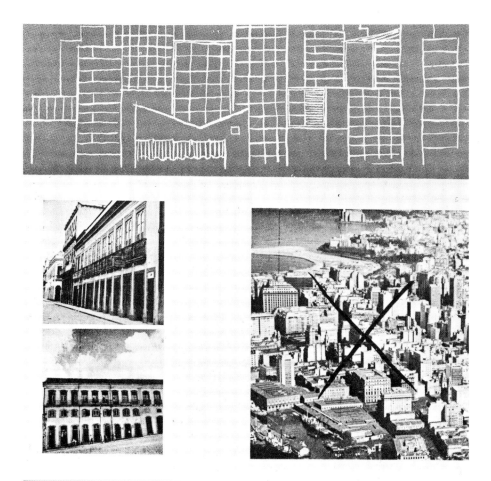

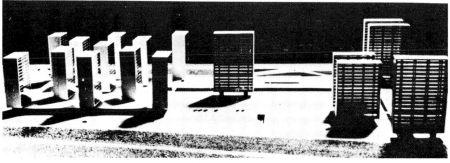

*Oscar Niemeyer, proposals for the Brasília Design Guide, Brazil, 1959.*

*Central office zone of Brasília, 1976, showing the adherence to general massing and design regulations.*

'City Planning Unity'. Historical towns, it argued, achieved unity through the repetition of restricted solutions, but: 'In the cities of today, on the other hand, modern architecture has been wooed by techniques which afford a vast range of possibilities and has fallen away from this ancient virtue, and become reduced to a conglomeration of structures, some of them of great merit, considered individually, but having nothing in common with one another and presenting as a group a deplorable picture of confusion and lack of harmony.' Such a fall from grace could only be corrected by the imposition of a stringent artificial control to take the place of the former limitations: 'It may be that Brasília will exercise a salutary influence on Brasilian architecture in the field of city planning, by disciplining the use of masses and open spaces and by restoring among architects the concern with unity.'

The chilling tone of this passage was reflected in the buildings which the policy engendered, and subsequent design guides have generally not felt it necessary to take such a universally disapproving line on the state of existing cities, but rather have sought out those aspects of their development which might be encouraged and those which should be suppressed. This approach was adopted, for example, by the San Francisco Department of City Planning in its preparation of citywide 'urban design guidelines' as a framework for more detailed urban design plans at district and neighbourhood levels. The framework depended first upon an analysis of the city as a set of fairly discrete 'design units', identifiable by the distinctive natural or man-made character peculiar to each. This definition of 'visual districts' indicated the qualities of each part of the city which could be enhanced, and urban design guidelines were then formulated to achieve this, under five specific headings: 'Urban Design Guidelines for Open Space and Landscaping'; 'Urban Design Guidelines for Streets'; 'Urban Design Policy for Protecting Street Views and Street Space'; 'Urban Design Guidelines for the Height of Buildings'; and 'Urban Design Guidelines for the Bulk of Buildings'.

Such an approach, permitting exceptions but offering a consensus view of the particular qualities of a city which each new development should respect, was obviously a more flexible form of urban design control than the Brasília example, although, like most such regulatory documents, it shared some of the historical pessimism of that policy, being based on the view that some distinctive quality had been, or was about to be, lost, and that restrictive legislation would be necessary to

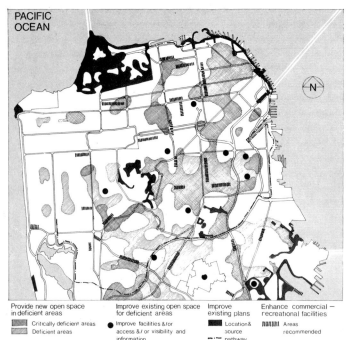

PROPOSED URBAN DESIGN GUIDELINES FOR OPEN SPACE

*San Francisco Department of City Planning, proposed urban design guidelines for open space, San Francisco, US, 1969–70.*

save it. For San Francisco, as for Toronto, London and many other cities, it was primarily the eruption during the 1960s of high buildings in the downtown area which persuaded planners of the need for such a policy, but this was not the only form of large-scale disruption to have this effect. In Britain, the first and most comprehensive attempt to define an urban design policy on a regional rather than individual city scale was made by the County Council of Essex in 1973, and was motivated by the expansion of suburban housing across the county and its effects upon the character of towns and villages. Under the project leadership of Melville Dunbar, a design guide for housing development in the county was prepared which amounted to a textbook of the aesthetics of town design, of appropriate road engineering standards and of domestic planning for privacy and amenity. Reinforced by case-study examples of permitted and unacceptable forms of development, and backed by the apparatus of planning approvals, developers were urged to choose between a 'new rural' or 'Arcadian' mode of residential layout in which landscape was to dominate, and a 'new urban' mode of mews and courts in which buildings formed enclosed urban spaces. The conventional 'suburban' mode in which neither landscape nor buildings dominate was to be avoided and in addition the traditional materials, construction details and landscape species of Essex were to be adopted.

The challenge offered by the Essex design guide to what had previously been assumed to be the largely impervious and universal tide of suburban

estates which spread across the country, was taken up by other authorities in the United Kingdom. For some areas, such as the Peak District National Park, the existence of a strong and largely intact vernacular meant that the design guide could consist primarily of an extensive description of a particular architectural language which all new building must adopt. The intention of such design guides was undoubtedly to take the principle of urban design control beyond both the rigidly restrictive edicts of Brasília and the somewhat loose formulations of city 'character' in San Francisco, to re-create the conditions of a genuinely creative tradition. Like all legislation, however, their wisdom tends to be retrospective, working best on well-rehearsed problems. The application of a traditional vocabulary to a non-traditional building problem, such as a superstore as occurred in the new Essex township of South Woodham Ferrers, may require a creative extension of that vocabulary in a way which a design guide cannot anticipate, and without which tradition becomes rapidly subverted into pastiche.

**References:**

Paul Zucker, *Town and Square*, Columbia University Press, New York 1959, p. 87.

*Módulo*, Vol. 2, No. 12, February 1959.

San Francisco Department of City Planning, *Preliminary Report No. 8: Urban Design Plans*, 1970.

County Council of Essex, *A Design Guide for Residential Areas*, 1973.

Peak Park Planning Board, *Building Design Guide: Peak National Park*, 1976.

## Village Projects

Despite its small scale, the village encapsulates the problem of consistency in urban design in a peculiarly intense way. Limited in extent and isolated in setting, its character is particularly susceptible to casual development, which, in logistic planning terms, may seem innocuous or even beneficial.

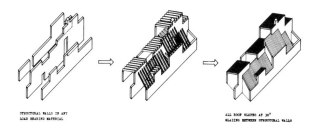

*James Stirling, Village Project for Team X, 1955.*

This problem motivated James Stirling's Village Project for Team X in 1955: '... a reaction to driving through country villages and finding at the other end perhaps half a dozen houses tacked on by the local authority, usually semi-d's, unsympathetic to the scale and materials of the village. One had to propose a system appropriate to the size and formation of the English village and, therefore, it had to continue the linear street pattern.' Stirling's 'system', comprising in principle three parallel structural walls with lean-to roofs, using 'any material, according to locality', thus offered an architectural language derived from a generic condition of the traditional village—the linear form. As Stirling himself noted, the English village also adopted another configuration at times, in its grouping of buildings around a common open space, and this clustering principle has provided the basis for several projects by Aldington and Craig, which have been recognized as outstanding additions to small existing communities.

In addition to being, in practical terms, a special case of certain general urban design problems, the village has also provided a metaphor for the larger town, a model doubly condensed in those miniature villages, like 'Legoland' in Jutland, which exert such a fascination on visitors. This sense of compacted scale is particularly vividly evoked in that most artful of villages, Portmeirion, built for himself on the North Wales coast by Clough Williams-Ellis, and provides a key to other projects for which the idea of 'village' is a central reference. reference.

An excellent example of this is provided by the design of Charles Moore and William Turnbull for Kresge College, part of the Santa Cruz campus of

*Aldington and Craig, village housing, Bledlow, Bucks, England, 1978, street view.*

*Aldington and Craig, village housing, Bledlow, 1978, view of inner court.*

*Charles Moore and William Turnbull, Kresge College, University of California at Santa Cruz, US, 1965–74, plan.*

the University of California. Built in a secluded forest setting, the community of 350 resident students with its library, dining hall and other common facilities is housed in an irregularly grouped sequence of stuccoed wood-frame buildings along a meandering street. This street is structured, first by the disposition of the main common buildings at its ends, like magnet stores in a shopping centre, and then by a series of idiosyncratic land-marks, or 'trivial monuments' as the architects called them, set out along its length—an entrance gate, a fountain, a speaker's rostrum painted red, white and blue, and so on. 'These are meant, without prejudicing the freedom of students to make their own new institutions, to signal to them where they are.' The jokey, theatrical element which this project shares with Portmeirion is not accidental. It makes it possible for the designer to offer an ordering framework without seeming to impose it, and to enrich his settings with historical or memorial anecdotes which everyone knows, without loss of pleasure, to have been made only yesterday. Perhaps for the city dweller it is almost impossible to approach the village in any other way.

### References:

*James Stirling—Buildings and Projects 1950–1974* (introduction by John Jacobus), Thames and Hudson, London 1975.

*James Stirling—RIBA Drawings Collection* RIBA Publications Ltd, London 1974.

Kent C. Bloomer & Charles W. Moore, *Body, Memory and Architecture*, Yale University Press, New Haven 1977.

*Blackpool Fun Fair, England, revolution ride, 1980.*

*Blackpool Fun Fair, monorail support, 1980.*

### Fun Fairs

Robert Venturi's seminal study of Las Vegas initiated an entirely new direction in architectural theory as a form of counter culture. Carried out as an urban design/visual perception study by Yale architectural students under Venturi's direction, it concluded that the 'commercial strip' and the elements which formed this part of the urban structure represented a significant part of the visual and physical environment of American cities. A more conventional view, shared by the majority of architects and planners, had been taken in Tunnard and Pushkarev's earlier study, which had dismissed the commercial strip as 'a visually aggressive and ubiquitous feature that is sometimes considered to be typical, even inevitable, in the urban fringe'. Venturi's view by contrast, was that outdoor advertising provides the population with perhaps the most significant everyday visual experience, in which pictorial composition, colour relationships, graphics and visual metaphors represent the best popular art. Sennett has supported this view, describing the southern entrance to Los Angeles as 'five miles of unrelenting neon, giving rise to the theory that electricity can induce an unending orgasm'.

Perhaps the purest examples of this contention, and hence the most suggestive models for a formal consistency based on this approach, are provided in fun fair architecture. Travelling fun fairs have long been a cult subject amongst aficionados entranced with the decorative elements of the machines dating back to the nineteenth century. Surprisingly little has been said, however, on the architecture of fun fairs with the exception of a 1978 American study by L. Wasserman which subsequently received an award in January 1979 from *Progressive Architecture*. Wasserman was specifically seeking points of reference and lessons from fun fairs for application in architectural theory, and was inspired by the quite phenomenal revival of fun fairs in the United States, which, with the singular exception of Disneyland, had seen a decline in the 1950s and 1960s and were now re-establishing themselves with the construction of the giant 'theme' parks. Of these, Knott's Berry Farm in California has some of the most advanced rides and structures, one of which (Montezooma's Revenge) was described by a visiting reporter as 'the most terrifying artifact I have ever set eyes on'.

The American architectural practice Cambridge Seven Associates of Cambridge, Mass., and New York prepared a detailed report in 1973 on amusement parks for the Inter-American Center Authority. They noted that in choosing a menu of rides, which is the primary attraction of an amusement park, the public should be offered a wide range of choice of experience. Analysis, the report said, should be primarily based on the character of the ride experience, and on the variables of body movement and the surrounding environment. Many rides have in common an experience of movement along a linear track or path. A ride with very high speed, strong gravitational forces, strong centrifugal forces and an element of fear offers one end of the experience spectrum. Other rides will have slow gentle movement through a series of changing surroundings. Among the several rides using rotational movement, there is a high-speed horizontal rotation, combined with up and down movement and horizon tilting. The Ferris Wheel, rotating vertically in a smooth and gentle sweep offers a dramatic spatial and viewing experience, a high outlook over the site. Several new forms of ride induce environmental enclosures, rooms that move and equipment that allows the rider to participate or fully propel himself.

It is possible to consider therefore that the basis of fairground rides could be used as an analytical tool of total urban experience. At one level they

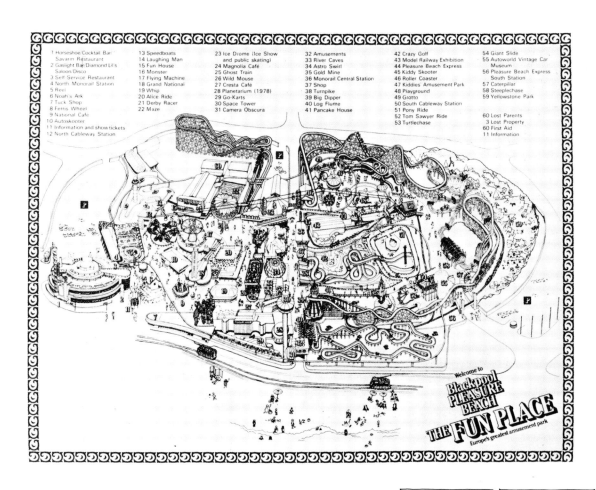

1 Horseshoe Cocktail Bar
 Savarin Restaurant
2 Gaslight Bar/Diamond Lil's
 Saloon/Disco
3 Self Service Restaurant
4 North Monorail Station
5 Reel
6 Noah's Ark
7 Tuck Shop
8 Ferris Wheel
9 National Cafe
10 Autoskooter
11 Information and show tickets
12 North Cableway Station

13 Speedboats
14 Laughing Man
15 Fun House
16 Monster
17 Flying Machine
18 Grand National
19 Whip
20 Alice Ride
21 Derby Racer
22 Maze

23 Ice Drome (Ice Show
 and public skating)
24 Magnolia Café
25 Cresta Café
26 Wild Mouse
27 Cresta Café
28 Planetarium (1978)
29 Go-Karts
30 Space Tower
31 Camera Obscura

32 Amusements
33 River Caves
34 Astro Swirl
35 Gold Mine
36 Monorail Central Station
37 Shop
38 Turnpike
39 Big Dipper
40 Log Flume
41 Pancake House

42 Crazy Golf
43 Model Railway Exhibition
44 Pleasure Beach Express
45 Kiddy Skooter
46 Roller Coaster
47 Kiddies Amusement Park
48 Playground
49 Grotto
50 South Cableway Station
51 Pony Ride
52 Tom Sawyer Ride
53 Turtlechase

54 Giant Slide
55 Autoworld Vintage Car
 Museum
56 Pleasure Beach Express
 South Station
57 Caterpillar
58 Steeplechase
59 Yellowstone Park

60 Lost Parents
 3 Lost Property
60 First Aid
11 Information

*Blackpool Fun Fair, aerial perspective, 1982*

*Blackpool Fun Fair, sequential photographs of the Ghost Train ride.*

*John Ferguson, interpretation of a Blackpool Fun Fair ride using the comic strip to portray sequential events and movement through space.*

provide a greatly heightened version of the everyday experience of sequential space, as described for example by Cullen, with experiences of danger, shock, surprise and changing light as exploited in the fairground Ghost Train. Alternatively, they can be seen in terms of a broader experience of fantasy and idealism. The huge numbers of people who visit Disneyland may do so because of a basic need to create fantasy in a popular dream world of illusions which for a day has more vivid reality than the monotonous environment left behind.

In the United Kingdom, the largest and best-known fun fair is at the coastal resort of Blackpool, which has been analysed in a recent paper prepared by Rosemary Ind with Alison and Peter Smithson. Though the layout is simple, resembling in principle a village green fair, it has an entity and coherence of its own. Dating back to 1910, the major architectural contributions were by Joseph Emberton between 1935 and 1956. The Fun House was described by Rosemary Ind and the Smithsons as an architectural promenade where entry into the building is via a carefully defined route of spatial and tactile experience. The Grand National Roller Coaster is a double car race, described as 'the plan which generates' and with its partially underground

track anticipates some of the recent transportation developments in the United States. Blackpool has more in common with Venturi's theories perhaps than Disneyland. It is a full-blooded fantasy world where popular art has not been diluted by prettiness or gentility. Some of the newer rides are ambitious attempts at integrating spatial effects. The Gold Mine ride at one point enters a restaurant building where diners become spectators sitting at terrace tables below which is an underground boat ride.

Tivoli in Copenhagen, on the other hand, is quite different in its intentions and techniques. More sophisticated than Blackpool, it forms an integrated piece of central city urban design. It has been referred to as a magic garden and its function as a city park for both inhabitants and tourists takes precedence over its fairground attractions. Dating back to 1843, it was largely destroyed under the German occupation during the Second World War. Now completely restored, it is an impressive combination of parkland, cafés and restaurants, firework displays, open-air theatre, ballet, symphony and jazz concerts and parades. Its fairground component is low key and the rides are not designed with the element of danger and surprise experienced at Blackpool. They are smaller and rely on magical effect and visual delight. The internal rides which include a small railway, the Blue Coach, provide a surreal experience more akin to Dali than the more typical haunted house ride. The architecture of most of the park is classical Chinese.

Disneyland in California preceded the more recent and more ambitious Disneyworld in Florida. The magic kingdom or miniature universe in Disneyland took the theme of popular fantasy based upon childhood memory much further and in a quite different direction to the traditional fun fair. The element of danger and surprise is deliberately missing. Peter Blake, writing in *The Art of Disney*, noted that Charles Eames was the first designer to recognize its importance in the 1950s, and further suggested that in Disneyworld, Disney had produced something as yet unattainable in real-life cities—a truly integrated scheme of multi-level mass transit systems, comprising people-movers, non-polluting vehicles, pedestrian malls and vast urban infrastructures. Disney used cartoonists to colour-code buildings and drew upon the expertise of film-makers to chart the progression of pedestrians through a sequence of urban spaces. Above all else, Blake claimed, he created an urban environment which endlessly fascinates and endlessly

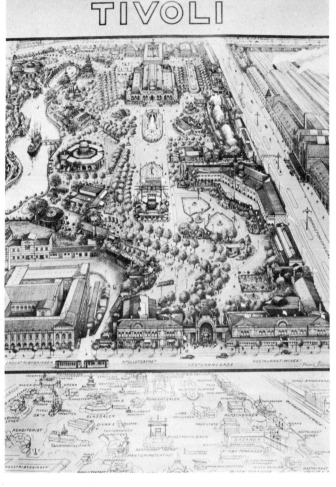

*◁ Tivoli Gardens, Copenhagen, Denmark.*

*Tivoli Gardens, Copenhagen, 'Blue Coach' sequence, 1978.*

*▷ Sleeping Beauty's Castle, Disneyland, California, US, using distorted scale and perspective.*

*'Mississippi' riverboat, Disneyland, California, the beginning of the theme park idea in the 1950s.*

*Tivoli Gardens, Copenhagen, Ferris Wheel.*

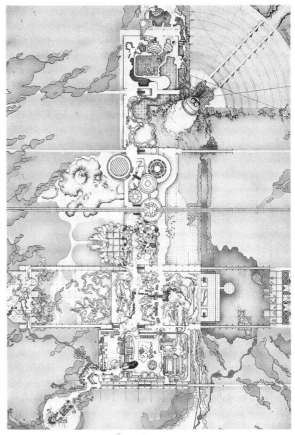

Wonderworld site plan, 1982.

attracts. Like Clough Williams-Ellis at Port-meirion, he deliberately used fake facades and a smaller-than-human scale. In Disneyworld, the reduced scale at pedestrian level becomes further reduced above, so as to create the illusion of greater height by the use of distorted perspective. Again, in Disneyland use is made of specific themes to break down the scale of the overall experience into a series of small, discrete worlds, such as the early twentieth-century Main Street, the nineteenth-century Mississippi river boat area, or the medieval fairy castle.

It has been suggested by John Pastier that both Disneyland and Las Vegas are colonies of Hollywood, and that there are distinct parallels between the two. Both places are theatrical experiences, employing vivid characteristics, solid and wholesome in the first case, ephemeral and mysterious in the second. Perhaps, as Charles Moore has remarked, as we become more enlightened 'we will understand the multiple realities of Disneyland and come to enjoy our cities as giant theme parks'.

Derek Walker's Wonderworld Project published in 1982 is, in many ways, the most advanced proposal for a theme park. Though theme parks do exist in Britain, such as Alton Towers in Staffordshire, none are comparable in scale to the American theme parks. Wonderworld is not only comparable in scale but adopts some of the marketing and financing techniques used in its American counterparts. The choice of site appears slightly curious. Located in derelict industrial land of the

steel town of Corby, which until recently was a designated new town, it is nevertheless strategically located to draw upon most of the major conurbations of England for its custom. If any criticism were to be made of Wonderworld, it would be its studied lack of vulgarity and the question whether the millions who are attracted to Blackpool exactly *because* of its vibrant vulgarity might be intimidated by Walker's finely designed megastructures. In detail, the entertainment projects proposed, such as the Ride through the Body for which Jonathan Miller acted as consultant, show a verve and imagination which is admirable.

**References:**

Venturi, Scott-Brown, Izenour, *Learning from Las Vegas*, MIT/Harvard 1972.

Tunnard & Pushkarev, *Man-Made America*, Yale University Press 1963.

R. Sennett, *The Uses of Disorder*, Pelican, London 1973.

L. Wasserman, *Merchandising Architecture: The Architectural Implications and Applications of Amusement Parks*, National Endowment for the Arts, Washington D.C. 1978.

R. Ind, A. and P. Smithson, 'Blackpool Pleasure Beach' in *Proceedings of the Second Conference on Twentieth Century Design History (1976)*, Design Council Publications, London 1976, pp. 38–43.

P. Eilstrup, *Tivoli*, Scandinavian Idea-Publishers, 1975.

J. Pastier, 'The Architecture of Escapism', *American Institute of Architects Journal*, December 1978, pp. 26–37.

*Architectural Design*, Vol. 52, Nos. 9–10, 1982.

Wonderworld model.

Wonderworld, 'Take a crazy cruise through the body in a carrot canoe, banana boat or sausage ship . . .'.

*Michael Graves, drawing for 'Roma Interrotta', 1978.*

## Competition: Roma Interrotta

Although not strictly speaking a competition, the invitation to twelve well-known theorists and practitioners of architecture and urbanism to rework, in whatever way they pleased, a one-twelfth segment of Giovanni Battista Nolli's 1748 plan of Rome, produced a similar result in freezing, as it were, the state of the art as interpreted at one point in time by the contenders. The relaxed terms of the contest made it both more confusing and more revealing than a conventional competition, and although the participants tended to convey the impression that they saw the whole thing as a bit of a joke, it was apparent from the amount of work they devoted to their entries that they took the joke rather seriously. Thus, once the initial witty or self-conscious stance had been established by each, the opportunity provided to comment on what urban design might mean in 1978 produced some interesting results which, in the absence of a functional programme, concentrated on the question of formal coherence.

The idea of the invitation came from Michael Graves, whose choice of Nolli's plan was not an arbitrary one. As he relates, Nolli's technique of drawing his plan, not at roof level, but as a horizontal section at ground-floor level, with commercial and residential buildings blocked in and spaces in public buildings shown as extensions of the outdoor streets and squares, projects a particular view of the city as a complex sequence of rooms which is unlike, on the one hand, the rigid separation of inside and out shown on medieval representations, and, on the other, the spatial continuity implied in modern plans. This led Graves, in his own entry, to define four archetypal forms of urban organization compatible with this view of the city, which he then combined and developed in his segment. The first of these four paradigms was 'the centroidal object in the landscape', a simple centralized volume inside and compact, isolated mass outside, exemplified by the Temple of Minerva Medica or Bramante's Tempietto. The second archetype is the figure-ground antithesis of the first, a single space read against a surrounding building, or building group, as at the Villa Madama. From these singular elements, the third and fourth archetypes build generic arrangements, the third being essentially a linear sequence of discrete spaces, as in the Villa Adriana, and the fourth a more fluid network of movements as seen in the complex of spaces forming the Church of the Trinita de Pellegrini.

Graves' careful definition of urban models and investigation of the subtle interrelationships possible between them, was echoed in James Stirling's contribution which, paradoxically, started from precisely the opposite pole. Beginning with the proposition that he would bring together all of his various projects to populate his rather empty section of Nolli's plan, Stirling went on to recast them as generic urban types appropriate to their new location. The 1975 project by the Hohenzollern Bridge and railway crossing of the Rhine at Cologne now provided a gateway funnel sucking urban motorway traffic under the Tiber; the 1969 Siemens headquarters was transformed into a platform building connecting both banks of the river; the water's edge condition along the Tiber banks was satisfied by the 1976 Government Centre for Doha; the 1965 Dorman Long project provided a wall building along the Gianicolo walls; and so on through some two dozen or more projects. Thus Stirling worked from a particular set of highly specific projects to define, like Graves, some universal conditions of urban design. He likened his 'contextual-associational' method to the historical process (in that any addition is seen as a confirmation and complement to that which exists), to Colin Rowe's concept of 'Collage City', and to the working method of one or two other designers, such as O.M. Ungers. He contrasted this to the 'rational' methods of most post-war planning by which sewers and roads determine the layouts of new buildings and 'expediency and commercialism' destroy existing cities.

This note of disgust at the state of contemporary urban development, and the part played in it by Modern architecture—'here termed "block modern" (cf: blockhouse, blockhead, blockbuster, blocked)'—was shared by Colin Rowe and his team: 'We assume that, on the whole, modern architecture was a major catastrophe—except as a terrible lesson—best to be forgotten; and, though we sometimes wonder how an idea—apparently so good—could so easily have been betrayed, we see no reason to indulge in pseudo-regrets or quasi-satirical demonstrations.' Instead Rowe, in three richly worked compositions for the Aventine, Palatine and Celio hills included in his sector, postulated a Rome which, with a little tinkering with history, might plausibly be interpolated as a natural extension of the old city. This suggestion of the search for improved urban form as the invention of an alternative, imaginary history, makes a fascinating contrast with Stirling's and Graves' 'end-seeking' hunt for universal urban types, and is supported by an elaborate and learned guide to the alternative history of the area, supplied by an erudite (and imaginary) Jesuit scholar. This technique, though quite unlike the others, achieved a result much in sympathy with them: 'We have attempted to constitute a fragment of ... a city of discrete set pieces and interactive local incidents, a city which represents coalition of intentions rather than the singular presence of any immediately apparent all-coordinating ideas.'

**References:**

*Roma Interrotta*, catalogue of exhibition in Rome, 1978, originated and promoted by Incontri Internazionali D'Arte, Rome.

*Architectural Design*, Vol. 49, No. 3–4, 1979.

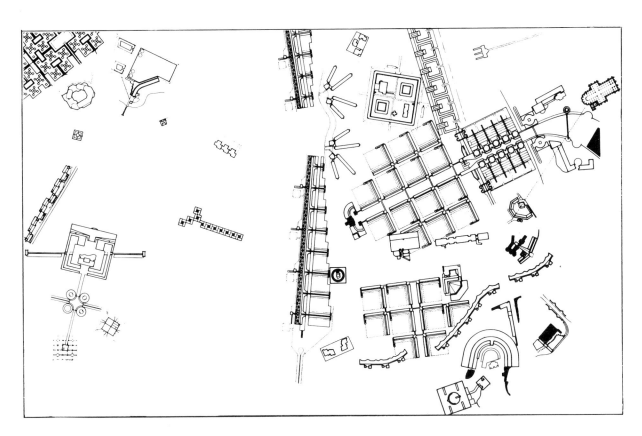

*James Stirling, drawing for 'Roma Interrotta', 1978.*

*Colin Rowe, drawing for 'Roma Interrotta', 1978.*

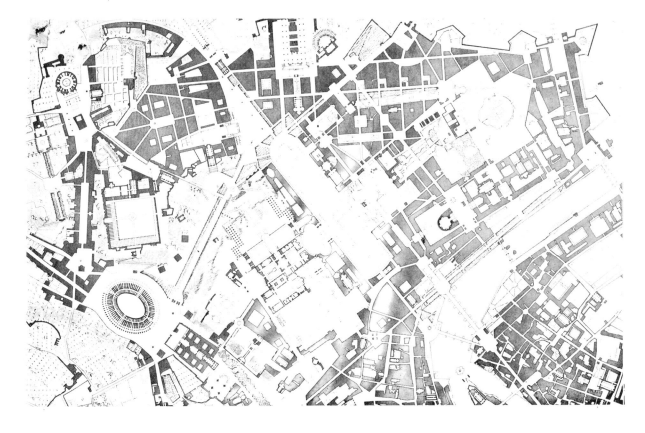

# PART FOUR
# FUTURE DIRECTIONS

THE PRECEDING CASE STUDIES CAN CERTAINLY NOT BE regarded as a representative sample of urban design projects of recent years. Selected as being among the most interesting and thoughtful of those available, they intentionally exclude the large number of banal and crude schemes which have disfigured our cities and which now make urban design an area of urgent and widespread concern.

If not typical, however, the case studies do illustrate the enormous variety of attitudes and preoccupations of designers in this field, a variety which it would be helpful to simplify by critical appraisal into that limited range which offers genuine directions for the future. Unfortunately this seems hardly possible. An urban design is a proposal to manipulate the future, to set out a pattern which will take years to implement and many more years to assess in use. The great majority of current urban design ideas are thus unrealized, or implemented only in small fragments and barely capable of objective appraisal.

Nevertheless, we can attempt a more limited assessment by setting these ideas against one another, testing their implications by reference to the alternative positions available, and can perhaps thus suggest some ways forward, not by virtue of what would be correct but rather in terms of what appears possible. Fortunately current theorists, although varying greatly in their solutions, do seem to share a preoccupation with a few key issues, consideration of which may provide us with a test of future directions.

Though it might be judged a secondary issue, a question of means rather than ends, a concern to define an appropriate technology for city building forms an important component of a wide range of urban design philosophies, and may provide us with a convenient starting point. After all, a faith in the 'technological fix' as a necessary part of a successful design strategy was central to the mainstream of the Modern Movement and, as Banham has noted,[1] the acid test of its members' orthodoxy. New technologies for distributing people and goods, for disposing of waste products, for provid-ing light, heat and air, and for overcoming the economic limitations of past construction methods, were all seen as being essential if conditions in industrial cities were to be made tolerable. In discussing the development of this view, Banham noted a watershed, about the year 1912,[2] after which the assumption was widely shared in progressive architectural circles that the technological developments in society at large and the construction industry in particular were irreversible, and salvation therefore depended upon more and more technological innovation.

Despite the setbacks and scepticism of recent years, this basic assumption is still held by an important group of environmental designers. Indeed, Buckminster Fuller, in 'An Open Letter to the Architects of the World' published in December 1979,[3] announced that the development of technology had reached a point some ten years previously at which that earlier hope had become capable of definitive realization: 'Neither the great political or financial power structures of the world, nor the population in general, realize that the engineering-integratable, invisible, metallurgical, chemical, electronic revolution now makes it possible to do so much with ever less pounds and volumes of material, ergs of energy, and seconds of time per given technological function that it is now possible to take care of everybody at that higher standard of living than any have ever known. It does not have to be you or me. Selfishness is unnecessary. War is obsolete. It could never have been done before. Only ten years ago the more-with-lessing technology reached the point where it could be done. Since then, it has made it ever easier to do so. It is a matter of converting the high technology from weaponry to "livingry"—and the essence of "livingry" is environmental controlling.'

If Buckminster Fuller thus insists that the principle of high technological salvation is intact and valid still, others have suggested specific forms which it might now adopt. Frei Otto's tent structures, for example, effortlessly enclosing huge areas of public space, provide a more flexible model for this enclosure than Fuller's own geodesic dome solution (as in the project for covering the centre of Manhattan with a two-mile diameter dome), while acknowledging Fuller's preference for tensile rather than compressive forces. Ironically, the names of both men have become so closely associated with their own particular preferred versions of the universal enclosure that these have become curiously private stereotypes—'Bucky's domes', and 'Frei's tents'.

A similar personal association occurs with the work of Zvi Hecker, although it may be argued that his preference for polyhedric geometries is a formal rather than a technological one. Nevertheless, in a project such as his 1969–71 proposals for Montreal, this preference clearly implies the obsolescence of the old orthogonal city structure as it is taken up and replaced by the new hexagonal technology. After all, what else but the massive and insupportable failure of the existing fabric could justify the adoption of such an alien new order? Wolf Pearlman suggested a similar position in his premiated entry for the Beaubourg competition. His research into environmental design and the geometry of polyhedra has developed totally new spatial concepts in urban design as exemplified by the competition entry for Old Jerusalem.

If Fuller's and Hecker's heroic versions of future technological deliverance are met with rather more scepticism today than in the past, this scepticism is most eloquently evoked in those imaginary urban projects drawn up in the late 1970s by Peter Cook, in which pristine megastructures are overwhelmed by natural, or random, events. Given Cook's earlier pedigree as a prime source of high-technology urban images in the Archigram group, the frisson

*Frei Otto (Engineer Buro Happold), Olympic Stadia, Munich, 1972.*

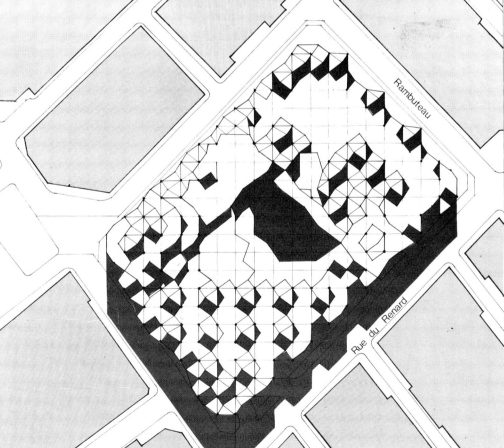

*Wolf Pearlman, premiated competition design for the Beaubourg Centre, Paris, France, 1971.*

*Zvi Hecker, proposals for Montreal, Canada, 1969–71.*

Beauborg Centre Competition    Wolf Pearlman

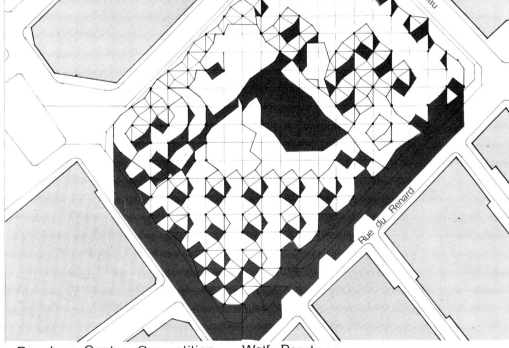

*Peter Cook, 'The Urban Mark', 1972.*

*Peter Cook, 'The Urban Mark', 1972.*

*Peter Cook, 'The Urban Mark Disintegrated', 1972.*

*Peter Cook, 'Arcadian City', 1977.*

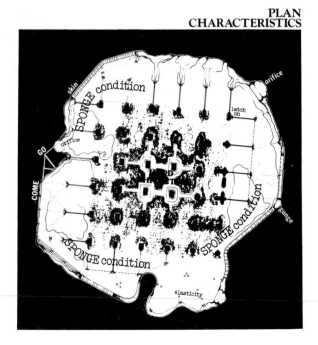

*Peter Cook, 'The Urban Sponge', 1978.*

generated by such illustrations as the 'Urban Mark' sequence is particularly disquieting. Perhaps it is unnecessary to insist upon too close a parallel with the spate of disaster movies which were contemporaneous, or with the spectacular celebrations of building failure devised by James Wines and SITE for Best Products in the USA, or indeed with the plague of actual building failures which become increasingly obtrusive at this time. Cook's visions of crumbling hardware invoked eighteenth-century landscapes in which fragments of lost civilizations were replaced by fragments of flawed technologies, but his reworking of the theme of ruin in Arcadia had a second and more optimistic thread. In the 'Urban Mark' itself, and in subsequent projects for 'Sponge', 'Lump' and 'Mound' buildings, the natural forms which appear to overwhelm the old architecture are ambiguous. In fact we become increasingly uncertain whether they are 'natural' or whether they are in fact the old structure in the process of metamorphosis. 'Remnants of the "high architecture" are having to co-exist with tatty, strange, ad-hoc elements (probably put there by laymen, not designers) ... Is it "dust-to-dust", "ashes-to-ashes"? Is it the end of our civilisation? No, surely not. *This* is a new architecture, infinitely more subtle and more responsive than that which went before...'[4]

Cook went on further to explore the ambiguities of architecture becoming ruins, ruins imitating nature, and nature posing as architecture, most notably in his 'Arcadian City' project of 1977. In his essay on the Arcadian myth, Erwin Panofsky has noted that 'Arcady, as we encounter it in all modern literature, and as we refer to it in our daily speech, falls under the heading of "soft" or "golden-age" primitivism',[5] and Cook's appeal for a 'soft' technology to supersede the old 'hard' urban structures undoubtedly describes an important future direction for urban designers (although we may note Panofsky's warning that the inhabitants of Arcady, while famous for their 'musical accomplishments,... rugged virtue, and rustic hospitality', were also noted for 'their utter ignorance and low standards of living').[6]

An interesting aside on Cook's search is provided by Emilio Ambasz, a designer who has provided some ingenious clues as to how a soft urban technology might operate, in his remark that 'Europe's eternal quest remains Utopia, the myth of the end. America's returning myth is Arcadia, the eternal beginning.'[7] Ambasz's designs for the latter in a project for a Cooperative of Mexican-American Grape Growers in California has close affinities with Cook's projects in its emphasis upon the interdependence of 'natural', 'cultivated' and 'built' structures—the grapevines, suspended on wire-grids, form a shady 'roof' to areas of settlement and cultivation below. While the pursuit of 'the eternal beginning' may be appropriate for the citizens of California, however, its offer by a Government agency to the poverty-stricken aboriginal population of the Peruvian Andes must seem ironic. Nevertheless, Ambasz's project for the Comision de Integracion Nacional demonstrates a similar novelty of approach. The 'hard' technology response to the problems of the inhabitants of the high Valle de Huallanco, which included isolation, illiteracy, disease, poverty and periodic devastation by sudden river floods, might have taken the form of a major dam-building project, or the resettlement of the population elsewhere. Ambasz proposed instead to construct a series of 12 metre square barges in Peru's idle shipyards and to tow these upstream to be anchored in one of a variety of appropriate configurations at each existing village, providing classrooms and communal areas, and places of refuge at flood time. His strategy of 'making peace with the river' was further developed by equipping some barges with paddle wheels to generate electricity from the river's current, mainly to refrigerate food and to receive UNESCO's satellite-linked educational television broadcasts. Finally, two old river gun-boats were to be refitted, one as a hospital ship and the other as an educational ship, first to tow the barges into position and then to visit the villages in rotation.

Ambasz also used the idea of the barge as a building which does not impose itself too per-

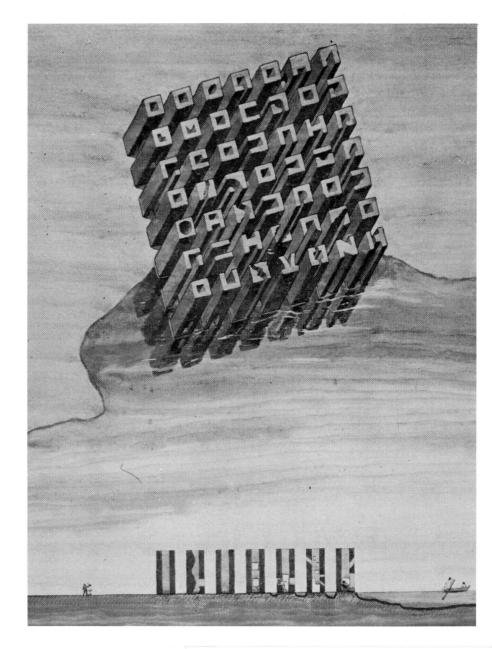

*Emilio Ambasz, Cooperative of Mexican-American Grape Growers, California, 1979.*

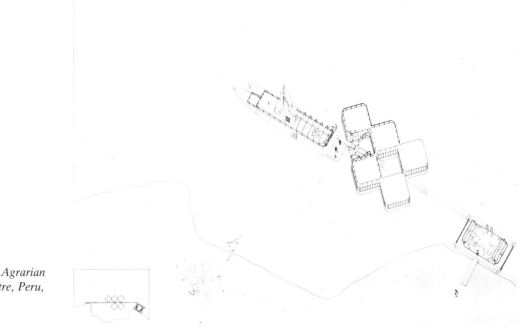

*Emilio Ambasz, Educational and Agrarian Community Centre, Peru, 1977.*

*Emilio Ambasz, Center for Applied Computer Research and Programming, Mexico City, 1976.*

manently upon the landscape in a quite different context in a design for a Center for Applied Computer Research and Programming (Centro Mexicano de Calculo Aplicado S.A.) outside Mexico City. Here a 150 metre square water basin would be required for site drainage and would act as the location for the office workspaces required by the programme, which would be provided in barges floated into appropriate positions and then settled in the shallow water by flooding their ballast tanks. Capable of being easily refloated and repositioned, the barges would again make use of the country's 'sole fully industrialized building industry', its shipyards. In a gesture once more reminiscent of Cook's 'Urban Mark', two large walls 28 metres high and 150 metres long contain two adjacent sides of the lagoon and act as a 'site mark' for further developments on the estate. One wall is a solar energy gathering device and the other an information wall displaying messages and information on current research projects. Finally, the computer terminals, reception areas, storage and cafeteria are housed under a large platform at the base of the information wall and looking out over the pool. Above this platform hovers a cloud, 'conceived as an architectural element', which is created by pressurizing through specially designed nozzles water which is pumped by windmills around the centre, and which cools the outdoor climate. Ambasz provides his own commentary on the transitional nature of this design on the road to Arcadia: 'The Users understand the architect's basic premise that "Nobody should have to work. If present circumstances so constrain us, at least it should be possible to do it from home. There is not, therefore, a real need for a large building but for a relatively small installation to house the computer and receive messages." But the Users also feel that they are not ready yet for such a radical arrangement. The building has been conceived, therefore, as composed of elements which may be progressively removed, as courage grows and the need for physical space diminishes. Then, only the silent walls and a single barge turned into an island of flowers will remain.'[8]

Ambasz's idyllic evocation of an alternative soft urban technology remains, however, overshadowed by the choices which customarily present themselves in the polarized forms of hardware comprising, on the one hand, the bristling high-tech Utopia offered by the Pompidou Centre, and on the other the gentle low-tech Arcadia of, say, Ted Cullinan's Minster Lovell Mill. But if these are the extremes of a range of possible current technologies, we may question whether, in terms of the city as a whole, these fiercely defended positions do represent exclusive alternatives; whether, that is, we can view the city as a consistent technological product at all. Certainly a great many urban concepts do seem to have taken technological purity as a desirable or necessary characteristic, whether they belong to the line that can be traced from la Città Nuova to La Défense, or alternatively from the Bund Für Heimatschutz to the Essex Design Guide.

Now this aim could be challenged in a number of ways. It could be argued that a mono-technic city, such as was implied by the Modern Movement, is a functionally inappropriate concept, better replaced by the notion of a bi-technic city comprising two distinct technological zones. Such was the basis of the Nazi *Blut und Boden* philosophy in which the monumental and technically advanced places of work and public ritual envisaged for the city centre by Albert Speer or Ernst Sagebiel contrasted with the vernacular hearth-and-home associations of the residential 'Schaffendes Volk' estates. Such also is surely the actual condition of most Western cities, divided into the technological zones of the commercial down-town or business districts on the one hand, and on the other the suburban 'houses with clapboard siding and a high-pitched roof and shing-

*Albert Speer, 'Cathedral of Light' designed for the Nazi Party rally at Nuremberg, West Germany in September 1938, showing another aspect of Speer's formalism.*

les and gaslight-style front porch lamps and mailboxes set up on top of lengths of stiffened chain that seemed to defy gravity....'[9] It could further be argued that such a bi-technic division is itself a crude simplification of the ancient association of the most advanced and expensive technology with the most powerful building types which themselves tend to congregate in the areas of highest land value. This suggests a picture of the city as a spectrum of technologies, hierarchically ordered, from the most exotic house of God, King, State or Business Corporation, to the most modest structure for the domestic pet.

There is also another way in which the idealization of a mono-technic city can be challenged by the reality of a multi-technic one, for at any one moment a city in fact comprises a very few examples of newly formed, precisely contemporary construction, together with a huge mass of steadily obsolescing material which is undergoing, to a greater or lesser extent, a continual process of modification. We may recognize this as a matter of fact, but we may also welcome it as a fundamental characteristic of a valid urban design approach, in which the city is seen as an unpredictable compound of technologies. Banal as this truism may be, there are few examples of designs which might suggest where such an approach would lead. While

designers have readily accepted fragments, or indeed whole envelopes of existing older structures into their compositions, they have generally regarded the technological purity of the new element to be sacrosanct. The history of modern architecture does however offer a few examples of multi-technic designs, from the transitional structures of Viollet-le-Duc to Le Corbusier's early collaging of rough stone walling with the quintessential image of industrialized technology at the Pavillon Suisse. In their designs for the National Gallery Extension at Stuttgart, James Stirling and Michael Wilford have developed a similar dialogue between two conventionally incongruent technologies of ashlar walling and painted steelwork, and the invitation to ask, as Jencks has done, 'What is the Machine Aesthetic doing on a Schinkelesque facade, with such obvious discontinuity?'[10] provides a challenge to the usual positions adopted in the argument as to what constitutes an appropriate contemporary technology in the context of the city.

It must be said, however, that for most urbanists the question of appropriate technology is not considered so much a matter of survival, as Buckminster Fuller would regard it, but rather as a route to the discovery, or authorization, of an appropriate formal language for the city, the problem of which forms a second common preoccupation among designers. Thus in the conventional development-control debate between private interest and public authority, materials, forms and patterns of elements may be sought to be 'in keeping' with existing models; that is to say, to 'represent' an equivalent technology to that used elsewhere. When carried through with conviction, as in Darbourne and Darke's housing development at Pershore, we may assume that the technology, and hence the formal language which derives from it, is precisely comparable to that used in the nineteenth-century terrace housing types they recall, although on reflection we may suppose that in fact the methods of manufacture and assembly of elements, of site erection and craft skills employed, have all been radically transformed in a piecemeal fashion in the intervening period. Again, in a development like François Spoerry's Port Grimaud, perhaps the most widely acknowledged recent example of the reproduction of an 'obsolete' building technology on a large scale, the use of reinforced-concrete box-plate piles and other modern techniques to support a Mediterranean fishing village in a former marsh is important only in so far as it sustains the twin formal requirements of a unified hand-made superstructure containing a maximum variety of

*François Spoerry, Port Grimaud, 1977.*

*Heinz Mohl, Schneider Store, Freiburg, 1978.*

conditions (the sales literature challenges the visitor to find any two houses which are identical).

While this example relies upon the panache with which a convincing authenticity is maintained, others frankly mimic (or 'echo') the forms generated by older technologies without concealing the fact that the means of construction have substantially changed. This strategy, which surely involved a good deal of hard swallowing by architects of the Modern Movement, attempts a reconciliation with the context on a formal level, while maintaining the uncompromising purity of a contemporary monotechnic language within its own boundaries, and has been widely adopted in sensitive central area locations, particularly in West Germany. In the medieval silver-mining town of Goslar, in Lower Saxony, for example, new department stores adopt the medieval configurations of irregular forms, stepped upper storeys, oriel windows and steeply pitched roofs without disguising their concrete frame-and-panel construction, and the same may be seen in Munich, Regensburg and, most inventively and idiosyncratically of all, in Heinz Mohl's design for the Schneider Store in Freiburg. Moderate and 'responsible' as this tempering of naked modernism might appear, the same strategy can be used to devastatingly subversive or simply playful effect, as Charles Moore has demonstrated with his reconstruction of the classical orders in stainless steel, neon tubes and water jets in the Piazza d'Italia, New Orleans.

Once again we are obliged to consider whether urban design implies a definition of the city as a homogeneous product, in this case in formal terms, and, again, we find that an assumption of this kind does seem to underlie a great many proposals, whether the preferred model be the vernacular village or the Ville Radieuse. Just as we were able to define a spectrum of attitudes to the future in terms of a choice of technologies, so we can define a similar range in formal terms. On the one hand we have Rob Krier's view that: 'We live in an era of unlimited technological and formal potential, and it is precisely this illusory progress which reveals itself as the Achilles' heel of the age, which bears all the marks of an experimental period of expansion. And yet we treat this freedom a bit too lightly. What I optimistically refer to as a period of expansion is seen by others as a symptom of cultural decline.'[11] In practice, Krier has adopted the severe and highly controlled vocabulary of the new Rationalism in order to arrest this 'cultural decline'. On the other hand, however, we have Venturi's preference for 'vital mess', and his model of 'the Strip' which draws precisely the opposite conclusion from the current unsatisfactory state of affairs: 'Henri Bergson called disorder an order we cannot see. The emerging order of the Strip is a complex order. It is not the easy, rigid order of the urban renewal project or the fashionable "total design" of the megastructures.'[12]

Fascinating as this range of opinions on the questions of technology and formal language may be, it is difficult to adopt a coherent position without considering a third area of common concern. For most statements of technical or formal position beg further questions about the scope and purpose of urban design itself: What is the nature of the design problem posed by urban design? What are the aims and limitations of the urban designer's activity? If we consider these questions while studying the proposals and statements of designers we must soon conclude that their arguments develop from very different assumptions as to the nature of their task. The identification of these attitudes may thus provide us with a useful appraisal of alternative future directions for urban design. In each case the initial premises lead to specific implications for the designer, and are open to particular critiques, some of which we have attempted to indicate.

## 4.1 URBAN DESIGN AS POLITICAL STATEMENT

'Mostly we talked cities and how to build them so they in turn might build better, more human, people.' (Ray Bradbury on conversations with Walt Disney)

'What today's Utopians in the West are trying to do is to find the technical means of resolving the urban crisis without changing the conditions that inevitably accompany capitalist development. But the urban crisis in the capitalist countries is a result of insurmountable social conditions.'[13] (M.V. Posokhin)

MIKHAIL VASSILYEVICH POSOKHIN, CHIEF ARCHItect of Moscow and director of its development plan to 1985, introduces the first and perhaps the clearest position which we might examine. 'The city is the most explicit and complete demonstration of the political beliefs and social patterns of its inhabitants, and designing within it is a political act. To behave as if this were not true is misguided.'

Now undoubtedly many people have recognized the truth of this position, which establishes the urban designer as the instrument of the society he serves. The validity of any choice on his part has to be tested against the requirements of that society. A decision, for example, to switch 'from the years-to-build, human-need exploiting cities to the in-one-day-air-deliverable-or-removable, human-need-serving, domed-over cities',[14] as Buckminster

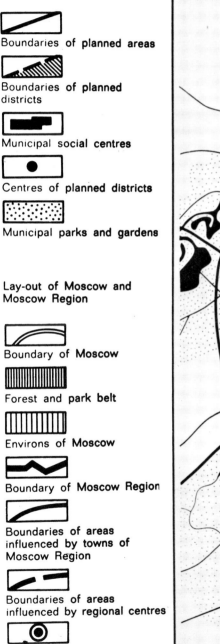

Boundaries of planned areas

Boundaries of planned districts

Municipal social centres

Centres of planned districts

Municipal parks and gardens

Lay-out of Moscow and Moscow Region

Boundary of Moscow

Forest and park belt

Environs of Moscow

Boundary of Moscow Region

Boundaries of areas influenced by towns of Moscow Region

Boundaries of areas influenced by regional centres

Industrial and social centres of local population zones

Regional centres

*M.V. Posokhin, Development Plan for Moscow to 1985.*

*Minoru Takeyama, Row House Project, Japan, 1974–78.*

*Minoru Takeyama, Row House Project, Japan 1974–78.*

*Christiana Free City, Copenhagen, c. 1978, mid section.*

Fuller suggests, is not simply a technical one, but implies a condition of society to support it. For this reason, as much as for ones of aesthetic or practical preference, Leon Krier, like William Morris before him, has advocated 'the reconstruction of an artisanal building culture' in opposition to industrialized building methods which have 'reduced manual labour to a stultifying and enslaving experience'.[15] Again we may suppose that if we take two contrasting examples of design, such as Minoru Takeyama's Row House projects developed between 1974 and 1978 and, say, the squatter settlement of Christiana in Copenhagen, we can infer the social order appropriate for each. The first appears as a sophisticated, industrialized product of a highly regulated society and the second, with its acceptance of varied uses and spontaneous adaptations of its buildings, a model of tolerant anarchism. However we cannot be certain of this on the evidence of the built form alone. Although the residents of Row-1 and Row-2 may have placed all design decisions for their environment in the hands of a single architect, they may enjoy a relaxed and liberal way of life, while some might find the demands of self-sufficiency in the Free Town (where there are no architects, or other professionals) tyrannical, or might regard it as no more than a necessary escape valve in an over-regulated society. The difficulty is that although each society clearly passes down to its urban designers instructions and limitations peculiar to itself, the reciprocal effect of their response is much less predictable. We may recognize the programme as symptomatic but so cannot categorize the form supplied to fulfil it. Thus, as Broadbent reminds us, 'A range of political regimes, from Jefferson's America to Stalin's Russia, to Hitler's Germany and even Mao's China, all used the neo-Classical or pared-down versions of it for their city centre monuments.'[16] This state of affairs is further confused by Leon Krier's claim that the very different architectural solutions offered by, for example, Frei Otto's Munich structures or Piano and Rogers' Pompidou Centre, 'try to achieve cultural aims which are very similar to the respectability of fascist monuments'[17], which themselves, to further compound our difficulties, have been modified by history, the Zepelinfeld for example into a baseball pitch and motor-cycle racing track.

We could argue then that Posokhin's analysis is correct, but inadequate as a programme of action for the urban designer. The categorization of urban design as political action is a necessary description but not a sufficient one.

## 4.2 URBAN DESIGN AS TECHNIQUE

PRECISELY THE OPPOSITE VIEW TO POSOKHIN'S IS adopted by those designers whose work suggests the existence of a value-free method of approach. The pursuit by Thiel, Appleyard and others of a more complete and precise method of describing the visual phenomena of the city suggests that such an annotative method would itself lead to the reform of the subject of its study. The line of enquiry begun at MIT in the 1950s has been further developed by Appleyard in his Environmental Simulation laboratory at the University of California, Berkeley, during the 1970s. There the search for an accurate method of simulating and testing alternative planning proposals has been substantially achieved by means of extremely realistic models through which a periscope with a tiny movable lens, mounted on an elaborate overhead gantry system, is remotely controlled in response to either hand or computer directions. Thus TV or movie film of a simulated walk or drive through a familiar environment with proposed developments incorporated can be made and debated by interested parties.

At MIT, the Architecture Machine Group has developed two extraordinary mixed-media projects, 'Movie Map' and 'Dataland', which use responsive computer techniques to provide a detailed journey through a chosen area. Seated before a 2.4 × 3.3 metre screen in an armchair equipped with joystick controls and touch-sensitive monitor screens, the viewer can zoom down from satellite pictures of, say, the East Coast of the United States into a particular city area, and then proceed along its streets. He may stop and look into or out of nearby buildings (provided, of course, the computer has previously been supplied with the appropriate slides or film), and add sound to the experience. The first Movie Map was made of Aspen, Colorado, for a conference there at which the system was demonstrated, and has been further developed in the more elaborate Dataland project, which can add 'virtual' objects to the screen to support the visual programme, such as a calculator or reference books, which can be manipulated by normal hand movements to the touch-sensitive monitors (to 'turn the pages' of books for example).

By means of such techniques, the urban designer can perform his main function, which is presumably seen as being to formulate and present the problem as accurately and vividly as possible. In this, the approach is similar to some other investigations of design methods which were made in the 1960s. Christopher Alexander's *Notes on the Synthesis of Form*,[18] for example, described a process for the design of an Indian village which attempted to reconcile all the functional requirements of the problem by its meticulous breakdown into its most basic statements and their subsequent recomposition according to rational, mathematical procedures. Again, to take an example which, if less intellectually rigorous, resulted in a considerably greater volume of building, Skidmore Owings and Merrill's use of 'Field Theory' in the late 1960s generated plans with highly elaborate octagonal geometries from the application of overtly neutral methods of activity analysis and grid overlays.[19]

It may be objected, however, that while an accurate statement of the problem is invaluable, and may lead to a more rational debate, it cannot in itself provide solutions. Further, the pursuit of apparently authoritative and neutral techniques may mask those value judgements which urban design problems invariably entail. A rhetorical commentary on the search for new descriptive and analytical methods to pin down such elusive problems is provided by those artists who have presented the record of the act of creating the work of art as the work itself, and in particular by Bernard Tschumi whose exhibition 'Manhattan Transcripts', held at Artists Space, New York in April 1978, set out to represent, by methods not dissimilar to those earlier identified at MIT, an urban sequence of events. In this case, however, the photographs, plans and schematic diagrams of movement recorded not a progression of landmarks, nodes and paths, but a violent crime and the murderer's subsequent movements to evade capture.

*Bernard Tschumi, 'The Manhattan Transcripts', sequence from MT2, 1978.*

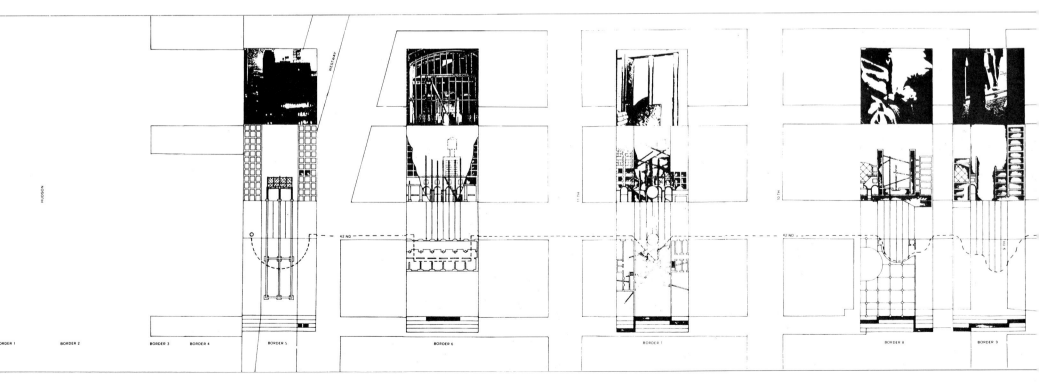

## 4.3 URBAN DESIGN AS MEDIATION

AN ALTERNATIVE VERSION OF THE VIEW OF URBAN design as an essentially neutral technique is provided by a number of studies in which the problem of values is recognized by devising design methods which allow conflicts to be expressed and then resolved. Urban design is then seen as a 'forum' or 'ring' and the urban designer as a chairman. N.J. Habraken's theory of 'supports' could be regarded in this way in that it sets out a literal framework for high-density housing within which a balanced reconciliation of public and private interests may be established. In his subsequent work with the Design Methods Group at the University of Eindhoven, Habraken further elaborated the design possibilities of his theory in considerable detail and published the results as *Variations: the Systematic Design of Supports*.[20]

Perhaps the purest illustration of this mediating function of urban design is provided by the various applications of operational games which have been developed for architectural and planning situations. Although primarily useful as educational tools, these games provide a useful alternative to mathematical techniques in modelling possible future results of complex and interrelated decisions, and allow the particular influences and effects of individual interests to become apparent. One such example is the 'Game for Alternative Policies' or GAP, devised by Drew Mackie and the Urban Design study group at Edinburgh University in 1979,[21] to explore alternative futures for the mining town of Newtongrange in Midlothian, and developed from earlier, more generalized games such as the early Cornell Land Use Game and Mackie's own prototype BUG (Basic Urban Game). A

*Lucien Kroll and Atelier, Development at University of Louvain, Belgium, 1976, medical student faculty.*

*Lucien Kroll and Atelier, Development at University of Louvain, Belgium, 1976.*

particularly interesting feature of these games is their often unexpected confirmation of the persistence of certain features which, in a real context, may well be assumed to be undesirable and capable of being 'designed out'. Thus Cedric Green has described the experience of running a game, SQUAT, one of a series which he designed under the general title INHABS (Instructional Housing and Building Simulation), whose rules simulated the basic conditions of unstructured initial development and relative material poverty found in many squatter settlements: 'The experience of running SQUAT with students of all kinds, western and not, was the same—anarchy. Even the rules of building economics were flouted, representing the squatter's use of scrap material. In every game it became necessary for the person running it to invent rules ad hoc to meet situations in which it seemed everything would break down and the exercise would have to be abandoned.... And when a group of players was put in authority over the others they invariably took draconian measures to "clean up" the settlement and sweep away everything that represented jerry-built constructions. Whatever set of rules was imposed to try to control future development or produce a better standard, unless the players were provided with higher purchasing power, the game ended there.'[22]

Now although both these studies and the previously described work by Appleyard and others are discussed here in terms of the primacy of techniques, this should not be taken to mean that their successful application is a mechanical process. On the contrary, the very considerable level of investigation and commitment which such methods may entail is illustrated by the work of Lucien

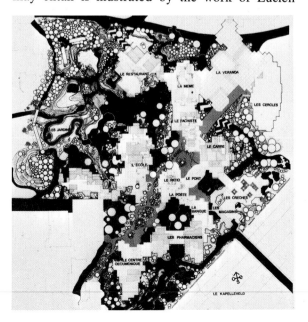

Kroll, which similarly attempts to open up the design process to users and place the designer in the role of an orchestrator. Kroll's method of working with his medical student clients on the campus of the University of Louvain resembled a gaming exercise in certain respects, and particularly in its allocation of roles to distinct groups of students with instructions to consider specific areas of the brief and then, when conflicts arose, its rearrangement of these groups with new interests. Again, his simultaneous use of several building methods, and delegation of certain choices of action to the builder, were governed by what amounts to rules of play, by which odd and unpredictable events occur spontaneously as the operations unfold.

Nicholas Negroponte has argued that this variety and sensitivity to particular, unique circumstances can be achieved in other ways: 'The industrial revolution brought sameness through repetition, amortization through duplication. In contrast, information technologies—soft machines—afford the opportunity for custom-made, personalized artifacts.'[23] Adopting a stance similar to Yona Friedman's, Negroponte has explored the possibility of computers 'making the built environment responsive to me and to you, individually, a right I consider as important as the right to good education'[24] both in terms of introducing direct user-participation in the design of the environment, and also by making that environment itself more 'intelligent' and capable of interaction with its inhabitants.

In all these cases, techniques are proposed to make the design problem more immediately comprehensible and the design process therefore less paternalistic and remote. To do this, the professional becomes less clearly a designer, and more the provider and mechanic of the enabling technique. It might be objected, however, that, apart from some net gain derived from a clearer appreciation of the problem, the overall effect of such techniques is simply to reallocate the burden of design decisions onto other shoulders, without providing any new understanding of the terms in which they should be resolved. It may be that such a reallocation is both necessary and a source of great vitality, but we may dispute Negroponte's claim that the central aim of urban design—the positive reconciliation of public and private realms—could be achieved in an unselfconscious and almost vernacular manner by the application of redistributive techniques alone.

## 4.4  URBAN DESIGN AS PRIVATE DISPLAY

ONE POSSIBLE VERSION OF BOTH THE VIEW OF URBAN design as a true representation of the social system and as an expression of user choice, is provided by the idea of the city as a battleground of competing private interests. There are obvious historical precedents for such a notion, as, for example, in the skylines of San Gimignano and, to a lesser extent, Bologna, which are still dominated by the unlikely towers competitively erected by feuding medieval families. Today, it is widely accepted, at least within the confines of shopping streets where considerable freedom for competitive display is allowed within the boundaries of shop windows, and rather less beyond.

Now it could be argued that the controls which customarily limit such display and restrict its proliferation in signs and advertisement beyond the shop window are misguided. The traditionally most highly regarded commercial spaces, like Times Square and Piccadilly Circus, are remembered for their unconstrained display of those elements which elsewhere are restricted in the interests of urban design. Not only do these restrictions prevent the development of new and unexpected urban forms (contemporary equivalents of the San Gimignano towers) but they tend to promote unimaginative, conforming solutions whose banality invites further controls. The problem of most urban spaces, so the argument runs, is not how to control unbridled vitality, but how to restore real signs of life.

A supporter of this view might take some encouragement from the work of Roger Walker in New Zealand, whose buildings celebrate the idea of advertisement, not by the use of applied signs but through the extraordinarily animated development of the building itself. Using a vocabulary incorporating a variety of ad hoc improvisations, Walker has demonstrated, in the Centre Point shopping centre and a greater number of private houses in North Island, the ability of unexpected architectural events to command attention.

The same may be said of SITE (Sculpture in the Environment), whose first experiments for Best Products depended upon destabilizing the predictable image of a supermarket shed by signs of spectacular building failure—a brick outer leaf peeling away, a parapet collapsing in a pile of bricks over the entrance canopy or an entrance formed within the jagged opening left by a corner of the building which slides away at opening time. These architectural jokes worked more dramatically as advertisements than would conventional signs

*SITE, Best Showroom, Houston, Texas, 1975, 'Indeterminate Facade'.*

*Roger Walker, Park Mews, Wellington, New Zealand, 1978.*

and evoked widespread reactions: 'Police and a frantic motorist bang at the door: "The wind is tearing apart your building!"... A local structural engineer, after careful study of the project: "I have dedicated my whole life to preventing things like this."... Customer to the store manager: "Your building is shrinking!"'[25] 'I knew I was on the right track when a Texan came along as we were building and said "That's what I always wanted to do—kick the shit out of it".'[26]

James Wines, Alison Sky and their group then went on to explore other surreal architectural devices, reversing wall and ground elements in a project for the Molino Stucky Mills in Venice, Italy and inserting the building under an undulating asphalt parking lot in a showrooms proposal for Best Products in Los Angeles. Besides acting as startlingly effective signs, these inversions also probe customary expectations of commercial architecture and, incidentally, provide an amusing commentary on the assumptions of development control. One of their proposals for a Best super-

*SITE, 'The Stucky Mills', Guideca Island, Venice, Italy, 1975, sponsored by Venice Biennale of Art and Architecture.*

*SITE, Best Showroom, Los Angeles, California, 1976, 'Parking Lot Project'.*

market, for example, involved burying it in a grove of trees. Now the device of calling for landscaping to hide obtrusive buildings is commonly applied by planning officers in the U.K., and, in such a case as a controversial hypermarket proposal for Carrefour set in a green-field site near Eastleigh in Hampshire, resulted in the building being designed with a surrounding trellis structure on outriggers from the main envelope to support a masking screen of creepers. But while the purpose of this vegetation was one of elaborately contrived camouflage, that in the SITE project was precisely the opposite, since no architectural device could have been more obtrusively unexpected in the middle of the urban parking lot than a rural copse.

The most elaborate philosophical investigation of private display as urban design was that carried out in 1968 by Robert Venturi, Denise Scott Brown, Steve Izenour and students at the Yale School of Art and Architecture, and published in 1972 as *Learning from Las Vegas*. Taking the length of Route 91 as it passes through Las Vegas as 'the archetype of the commercial strip, the phenomenon at its purest and most intense', they explored what they believed to be a fundamental but neglected urban type, 'as important to architects and urbanists today as were the studies of medieval Europe and ancient Rome and Greece to earlier generations' but which, 'from ignorance, we define today as urban sprawl'.[27]

From this premise, and accepting the commercial strip on its own terms, Venturi and his team developed a critique of architecture and urban design which paralleled that offered by Rudofsky and others in respect of vernacular sources by opposing an alternative, apparently unselfconscious and vital tradition to the conventional culture of professional architecture. Their study concluded with a theory of 'Ugly and Ordinary Architecture' in which the characteristics of the strip and of modern architecture were contrasted: 'Decoration by the attaching of superficial elements' in the former against 'Unadmitted decoration by the articulation of integral elements' in the latter; 'Symbolism' against 'Abstraction'; 'Expedient' against 'Heroic'; and so on.

Venturi's position on the exuberant display of the strip is somewhat different from that of Walker or Wines, both of whom make compelling visual images of their buildings using dramatic variations of the conventional language of architecture. SITE'S images of reversal and collapse, for instance, are witty and 'artistic' manipulations of the spectator's expectations, much as were Giulio Romano's Mannerist disturbances of the classical language of Renaissance architecture four centuries earlier. Venturi on the other hand proposes a new insight, a ready-made collection of values and techniques quite different from those normally adopted by architects. While Wines' jokes are more effective for being unexpected and uncommon, Venturi's strip is offered as a universal, a generic model of one possible form of urbanism.

And yet it is difficult to see what kind of relationship this model could strike up with the conventional modes of architecture. Venturi castigates the efforts of the Strip Beautification Committee to apply conventional notions of improvement such as tree planting and unification of building treatments, since these misunderstand and compromise its real character. But if the efforts to make the strip conform to 'Architecture' are doomed, the converse seems hardly more promising. Venturi catalogues the efforts of modern architecture to absorb earlier models, such as nineteenth-century industrial buildings, Italian hill-towns and Cape Kennedy, and ranges these as symptomatic of the architectural method with which the 'vital mess' of the strip contrasts. And if those sources could not be enlisted without some loss of their original virtue, it seems hardly possible that assimilation of the strip would be more successful.

If Venturi's message is thus for architects a difficult one to apply, and perhaps more exhilarating in its iconoclasm than in its formulation of new models, it does carry one straightforward exhortation for the urban designer which contrasts with other views we have considered. 'The commercial strip . . . challenges the architect to take a positive non-chip-on-the-shoulder view. Architects are out of the habit of looking nonjudgmentally at the environment, because orthodox Modern architecture is progressive, if not revolutionary, utopian, and puristic; it is dissatisfied with *existing* conditions. Modern architecture has been anything but permissive: Architects have preferred to change the existing environment rather than enhance what is there. . . . For the artist, creating the new may mean choosing the old or the existing. Pop artists have relearned this. Our acknowledgement of existing, commercial architecture at the scale of the highway is within this tradition.'[28]

## 4.5 URBAN DESIGN AS PUBLIC PRESENCE

ONE WAY OUT OF THE IMPASSE SUGGESTED BY Venturi's analysis, of a messy environment which immediately loses its saving characteristic, its vitality, as soon as one attempts to regulate it or absorb it into a public culture, is to regard the public presence not as an ordering discipline for the private display, but simply as a third party, a connective theme which surfaces from time to time at significant points in the city. This approach is suggested by Emilio Ambasz in his 1975 project for Grand Rapids, Michigan, in which an abandoned Federal Building is rehabilitated as a new Community Arts Center. Between the wings of the Beaux-Arts building, Ambasz proposed the insertion of a large inclined plane acting both as a translucent canopy to the enclosed forecourt of the building and as a monumental flight of steps up to the Grand Foyer at first floor level. On either side of this stairway water was intended to flow down the inclined surface as a silent cascade visible from across the public space facing the building. Apart from these specific functions, however, the tilted plane was envisaged as the first of a series and 'as an architectural sign whenever there is a need to identify other abandoned city buildings recovered by and for the Community Arts Center.'[29]

It could be argued that this idea is a variant of the nineteenth-century habit of evoking a civic presence through the construction of key public buildings, but with the Victorian use of recognizable and prestigious architectural languages replaced by an equally arbitrary but memorable formal device, which Ambasz proposed to reinforce by secondary features, such as a change in the materials of the pavements as they passed under the tilted planes projecting out from the public buildings. Now while this would undoubtedly clarify and locate the presence of the community in built form, it could be said to have isolated and limited it, so that it becomes, in effect, another supermarket chain competing for attention.

An alternative approach to reinforcing the public presence would then be not to localize it in public buildings, but to allow it to invade private ones, and erode the conventional demarcation lines of public and private space. It could be said that those commercial developments which trade some planning gain (building height perhaps) for space at street level, and thus hand over space to public 'piazzas' are contributing to such a process, but in practice the public gain is often no more than token. A more fundamental probing of the boundary is suggested by Herman Hertzberger in a num-

ber of his building commissions in which he has encouraged or persuaded his clients to re-examine their needs for territorial limits. In the offices at Apeldoorn, for example, the customary single formal office entrance is replaced by a number of low-key points of entry around the perimeter of the building, which lead by way of internal streets to the coffee bar and other facilities inside. Office workers are free to take breaks at times to suit themselves, and their families are then encouraged to meet them and use the office facilities during the day. Thus the extension of public accessibility into normally reserved areas raises corresponding questions about the relationship between work, family and leisure. In his music centre at Utrecht, Herzberger poses a similar challenge in relation to cultural activities.

Ambasz and Hertzberger thus provide us with

two models of the representation in urban design of the public presence, one independent and a counterpoint to the mixture of private uses, and the other engaging them and challenging their assumed terms of accessibility and in the process the whole nature of social patterns of life. Both undoubtedly have considerable relevance for the future. Regarding the second, for instance, a continuation of the search for a more rational duplication of scarce facilities, such as office car parks and school sports facilities, outside their hours of primary use, will tend to erode the idea of exclusive functions on economic grounds alone. For our purposes, however, both Ambasz's and Hertzberger's initiatives perhaps suffer from the limitation of deriving their strength and clarity primarily from the fact that they are each the product of a single designer.

*Emilio Ambasz, Community Arts Center, Grand Rapids, Michigan, US, 1975–79.*

*Herman Hertzberger (with Lucas and Niemeyer), Centraal Beheer Office Building, Apeldoorn, Netherlands, 1972, cutaway section.*

*Herman Hertzberger, Vredenburg Music Centre, Utrecht, Netherlands, 1979, plan.*

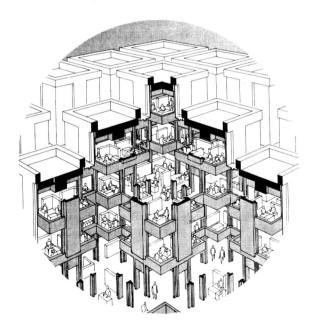

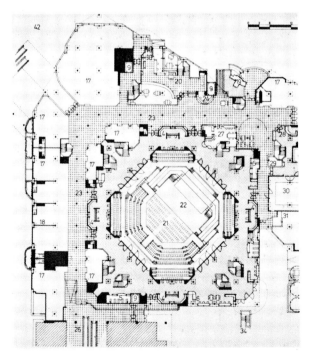

## 4.6 URBAN DESIGN AS THEATRE

IF THIS CRITICISM IS FELT TO BE VALID WE MIGHT search for an elaboration of the public presence from a single committed gesture into an extended pattern of actions which a number of designers might develop over a period of time. This suggests the analogy of theatre, and the urban designer as producer or script-writer. We have already seen this idea in Shepherd Fidler and Cullen's winning Telford competition entry, and their explanation that they sought to provide 'the plot' which would then be elaborated by individual designers into 'the story'. In another town design, for a new community near Aberdeen called Maryculter, Gordon Cullen with Kenneth Browne, Dan Donohue and David Gosling proposed a similar strategy of

sequentially experienced town events around a circuit form, culminating in a central citadel focus. The problem of artificially creating a new village with the authenticity of one which has developed over a long period of time is then resolved by considering it as a 'story' or 'score' developed around themes suggested by the landscape, the context of appropriate local vernacular forms (in this case, for example, the traditional protective enclosures of the kale yards) and the 'characters' assumed to be present in the 'cast'.

Of course there are other forms of theatre besides the charming and wholesome performances in which Cullen invites us to participate. An extraordinary recent example of urban design as theatre is to be seen in Domenig's design for the Zentrals-

*Gosling, Cullen and Donohue, Maryculter New Town, Aberdeen, 1974.*

*Gordon Cullen, Maryculter New Town, Aberdeen, 1974, sequential study.*

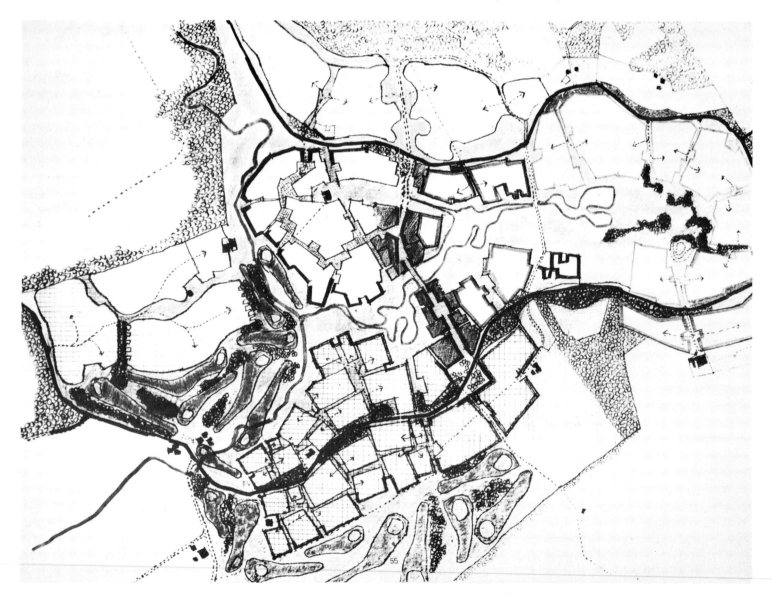

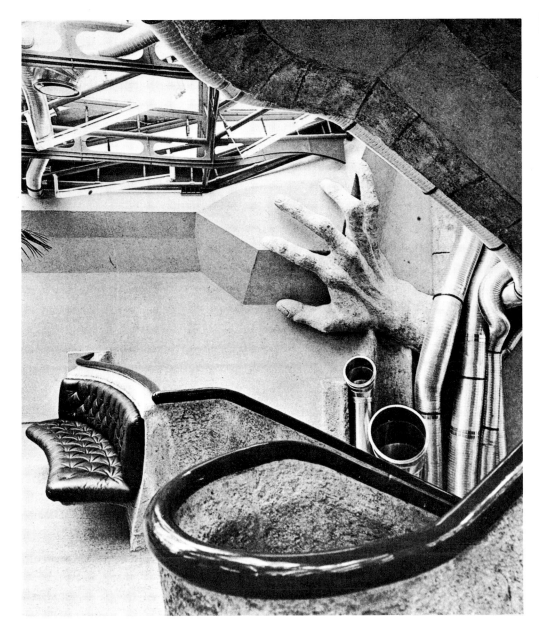

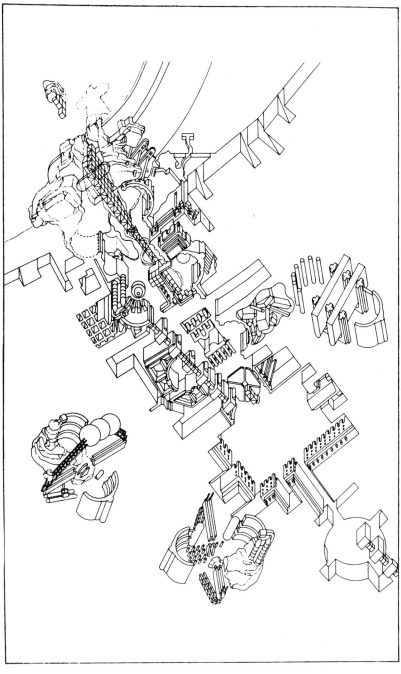

*Günther Domenig,*
*Zentralsparkasse Bank,*
*Favoriten, Vienna, 1979.*

*Bernard Tschumi,*
*'Joyce's Garden',*
*manifesto 4, 1977.*

parkasse bank in Vienna.[30] Bearing a resemblance to the wilder fantasies of the Swiss artist, H.R. Giger (set designer of early scenes in the horror movie *Alien*), the building resolutely rejects conventions of structure, form, permanence and security normally associated with a city bank building. Comparisons might be drawn with Gaudí or Van der Velde's work earlier in the century, but this design has a different intent as a theatrical statement. The incredible appearance of the street facade is surpassed by the interior design with its connotations of the human organism. Public reaction has been surprisingly mixed rather than, as one might have supposed, uniformly hostile, with comments ranging from 'a disgrace to the

district' and 'a monkey cage' to 'a super-style building' and 'at last something different'. Perhaps it achieves the same impact intended by Franz Kafka in his short story *Metamorphosis*[31] describing the transformation of a human being into a giant insect—a reaction of shock but not necessarily a lack of acceptance.

As Tschumi reminds us, there is also the theatre of Cruelty, and of the Absurd: '... architecture does not choose sides. It happens underneath the stadium arches where fans bash one another with bicycle-chains ... Architecture is defined by the actions it witnesses as much as by the enclosures of its walls. Murder in the street differs from Murder in the Cathedral in the same way as love in the

street differs from the Street of Love. Radically.'

Tschumi has gone further, in using a literary work, James Joyce's *Finnegan's Wake*, as the 'script' for an urban design project linking Covent Garden through to the River Thames, in which architectural elements are counterparts of the fictional characters and their associations. One problem with this approach, which Tschumi neatly describes as 'function follows fiction', is that, as we saw in the case of Telford, the functions have a nasty tendency to ignore the script. If we are to have a scripted performance at all then, rather than a piece of improvised theatre, we may have to limit the repertoire to certain sustainable forms.

## 4.7 URBAN DESIGN AS THE GUARDIANSHIP OF URBAN STANDARDS

PRESUMABLY THE MOST STRAIGHTFORWARD SOURCE OF durable forms is the city itself. If we chose to regard it not as a blank site for the construction of solutions to urban problems, but as a species of viable organisms which have already defined the generic type-solutions available to use and which need not be re-invented but only reapplied, then we would switch our attention from methods and analogies and look to the city itself as our primary source. Anthony Vidler has suggested that in the work of Aldo Rossi, Leon Krier and the 'rapidly multiplying examples' of the new Rationalists, such a source has become sufficiently well established for it to constitute a 'third typology', as powerful an inspiration of architectural order as the earlier typologies of the natural order, symbolized by the primitive hut, and the industrial order symbolized by the machine.[32] Until the point at which it was destroyed by the disastrous innovations of the twentieth century, the city is seen as having developed certain 'type' elements, rather in the sense that Le Corbusier intended the term in relation to 'objet-types', as universal solutions of great simplicity and integrity, arrived at over a period of time by the operation of anonymous forces of selection. In the case of the city, the type-solutions include the quarter, the block, and a variety of urban-space types such as streets, avenues, squares, arcades and colonnades.

This attempt to identify the essential components of cities-as-they-actually-are, and then classify them, is similar in intention to Lynch's analysis (although Lynch's methods and categories are, of course, quite different) and again to Camillo Sitte's. Indeed, Sitte's comparative appraisal of city squares in *Der Städtebau* forms a direct precedent for the urban specimen collections which accompany many new Rationalist investigations of the city and its element types. Of these perhaps Rob Krier's collection of squares, illustrated as the 'Morphological series of Urban Spaces' in his book *Urban Space* (originally published in Germany as *Stadtraum*) is the most comprehensive,[33] while his brother Leon has compiled a morphology of quarters,[34] and, with Enrico Guidoni and others, of city blocks.[35] The relationships between these physical components of the traditional city have also been studied, and encapsulated in Leon Krier's 'three models to conceive urban spaces', which again perhaps recall Le Corbusier and his 1929 formulation of four alternative methods of architectural composition.

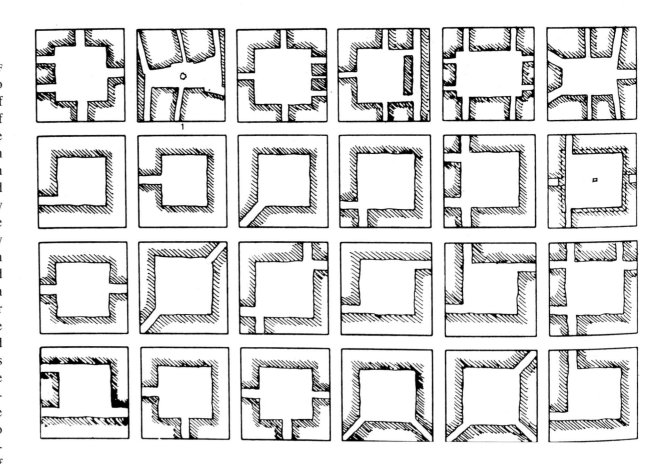

*Rob Krier, 'Variations on a four-sided square', 1979.*

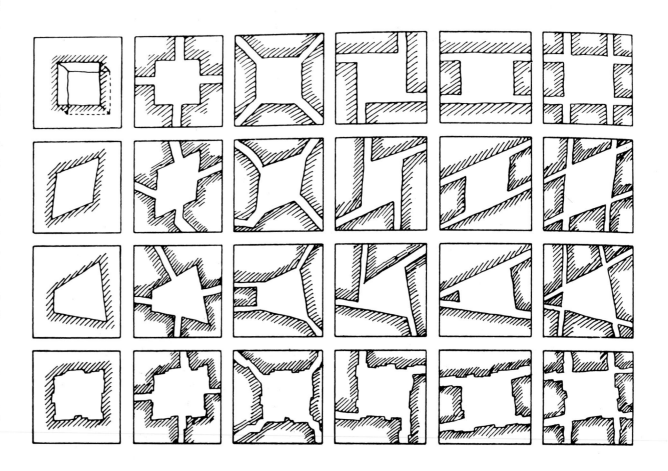

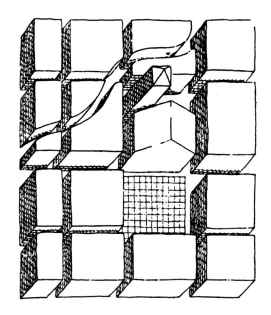

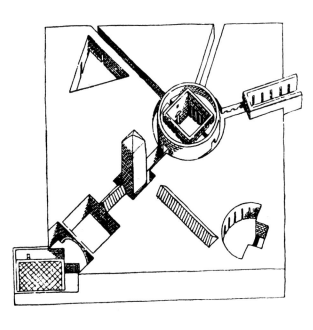

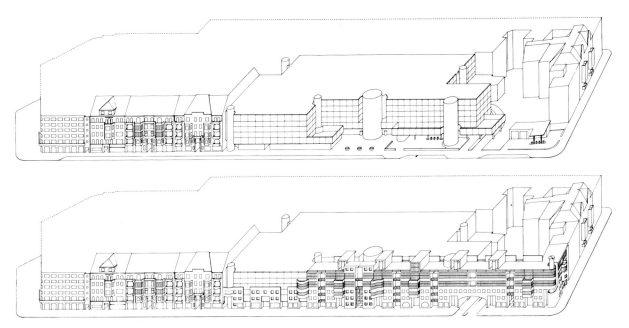

*Leon Krier, 'Three Models of Urban Space', 1979.*

*James Stirling, Michael Wilford and Associates, Meineke Strasse, Berlin, 1976, projections of existing and proposed frontages.*

This view of urban design, which sees its central purpose as the protection and restoration of the fundamental characteristics of the nineteenth-century city, is exemplified by James Stirling and Michael Wilford's hypothetical reconstruction of Meineke Strasse in Berlin. While one side of this street retains the older pattern of development, most of the other has been eroded by commerical developments which typify the post-War pattern. The blank elevation of a parking garage has been pushed back from the old building line to leave an empty strip behind the pavement, the formal lines of trees down each footpath have been arbitrarily removed, and the corner of the city block where Meineke Strasse meets Leitzenburger Strasse has been blown open. The problem for the urban designer then becomes to recover the old city form-types of street and block, and this is done by the insertion of new accommodation along the old building line and the restoration of the corner in a celebratory 'hinge'.

There must be much to recommend an urban design strategy which aims to draw attention to certain stable formal categories, drawn from the analysis of existing cities, and to use these as the agreed basis for future action. A critique of the new Rationalist version of that plan might then begin by asking whether the analysis is a complete one. It is of course selective, in the sense that Leon Krier's three models specifically exclude a fourth

permutation of his constraints, the one in which blocks are 'precise spatial types' and the spaces are what remain. This corresponds to the Ville Radieuse model which is rejected as a recent aberration, a mistake which must be repealed in a manner exemplified by Rodrigo Pérez de Arce's projects for the 'reurbanization' of Le Corbusier's and Louis Kahn's Capitol areas of Chandigarh and Dacca, by 'reversing the process of analytical de-composition' and filling their empty spaces with blocks, streets and squares.[36]

While this may be regarded as the rejection of an 'artificial' alternative, there is another sense in which the new Rationalist analysis is selective in its approach to the 'third typology', in that it seems in practice to show a preference for a specific urban prototype, the nineteenth-century European city with orthogonal street pattern. This preference is heavily reinforced by the use of an architectural language which Colin Rowe has aptly described as 'the tricking out of Beaux-Arts plans with neo-primitive facades'.[37] Although by no means an inevitable accompaniment of the original analytical intention to seek basic urban solution-types, the choice is not an arbitrary one, but as Leon Krier has set out, forms part of a package of social and architectural intentions which together constitute 'the great themes of this movement' and which are worth listing here:

'1 The physical and social conservation of the

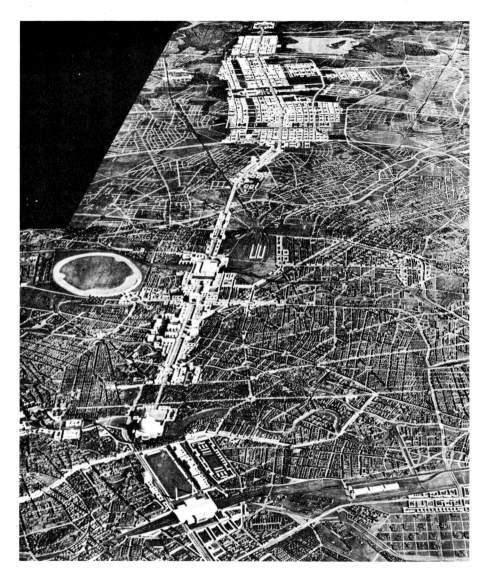

*Rob Krier, Plan for the expansion of Stuttgart, 1973.*

▷
*Albert Speer, Die Nord-Süd Achse, Berlin, 1939.*

historical centres as desirable models of collective life.

'2 The conception of urban space as the primary organising element of the urban morphology.

'3 The typological and morphological studies as the basis for a new architectural discipline.

'4 The growing conscience that the history of the city delivers precise facts, which permits one to engage an immediate and precise action, in the reconstruction of the street, the square, the quartier.

'5 The transformation of housing zones (dormitory cities) into complex parts of the city, into cities within the city, into quartiers which integrate all the functions of urban life.

'6 The rediscovery of the primary elements of Architecture, the column, the wall, the roof, etc.'[38]

The conviction and consistency with which this programme is presented should not prevent us from examining the logic of its urban design component, and in particular its assertion that the study of the historical form-types does provide us with a

relevant and useful basis on which to proceed. It is, after all, not long ago that those same form-types were being condemned as 'a picture of the seventh circle of Dante's Inferno', and the nineteenth-century city 'as it exists in actuality', as 'an absurdity'.[39]

It might be argued that that particular model of the third typology has been undermined by forces additional to the preferences of the Modern Movement, and that these must be recognized in any new approach. This argument was developed in a project run by Cornell University with O.M. Ungers, Rem Koolhaas and others, at the Sommer Akademie of Berlin in 1977, which sought to define an effective urban design strategy for that city. They concluded that 'the current opinion whereby the historic quarters of the city can be preserved and saved only through additional and integrant building stems from erroneous assumptions and is therefore illusory'.[40] The fallacy arises from the depopulation of the city, which undermines all the bases upon which a return to the historic forms

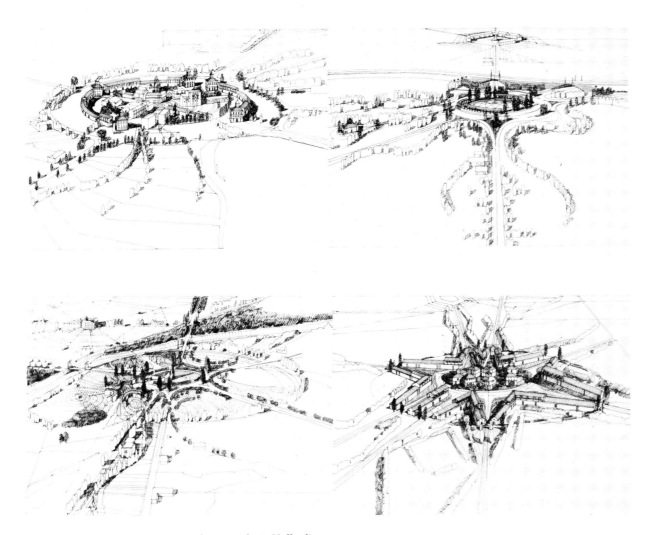

Paolo Portoghesi, Vallo di Diano, junctions. Top left *the junctions recover existing architecture with a design which connects new and old streets.*

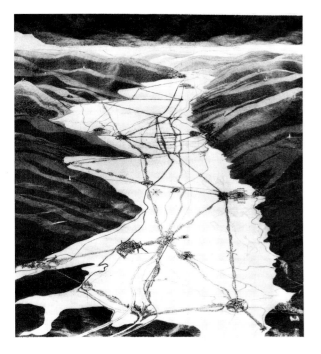

Paolo Portoghesi, Vallo di Diano, 1981, nodal system for the valley plan.

ignore the activities and events which the city contains (except perhaps those which celebrate the virtues of 'collective life') in defiance of the view expressed by Tschumi that 'What matters is that there is no architecture without the relationship between *live actions* and the spaces themselves.' By contrast, one might compare Venturi's strip, which, although generated by private display, works as an overall system to identify variations in intensity of use and points of focus of activity as they come into effect. One might suggest then that the new Rationalist analysis of existing city form has identified those formal elements and structures which tend to stability and uniformity, but has omitted those equally pervasive structuring principles which tend to variety and change. This does not diminish the value of the first analysis, but might reinforce the argument that the analysis can be separated from the formal preferences which the new Rationalists attach to it. These, as we have seen, are also heavily loaded with images of collective stability and control and give rise to schemes which sometimes directly recall earlier authoritarian models, as in Rob Krier's proposal for the westward axial expansion of Stuttgart which, superficially at least, bears a striking similarity to Albert Speer's monumental plans of 1939 for the Grosse Achse in Berlin.

A proposal by Paolo Portoghesi in 1981, was intended to unite the dispersed residents of an Italian rural valley (Vallo di Diano, Salerno) into a coherent community. The urban forms used were unashamedly historicist, reflecting both Baroque and Islamic architecture, though in technological or functional terms the proposals reflect contemporary thought. The design has the appearance of an illustration from fiction, almost theatrical in quality. Portoghesi allocates these formal villages in a tight network on the lower slopes of the valley rather than in the valley base which provides the background to a formal network of radiating roads. The junctions of these radiating roads form different nodal points with contrasting forms giving, as Peter Buchanan says, 'a spectrum of urban space and activities suited to a richly varied and contemporary lifestyle (*The Architectural Review*, December 1981). Each node represents different functions—commerce, culture, local government and recreation. The centre of the valley is accentuated by a long lake created from further excavation of the river bed. Whilst the scheme resembles, on a larger scale, the work of Clough Williams-Ellis at Portmeirion, it is, in actuality, firmly in the realm of urban design as theatre.

could be undertaken, so that 'In Berlin in particular the consequences of the theory of a restored city, in the sense of an historic reconstruction, would be the reverse of those expected, since the inexorable depopulation process would only be camouflaged and all action taken to improve reality would be pointlessly deferred to the consequent disadvantage of the city.' In order to reconcile the strategy to these new circumstances, it was proposed that investment should be restricted to a series of historic enclaves, allowing existing developments in the intervening spaces to wither away and leave, in effect, a 'city-archipelago' of 'urban islands', 'a federation of single towns with different structures, developed in a deliberately authentic manner'.

Although the result is not incompatible with the preferred pattern of quarters, blocks and streets, it suggests that the new Rationalist description of the city may be too restrictive, too insensitive to forces within it which themselves provide it with structure and form. The description seems in fact largely to

*Clough Williams-Ellis, Portmeirion, 1925–79.*

## 4.8 URBAN DESIGN AS COLLAGE

THE VILLAGE OF PORTMEIRION, STANDING ON AN isolated peninsula at the head of Cardigan Bay in North Wales, now attracts over 100,000 visitors each year to what is in effect a private architectural collection accumulated between 1925 and 1979 by Clough Williams-Ellis. As a piece of urban design, it is certainly theatrical, but not in the sense of a linear plot which we have discussed earlier. It is also nostalgic in its reference to a vernacular model, the Mediterranean fishing village of Portofino,

although not in the sense of a consistent reproduction as at Port Grimaud. Instead, and assisted by an isolation which allowed him both to protect the 'health and virginity' of 'my "New Model"'[41] from commercial vulgarization and also to ignore the local vernacular which on a more public site he would have felt obliged to acknowledge, Williams-Ellis cultivated 'a glorious medley of Italy, Wales, a pirate's lair, Cornwall, baroque, reason and romance'.[42] In being thus an assemblage of buildings of different periods and styles, using differing technologies and materials, and gathered over a

period of time, Portmeirion might well be regarded as a further viable model of the city in miniature.

We have suggested earlier that an implicit and arguable assumption of many urban design philosophies is the desirability of a particular technological or formal hegemony, so that such philosophies seem to imply that they will only really have been tested and their merits really appreciated when all opposing systems have been suppressed and the preferred models universally applied. We have also suggested that since few societies would wish or could afford to impose such an urban purity, it would seem worthwhile to develop a strategy that could not only accommodate this fact, but, like Portmeirion, could make a virtue of it.

Such an approach has been investigated by Colin Rowe and Fred Koetter, and the result christened by them 'Collage City'.[43] To envisage a model for such a place they compare two monumental palace complexes, the Villa Adriana at Tivoli and the Palace at Versailles. The second, controlled by a single conception, is complete and stands for the elusive purity and hegemony sought by much urban design. The Villa Adriana, however, consists of a number of discrete component areas, each different in character and organization, a fragment of some other whole, which are brought together in a fortuitous and pragmatic assembly, a collage in which the dialectic between dissimilar components is as important as the parts themselves.

Rowe and Koetter go on to explore the implications of this idea, and to draw upon related ideas which contribute to it. Claude Lévi-Strauss' notion of the *bricoleur*, for example, is invoked as a possible source of design attitudes for the urban collagist. In *The Savage Mind* Lévi-Strauss distinguishes the *bricoleur* from the engineer or scientist 'by the inverse functions which they assign to events and structures as means and ends, the scientist creating events . . . by means of structures and the "bricoleur" creating structures by means of events'.[44] Again, their attitude to tools is contrasted, the engineer subordinating the task to the availability of raw materials and a purpose-designed set of tools, while the *bricoleur* improvises with a magpie collection of ready-made tools which will be reused for quite different projects.

Through such analogies, and by the investigation of the philosophical implications of the design principle, Rowe and Koetter developed an elaborate and subtle appreciation of the pluralist approach. Against it, one might object that it would hardly be amenable to prescription. Indeed, by its avoidance of simple and unitary goals it would be peculiarly difficult for either lay or professional bureaucracies to control, and in place of 'the blinding self-righteousness of unitary conviction' it would be necessary to recognize 'a more tragic cognition of the dazzling and the scarcely to be resolved multiformity of experience'.[45] If the freedom is thus a demanding one, we can at least be comforted by Rowe's thought that it 'might be a means of permitting us the enjoyment of Utopian poetics without our being obliged to suffer the embarrassment of Utopian politics'.[46]

*Versailles, France, view from 'Collage City'.*

*Villa Adriana, Tivoli, view from 'Collage City'.*

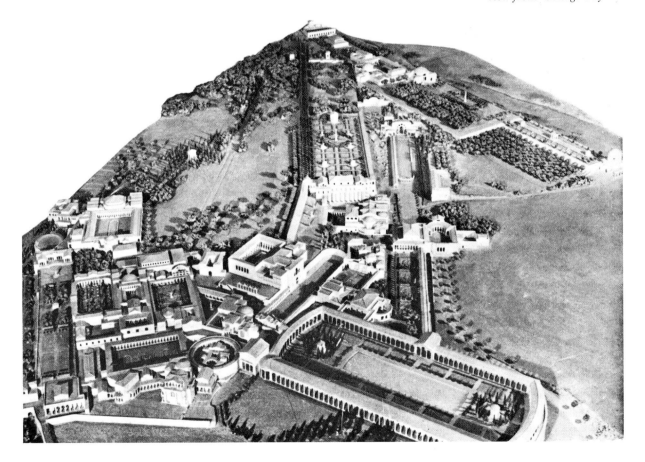

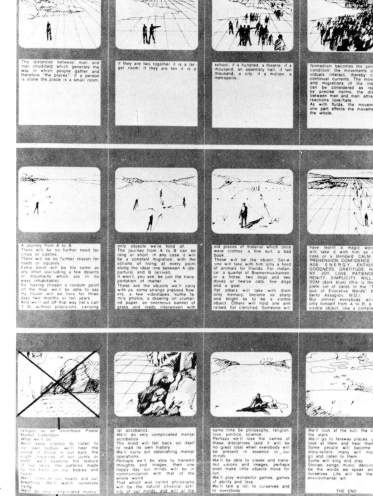

*Superstudio, 'Cinque storie del Superstudio', 1972.*

As a final postscript to this review of possible future directions for urban design, we might take the Italian Superstudio group's cartoon strip 'Vita, Educazione, Cerimonia, Amore, Morte—Cinque storie del Superstudio'. Entitled 'Life—or the public image of truly modern architecture' and subtitled 'Supersurface—an alternative model of life on earth', it proposes perhaps the ultimate statement of post-industrial urbanism: 'If the instruments of design have become as sharp as lancets and as sensitive as sounding lines, we can use them for a delicate laboratory. Thus beyond the convulsions of over-production, a state can be born of calm in which a world takes shape without products and refuse, a zone in which the mind is energy and raw material and is also the final product, the only intangible object for consumption. The designing of a region free from the pollution of design is very similar to a design for a terrestrial paradise.... This is the definitive product. This is only one of the projects for a marvellous metamorphosis.'[47]

## NOTES

1 Reyner Banham, *Theory and Design in the First Machine Age*, The Architectural Press, London 1960, pp. 11–12.
2 Banham, *ibid*.
3 Published in *The Architects Journal*, 12 December 1979, p. 1243.
4 Peter Cook, 'Melting Architecture', catalogue to exhibition at Art Net, London, 1–20 December 1975.
5 Erwin Panofsky, *Meaning in the Visual Arts*, Doubleday Anchor Books, Doubleday & Co. Inc., Garden City, New York 1955, Chapter 7, 'Et in Arcadia Ego', p. 297.
6 Panofsky, *ibid*., p. 297.
7 Translated from the introduction to the monograph *La Arquitectura Alternative de Emilio Ambasz* by Marina Waisman, published by Editorial Summa, Buenos Aires, September 1977, p. 15.
8 Waisman, *ibid*., p. 11.
9 Tom Wolfe, 'The "Me" Decade', *Harpers and Queen*, January 1977, p. 48.
10 Charles Jencks, 'A note on Stirling's Stuttgart Drawings', *Architectural Design*, Vol. 49, No. 8–9, 1979, p. 234.
11 Rob Krier, *Urban Space*, Academy Editions, London 1979, p. 170.
12 Robert Venturi, Denise Scott Brown, Steven Izenour, *Learning from Las Vegas: The Forgotten Symbolism of Architectural Form*, MIT Press, Cambridge, Mass. 1977, p. 52.
13 M.V. Posokhin, *Cities to Live In*, Novosti Press Agency Publishing House, Moscow 1974, p. 59.
14 Buckminster Fuller, 'An Open Letter to the Architects of the World', *op. cit.*
15 *Rational Architecture*, Editions des Archives d'Architecture Moderne, 1978, p. 41.
16 Geoffrey Broadbent, 'Neo-Classicism' in *Architectural Design*, Vol. 49, No. 8–9, 1979, p. 55.
17 *Rational Architecture*, *op. cit.*, p. 41.
18 Christopher Alexander, *Notes on the Synthesis of Form*, Cambridge, Mass. 1964.
19 *Progressive Architecture*, March 1969, pp. 94–113.
20 N.J. Habraken *et al*, *Variations: the Systematic Design of Supports*, MIT Press, Cambridge, Mass. 1976.
21 *Gaming Alternative Policies in Newtongrange*, University of Edinburgh, Department of Urban Design and Regional Planning, May 1979.
22 Cedric Green, 'Purpose-Designed Games', Paper to EPA Conference, Edinburgh, March 1978.
23 Nicholas Negroponte, *Soft Architecture Machines*, MIT Press, Cambridge, Mass. 1975, p. 145.
24 Negroponte, *ibid*., preface.
25 *6 Projects by S.I.T.E.*, Environmental Communications, Venice, California 1974.
26 Peter Marsh, 'Vintage Year', article in *Building Design*, November 18, 1977.
27 *Learning from Las Vegas*, *op. cit.*, p. xi.
28 *Ibid*., pp. 3–6.
29 Emilio Ambasz, notes on 'Project: Community Arts Center, Grand Rapids, Michigan', 1975.
30 'Banca Viennese', *Domus*, No. 602, January 1980, pp. 14–19.
31 Franz Kafka, *Collected Short Stories*, first published by Heinrich M. Sohn, Prague 1936.
32 Anthony Vidler, 'The Third Typology', essay in *Rational Architecture*, *op. cit.*, pp. 28–32.
33 Rob Krier, *op. cit.*
34 Leon Krier, 'The Cities Within the City II: Luxembourg', in *Architectural Design*, Vol. 49, No. 1, 1979, pp. 18–32.
35 *Lotus International* 19, June 1978.
36 *Ibid*., pp. 98–101.
37 Colin Rowe, foreword to Rob Krier, *op. cit.*, p. 9.
38 *Rational Architecture*, *op. cit.*, p. 42.
39 Quotations from Le Corbusier, *The City of Tomorrow*, The Architectural Press, London 1971 (originally published as *Urbanisme* in 1924).
40 *Lotus International* 19, June 1978, 'Cities Within the City', pp. 82–97.
41 Clough Williams-Ellis, *Portmeirion—The Place and its Meaning*, published by Portmeirion Ltd., Penrhyndeudraeth 1973, p. 14.
42 Christopher Hussey, 'Prologue' to *Portmeirion—The Place and its Meaning*, *ibid*., p. 8.
43 Colin Rowe and Fred Koetter, 'Collage City', *The Architectural Review*, August 1975 and MIT Press 1979.
44 Claude Lévi-Strauss, *The Savage Mind*, Chicago 1969, p. 16, quoted by Colin Rowe and Fred Koetter, 'Collage City', *The Architectural Review*, p. 83.
45 Rowe and Koetter, *ibid*., p. 86.
46 *Ibid*., p. 90.
47 *Casabella*, No. 367, 1972, pp. 15–26.

# PART FIVE
# CONCLUSION

THIS BOOK IS INTENDED PRIMARILY AS A REVIEW OF some of the principal urban design themes and projects to have appeared in the last 30 or so years, rather than as a polemical argument in favour of a specific view. Nevertheless, several readers of early drafts of this manuscript have made the very reasonable suggestion that such a review ought to be accompanied by a statement of the authors' own position in relation to the material presented. And since the book is the work of two authors, we have thought it best to give two such postscripts to the great diversity of material we have examined, offering our individual views on where it leaves us, and on the direction which urban design might now most fruitfully adopt.

## 5.1 DAVID GOSLING: THE NEED FOR AN URBAN DESIGN PLAN

IT IS INEVITABLE WHEN CONSIDERING A SUBJECT AS complex as urban design that definitive opinions must vary from one person to the next. In the introduction to this book, we noted that perhaps the real contribution currently being made towards the progress of urban design occurs in competitions; the most well-known of which is the 1979-80 Les Halles competition in Paris. Yet here this same difference of opinion was manifest amongst the distinguished international jury. As Bruno Zevi noted in an article in *L'Espresso* (February 17th, 1980), there were '... very violent disagreements between jury members, who were never able to arrive at a majority vote, at best nine out of twenty'.

The results of competitions, unlikely to be built, throw up an immensely rich spectrum of ideas about the future city, far more imaginative and appealing than the huge redevelopment projects which actually are built. The little publicized Tegeler Hafen competition in Berlin, for example, the results of which were announced in November 1980, included schemes by figures such as Charles Moore, Arata Isozaki and Leon Krier. Indeed, the German competition system has perhaps done more than any other in the world to promote and encourage adventurous architecture and urban design.

In human terms, however, urban design should perhaps be an attempt to satisfy the needs and aspirations of the inhabitants of any urban community in response to their visual environment. The work of Kevin Lynch and Donald Appleyard described earlier was the most direct attempt to discover how people perceived and responded to their environment and to express these responses in a graphic form which could be translated into planning analyses and possibly proposals. A more theoretical but no less valid approach was that of the environmental psychologists, the most notable of whom in the United Kingdom are Terence Lee and David Canter of the University of Surrey. Lee, in particular, recognized the need for a 'cognitive map' or 'socio-spatial schema'.

Some 20 years after Lynch's pioneering work, the physical planning process still does not include the visual design process as part of the normal sequence of work. Certainly, many planning teams now make visual analyses of the urban environment, but they stop short of any definitive attempt at a three-dimensional proposal related to their understanding of the responses of the citizen. Exceptions are to be found, particularly in the work of the American practice, Arrowstreet.

Gordon Cullen's work, which goes back further than Kevin Lynch's, recognizes the need to respond to the qualities of the visual environment. Even more importantly, Cullen indicated that the secret of the creation of a visually satisfactory urban complex lies in the recognition of movement as part of the design process (serial vision). Appleyard developed this theme through the use of ambitious video and filming techniques, but again this important aspect of urban design is rarely to be found in the work of planning teams.

A Saudi Arabian study by Farhat Khorshid Tashkandi for an MIT Research Project is an example of urban design analysis applied to totally different cultural and ethnic settlements. Salman Al-Sedairy, a Saudi Arabian government chief architect, is perhaps one of the first public architects to incorporate urban design procedures at the very largest scale. Taking large groups of New Town plans and using an international design team, he has evolved a methodology of integrative social, economic and physical planning right down to the detailed design of houses and the immediate landscaping. Urban design is a significant part of this process.

The present preoccupation among a new gener-

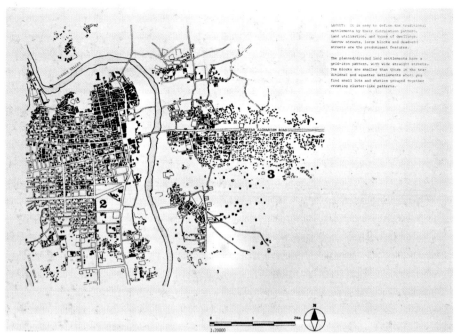

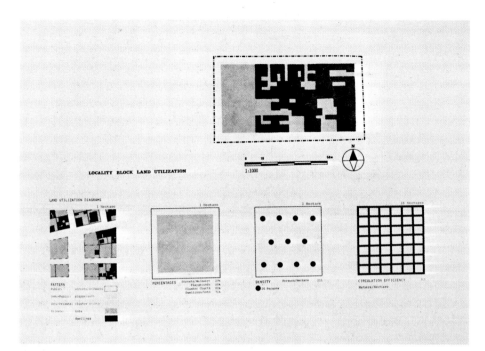

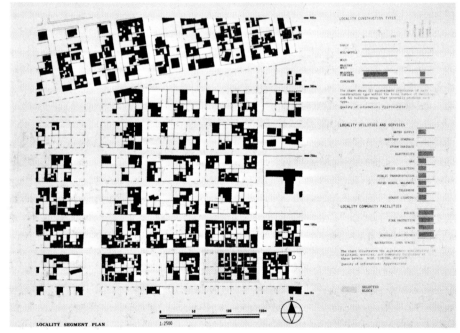

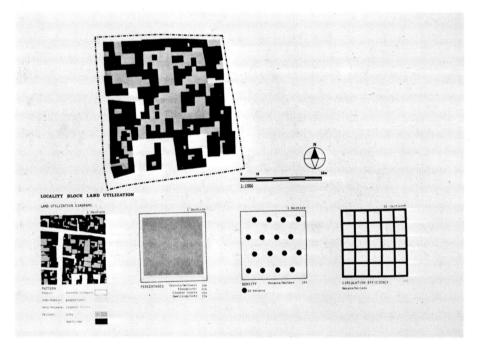

*F.K. Tashkandi, M. I. T. studies of Arabian settlements, 1979.*

ation of urban designers with historicism and morphology seems to have some dangerous precedents. An obsession with Neo classicism can be found in many of the totalitarian political regimes of the twentieth century. It may be seen as a tangible expression of power, and although highly skilled designers may conjure up visions of the ordered city for quite different political reasons and ideals, it appears, nevertheless, to be a super-imposition of the political ruler and the designer upon the people, for the good of the people. Other authorities have referred to these designers, some-what patronizingly, as the 'Lamborghini Marxists'. It has to be said that the 'People's Palaces' they provide often seem remote from the true wishes of the people.

Early in 1971, UNICEF (The United Nations Children's Fund) stated that only 10% of children in Third World countries ever receive medical attention of any sort. It begs the question whether the majority of the world's population need de-signers in the conventional sense when adequate food and shelter is their primary need. In under-developed or developing countries perhaps more self-determination for the urban poor rather than less is called for. The lessons in Latin America described by John Turner and others indicate that reconstruction and self-determination are often a more satisfactory answer in psychological and prac-tical terms for the inhabitants of squatter settle-ments than the forceful removal of families to government-controlled housing projects. It is a case of the citizens creating their own urban design schema. This is not to deny that many of these groups received technical help from architects and others, but the final decision on the form of their urban complexes lay with the residents and not the technicians. Nor is self-determination necessarily confined to Third World countries. Cooperatives in Glasgow and the north-east of England or protest groups in the black ghettoes of North America are all indications of an alternative approach to urban

*Street scene, Moss Side, Manchester, 1981.*

*Destroyed school building, Moss Side, Manchester, England, 1981.*

*Unoccupied housing project known as the 'Weetabix', Belfast, Northern Ireland (photographed 1980).*

development. Jane Jacobs, in her analysis of American cities, and, more forcibly, Richard Sennett in *The Uses of Disorder*, make the case for an almost anarchistic variety and degree of self-determination.

Events in mainland Britain during the summer of 1981 mirrored the street violence of Belfast over the last decade. But in London's Brixton, Liverpool's Toxteth, or Manchester's Moss Side, the root causes were not sectarian, political or even tribal (as some observers have described the civil disturbances of Belfast). Though strenuously denied as the basic underlying cause, it is evident that bad housing conditions, social and economic

deprivation and the present spectre of permanent unemployment for the young all contributed to the explosion of violence witnessed in the inner areas of major British cities in 1981. This, combined with an antagonism between the police and the indigenous population, particularly in Toxteth, has brought frightening visions that George Orwell's prophesies[2] might yet be fulfilled. *The Sunday Times*[3] noted that 'There is a message here . . . just as important as any of the immediate causes and effects of the recent riots. Traditionally, our approach to groups at the bottom of the economic heap has been twofold. First, allay poverty, bad housing, poor education. . . . People with property

will tend to move out, insurance rates will tend to rise further, local rates will be heavy, good teachers harder to keep . . . in short, economic forces will create more and tighter informal ghettoes.' *The Guardian*,[4] commenting on the concern expressed by the chairwoman of the Liverpool Police Committee (Lady Margaret Simey), remarked that in 'Toxteth they [the police] are faced with a vital community which has its own coarse inner energy and customs which could not be further from [that] simplistic image. Large families live contentedly or noisily on top of one another . . . but the community works and could do wonders by itself with more attention and the right kind of social decisions at

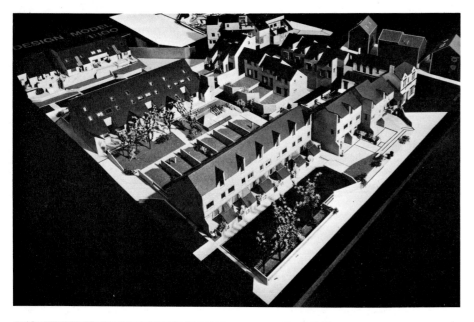

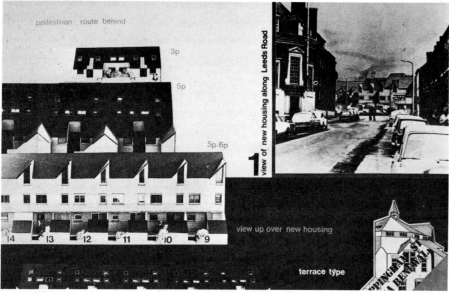

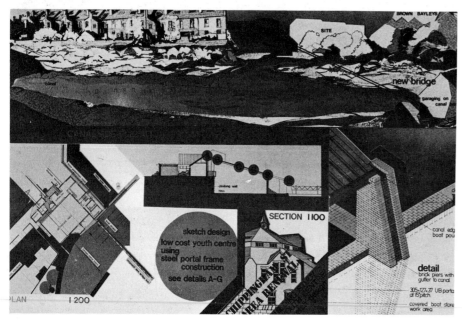

*Chris Liddle, social preservation and rehabilitation scheme, Attercliffe, Sheffield, England (Sheffield University thesis project, 1976).*

local and national level.' It has been said in the previous paragraphs that perhaps a positive direction for urban development in underdeveloped and developing countries is a degree of self-determination. Perhaps this is equally true for developed countries or even for 'post-industrial' societies such as Britain, especially in multi-racial communities such as Liverpool's Toxteth.

Even where applied design is considered to be necessary, popular response does not seem to favour grand Neoclassical projects, but rather the application of humour and wit. The Best supermarkets in the United States by SITE are an example; Clough Williams-Ellis' Portmeirion Village is another type of theatrical display; while a recent example of the application to urban design of the lessons of fun fairs and Disneyland, discussed in Part Three of this book, is Jean and Martine Patton's attractive submission for the Les Halles competition.

Among groups of designers, perhaps the most sensitive to changes in the climate of design today is the student body, whose annual output in school exhibitions provides an enormously varied and relevant commentary on both current and anticipated future issues. Five projects from Sheffield University which won RIBA Urban Design Prizes illustrate what might be regarded as a mainstream position reflecting the substantive shift of interest from the early 1970s onwards towards projects investigating the existing fabric of cities. The authors tended to reject 'high-technology solutions' in favour of generating 'idiosyncratic environments by turning building complexes inside out', and stressed the importance of human scale within an urban form structured so as to become readable and memorable (Macdonald and Lees 1975). Degraded urban environments were selected so that an urban design system of incremental renewal rather than comprehensive redevelopment was achieved (Liddle 1976), with projects tackling the housing problem at local level but setting the solution within the framework of a physical development plan for the city regions (Greenwood and Mathieson 1978). By 1981, however, Gregory Penoyre, who won both the RIBA 1981 Urban Design Prize and 1982 *Architectural Design* Project Award (student section), showed a change in emphasis at Sheffield towards a much more formal and historicist approach seen at the Royal College of Art in London for a number of years previously.

In contrast to the low-technology solutions discussed above, the work of students at the RCA, where some extremely distinguished architectural

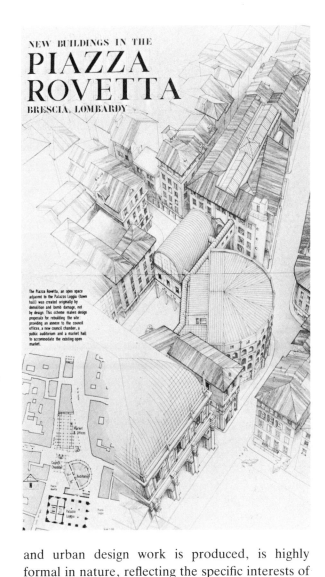

## NEW BUILDINGS IN THE
# PIAZZA ROVETTA
### BRESCIA, LOMBARDY

The Piazza Rovetta, an open space adjacent to the Palazzo Loggia (town hall) was created originally by demolition and bomb damage, not by design. This scheme makes design proposals for rebuilding the site: providing an annexe to the council offices, a new council chamber, a public auditorium and a market hall to accommodate the existing open market.

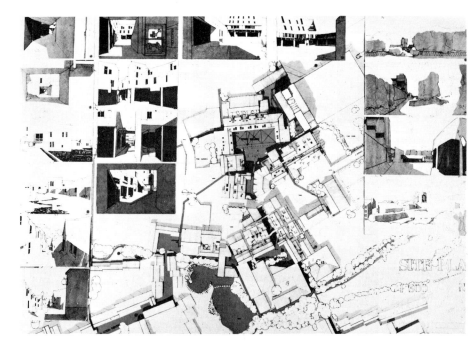

*Gregory Penoyre, redevelopment of central Brescia, Italy (Sheffield University thesis project, 1981).*

*Bob Macdonald and Dave Lees, Mosborough New Town, Sheffield, England, site plan and urban design sequence study (Sheffield University thesis project, 1975).*

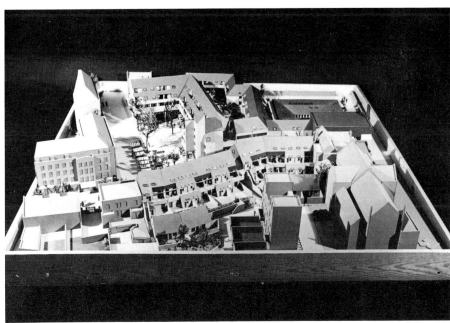

*Anne Greenwood and Richard Mathieson, redevelopment of Wapping, London, England (Sheffield University thesis project, 1978).*

and urban design work is produced, is highly formal in nature, reflecting the specific interests of the design tutors, and has been described as 'a reaction to our everyday environment, which grows increasingly abstract'. Land settlement patterns and building types are questioned as well as distinctions between public, private and semi-public realms. Architectural symbolism is seen as an important part of the course.[5] The RCAs department of architecture is particularly interesting since it was not founded within the framework of a formally recognized RIBA course, though such recognition was given in 1983. The department, headed by John Miller, has a small but distinguished team of architects including Christopher Cross, Ed Jones and Su Rogers, who teach a small group of post-graduate students, including furniture designers and landscape architects as well as graduate architects. The impressive consistency of their beautifully drawn, highly formal designs indicates a philosophy of design not really seen in any other British school of architecture. The particular emphasis on contextual problems makes the work of the RCA all the more relevant to urban design.

*Bob Macdonald and Dave Lees, Mosborough New Town centre, model.*

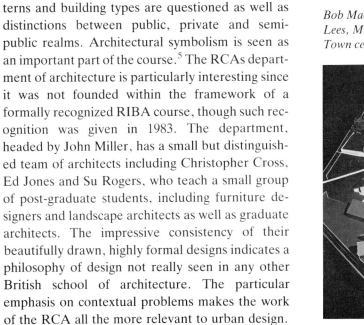

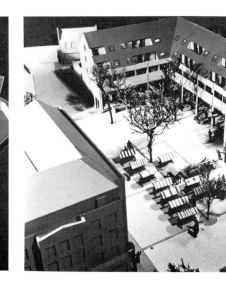

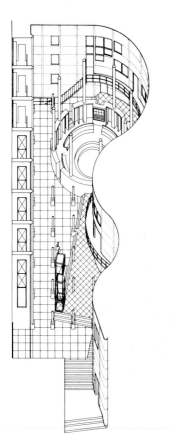

*Royal College of Art student projects, 1980, City of London studies.*

▽ *Sheila O'Donnell, Metal Exchange (Royal College of Art student project, 1980).*

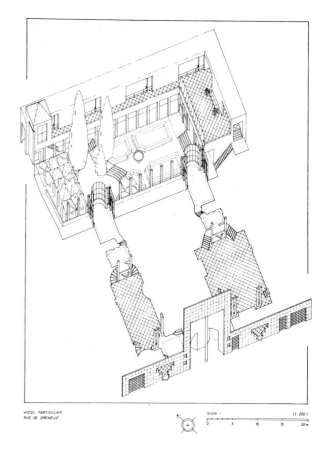

△ *Ed Bonness, 'Hôtel Particulier' (Royal College of Art student project, 1980).*

▽ *Ian Grant, Metal Exchange (Royal College of Art student project, 1980).*

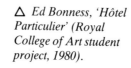

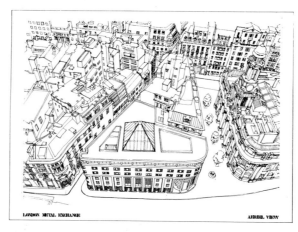

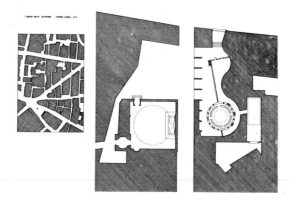

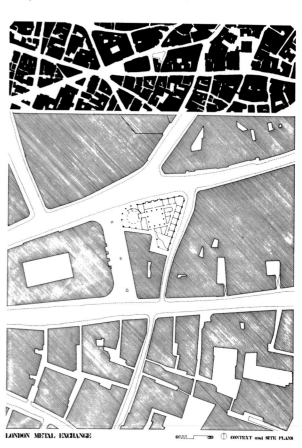

The Architectural Association school in London has been the centre of radical ideas for many years, attracting not only talented students from all over the world, but also major theorists and designers as tutors. The School of Architecture is administered through a teaching unit system whereby students elect to join a specific unit in the first year, intermediate school, or Diploma school. Because these units have been run by tutors as diverse as Peter Cook, Rem Koolhaas, Ron Herron, Bernard Tschumi, Leon Krier, Brian Anson and Tom Wooley, a great diversity of thinking is inevitably reflected in work of the students whom they teach, resulting in projects which are a test bed of new architecture and urban design.

We have tried to make it clear in this book that the present planning systems are woefully inadequate for producing urban environments which satisfy the aspirations of the citizens. Whether an almost anarchistic self-determination or an analytical cooperative approach is the answer, clearly some alternative has to be found. This final comment might appropriately apply to the planning dilemma of London Docklands. Here is a great area of derelict land with vast waterways in the heart of one of the world's great capital cities. The conflicting ideas of the public authorities and the plethora of land-use, traffic and economic surveys and plans have brought no solution. Neither will a series of developers' submissions, nor the creation of an Enterprise Zone create a satisfactory answer. The area is the very core of the city; it is the biggest development project in London since the work of Wren, and it is likely to be the last major urban development in Britain this century.

In 1981, a study was commissioned by the London Docklands Development Corporation, and David Gosling Associates were invited to join Edward Hollamby, Chief Architect, in the preparation of a comprehensive urban design study for the Isle of Dogs which included the Enterprise Zone. The small team was established in mid-1981, with Gordon Cullen joining later that year. The final report was published in late 1982.[6] It is probably premature to discuss whether the study itself was successful, but the actual execution of the work created unforeseen difficulties.

The alternative planning options presented by Gosling Associates tried to indicate the potential variety of opportunities and design approaches. The proposals were seen as an amalgam of the public and the private realms. The public realm concerned the public spaces formed by new and existing buildings, public movement systems

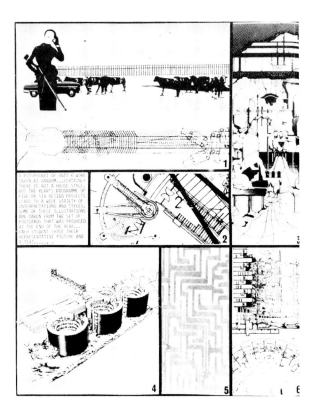

*Architectural Association*
*Unit 6 student projects,*
*tutor Rem Koolhaas.*

*Architectural Association*
*Unit 6 student projects,*
*1978, tutor Ron Herron.*

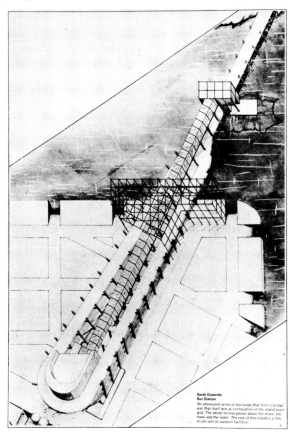

The game of architecture is an intricate play with rules that you may break or accept. These rules, like so many knots that cannot be untied, have the erotic significance of bondage: the more numerous and sophisticated the restraints, the greater the pleasure.

# ropes and rules

*Bernard Tschumi,*
Advertisements for
Architecture, *1978.*

*Architectural Association*
*Unit 2 student projects,*
*1976, tutor Leon Krier.*

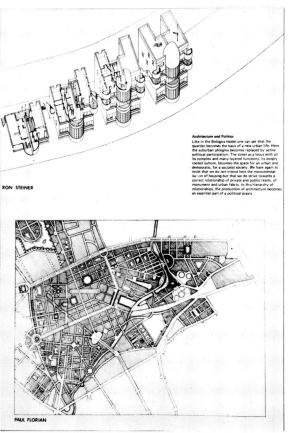

including pedestrian routes, access roads and rapid transit systems and the squares, streets, arcades, parks and open spaces which form the urban morphology or physical shape of the plan. This is not to say that a plan should establish hard rules which inhibit development, but rather that visual and social success is only possible within a public framework which has sufficient coherence and identity. The urban design plan was thus intended to stimulate ideas for development and weld together the existing community which forms the urban crust around the perimeter of the island with its vast spaces of water and vacant land inside forming the basis of the new development. The four options contained in the plan represent a summary of the way in which the initial conceptual studies relate to the final plans. Options one and two put forward proposals for a high-technology development and a water-based development. Option three was a mid-programme study which investigated the urban structure implications of the Greenwich axis and option four represented an interpretation of the marketing strategy requirements of the Development Corporation. Of the four plans, option three perhaps came closest to an authentic urban design plan.

In the whole of the peninsula forming the Isle of Dogs, Island Gardens at the southern tip is the only major public area giving a dramatic view out of the island towards Greenwich. The vista can only be described as breathtaking and is one of the major visual attributes of the area. The view from the Monument on the rise at Greenwich gives an

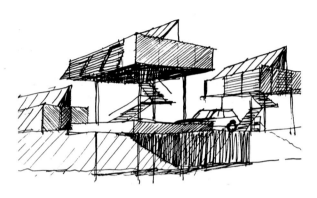

*David Gosling, preliminary studies for low-density, water-based housing, Blackwall Basin, Isle of Dogs, London.*

*Russ Davenport and Bill Taylor, Theme Park, Isle of Dogs, London, England (Sheffield University student project, 1982).*

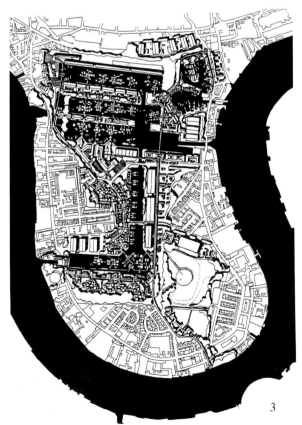

*David Gosling, preliminary urban design studies, Isle of Dogs, London, 1981, 1 theme park development, 2 structure plan and 3 water-based development.*

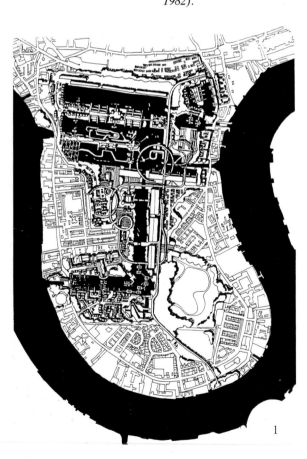

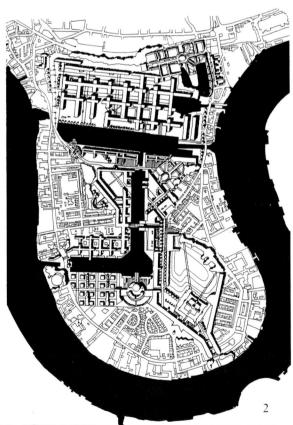

*Barry Maitland, Option 1, David Gosling and John Ferguson, Options 2, 3, 4, Isle of Dogs urban design plans.*

*Approved plan for the Isle of Dogs by London Docklands Development Corporation Team (chief architect E. Hollamby) 1982, illustrating the pragmatic approach to planning issues.*

equally good, though less dramatic, view of the island. The significance of this view is that there is a direct axis towards St Anne's Church, Limehouse, designed by Hawksmoor in 1714, on the north-western boundary of the isle. Because this axis crosses key points within the island including the Mudchute and the centre of the Glengall Bridge across the Millwall Dock, it provides an important key to the possible visual structure of the future Isle of Dogs and in itself acts as an urban generator. The axis takes on the mystical form of a ley-line with a significance beyond the linking of two monuments, and provides a series of reference points which enhance the visual structure. The plan provides a structural spine for development and relates the island to significant urban structures on the exterior. It relates one district to another by means of vistas (established in previous centuries), topographical relationships (Mudchute to Greenwich Hill), movement systems (river pedestrian tunnel, pedestrian paths, rapid transit) and the counterpoint of new buildings (new belvederes on the Mudchute, new towers proposed in the district core—the towers of St Anne's, Limehouse and Greenwich Palace). A narrow-gauge rail or tramway system enhances the axis and provides easy access for workers within the Enterprise Zone and outside it as well as a much-

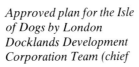

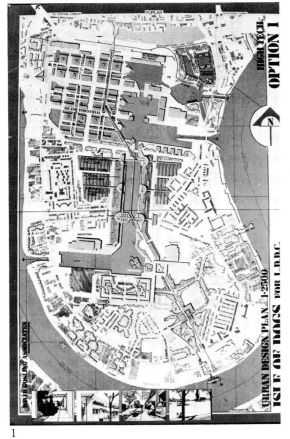

1

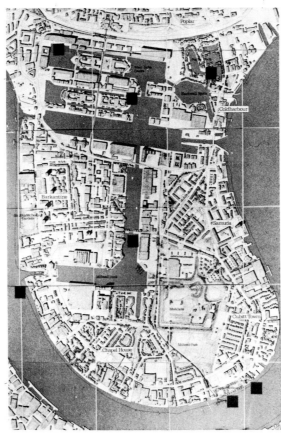

2

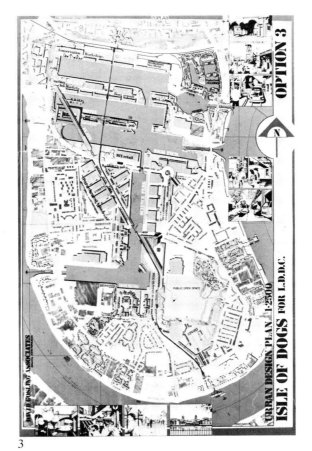

3

4

needed efficient public transport system for the residents. The ride sequence from one end of the island to the other could be spectacular, crossing major water basins, passing through or between buildings and utilizing old, high-level viaducts such as that adjacent to the Mudchute.

Nevertheless, the report finally presented to the Development Corporation Board in 1982 included the plan approved by the Chief Architect, Edward Hollamby. It represents a pragmatic planning approach which examines all existing and future planning constraints, alternative schemes put forward by various developers and incorporates planning decisions by the Development Corporation including the retention of the dock basins and the designation of major conservation areas. In spite of the worthy aims of such a plan, there appears to be no strong structural or visual framework and one suspects that the ensuing development will be merely an amalgam of developers' schemes with a lost opportunity in this century to recreate a coherent entity in metropolitan London.

By contrast, the visual appraisal and structure plan by Gordon Cullen provides a vocabulary of eye-level planning which defines identities and networks. It relates studies of key areas of existing development around the perimeter of the Isle of Dogs to suggestions for environmental improvement and a study of the inner core for new development. Beautifully drawn, it however still fails to provide a strong enough framework to guide developers, as does the pragmatic plan produced by the Corporation team responsible to Hollamby.

The unfortunate conclusion which may be drawn from this exercise in the preparation of an actual urban design plan, is that, in spite of some 30 years of development work in urban design theory, the disparities of approach cause confusion and contradiction. There must be a way of producing a consistent, practical imaginative approach to urban design. The wealth of examples presented in this book indicate no shortage of ideas, but rather lack of direction and agreement.

Perhaps there are other alternatives to this dilemma. If the three-dimensional urban design plan of the public realm indicated a conflict of three distinct philosophical approaches, then two im-

*Gordon Cullen: aerial view of Isle of Dogs, 1982.*

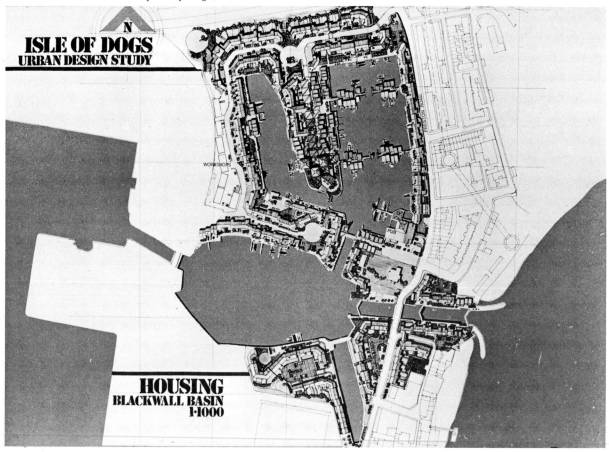

*David Gosling and John Ferguson, Isle of Dogs urban design study, detail of proposed Poplar Dock housing, 1982.*

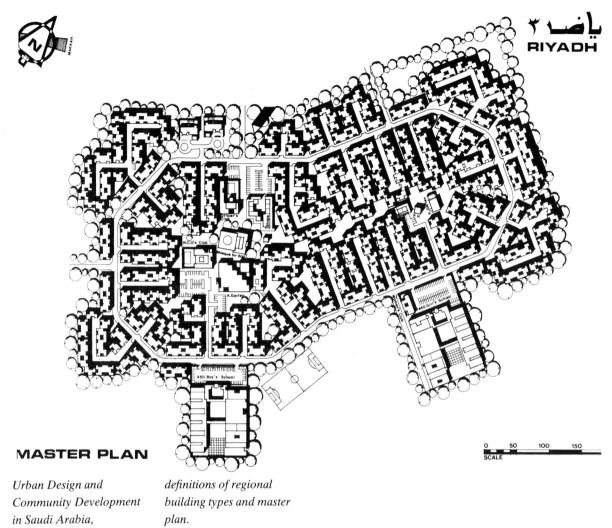

**MASTER PLAN**

يــاض٣
**RIYADH**

*Urban Design and Community Development in Saudi Arabia,* *definitions of regional building types and master plan.*

SCALE  0  50  100  150

portant studies published in 1983 might indicate a more positive alternative approach.

The vast construction programme over the last decade in the Kingdom of Saudi Arabia has revealed strengths and weaknesses in the planning framework. Much has depended, until comparatively recently, on the abilities or otherwise of foreign consultants from all over the world. Since the beginning of 1980, however, a totally new direction in not only physical planning and architecture but, more importantly, in urban design, has been shown by a young multi-national team in the Ministry of the Interior led by the Director General of Projects, Salman Al-Sudairy. The team, charged with an extremely large construction programme of new towns throughout Saudi Arabia has evolved an urban design process for this programme. This process is shortly to be published in two volumes of an urban design manual, *Urban Design and Community Development in Saudi Arabia* and a landscape design manual written by Salman Al-Sudairy and Louis May, *Landscape in Saudi Arabia*.

A distinction should be made between the design guides published over the last decade in England by various county councils and this new work. Whereas the former tended to 'instruct' architects about the *detailed* design of individual buildings, particularly in a residential context, the Saudi Arabian studies attempt to set a frame of reference

| الطراز المعماري Spatial Model | طراز الإنشاء Construction Model | النوع الأقليمي الأساسي Basic Regional Type | تأثير الأسلوب Stylistic Influence | التعريف الكامل للنوعية الأقليمية Full definition of Regional Type | |
|---|---|---|---|---|---|
| اسكن ذوالباحة Patio house | + حائط الحمل Bearing wall = | | + اسلوب نجدي Najde style = | | Center الوسطى |
| السكن ذوالباحة Patio house | + الهيكل Skeleton = | | + تأثير العراق والفارسي Mesopotamian and Persian influence = | | East الشرقية |
| البرج Tower | + حائط الحمل Bearing wall = | | + التأثير اليمني Yemeni influence = | | South الجنوبية |
| البرج Tower | + الهيكل Skeleton = | | + التأثير التركي والمصري Turco-Egyptian influence = | | West الغربية |

which gives a greater degree of creativity to the architect and urban designer. They stress, for example, with extensive use of diagrams and photographs, the evolution of traditional communities in the country as a response to extreme climatic conditions as well as a strong Islamic cultural heritage. They do not, however, impose historicist solutions upon the designer but indicate the way in which the cluster grouping of small villages and towns, focusing upon a central mosque and square, generated a movement system catering for pedestrians in a hot, dry climate. Houses are seen as cellular groups within an informal geometry with no grand formal spaces except for the central square. 'The house groupings relate more to pedestrian destinations than accidents of place and time, but always at a scale of people on foot in such a way as to create shade and small intermediate meeting places.' Thus the emphasis on orientation, landscape structure, microclimate protection, and view corridors fall into the realm of urban design, as opposed to the English design guides which tend to relate to detailed architectural design.

Following the 1967 urban riots in the United States in many of the major cities, poverty, social and economic deprivation and segregation were seen as root causes. Amongst efforts to combat the decline of the cities were the Council on Urban Design set up by Mayor John Lindsay in New York City and the Community Design Center which spread across the country with volunteer architects, teachers and students, as well as the R/UDAT[7]. Starting with a study of Rapid City, South Dakota in 1967, four volunteer teams were established who worked with all members of specific communities who requested aid. The professional services were free and the communities were only called upon to bear the expenses of the visits. Usually, each team contained four members who represented a variety of professions depending on the requirements of the particular study. Architects were invariably represented in the teams which also included economists, planners, engineers, sociologists and geologists. Each visit occupied an intensive four-day study which involved a physical inspection of the area by foot, bus and helicopter on the first day and talks between the mayor, council, planning board, chamber of commerce and banking community. On the second day was a town meeting open to all interested citizens including an input from non-establishment groups (neighbourhood organizations, block groups, ethnic and minority representatives) who were usually called back for further discussions. This was followed by a team work session to synthesize experiences. The third day of the visit was a twenty-four hour session of production work on the report providing a comprehensive framework for recommendations with a final report (some 60 to 100 pages long) printed during the visit. On the final day, a press conference was held followed by a town meeting in the evening using the finished report and a slide show. Organizing a visit generally took up to twelve months of pre-planning and there was a highly organized follow-up programme. In their own document, published in 1983, R/UDAT say: 'The extent of the R/UDAT exercise is unequalled to any other urban design activity over the past decade. No consultant organization worked so closely with so many communities or government agency with such a rich variety of issues'.

They say that for urban design to be successful, the effort is as important as the product, that it must examine all elements of the community, that it must be inter-disciplinary and not the work of a single profession and, above all, there must be citizen participation. In addition, sponsorship from a particular community must be from a variety of sources and not reflect the pressures of one particular interest group. Successful media coverage is seen as essential. The urban design group felt that if public/private partnership in urban design is to work, government and community must mutually understand the development process and how to make it operate in the best *public* interest. They must minimize the conflict of goals, improve quality, remove obstacles and misunderstandings and maximise public good relative to private gain.

Amongst the 75 communities studied were Springfield (where the main issue was conservation), Lansing (the problems of downtown), Kansas City (growth), Denver (transportation), Trenton (neighbourhoods), South End, Boston (social issues), New Orleans, Vancouver (parks, open spaces) and Louisville (process/direction).

In contrast to this American experience, the results of public urban design participation in Britain has been less satisfactory. It is worth noting that urban unrest reached the major British cities in 1980 some 13 years after the United States, yet in the last three years there has been an apparently complacent attitude on the part of the professional bodies. The R/UDAT experience might indicate an alternative way forward.

Of particular note is the way in which the urban design team involved the total community in these exercises. It seems slightly ironic that in Britain, where there has been sophisticated planning legislation and consultative machinery for many decades, there are few occasions when consultation with local communities and action groups is made. Perhaps the London Docklands proposals would have achieved more positive results had they been the outcome of such consultation.

## NOTES

1 *Urban Dwelling Environments in Rapidly Growing Cities. Case Study: Khamis Mushait, Saudi Arabia*, MIT, May 1979.

2 George Orwell, *Nineteen-Eighty-Four*, Penguin Books, 1954 (first published 1949).

3 Graham Searjeant, 'Ottowa's dim message to Liverpool 8', *The Sunday Times*, July 26th, 1981.

4 Philip Jordan, 'An angry voice in Toxteth', *The Guardian*, August 1st, 1981.

5 *Architectural Design*, Vol. 46, No. 7, July 1976, pp. 394–422.

6 E. Hollamby, D. Gosling, G. Gullen *et al.*, *Isle of Dogs: Urban Design Plan: A Guide to Design and Development*, London Docklands Development Corporation, November 1982.

7 American Regional/Urban Design Assistance Team, 1967–83.

## 5.2 BARRY MAITLAND: TOWARDS A MINIMAL THEORY OF URBAN STRUCTURE

IT HAS BEEN SUGGESTED EARLIER THAT A LARGE part of the current interest in urban design springs in the first place from a critique of contemporary architecture and town planning, which is essentially formal in nature (3.4). That is, criticism tends to begin with the observation that, whether or not regional, economic, social and transportation strategies are effective, and whether or not the individual buildings we occupy are satisfactory, the form of the cities which results from the sum of these actions is largely incoherent, hostile, unintelligible and inconsequential.

Many urban designers would be reluctant to accept that their critical stance is, at least initially, formal, perhaps in part because the vocabulary available to explain this position seems unconvincing and inadequate. Talk of 'visual qualities' and 'townscape values' seems uncomfortably imprecise and apparently concerned with a secondary, superficial level of design. Yet the fact is that without a clear sense of formal structure for the material he is attempting to manipulate, the urban designer can make only disconnected and arbitrary gestures. Lacking such a coherent basis he will always be dependent on conventional responses which may be quite inappropriate to the case in hand. Indeed, it could be argued that if the urban designer has any function, it is to provide the architect and town-planner with formal constructs which can guide their decisions.

Many of the urban design theories we have considered can be regarded as attempts to set out such a framework which, it is worth noting, must, like any other formal system, provide two things to be effective: firstly, it must define the elements which are to be employed, and secondly the rules for their association. In the case of language, for example, the formal system must provide both a vocabulary and a grammar; in music both notes and the ways in which they may be harmonically, rhythmically and melodically combined; in mathematics both numbers and the rules for their addition, subtraction, multiplication and division. Unlike music and mathematics, but in common with architecture, however, a formal system valid for urban design purposes must have one further quality, namely that it must correspond with the functional organizations which inhabit it. This isomorphism between formal and functional structures must be maintained to a reasonably high degree of approximation, for although the two are constantly undergoing change at variable rates (new social patterns occupying old forms, for example) so that the former can be read as having an independent existence, it is nevertheless tied to its essential purpose as a means of organizing the settings for everyday life.

It is possible to look back over the theories we have discussed in terms of their ability to satisfy these three basic requirements of a comprehensive urban design strategy. Sitte's analysis for example, although offering some advice on the disposition of urban elements, is primarily concerned with the investigation of that one element, the square, which he felt to be the key to effective urban design. This concentration on defining and elaborating the elements—the first of our three characteristics of a complete formal system—is true also of a number of other theorists we have considered. Unwin, while covering a much broader field than Sitte, with many practical observations on street alignment and housing layout, for example, offers numerous models for other generic urban element types, such as town edge conditions, gateway buildings, bridge buildings, and so on. Similarly Rob Krier devotes considerable effort to an encyclopaedic analysis of possible element configurations, particularly squares and circuses, as 'typological and morphological elements of the concept of urban space'.

A different definition of categories, as conceptual rather than concrete elements, is offered by Lynch in *The Image of the City*, and it is perhaps here that the lack of a correspondingly exacting investigation of the relations which govern the elements becomes most telling. For while the abstract nature of Lynch's elements—paths, edges, nodes, districts, landmarks—gives them the power of universally applicable concepts, it also makes them elusive. When every street is potentially a path, every corner a node and every outstanding feature a landmark, what, if anything, governs their frequency and the relations between them? The book suggests that these questions will be answered by analysis of the existing context in each case, and that the somewhat arbitrary element patterns which result will thus at least have the justification of precedent, if not rational explanation. Lynch recognized, in fact, that, in his book, 'most of the work was confined to the identity and structure of single elements' and looked forward to further studies 'directed toward a future synthesis of city form considered as a whole pattern'.[1]

If we can then maintain that some analyses (and we could add others, such as those of Charles Moore and Christian Norberg-Schulz which have similarly offered lists of generic urban categories) have been limited by an absence of effective rules of association for the elements they defined, we could list a complementary set for which the opposite is true. Both Cullen and Appleyard, for example, concentrate upon the sequential experience of the city and the ways in which a moving observer perceives it in terms of the changing relationship of its parts. This direction of attack has the disadvantage that, except in certain limited conditions, as in the case of the urban motorway, the city is not experienced in the highly controlled linear sequence, from set beginning to set end, of a film, but rather as a highly variable and unpredictable set of individual movements across a stable pattern. Without a corresponding definition of the elements of that pattern, the approach seems, like those discussed above, to stop short of defining a complete formal system, and thus to suffer from a similar elusiveness when called upon to create that 'synthesis of city form' which Lynch anticipated.

A number of the projects we have examined have, however, been based upon potentially complete and consistent formal propositions, as with the three very different models framed by Leon Krier, Mel Dunbar and Christopher Alexander. In the first, Krier defines both the essential elements of the city in terms of the street, the square and the *quartier* and also 'the conception of urban space as the primary organizing element'[2] in its three permitted forms of association. With the Essex design guide, Dunbar similarly sets out a comprehensive vocabulary and grammar of design, while Alexander's 'pattern language' achieves the same end through the establishment of a network of 253 related patterns. Moreover, all three theories have a great deal to say about the relationship of the formal system to the reality they serve—that is they can all be examined in terms of the third necessary requirement which we have specified for a formal system suitable for urban design. Krier claims that his model must be 'part of an integral vision of society, it has to be part of a political struggle' or else it will merely be 'reduced to a style'.[3] The Essex design guide, on the other hand, seems to belong to 'that grand and endlessly running British cultural project to make the institutions of the present day seem like those of pre-industrial, agrarian, village society',[4] while Alexander's urban design patterns are embedded in a network which includes regional and even global strategies, in such a way that 'every individual act is always helping to create or generate these larger global patterns'.[5]

Now we might ask whether it is really essential for us to take on board the restoration of 'an artisanal building culture',[6] or the reproduction of a 'saccharine history',[7] or the restructuring of whole metropolitan regions, in order to achieve an effective form of urban design. From the point of view of that more limited objective, might it not be possible to define firstly those aspects of reality which seem to have been particularly troublesome for urban design theories to contain, and then devise a formal system which can respond to them? And if this might seem a useful programme to attempt, might we not then add that the formal system should be as simple as possible, establishing a minimal position, in the hope that this might generate 'common types' of the sort which Patrick Hodgkinson notes as underlying the successful urban solutions of earlier periods.

Although it would be repetitive to list all of the difficult aspects of urban phenomena to which a design strategy might respond, there are a few specific questions which have shown up the inadequacies of current methods particularly clearly in recent years, and to which a coherent approach might be expected to address itself. Firstly, it has become apparent that the scale of implementation of urban projects—the scale of development agencies, of land acquisition and of construction programmes—has become so variable that this factor in itself acts against any coherent scaling of the urban environment. We might hope then that our formal structure would act as a scaling device, providing a city-wide framework appropriate to the way in which the city is used, irrespective of the way in which it is made. Secondly, the structure should have the ability both to survive, and to provide a comprehensible context for, change in the urban fabric, whether that change be the internal piecemeal renewal of the *favela*, the generation of a new green-field settlement, or the decline of an established area now by-passed by new industrial and transportation patterns. That is to say that the formal structure should not only be able to accept change, but should itself reflect the way in which change occurs. Thirdly, we might hope that our design structure would relate and reconcile the increasingly isolated and specialized single-use zones which the modern city generates.

There are, of course, many other difficulties which should be considered, but these three seem particularly representative of the tendencies which cause disquiet at the form of the modern city, and call into being the need for some kind of interven-

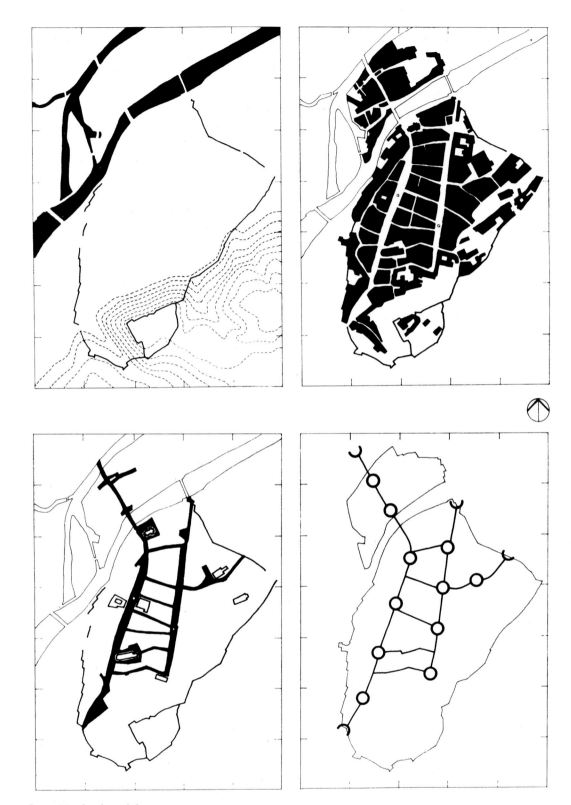

*Barry Maitland, nodal urban design structure, 1980.*

tion which we may call 'urban design'. Where then might we hope to find a formal structure appropriate to these requirements? It is a curious thing that so many of the ideas we have considered are of the form 'the city ought to be . . .', and so few of the type 'the city is . . .'. For if there are indeed any general propositions we can make about urban structure, and the way it can respond to change, we might expect to find evidence of them in the existing urban fabric itself. In fact, an increasing amount of attention has recently been paid to this point, with a number of research projects undertaken into the quantitative and qualitative evaluation of conventional urban components and their arrangements.[8] And we might expect to find these traces most clearly in areas of established building which have undergone relatively unpremeditated cycles of development. From a study of these areas it is possible to develop the following general argument.

The mass of construction which makes up a city contains variations of use and levels of activity which articulate that urban mass both functionally and visually. This differentiation tends to occur around points of focus, or nodes, which generally relate to local intensifications of form (crossroads for example). The frequency of these nodes is thus a basic characteristic of the city, and the network they produce creates a fundamental structure in terms of both our use and understanding of it. Node frequency is dependent in part upon the level of surrounding activity, and hence upon such variables as density of land usage, but it is also related to the tolerance or ability of the pedestrian to move about the city. The latter relatively invariant factor makes it possible to postulate a 'standard' or 'median' node interval which will operate within a middle range of activity levels, and indeed analysis of a great number of older towns suggests that an interval of about 200 metres does commonly occur. In certain cases however, as within the densely packed mass of certain medieval walled towns for example, this might reduce as far as 100 metres, while low-density suburban areas often lack significant functional differentiation below 400 metres.

The generic net of nodes at 200-metre intervals exists only as a first approximation to an urban structure, however, and is subject to modification by a number of factors. In older settlements topography acts upon this model in quite specific and predictable ways to adapt it to the local case. Again, important routes passing through the net produce dominant linear sequences, or 'strings' of nodes within the general pattern. The combination of these two factors then produces an enormous variety of specific solutions. The example of the small Bavarian town of Landshut may serve to illustrate just one possible minor variation. The town stands on land contained by a curve of the River Isar to north and west, and high ground to south and east, and is based upon one major street, Altstadt, along which, from the river bridge at its north end to a city gate at its south end, the major public buildings are ranged at 200-metre intervals to form a classic string, reinforced by monuments and interspersed with commercial uses. Parallel to

this, and 200 metres to the east, a second street, Neustadt, accommodates secondary commercial uses, its length again articulated into major intervals of 200-metre length by fountains, and connected by numerous cross streets to the Altstadt to form a double-string or 'ladder' arrangement.

It should be noted that although the node structure is closely related to the distribution of uses within the town, it is also independent of any specific economic or social configurations. Thus, in the medieval hill-towns of Umbria, for example, it expresses itself in the pattern of churches and associated piazzas, whereas in nineteenth-century English industrial towns a corresponding pattern is traced through the rows of terrace houses, but now by corner shops and pubs. Indeed, the particular sensitivity of retail and service uses to levels of surrounding activity makes them especially helpful in identifying this structure, and it is interesting that in the highly specialized case of controlled urban design represented by the large, planned shopping centres, a very similar set of rules to those described above (200-metre maximum walking distance between 'magnet' stores, with carefully organized hierarchy of secondary uses between) is applied.

What the node structure does is to describe a hierarchy of accessibility and activity levels, and hence also of land value, privacy and susceptibility to change, across the urban mass. To take the case of the industrial towns, for instance, houses occurring at node points would become converted to corner shops, and then, as the patterns of retailing coarsened after 1950, reconverted back to residential use or perhaps changed to some service trade. When slum clearance and redevelopment occurred, the more expensive shops and pubs on the node locations would often remain, presiding over a wasteland until the fabric filled in again around them.

It will be seen that the formal structure sketched out above contains elements familiar from previous theories we have considered, and in particular those of Lynch and Alexander (who suggests 'nodes of activity throughout the community, spread about 300 yards apart'[9]). Similarly, it is not dependent on the availability of surplus wealth and would thus be valid as a basis for the most marginal settlement, although it can also act as a 'deep structure' for the subsequent elaboration of architectural events. And although it appears as a rather general strategic idea, it carries quite specific and detailed implications for local decisions about land use, for example, or the size of development

packages, or the appropriateness of particular architectural statements. Avoiding prescriptions which are rapidly overtaken by cultural, technological or economic events, but rather, by attempting to identify the essential features of the way cities are actually used and perceived, setting out a matrix within which unpredictable events can naturally occur, it is possible to describe the structure as 'minimal'.

In a scheme prepared for the Isle of Dogs Enterprise Zone in London in 1982, the concept of the node structure was utilized. The scheme showed specific building proposals for the whole area, but this was no more than an attempt to indicate the character of one type of solution, which would be 'well-formed' in terms of the underlying node structure, and which would demonstrate the range of development options possible on the site. The proposed node structure makes use of a number of the net and string features investigated in the model, adopted as appropriate to the conditions occurring at different locations within the Isle of Dogs. Because of the extended form of the central development zone, a spine string sequence was proposed from north to south, related to the route of a planned rapid transit system.

Whether this or some alternative model be adopted, it is surely the case that there now exists a real need for simple, flexible working concepts of this type to become generally available, in order that the great vitality and breadth of urban design ideas which we have attempted to review in this book may now make some broader impact upon the shaping of our cities.

**NOTES**

1 Kevin Lynch, *The Image of the City*, MIT Press, Cambridge, Mass. 1977, p. 118.
2 *Rational Architecture*, Archives d'Architecture Moderne, Brussels 1978, p. 42.
3 *Ibid.*, p. 39.
4 Richard Hill, 'Architecture: The Past Fights Back', *Marxism Today*, November 1980, p. 24.
5 Christopher Alexander *et al.*, *A Pattern Language*, Oxford University Press, New York 1977, p. XIX.
6 *Rational Architecture*, *op. cit.*, p. 41.
7 Richard Hill, *op. cit.*, p. 24.
8 For example, K. Zekavat, Ph.D. Thesis *The Urban Street*, on the characteristics of urban streets, and in particular the 'primary urban corridor', Sheffield University, 1981. See also *On Streets* (ed. Standford Anderson), Institute for Architecture and Urban Studies, MIT Press, Cambridge, Mass. 1978.
9 Christopher Alexander, *op. cit.*, p. 166.

# APPENDIX

Attitudes of urban designers to their subject are just as varied as are those of architects and planners to theirs. An appraisal of the main lines upon which these attitudes are formed has been undertaken by Javier Cenicacelaya Marijuan[1] and a summary of his main conclusions may provide a reference for many of the issues raised in this book. Marijuan defines a series of approaches to urban design, which can be classified in three broad groups:

A. Dependent on a particular politico-cultural system:
  A1 Marxist
  A2 Utopian
  A3 Capitalist
B. Related to a variable politico-cultural system:
  B1 Mathematical, economic
  B2 Descriptive, Functionalist
  B3 Morphological—B3.1 Analysis of human geography; B3.2 Morphology of the plan; B3.3 Network analysis
  B4 Historical
C. Not dependent on any politico-cultural system:
  C1 Perceptual—C1.1 The City as an image; C1.2 The City as sequences; C1.3 The City as underrated architecture.

A brief description of what is meant by each of these categories runs as follows:

A1 Marijuan argues that Marxist theory predicates an attitude towards the city as well as towards society in general. According to such an analysis, the city is seen as representing the state of the class struggle within it, and the ultimate objective of the urban designer is to eliminate inequalities in the benefits which the city offers to its citizens.

A2 The utopian concept refers to Plato's proposal that a perfect environment is the result of a perfect society. Thus utopian planning proposals historically have been based upon particular utopian concepts of society, and assumed the creation of a new mentality in mankind. Most such proposals have adopted rigid geometrical forms.

A3 The capitalist view of the city is held to be that of a field in which forces struggle for predominance in urban life. The forces are related to particular power structures, such as government, church or multi-national companies, and the city reflects an equilibrium of power, whether relative or absolute. The emphasis in the city structure may variously be on protection, beauty, identity or other general ideas of an optimal situation.

B1 The term 'mathematical-economic' does not necessarily imply a geometric proposal for the city and its growth. Rather it refers to a consideration of the city as a field of complex needs which are to be satisfied. The city is analysed within the framework of an interchange of goods and services. The main objective is to achieve an adequate infrastructure for the city and its hinterland based upon a highly detailed analysis of networks and interrelationships. Mathematical models for retail distribution may be considered as an example of network theory. The work of the Cambridge School has been developed from related concepts of architecture as geometry. Architectural form is reduced to geometric conditions and architectural space becomes pure space. Urban structure is seen as a mathematical relationship of distance between different activities.

B2 The functionalist view arose out of a reassessment of the major European industrial cities at the beginning of the twentieth century. Building on the work of Tony Garnier, Le Corbusier proposed such a view in which the functions of the city —living, working, leisure and transportation— were identified as discrete systems both for analytical purposes and as criteria for future proposals.

B3 The term 'morphological' is intended to cover those approaches which concentrate upon classification and study of the form of cities.

B3.1 The study of human geography emphasizes the importance of topographic factors in the determination of its form. Cities may be classified as those sited on hillsides, river crossings, coastal sites and so on. Such analysis tends to be more descriptive than explanatory.

B3.2 The morphology of the plan produces a classification of city plans in such terms as reticular, radial, linear, concentric and policentric, and aims to establish underlying principles of formation.

B3.3 In the context of morphological approaches, network analysis takes as its point of departure the hypothesis that the city or its hinterland is structured by networks, and it is then analysed through the observation of the elemental categories in different areas, and the combination of categories.

B4 The historical approach stems from the study of classical cultural periods of urban history and is epitomized in the works of Lewis Mumford and Patrick Geddes among others. Architecture is considered as the main element in the construction of the city throughout history and with it comes the sense of permanence, locus, individuality and memory.

**C1** The study of perception and interpretation of the environment attaches great importance to the attitude of the individual and to his relationship with the city and surrounding world. Marijuan asserts that it is based upon the preoccupations of psychologists and sociologists and cites Goodey to confirm this view. Goodey notes that: 'the basic motive for interpretation should be *the right to know*, the right tŏ acquire knowledge and interpretation about the environment'. In fact, this particular approach has been pioneered as much by architects and urban designers as by psychologists and sociologists.

**C1.1** This approach, mainly developed by Lynch, is analysed through five main constituent elements —Paths, Edges, Nodes, Landmarks and Districts —with the interrelationship between the elements.
**C1.2** In this group is the type of study developed by Gordon Cullen. Based upon architecture and the spaces generated, the city is seen as a succession of sequences and as a chain of different events.
**C1.3** 'The city as underrated architecture' relates to a range of recent attitudes, from a total rejection of conscious design to a renewed interest in vernacular models, which share two underlying assumptions: firstly that architecture is a particularly truthful record of its period, and secondly that any previous period is better than today. According to this view, the accumulation within the city of past forms is not only justified but highly desirable, and, manifesting itself variously in picturesque, vernacular and pop design, it regards the city as a theatre.

Each of the groups of attitudes which Marijuan identifies makes a specific response towards common issues of urban design. It attaches greater or lesser importance to the role of the individual as an agent in effecting the urban environment and to the relevance of strictly architectural influences. Again, it may be primarily concerned with urban design questions operating at the most local scale, or alternatively at a wider level. The preoccupations of the various schools of thought with regard to these key issues may be represented in tabular form (see below).

**Reference:**
Javier Cenicacelaya Marijuan, *Towns in Expansion, Historicist Approach or Perceptual Approach*, M.A. Dissertation in Urban Design, Oxford Polytechnic 1978.

| | B1 Mathematical Economic | B2 Functionalist in the City | B2 Functionalist in the Territory | B3.1 Morphological Human Geography | B3.2 Morphological The Plan | B3.3 Morphological Network Analysis | B4 Historical | C1.1 Perceptual City Image | C1.2 Perceptual City as Sequences | C1.3 Perceptual City as Theatre |
|---|---|---|---|---|---|---|---|---|---|---|
| *Scale of the Field of Analysis:* | | | | | | | | | | |
| —Part of the City | | | | | * | * | * | * | * | * |
| —The City as a Whole | * | * | | | * | * | * | * | * | * |
| —The City Hinterland | * | * | | * | * | * | | | | |
| —The Region | * | | * | * | | | | | | |
| *Importance Given to Architecture:* | | | | | | | | | | |
| —Very important | | | | | | | * | | | |
| —important | | * | | * | * | | | * | * | |
| —Not very important | | | | | | * | | | | * |
| —Not considered | * | | * | | | | | | | |
| *Importance Given to the Individual:* | | | | | | | | | | |
| —Very important | | | | | | | | * | * | * |
| —Important | | | | | | | * | | | |
| —Not very important | | | | | | | | | | |
| —Not considered | * | * | * | * | * | * | | | | |

# BIBLIOGRAPHY

## URBAN PROBLEMS

### GENERAL:

**Books:**

ABRAMS, C., *The City is the Frontier,* Harper Colophon Books, New York, 1965

BENEVELO, L., *The History of the City,* Scolar Press, London, M.I.T. Press, Cambridge, Mass., 1980

DAVIDOFF, P., 'Normative Planning' from *Planning for Diversity and Choice*, ed. Anderson, S., M.I.T. Press, Cambridge, Mass., 1968

DYOS, H.J., *The Study of Urban History*, Arnold, London, 1968

GUTKIND, E.A., *International History of City Development*, Vol. 1. *Urban Development in Central Europe*, Collier-Macmillan, London, 1964

HALL, P., *Great Planning Disasters*, Penguin Books, Harmondsworth, 1981

HARVEY COX, W., *Cities: The Public Dimension*, Penguin Books, Harmondsworth, 1976

JACOBS, J., *The Death and Life of Great American Cities,* Penguin Books, Harmondsworth, 1965 (first published U.S.A. 1961)

JOHNSTON, R.J., *City and Society*, Penguin Books, Harmondsworth, 1980

MUMFORD, L., *The City in History*, Penguin Books, Harmondsworth, 1961

RASMUSSEN, S.E., *London, The Unique City*, University of Chicago Press, 1982 (first published 1934)

REPS, J.W., *The Making of Urban America*, Princeton University Press, 1965

**Articles:**

DAVIS, K., 'The Urbanization of the Human Population', *Scientific American* 213, September 1965, pp. 40–53

## URBAN ECONOMIC PROBLEMS

**Books:**

AMBROSE, P. AND COLENUTT, R., *The Property Machine,* Penguin Books, Harmondsworth, 1975

BADCOCK, B., *Unfairly Structured Cities*, Blackwell, Oxford, 1983

BERRY, B.J.L., 'General Features of Urban Commercial Structure' in *International Structure of the City*, ed. Bourne, L.S., Oxford University Press, New York, 1971

COUNTER-INFORMATION SERVICES, *The Recurrent Crisis of London*, London, 1972

DALTON, G., *Economic Systems and Society: Capitalism, Communism and the Third World*, Penguin Books, Harmondsworth, 1977

GALBRAITH, J.K., *The New Industrial State*, Penguin Books, Harmondsworth, 1977

GOSLING, D. AND MAITLAND, B., *Design and Planning of Retail Systems*, Architectural Press, London, 1976

## URBAN SOCIAL PROBLEMS

**Books:**

ALLAUN, F., *No Place Like Home—Britain's Housing Tragedy*, Andre Deutsch, London, 1972

BADCOCK, B., *Unfairly Structured Cities*, Blackwell, Oxford, 1983

COATES, K. AND SILBURN, R., *Poverty—the Forgotten Englishmen*, Penguin Books, Harmondsworth, 1981

FIELD, A.J., *City and Country in the Third World*, Schenkman, U.S.A., 1970

GALLET, P., *Freedom to Starve*, (El Padre) Les Editions Ouvrieres, France, 1967

HAUSER, P.M., 'The Changing Population of the Modern City' in *Cities and Society*, ed. Hatt, P. K., and Reiss, A.J., Collier-Macmillan, London, 1957

LLOYD, P., *Slums of Hope—Shanty Towns of the Third World*, Penguin Books, Harmondsworth, 1979

LOPES DE ALMEIDA, F., *A Questão Urbana na América Latina*, Forense-Universitária, Rio de Janeiro, 1978

MINGIONE, E., *Social Conflict and the City*, Blackwell, Oxford, 1981

NIEDERGANG, M., *The Twenty Latin Americas* (Les 20 Amériques Latines), Plon, Paris, 1962

HARVEY, D., 'Social Processes, Spatial Form and the Redistribution of Real Income in an Urban System' in *The City, Problems and Planning* ed. Stewart, M., Penguin Books, Harmondsworth, 1972

KNEESE, A.V., *Economics and the Environment*, Penguin Books, Harmondsworth, 1977

MARRIOTT, O., *The Property Boom*, Pan Books, London, 1969

MARX, K., *Capital*, International Publishers Edition, New York, Vol. 1, 1967

**Articles:**

AGERGARD, E., OLSEN, P.A., ALLPASS, J., 'The Interaction between retailing and the urban centre structure: A theory of spiral movement', Institute for Center-Planlaegning, Lyngby, Denmark, 1968

DAVIS, KINGSLEY, 'The Urbanization of the Human Population', *Scientific American* 213, September 1965, pp. 40–53

## URBAN PHYSICAL PLANNING PROBLEMS AND SOLUTIONS

**Books:**

BANHAM, R., *Los Angeles: The Architecture of Four Ecologies*, Penguin Books, Harmondsworth, 1973

CHAPMAN, S.D. (ed.), *The History of Working Class Housing*, David and Charles, London, 1971

GOODMAN, R., *After the Planners*, Pelican Books, Harmondsworth, 1972

HALL, P., *Urban and Regional Planning*, Penguin Books, Harmondsworth, 1975

RITTEL, HORST, W.J. AND WEBBER M., 'Wicked Problems' in *Manmade Futures*, ed. Goss, N., Elliott, D. and Roy, R., Hutchinson Educational in Association with the Open University Press, London, 1974

SITTE, CAMILLO, *The Art of Building Cities* (translated by Stewart, C.T.), Reinhold Publishing Corp., New York, 1945

SUTCLIFFE, A., *Towards the Planned City—Germany, Britain, the United States, France 1780–1914*, Blackwell, Oxford, 1981

WEBBER, M., 'Permissive Planning' in *The Future of Cities*, ed. Blowers, A., Hamnet, C. and Sarre, P., Hutchinson Educational in association with the Open University Press, London, 1974

WHITTICK, A., *Encyclopedia of Urban Planning*, McGraw Hill, New York, 1974

PACIONE, M., *Problems and Planning in Third World Cities*, Croom Helm, London, 1981

PATRICK, J., *A Glasgow Gang Observed*, Eyre Methuen, London, 1973

PERLMAN, J.E., *The Myth of Marginality*, University of California Press, Berkeley, 1976

ROBERTS, R., *The Classic Slum: Salford Life in the First Quarter of the Century*, Penguin Books, Harmondsworth, 1973

SCHLYTER, A. AND GEORGE, T., *The Development of a Squatter Settlement in Lusaka, Zambia*, National Swedish Inst. for Building Research, Gävle, Sweden, 1979

SENNETT, R., *The Uses of Disorder: Personal Identity and City Life*, Penguin Books, Harmondsworth, 1970

STEWART, M., *The City: Problems of Planning*, Penguin Books, Harmondsworth, 1972

TURNER, J.F.C., AND FICHTER, R., *Freedom to Build* Macmillan, New York, 1972

WARD, C., *Tenants Take Over*, Architectural Press, London, 1974

WARD, C., *Housing—an Anarchist Approach*, Freedom Press, London, 1976

WARD, C., *The Child in the City*, Penguin Books, Harmondsworth, 1979

WATES, N., AND WOLMAR ,C. (eds.), *Squatting*, Bayleaf Books, London, 1980

YOUNG, M. AND WILLMOTT P., *Family and Kinship in East London*, Routledge and Kegan Paul, London, 1957

**Articles:**

LUPSHA, P., 'On Theories of Urban Violence', *Urban Affairs Quarterly*, Vol. 4, 1969

MUSTAFA HAG, BAGI AHMED, 'Solutions to Low Income Housing Problems in the Sudan', University of Sheffield Ph.D. dissertation, 1978

PAHL, R., 'Will the Inner City Problem ever go away?' from *Town and Country Planning Summer School*, U.K., 1978, Report of Proceedings

TURNER, J.F.C., 'The Squatter Settlement: Architecture that Works', *Architectural Design*, August 1968

## ECOLOGICAL PROBLEMS

**Books:**

ARVILL, R., *Man and Environment: Crisis and the Strategy of Choice*, Penguin Books, Harmondsworth, 1976

DA CUNHA CAMERGO, JOSE GERALDO, *Rural Urbanization*, National Inst. for Settlement and Land Reform INCRA, Brasília, 1971

DESHUSSAS, J., *Delivrez Promethee*, Flammarion, Paris, 1979

GOUDIE, A., *The Human Impact—Man's Role in Environmental Change*, Blackwell, Oxford, 1981

LANDSBERG, H.E., *The Urban Climate*, Academic Press, New York, 1981

PERRY, A.H., *Environmental Hazards in the British Isles*, George Allen and Unwin, 1981

WHITTOW, J.B., *Disasters—the Anatomy of Environmental Hazards*, Penguin Books, Harmondsworth, 1980

**Articles:**

GOSLING D., 'O Desenvolvimento das Faixas Pioneiras na Amazonia', Ministry of the Interior, Brazil, 1976

SCOTT, G., 'The Amazon—Saving the Last Frontier', *Time Magazine*, October 18, 1982, pp. 48–55

## URBAN PROBLEMS: DESIGN FRAMEWORKS

**Books:**

LÜCHINGER, A., *Strukturalismus in Architektur und Städtebau*, Krämer, Stuttgart, 1981

MÜLLER, W., *Städtebau*, B.G. Teubner, Stuttgart, 1979

PAPANEK, V., *Design for the Real World*, Thames and Hudson, London, 1972

RYKWERT, J., *The Idea of a Town*, Faber and Faber, London, 1976

SCHUMACHER, E.F., *Small is Beautiful*, Abacus (Sphere Books) London, 1974 (pub. Blond & Briggs, London, 1973)

TOFFLER, A., *Future Shock*, The Bodley Head, London, 1970

**Articles:**

ALEXANDER, C., 'A City is not a Tree', *Architectural Forum*, New York, April 1965, pp. 58–62 and May 1965, pp. 58–61

ALLSOP, K., 'Mr. Vorster's Showplace', *New Statesman*, 26th March, 1971

GOSLING, D., 'Brasília', *Third World Planning Review*, Spring 1979, Liverpool University Press, pp. 41–56

ROWE, C. AND KOETTER, F., 'Collage City', *Architectural Review*, London, August 1975

## URBAN DESIGN THEORIES

*Urban Design Theories with Historical Reference*

**Books:**

AL-SUDAIRY, S. (ed.) *Urban Design and Community Development in Saudi Arabia*, Ministry of the Interior, Saudi Arabia, 1983

AL-SUDAIRY, S. AND MAY,L., *Landscape Architecture in Saudi Arabia*, Ministry of the Interior, Saudi Arabia, 1983

CROUCH, D.P., GARR, D.J., MUNDIGO, A.L., *Spanish City Planning in North America*, M.I.T. Press, Cambridge, Mass., 1982

GUIDONI, E., *Primitive Architecture*, Academy Editions, London, 1975

HEYDEN, D. AND GENDROP, P., *Pre-Columbian Architecture of Mesoamerica*, Academy Editions, London, 1975

HOAG, J.D., *Islamic Architecture*, Academy Editions, London, 1975

LE CORBUSIER AND PIERREFEU, F., *The Home of Man*, Architectural Press, London, 1948 (Translated by Entwistle, C. and Holt, G. from *La Maison des Hommes*, Librairie Plon, Paris, 1941)

LE CORBUSIER, *Oeuvre Complète 1946–1952*, W. Boesiger aux Editions Guisberger, Zurich, 1955

LE CORBUSIER, *L'Art Decoratif d'Aujourd'hui*, Editions Vincent, Freal and Cie, Paris, 1925 (reprinted 1959)

LE CORBUSIER, *The Radiant City*, Faber and Faber Ltd., London, 1967 (Translated from *La Ville Radieuse*, Vincent, Freal and Cie, Paris, 1933)

LE CORBUSIER, *The City of Tomorrow*, Architectural Press, London, 1971 (translated by Etchells, F. from *Urbanisme*, Editions Cres, Paris, 1924)

LE CORBUSIER, *Sketchbooks*, edited by Le Fondation Le Corbusier and the Architectural History Foundation, notes by Francoise de Franclieu, Vols. 1 (1914–1948) 2 (1950–1954) 3 (1954–1957) 4 (1957–1964) M.I.T. Press, Cambridge, Mass., 1981, 1982

MORGAN, W., *Prehistoric American Architecture in the Eastern United States*, M.I.T. Press, Cambridge, Mass., 1980

O'CONNOR, A., *The African City*, Hutchinson, London, 1983

RAMADAN, A.M., *Réflexions sur L'Architecture Islamique en Libye*, La Maison Arab du Livre-Tunis, 1976

RUDOFSKY, B., *Architecture without Architects*, Doubleday & Co., New York, 1964/Academy Editions, London, 1977, 1981

SERAGELDIN, I. AND EL SADEK, S., *The Arab City: Its Characters and Islamic Cultural Heritage*, Arab Urban Development Institute, Saudi Arabia, 1981

SITTE, C., *Der Städtebau nach seinen Künstlerichsen Grundsätzen*, 1889 (translated into English in 1945 by Stewart, C.T. as, *The Art of Building Cities*, Reinhold Publishing Corp., New York, 1945)

TAFURI, M. AND DAL CO, F., *Modern Architecture*, Academy Editions, London, 1980

UNWIN, R., *Town Planning in Practice*, T. Fisher Unwin, London, 1919

VARANDA, F., *The Art of Building in Yemen*, M.I.T. Press, Cambridge, Mass., 1982

**Articles:**

GINDROA, R., 'Studies in visual structure for urban environments. Monumental v. Popular', in *Urban Structure*, ed. David Lewis, Elek Books, London (*Architects Year Book XII 1968*)

## URBAN DESIGN THEORIES: UTOPIAS

**Books:**

ALEXANDER, C. ET AL, Volume 1, *The Timeless way of Building*, Volume 2, *A Pattern Language*, Volume 3, *The Oregon Experiment*, Oxford University Press, London, 1977

ASIMOV, I., *Foundation*, Panther Books/Granada Publishing Ltd., London, 1979 (first published 1951)

BUCKMINSTER FULLER, R., *Utopia or Oblivion: the Prospects for Humanity*, Allen Lane, Penguin Books, Harmondsworth, 1970

BUCKMINSTER FULLER, R., 'The Comprehensive Man', (written 1959) from *The Buckminster Fuller Reader* ed., Meller, J., Penguin Books, Harmondsworth, 1972

CASSIRER, E., *An Essay on Man*, Yale University Press, New Haven, 1963

FISHMAN, R., *Urban Utopias in the Twentieth Century*, Basic Books Inc., New York, 1977

FRIEDMAN, Y., *Towards a Scientific Architecture*, (Trans, Lang, C.) M.I.T. Press, Cambridge, Mass., 1975

GARNIER, T., *Cité Industrielle*, (1904) Academy Editions, London, 1984

GOODMAN, P. & P., *Communitas: Means of Livelihood and Ways of Life*, Vintage Books, New York, 1960

HABRAKEN, N.J., *Supports:An alternative to mass housing*, (Trans. Valkenburg, B.) Architectural Press, London, 1972 (first published Holland, 1961)

HABRAKEN N.J. ET AL, *Variations: the systematic design of supports* (Trans. by Wiewel, W.) ed. Gibbons, S. M.I.T. Press, Cambridge, Mass., 1976

HAYDEN, D., *Seven American Utopias: The Architecture of Communitarian Socialism, 1790–1975*, M.I.T. Press, Cambridge, Mass., 1976

KOPP, A., *Constructivist Architecture in the USSR*, Academy Editions, London, 1983

KRIER, L. ET AL, *Rational Architecture*, Archives d'Architecture Moderne, Brussels, 1978

MARTIN, L. AND MARCH, L. (eds.), *Urban Space and Structures*, Cambridge University Press, London, 1972

MARX, K., *The Revolution of 1848: Political Writings, Volume I* (ed. Fernbach, D.), Penguin Books, Harmondsworth, 1978

MUMFORD, L., *The Human Prospect*, Beacon Press, Boston, Mass., 1955

POPPER, K.R., *The Poverty of Historicism*, Routledge & Kegan Paul, London, 1963

RABBIT, P., *Drop City*, Olympia Press, New York, 1971

ROSENAU, H., *Boullée and Visionary Architecture*, Academy Editions, London, 1976

SANT' ELIA, A., *The New City*, 1914 Nuove Tendenze exhibition catalogue, Famiglia Artistica, Milan, May-June 1914

SERT, J.L., *Architecture, City Planning, Urban Design*, Verlag für Architektur, Zurich, 1967

TAFURI, M., *Architecture and Utopia: Design and Capitalist Development* (Trans. Luigia la Penta, B.), M.I.T. Press, Cambridge, Mass., 1976

VITRUVIUS, *Ten Books on Architecture* (Trans. Morgan, M.H.), Dover Publications Inc., New York, 1960

**Articles:**

FRAMPTON, K., 'Notes on Soviet Urbanism, 1917–32' in *Architects Year Book XII*, Elek Books, London, 1968

FREIDMAN, Y., 'Towards a coherent system of planning', in *Architects Year Book XII*, Elek Books, London, 1968

VIDLER, A., 'The idea of unity and Le Corbusier's urban form', in *Architects Year Book XII*, Elek Books, London, 1968

## URBAN DESIGN THEORIES ARTS AND SCIENCES

**Books:**

AMERICAN REGIONAL/URBAN DESIGN ASSISTANCE TEAM (R/UDAT), *Urban Design, News from the Front*, American Institute of Architects, 1983

APPLEYARD, D., LYNCH, K., MYER J.R., *The View from the Road*, M.I.T. Press, Cambridge, Mass., 1964

ARNHEIM, R., *Art and Visual Perception: A Psychology of the Creative Eye*, Faber and Faber Ltd., London, 1956

BLOOMER, K.C. AND MOORE, C.W., *Body, Memory and Architecture*, Yale University Press, New Haven, 1977

BROADBENT, G., BUNT, R., JENCKS, C., *Signs, Symbols and Architecture*, J. Wiley, England, 1980

CANTER, D., *The Psychology of Place*, St. Martin's Press, New York, 1977

CONZEN, M.R.G., *The Urban Landscape*, ed. Whitehead, J.W.R., Academic Press, London, 1981

CULLEN, G., *Townscape*, Architectural Press, London, 1961

DOWNS, R.M. AND STEA, D., *Maps in Minds: Reflections on Cognitive Mapping*, Harper and Row, New York, 1977

EISENSTEIN, S., *The Film Sense*, Meridian Books, New York, 1957

GIBSON, J., *The Perception of the Visual World*, Houghton Mifflin & Co., Boston, Mass., 1950

GIEDION S., *Space, Time and Architecture*, Harvard University Press, Cambridge, Mass., 1959 (first published 1941)

GILLIAM, T., *Animations of Mortality*, Eyre Methuen, London, 1978

KATZ, D., *Gestalt Psychology* (Trans. Tyson, R.),

Methuen, London, 1951

KEMMERICH, *Lasergraphy—medium for stage design and architecture*, Verlag Callwey, Munich, 1975

KEPES, G., *The New Landscape*, Paul Theobald, Chicago, 1956

KOOLHAAS, R., *Delirious New York*, Academy Editions, London, 1978

LAYBOURNE, K., *The Animation Book: a complete guide to animated film making*, Crown Publishers, New York, 1979

LYNCH, K., *The Image of the City*, M.I.T./Harvard University Press, 1960

LYNCH, K., *Site Planning*, M.I.T. Press, Cambridge, Mass., 1971

LYNCH, K., *What Time is this Place?*, M.I.T. Press, Cambridge, Mass., 1972

LYNCH, K., *Managing the Sense of a Region*, M.I.T. Press, Cambridge, Mass., 1976

MOHOLY-NAGY, L., *Vision in Motion*, Paul Theobald, Chicago, 1956

NEWMAN, O., *Defensible Space: People and Design in the Violent City*, Architectural Press, London, 1972

NORBERG-SCHULZ, C., *Intentions in Architecture*, Universitetsforlaget, George Allen & Unwin, London, 1963

NORBERG-SCHULZ, C., *Existence, Space and Architecture*, Studio Vista, London, 1971

PIAGET, J. AND INHELDER, B. *The Child's Conception of Space*, London, 1956

REITBERGER, R. AND FUCHS, W., *Comics: Anatomy of a Mass Medium*, Studio Vista, London, 1972 (from *Comics: Anatomie eines Massenmediums*, Heinz Moos Verlag, Munich, 1971)

DI SAN LAZZARO, G., *Klee* (Trans. Hood, S.), Thames and Hudson, London, 1957

SWALLOW, N., *Eisenstein: a documentary portrait*, George Allen & Unwin, London, 1976

VENTURI, R., BROWN, D.S. AND IZENOUR, S., *Learning from Las Vegas*, M.I.T. Press, Cambridge, Mass., 1972

WINGLER, H., *Bauhaus: Weimer, Dessau, Berlin, Chicago*, M.I.T. Press, Cambridge, Mass., 1969

WULF, F., *Uber die Veranderung von Verstellungen (Gedachtnis und Gestalt)*, 1922 from W.D. Ellis, *A Source book of Gestalt psychology*, Routledge and Kegan Paul, London, 1938

**Articles:**

APPLEYARD, D., 'City Designers and the Pluralistic City' in Rodwin L. (ed.), *Planning Urban Growth and Regional Development: the Exercise of the Guayana Program of Venezuela*, M.I.T. Press, Cambridge, Mass., 1969

BROWNE, K., 'Manchester Re-United' *Architectural Re-view*, August 1962, pp. 116–120

CULLEN, G., 'A Town Called Alcan' (1964), 'Four Circuit Linear Towns' (1965), 'The Scanner' (1966), and 'Notation' (1968), published by Alcan Industries, London

GOSLING, D. CULLEN, G., FERGUSON, J., 'Church Village: urban design proposals for central Bridgetown, Barbados', Central Bank of Barbados and Commonwealth Fund for Technical Cooperation, London, 1978

GRAPHIS, (Switzerland) Special Issue, 'The Art of the Comic Strip', No. 159, Vol. 28, 1972/73 and No. 160, Vol. 28, 1972/73

HINKS, R., 'Peepshow and the Roving Eye', *Architectural Review*, August 1955

MAITLAND, B., 'A Minimal Urban Structure', Ph.D. Dissertation, University of Sheffield, 1982

THIEL, P., 'A Study of the Visual Representation of Architectural and Urban Space-Time Sequences', unpublished paper, University of California, Berkeley, 1958

# APPLICATIONS

## A METABOLISTS (JAPAN)

### Books:

BANHAM R., *Megastructure: Urban Futures of the Recent Past*, Thames & Hudson, London, 1976

BOYD R., *Kenzo Tange*, George Braziller, New York, 1962

BOYD R., *New Directions in Japanese Architecture*, Studio Vista, London, 1968

CHAITKIN W. ET AL, *Arata Isozaki*, Architectural Design Profile, Academy Editions, London, 1977

ROSS M.F., *Beyond Metabolism—The New Japanese Architecture*, McGraw Hill, New York, 1978

TANGE K. AND KULTERMANN U., *Architecture and Urban Design*, Verlag für Architektur, Zurich, 1970

### Periodicals:

*Architectural Design*, Vol. 34 No. 10, October 1964, pp. 479–524

*Architectural Design*, Vol. 37 No. 5, May 1967, pp. 207–216

*Japan Architect*, 'Kiyonori Kikutake—Reconstruction of Mass Housing', June 1972, pp. 23–58

## B NEW TOWNS

### Books:

CANDILIS, JOSIC, WOODS, *Toulouse le Mirail, Birth of a New Town*, Krämer, Stuttgart, 1974

CHEESMAN R., LINDSAY W., PORZECANSKI M., *New Towns: The data bank, its construction and origin*, Working Paper 63, Centre for Land Use and Built Form Studies, University of Cambridge, 1972

COOPER, LINDSAY, TAYLOR, *New Towns: analysis of land uses*, Working Paper 72, Centre for Land Use and Built Form Studies, University of Cambridge, 1973

EVANS H. (ed.), *New Towns—The British Experience*, Charles Knight, London, 1972

GOSLING D. (ed.), *Irvine New Town Plan*, Irvine Development Corporation, 1971

INTERNATIONAL FEDERATION FOR HOUSING AND PLANNING, *New Towns in National Development*, IFHP, The Hague, Netherlands, 1980

LING A. AND ASSOCIATES, *Runcorn New Town*, Runcorn Development Corporation, 1967

LLEWELYN-DAVIES, WEEKS, FORESTER-WALKER, BOR, *The Plan for Milton Keynes Vols. I and II*, Milton Keynes Development Corporation, 1970

LONDON COUNTY COUNCIL, *The Planning of a New Town —Hook, Hampshire*, London County Council, 1961

MERLIN P., (translated Sparks M.), *New Towns*, Methuen, London, 1971

OPHER P. AND BIRD C., *Architecture and Urban Design in Six British New Towns (Warrington, Runcorn, Irvine, East Kilbride, Cumbernauld and Milton Keynes)*, Joint Centre for Urban Design, Oxford Polytechnic, 1980

OSBORN F.J. AND WHITTICK A., *New Towns*, Leonard Hill, London, 1977

PORZECANSKI M., CHEESMAN R., LINDSAY W., *New Towns: The evolution of planning criteria*, Working Paper 64, Centre for Land Use and Built Form Studies, University of Cambridge, 1972

THOMAS R. AND CRESSWELL P., *The New Town Idea*, Social Sciences: Urban development Unit 26 Course, Open University, Open University Press, 1973

WILSON L.H., *Cumbernauld New Town: Preliminary Planning Proposals*, Cumbernauld Development Corporation, 1958

### Periodicals:

*American Society of Planning Officials Journal*, Vol. 38 No. 7, pp. 163–165, August, 1972

*Architects' Journal*, Vol. 144 No. 20, p. 1184, 1966, Runcorn New Town Centre

*Architects' Journal*, Vol. 151 No. 9, pp. 526–528, March 1970, Irvine New Town Centre

*Architects' Journal*, Vol. 157 No. 37, pp. 616–619, September 1971, Irvine New Town Plan

*Architects' Journal*, Vol. 155 No. 25, pp. 1377–1392, June 1972, Runcorn Shopping City

*Architects' Journal*, Vol. 164 No. 31, pp. 211–222,

August 1976, Irvine New Town Centre

*Architectural Design*, Vol. 33 No. 5, pp. 209–225, May 1963, Cumbernauld New Town Central Area

*Architectural Design*, Vol. 37 No. 1, p. 25, January 1967, Runcorn New Town Centre

*Architectural Design*, Vol. 42 No. 6, pp. 372–378, June 1972, Runcorn Shopping City

*Architectural Design*, Vol. 43 No. 6, June 1973, Milton Keynes

*Architectural Design*, Vol. 44 No. 8, August 1974, Milton Keynes

*Architectural Design*, Vol. 45 No. 12, December 1975, Milton Keynes

*Architectural Review*, Vol. 141 No. 839, pp. 8–9, 11, 14–15, January 1967, Rutherglen Town Centre, Runcorn New Town Centre

*Architectural Review*, Vol. 153 No. 911, pp. 42–43, January 1973, Irvine New Town Leisure Centre

*Bauen & Wohnen*, (Zurich, Switzerland), No. 12, pp. 469–477, December 1967, Runcorn New Town Centre

*Bauen & Wohnen*, B1 52aE No. 9, p. 302, 1969, Irvine New Town, Foreshore Development

*Neue Laden* (Stuttgart, Germany), E5162F, pp. 13–15, Runcorn New Town Centre

*Royal Institute of British Architects Journal*, Vol. 79 No. 10, pp. 435–436, October 1972, Irvine New Town Plan

*Zodiac* (Italy and Milan), No. 18, pp. 139–146, March 1969, Runcorn New Town Centre

## C PEDESTRIANISATION

### Books:

ANTONIOU J., *Planning for Pedestrians*, Architectural Press, London, 1976

BEAZLY E., *Design and Detail of Space Between Buildings*, Architectural Press, London, 1967

BOEMINGHAUS D., *Wasser in Stadtbild*, Callwey, Munich, 1980

BRAMBELLA R. & LONGO G., *For Pedestrians Only*, Whitney Library of Design, New York, 1977

BUCHANAN C., *Traffic in Towns*, Penguin Books, Harmondsworth, 1963

GREATER LONDON COUNCIL, *The Design of Urban Space*, Department of Architecture and Civic Design, Greater London Council, 1980

HALPRIN L., *Cities*, Reinhold, New York, 1963, revised edition (MIT Press) 1972

LEEDS, *Leeds: Pedestrian Streets*, report prepared by the Project Planning Section, Planning and Property Department, Civic Hall, Leeds, England, 1972

PETERS (hrsg.), *Stadt für Menschen (Town for People)*, Callwey, Munich, 1973

PETERS (hrsg.), *Fussgängerstadt (City for Pedestrians)*, Callwey, Munich, 1977

RUDOFSKY B., *Streets for People*, Braziller, New York, 1969

TANDY C. (ed.), *Handbook of Urban Landscape*, Architectural Press, London, 1972

UHLIG K., *The Pedestrian Orientated Town*, Verlag Gerd Hatje, Stuttgart, 1979

UHLIG K., *Pedestrian Areas*, Academy Editions, London, 1979

## D REHABILITATION

### Books:

BENSON J., COLOMB P., EVANS B., JONES G., *Housing Rehabilitation Handbook* Architectural Press, London, 1980

DEPARTMENT OF THE ENVIRONMENT, *Housing Act 1974: Renewal Strategies*, Circular 13/75, H.M.S.O., London, 1975

GIBSON M.S. AND LONGSTAFF M.J., *An Introduction to Urban Renewal*, Hutchinson, London, 1982

MARKUS T.A. (ed.), *Building Conversion and Rehabilitation*, Newnes-Butterworth, London, 1979

ROCK D., *The Grassroots Developers: A Handbook for Town Development Trusts*, Royal Institute of British Architects, London, 1980

### Periodicals and Articles:

*Architects Journal*, Vol. 166 No. 40, pp. 630–636, October 1977

*Architects Journal*, Vol. 168 No. 35, pp. 377–389, August 1978

*Interim Report (2)*, 'ASSIST in Govan', 1972/75

MACKIE R., 'Cellular Renewal: A Policy for the older housing areas', *Town Planning Review 45*, pp. 274–90

WORTHINGTON J. ET. AL, *Series: Architects' Journal*, The re-use of redundant buildings, 22 March 1978 to 22 October 1980

## E TECHNICAL APPLICATIONS

### Archigram

### Books:

COLLINS G.R., *Visionary Drawings of Architecture and Planning, 20th Century through the 1960s*, MIT Press, Cambridge, Mass., 1979

COOK P., CHALK W., CROMPTON D., GREENE D., HERRON R., WEBB M. (eds.), *Archigram*, Praeger, New York, 1973

### Periodicals and Articles;

'Pop-Arkitektur', *Aftonbladet* (Stockholm), 23 May 1965

'Archigram's Exhibitions', *Architectural Association Quarterly*, July 1969

'Leaves from the Silver Book', *Architectural Design*, November 1965

'Cushicle and Auto-environment', *Architectural. Design*, November 1966

'House 1990', *Architectural Design*, March 1967

'Archigram at the Milan Triennale', *Architectural Design*, July 1968

'Instant City in Progress', *Architectural Design*, November 1970

'Archigram 1970–71', *Architectural Design*, August 1971

'Plug-in City Study', *Architectural Forum*, (New York) No. 8, September 1964

'Archigram', *Architecture USSR 728*, (Leningrad) 1971

'Experiments and Utopia', *Bauen and Wohnen* (Zurich), May 1967

'Review of Experimental Architecture', *Bauwelt* (Berlin), 21 February 1972

'Instant City', *Design Quarterly*, (Minneapolis) 1970

'Cushicle', *Domus* (Milan), December 1967

'Control and Choice', *Domus* (Milan), 458 1968

'Instant City', *Domus* (Milan), 477 1969

'Archigram'—Special Issue, *Hogar y Arquitectura* (Madrid), No. 72 September/October 1967

'Walking City', *IN* (Milan), No. 2/1, January/February 1971

'English Architects' *Kenchiku Bunka* (Tokyo), January 1967

Archigram Special Issue, *Kenchiku Bunka*, No. 279 1970

'Recherches', *L'Architecture d'Aujourd'hui* (Paris) June/July 1964

'Metamorphosis', *L'Architecture d'Aujourd'hui*, December 1967

'Archigram Group—Instant City', *L'Architecture d'Aujourd'hui*, October/November 1969

'Monte Carlo', *L'Architecture d'Aujourd'hui*, November 1970

'The Visionary Tradition in Architecture', *Metropolitan Museum of Art Bulletin* (New York), April 1968

'The New Architecture', *Newsweek* (New York), 19 April 1971

'Archigram, the name and the magazine', *Perspecta 11*, Yale University, 1967

'Plug-in City', *Sunday Times Colour Supplement* (London), 20 September 1964

**Louis Kahn (Philadelphia Plan)**

**Books:**

GIURGOLA/MEHTA, *Louis I Kahn*, Verlag für Architektur, Zurich, 1975

SCULLY V. JR., *Louis I. Kahn*, Braziller, New York, 1962

**Periodicals and Articles:**

BACON E.N., 'Urban Designs of Today', *Progressive Architecture*, Vol. XXXVII, pp. 108–9, August 1956

'Louis Kahn's Blueprint for Revolution', *Greater Philadelphia Magazine*, Vol. LI, pp. 68–72, September 1960

GUTHEIM F., 'Philadelphia's Redevelopment', *Architectural Forum*, Vol CV, pp. 128–36, December 1956

HUXTABLE A.L., 'In Philadelphia an Architect', *New York Times*, June 11, 1961

SMITHSON A. (ed.), 'CIAM, Team 10', *Architectural Design*, Vol. 30, pp. 192–93, May 1960

SMITHSON A. AND P., 'Louis Kahn', *Architects Year Book*, Vol IX, pp. 102–18, 1960

**Kenzo Tange (Tokyo Bay Plan)**

**Books:**

BOYD R., *Kenzo Tange*, Braziller, New York, 1962

**Periodicals and Articles:**

'A Central Core for Tokyo City', *Shinkenchiku (now Japan Architect)*, June 1958, pp. 6–26

'Architecture and the City. Contemporary Architecture of the World', *Shokokusha Publishing* (Tokyo), October 1961, pp. 86–100

TANGE K., 'Lineage of Urban Design', Special Issue of *Japan Architect*, September/October 1971

**F TRANSPORTATION SYSTEMS**

**Books:**

ALTSHULER A.A., WOMAK J.P.E., PUCHER, J.R., *The Urban Transportation System*, MIT Press, Cambridge, Mass., 1979

BERRY, BLOMME, SHULDINER, JONES, *The Technology of Urban Transportation*, Northwestern University Press, Evanston, Illinois, 1963

CRESSWELL R. (ed.), *Urban Planning and Public Transport*, Construction Press, Lancaster, England, 1979

ENGLEBRECHT P. AND AMPENBERGER K., *General reflections on the compatibility of rapid transit rail systems*, UITP-Review, Brussels, Vol. 22–2/1973

KICHENSIDE G., *A Source Book of Miniature and Narrow Gauge Railways*, Ward Lock, London, 1981

LATVALA E.K., *The TTI Hovair PRT System*, Society of Automotive Engineers (USA), 1973

LESSMANN H., *Moderner Tunnelbau bei der Münchner U-Bahn*, Springer Verlag, Berlin, 1978

MATTHEW R. JOHNSON-MARSHALL & PARTNERS, *Minitram in Sheffield*, Department of the Environment: Transport and Road Research Laboratory, 1974

MEYER, KAIN, WOHL, *The Urban Transportation Problem*, Harvard University Press, 1965

PRIDEAUX J.D.C.A., *The English Narrow Gauge Railway*, David & Charles, Newton Abbot, England, 1978

PRINCE, E.J., *The Best of Both Worlds—Transportation Planning for Irvine New Town*, Irvine Development Corporation, 1971

RICHARDS B., *New Movement in Cities*, Studio Vista, London, 1966

SMITHSON A. & P., *Team 10 Primer*, Standard Catalogue Co., London, 1965

THOMSON J.M., *Great Cities and their Traffic*, Penguin Books, Harmondsworth, 1977

**Periodicals & Articles:**

'Cabtrack', *Architects' Journal*, No. 20 Vol. 153, pp. 1112–1123, 19 May 1971

'Mobility' (Brian Richards ed.), *Architectural Design*, Special Issue, September 1968

FRANZEN U., 'Urban Design for New York', *Architectural Record* (New York), September 1975

SCOTTISH LOCAL AUTHORITIES SPECIAL HOUSING GROUP, *Roads in Housing Developments*, Conference Papers/Study Team Report, March 1977

**G ENERGY EFFICIENT DESIGN**

**Books:**

BOCKRIS J. O'M., *Energy: The Solar-Hydrogen Alternative*, Architectural Press, London, 1975

HOLTHUSEN T.L. (ed.), *The Potential of Earth-Sheltered and Underground Space: Proceedings of the Underground Space Conference and Exposition*, Kansas City, June 1981, Pergamon Press, New York, 1981

KNOWLES R., *Sun Rhythm Form*, MIT Press, Cambridge, Mass., 1982

KONYA A., *Design Primer for Hot Climates*, Architectural Press, London, 1980

SZOKOLAY S.V., *Solar Energy & Building*, Architectural Press, London, 1975

**Periodicals & Articles:**

'Resolute Bay New Town,' Report by Ralph Erskine, *Architectural Design*, Vol. 47 No. 11–12, 1977

International Union of Architects, '1978 Congress Mexico City,' report by Sheffield University Department of Architecture

'Primo Concurso Europeo Sul Solare Passivo—Ingliterra progetto', *L'Industria della Construzioni* (Italy), Numero 134, pp. 28–29, December 1982

'Proceedings Colloque Solaire International, Experimentation de Maisons Solaires Passives,' Nice, MIS, 1980, pp. 117–124

*RIBA Journal*, April 1979, pp. 169–170, Sheffield's Ecotecture Prototype House

*Techniques et Architecture* (Paris), No. 347, May 1983, pp. 146–147

WACHBERGER M. (ed.), 'Building with the Sun', *E+P* (Vienna) 1983, pp. 62–63, 'Wettbewerbsentwurf: Reihenhaussiedlung in Sheffield'

**H SOCIAL SOLUTIONS**

**Books:**

BANHAM R., *The Age of the Masters*, Architectural Press, London, 1975

BLACK W.J., *Visions of Harlem*, McGraw-Hill, New York, 1982

CONWAY D.J., *Human Response to Tall Buildings*, McGraw-Hill, New York, 1977

DARKE J. AND DARKE R., *Who Needs Housing?*, Macmillan, London, 1979

FRANCIS M., CASHDAN L., PAXSON L., *The Making of Neighbourhood Open Spaces*, Center for Human Environments, City University of New York, 1981

JOEDICKE J., *Architektur im Umbruch*, Karl Krämer Verlag, Stuttgart, 1980

MICHELSON W., *Environmental Choice, Human Behaviour and Residential Satisfaction*, Oxford University Press, 1977

RAPOPORT A., *Human Aspects of Urban Form: Towards a Man Environment Approach to Urban Form and Design*, Pergamon Press, New York, 1977

RAPOPORT A., *The Meaning of the Built Environment*, Sage Publications, London, 1983

*Richard Meier, Architect: Buildings & Projects 1966–1976*, (Introduction by Kenneth Frampton), Oxford University Press, New York, 1976, pp. 204–233

SACK R.D., *Conceptions of Space in Social Thought: A Geographical Perspective*, Macmillan, New York, 1980

SOMMER R., *Public Space: The Behavioural Basis of Design*, Prentice-Hall, London, 1969

WARD C., *The Child in the City*, Architectural Press, London, 1971

**Periodicals and Articles:**

BROADBENT G., 'Bofill', *Architectural Design*, Vol. 45 No. 7, July 1975, pp. 402–417

BROADBENT G., 'The Taller of Bofill', *Architectural Review*, Vol. 154 No. 929, November 1973, pp. 289–297

'Byker by Erskine', *Architectural Review*, Vol. 156 No. 934, December 1974, pp. 346–362

'Alexandra Road', *Architectural Review*, Vol. 166 No. 990, August 1979, pp. 76–92

'Farum Midtpunkt', *Arkitektur*, (Denmark), No. 1 1976, pp. 1–11

DARKE J., 'Public Housing ; The Politics of Aesthetics' (Sheffield University Paper, March 1979), *Slate*, No. 16, 1980, pp. 4–9

EGELIUS M. (ed.), 'Ralph Erskine—the Humane Architect', Special Issue of *Architectural Design*, No. 47 November/December 1977

GOSLING D., STEVENS P., DYER T., 'The Cave Hill Plan', Ministry of Home Affairs, Government of Barbados, November 1964. Also *Architectural Review*, Vol. 139 No. 830, pp. 287–8 'Cave Hill Plan'

BENTON T., 'The Rise and Fall of Quarry Hill', *The Architect* (U.K.), June 1975, pp. 25–28

## I SOCIALIST APPLICATIONS

### Soviet Union (USSR)

**Books:**

BARANOV N.V., 'Urban Planning' in *Great Soviet Encyclopedia*, Vol. 7, Macmillan, New York, 1975

DIAMIO A.J., *Soviet Urban Housing: Problems and Policies*, Praeger, London, 1974

HAMILTON F.E.I., LAPPO G.M., 'Trends in the Evolution of settlement patterns in the Moscow Region', in *Soviet Geography Review & Translation*, 14(1) 1973

HAMM M.F. (ed.), *The City in Russian History*, University of Kentucky Press, 1976

OSBORN R.J., *Soviet Social Policies, Welfare, Equality and Community*, Dorsey Press, Harewood, Illinois, 1970

POSOKHIN M.V., 'According to the General Plan: Setting and Example for the Entire Country' in *Current Digest of the Soviet Press* 25(23), 1973

Report of the USSR delegation to the XXXVIII Session of the UN ECE Committee on Housing, Building and Planning, *Urban Development in the USSR*, Moscow, 1977

Report of the USSR delegation to the XXXVIII Session of the UN ECE Committee on Housing, Building and Planning, *The Policy of Land Use in the USSR*, Moscow, 1977

State Committee for Civil Construction and Architecture, *New Towns in the USSR* Moscow, 1977

State Committee for Civil Construction and Architecture, *Master Scheme of residential distribution on the territory of the USSR*, Moscow, 1977

State Committee for Civil Construction and Architecture, *Current Trends and Policy in the Field of Housing, Town Planning and Building in the USSR*, Moscow, 1978

UNDERHILL J.A., *Soviet New Towns: Housing and National Urban Growth Policy*, United States Department of Housing and Urban Development, Washington D.C., 1976

WHITE P.M., *Urban Planning in Britain and the Soviet Union: A Comparative Analysis*, University of Birmingham, Centre for Urban and Regional Studies, Research Memorandum No. 70, March 1979

WHITE P.M., *Soviet Urban and Regional Planning*, a bibliography with abstracts, Mansell Publishing, London, 1980

### Eastern Europe

**Books:**

GADEK Z., *The Creation of Multi-Use Buildings*, Polytechnic of Cracow, Poland, 1971

GADEK Z., *Multi-Use System*, School of Architecture, Kingston-upon-Hull, 1974

OSROWSKI W., *Urbanistyka Wspotczesna*, Arkady, Warsaw, 1975

SZAFER T.P., *Nova Architektura Polska 1966–1970*, Wydawnictwo Arkady, Warsaw, 1975

SZAFER T.P., *Nova Architektura Polska 1971–1975*, Wydawnictwo Arkady, Warsaw, 1979

### China

**Books:**

BOYD A., *Chinese Architecture and Town Planning, 1500BC–AD1911*, Alec Tiranti, London, 1962

Committee of Concerned Asian Scholars, *China: Inside the People's Republic*, Bantam, New York, 1972

**Articles:**

*Architectural Design* (China: Special Issue), Vol. 44 No. 3, March 1974

CHENG, SEN-DON, 'The Growing Metropolis', *Geographical Review*, Vol. LV No. 3, July 1965

*L'Architecture d'Aujourd'hui* (Paris), China (Special Issue), February 1979

PENN C., 'Chinese Vernacular Architecture', *Royal Institute of British Architects Journal*, October 1965

SAWYERS L., 'Urban Planning in the Soviet Union and China', *Urban Planning*, pp. 35–47, March 1977

THOMPSON R., 'City Planning in China: World Development 1974'

WEBB S., 'China: The road to wisdom has no end', *Architectural Design*, Vol. 44 No. 4, pp. 218–222, April 1974

## J SQUATTER SETTLEMENTS

**Books:**

ALVES M.M., *Lages, a Força do Povo*, Brasiliense, São Paulo, 1980

BRANDT W., *North-South: A Programme for Survival*, Pan, London, 1980

DRAKAKIS-SMITH D., *Urbanisation, Housing and the Development Process*, Croom Helm, London, 1981

ENGELS F., *The Housing Question*, Moscow Publishers Edition, 1975

FIELD A.J., *City and Country in the Third World: Issues in the Modernization of Latin America*, Schenkman, Cambridge, Mass., 1970

PACIONE M. (ed.), *Problems & Planning in Third World Cities*, Croom Helm, London, 1981

PAYNE G., *Urban Housing in the Third World*, Routledge & Kegan Paul, London, 1977

PERLMAN J.E., *The Myth of Marginality: Urban Poverty & Politics in Rio de Janeiro*, University of California Press, 1976

ROBERTO M.M.M., *Competition Report for the Redevelopment of the Alagados Favela*, Bahia, Salvador, Brazil, 1972

SANTOS, C.N. DOS, *Some considerations about the possibilities of squatter settlement redevelopment plans: the case of Bras de Pinã*, Paper, M.I.T., 1971

SANTOS, C.N. DOS, 'Velhas Novidades nos Modos de Urbanização Brasileiros' in Valladeres L. (ed.), *Habitação em Questão*, Zahar, Rio de Janeiro, 1978

SCHLYTER A. AND T., *George—The development of a squatter settlement in Lusaka, Zambia*, Byggforskningsradet, Sweden, 1979

SEELIG M.Y., *The Architecture of Self Help Communities*, Architectural Record Books, New York, 1978

TURNER J.F.C. AND FICHTER R. (eds.), *Freedom to Build*, Macmillan, New York, 1972

TURNER J.F.C., *Housing to People: Towards Autonomy in Building Environments*, Boyars, 1976

WATES N.E. AND WOLMAR C. (eds.), *Squatting*, Bayleaf Books, London, 1980

**Periodicals and Articles:**

AIKEN S.R., 'Squatters & Squatter Settlements in Kuala Lumpur', *Geographical Review*, Vol. 71 No. 2, pp. 158–175, 1981

ALTMANN J., 'Self-Help Housing in Urban Squatter Settlements', *Habitat International*, Vol. 6 No. 4, pp. 417–424, 1982

BAYTIN N., 'The Metamorphosis in squatter settlement areas in Turkey', *International Journal for Housing Science*, Vol. 6 No. 1, pp. 27–39, 1982

BRAGA T., 'Uma Favela Modelo', *Opinião*, Rio de Janeiro, 2–8 Julho 1973, p. 5

CHOGUILL C., 'Regional Influence upon future urban development in Bangladesh', Dacca: United Nations Development Programme/United Nations Centre for Human Settlements/Bangladesh Urban Development Directorate, 1980

CHOGUILL C., 'An analysis of squatter resettlement programmes in Bangladesh', *Urban and Regional Planning in Developing Countries*, Proceedings of PTRC Summer Annual Meeting, London, 1980, pp. 73–82

CHOGUILL C., 'Linking planning and Implementations: The Mirpur Resettlement Project', *Ekistics* 49, 1982

EKE E.F., 'Changing Views on Urbanization, Migration and Squatters', *Habitat International*, Vol. 6 No. 1–2, pp. 143–163, 1982

GARG S.C., 'Strategy for housing the poor in Bhopal, India', *Ekistics*, Vol. 48 No. 286, pp. 79–88, 1981

GOSLING D., 'Housing Case Study in Brazil (II)', *Architectural Design*, Vol. 46, pp. 38–41, January 1975

HARRIS H., 'Limitation of Self-Help', *Architectural Design*, No. 43, pp. 230–1, 1976

JIMENEZ E., 'The Value of squatter settlements in developing countries', *Economic Development & Cultural Change*, Vol. 30 No. 4, pp. 739–752, 1982

JOHNSTONE M., 'The Evolution of squatter settlements in Peninsular Malaysian cities', *Journal of South-East Asian Studies*, Vol. 12 No. 2, pp. 364–380, 1981

KEARNS K.C., 'Urban Squatter Strategies—Social Adaptation to Housing Stress in London', *Urban Life*, Vol. 10 No. 2, pp. 123–153, 1981

LEEDS A., 'The Significant Variables determining the Character of Squatter Settlements', *America Latina*, pp. 44–85, 1969

MORAN E.F., 'A House of my own —social organisation in the squatter settlements of Lima, Peru', *International Migration Review*, Vol. 16 No. 3, pp. 684–685, 1982

PAYNE G., 'Housing: Third World Solutions to First World Problems', *Built Environment*, Vol. 5 No. 2, 1979, pp. 99–100

PORTES M., 'The challenge of squatter settlements with special reference to Latin America', *Latin American Research Review*, Vol. 16 No. 3, pp. 225–235, 1981

STEPICK A., MURPHY A.D., 'Comparing squatter settlements and government self-help projects as housing solutions in Oaxaca, Mexico', *Human Organization*, Vol. 39 No. 4, pp. 339–343, 1980

STRASSMANN W.P., 'Upgrading in squatter settlements —test of a Marxist hypothesis', *Journal of Economic Issues*, Vol. 16 No. 2, pp. 515–523, 1982

TALIB K., HAZEM M., 'Squatter resettlement in Saudi Arabia', *International Journal for Housing Science*, Vol. 6 No. 4, pp. 343–359, 1982

TURNER J.F.C., 'Housing Priorities, Settlement Patterns and Urban Development in Modernising Countries', *Journal of the American Institute of Planners*, No. 34, pp. 354–63, 1968

## K PROFESSIONAL SOLUTIONS

**Books:**

*Stirling James*, Royal Institute of British Architects, Heinz Gallery Exhibition Catalogue, RIBA Drawings Collection, 1974

STIRLING J., *Buildings and Projects 1950–1974* (Introduction by John Jacobs), Thames and Hudson, London, 1975

STIRLING J., *Bauten und Projeckte*, Verlag Gerd Hatje, Stuttgart, 1975

*Architectural Design*, Special Profile, 'James Stirling', Academy Editions, London, 1983

**Periodicals and Articles:**

*Architectural Review*, Vol. 160 No. 957, Nov. 1976 'Stirling in Germany', pp. 289–296

LE CORBUSIER, 'Precisions', Editions Vincent, Freal & Cie, Paris 1929

LE CORBUSIER ET PIERRE JEANNERET, *Oeuvre Complete 1929–1934*, Les Editions Girsberger, Zurich, 1957

ROWE C., 'The Blenheim of the Welfare State', *Cambridge Review* 31, October 1959

## L CENTRAL AREA PROJECTS

**Books:**

ANSON B., *I'll Fight You For It*, Cape, London, 1981

Department of the Environment, Report of a Study of General Development Areas 1969–76, *Circular* 14/75, H.M.S.O., 1978

GOSLING D AND MAITLAND B., *The Design and Planning of Retail Systems*, Architectural Press, London, 1976

JENCKS C., *Skyscrapers-Skycities*, Academy Editions, London, 1980

PORTMAN J. AND BARNETT J., *The Architect as Developer*, McGraw-Hill, New York, 1976

**Periodicals and Articles:**

*Architects' Journal*, Vol. 168 No. 31, 2 August 1978, Norman Foster proposals for Hammersmith, London, pp. 202–203

*Architects' Journal*, Vol. 170 No. 32, 8 August 1979, Richard Rogers scheme for Coin Street, London, pp. 270–271

*Architectural Design*, Special Issue No. 47, Feb 1977, Centre Pompidou

*Architectural Review*, Vol. 152 No. 908, October 1972, 'Brunswick Centre', pp. 196–218

*Architectural Review*, Vol. 161 No. 962, April 1977, 'Market Values at Eldon Square', pp. 212–226

'Covent Garden's Moving: Covent Garden Area Draft Plan', Consortium of Greater London Council, City of Westminster, London Borough of Camden, 1968

## M UNIVERSITIES

**Books:**

ARUP ASSOCIATES, *Loughborough University of Technology Master Plan Development*, Interim Report, 1967

DEUTSCHE BAUZEITSCHRIFT, *Bauten Für Bildung und Forschung*, Verlagsanstalt Koch, Stuttgart, 1971

FINGER, *Hochschulbauten—Institutsgebäude*, Callwey, Munich, 1973

TESTA, *New Educational Facilities*, Verlag für Architektur, Zurich, 1975

UNESCO, *Planning Buildings and Facilities for Higher Education*, McGraw-Hill, New York, 1976

WILD, *Bauten für Berufsausbildung*, Callwey, Munich, 1970

## M UNIVERSITIES

**Articles:**

*Architectural Record*, 'Campus Planning and Design', editors of Architectural Record, 1972

Architecture and Competitions, *International Quarterly*, No. 104, Buildings for Further Education, Karl Krämer Verlag, Stuttgart

## N FORMAL SOLUTIONS

**The Rationalists**

**Books:**

KRIER L., *Architecture Rationelle*, Editions Archives

d'Architecture Moderne, Brussels, 1978

KRIER L., CULOT M., SCHOONBRODT, *La Reconstruction de Bruxelles*, Editions Archives d'Architecture Moderne, Brussels, 1980

KRIER L., *Drawings 1967–1980*, Editions Archives d'Architecture Moderne, Brussels, 1981

KRIER L. AND CULOT M., *Contre Projets*, Editions Archives d'Architecture Moderne, Brussels

KRIER R., *Urban Space*, Academy Editions, London, 1979

KRIER R., *On Architecture*, Academy Editions, London, 1982

KRIER R., *Architectural Composition*, Academy Editions, London, 1984

PANERAI P., DEPAULE J-CH., DEMORGAN M., VEYRENCHE M., *Elements d'Analyse Urbaine*, Editions Archives d'Architecture Moderne, Brussels

ROSSI A., *Architecture of the City*, Oppositions Books, MIT Press, Cambridge, Mass., 1981

ROSSI A., *A Scientific Autobiograph*, Oppositions Books, MIT Press, Cambridge, Mass., 1981

SHARP D., (ed.) *The Rationalists*, Architectural Press, London, 1978


**Periodicals and Articles:**

*Architectural Design*, June 1975, pp. 365–370, Alan Colquhoun: 'Rational Architecture'

*Architectural Design*, Vol. 47 March 1977, pp. 187–213, 'Tafuri, Culot, Krier: The Role of Ideology'

*Architectural Design,* April 1978, pp. 218–266, 'Urban Transformations'

*Architectural Design*, Special Issue No. 48 April 1978 'Urban Transformations' (Krier L. ed.)

*Architectural Design*, Robert Krier: 'Typological and Morphological Elements of the Concept of Urban Space', January 1979 pp. 2–17, also Krier L. 'The Cities within a City' *op. cit.*, pp. 18–32

*Architectural Design*, Special Issue No. 51 January/February 1981, 'From Futurism to Rationalism', the origins of modern Italian architecture (Gargus J. ed.)


### O HISTORIC CITY CONSERVATION

**Books:**

FIELDEN B.M., *Conservation of Historic Buildings*, Butterworths, London, 1982

FUNDAÇÃO JOÃO PINHEIRO, *Plano de Conservação, Valorização e Desenvolvimento de Ouro Preto e Mariana*, Pub. Fundação João Pinheiro, Belo Horizonte, Brazil, 1975

GREATER LONDON COUNCIL, *Historic Buildings in London*, an Inventory of Historic Buildings owned by the Greater London Council, Academy Editions, London, 1975

MCNULTY R.H. AND KLIMENT S.A., *Neighbourhood Conservation*, Whitney Library of Design, New York, 1980

OPHER P. AND SAMUELS I., *New Use for Old Stones*, Council of Europe, Strasbourg, 1982

SCOTTISH CIVIC TRUST, *New Uses for Older Buildings in Scotland*, H.M.S.O., London & Edinburgh, 1981


### P DESIGN GUIDES

**Books:**

*Brasília: História, Urbanismo, Arquitetura, Construção* Acropole, São Paulo, Brazil, 1960

COUNTY COUNCIL OF ESSEX, *A Design Guide for Residential Areas*, Essex County Council, 1973

EPSTEIN D.G., *Brasília, Plan and Reality*, University of California Press, 1973

EVENSON N., *Two Brazilian Capitals*, Yale University Press, 1973

GOODEY B., *The Essex Design Guide: Initial and Related Sources*, Joint Centre for Urban Design, Oxford Polytechnic Research Note 9, 1982

JOHNSON MARSHALL P. & ASSOCIATES, *Design Briefing in Towns*, Report to the Scottish Development Department, Edinburgh, 1978

Monographs produced by the Department of Architecture and Urban Planning at the University of Brasília:
  a) KOHLSDORF M.E., *Gestalt Urbana: Consideracoẽs sobre os espaços do plano-pilôto de Brasília 1975*
  b) FARRET R.L., *Brasília un enfoque regional 1975*
  c) HOLANDA F. DE, *O centro urbano de Brasília 1975*
  d) KOHLSDORF G. (ed.), *Processo de Produção do Habitat popular urbano*

MORELY S., *Positive Planning and Direct Development by local authorities*, Planning Study 9, Polytechnic of Central London, 1980

NIEMEYER O., *Minha experiencia em Brasília*, Editôra Victoria, 1961

NIEMEYER O., (design framework for Brasília), *Módulo*, Vol. 2 No. 12, Rio de Janeiro, February 1959

PASTORE J., *Brasília a Cidade e o homen*, Editôra da Universidade de São Paulo, Brazil, 1969

PEAK PARK PLANNING BOARD, *Building Design Guide*, Peak National Park, Derbyshire, England, 1976

*Plano Estrutural de Organização Territorial do D.F.*, Convênio Seplan/D.F. Brasília, 1977 (2 Volumes)

SAN FRANCISCO DEPARTMENT OF CITY PLANNING, *Preliminary Report No. 8: Urban Design Plans*, 1970

STÄUBLI W., *Brasília*, Leonard Hill, London, 1966

ZUCKER P., *Town & Square*, Columbia University Press, New York, 1959


### Q FUNFAIRS, ARCHITECTURE OF FANTASY

**Books:**

BRAITHWAITE D., *Fairground Architecture*, Hugh Evelyn, London, 1968

BRAITHWAITE D., *Savage of King's Lynn*, Patrick Stephens, Cambridge, 1975

EILSTRUP P., *Tivoli: Story of a fairytale garden*, (Arnoldi J. translator), Scandinavian Idea Publishers

IND. R. AND SMITHSON A. AND P., 'Blackpool Pleasure Beach' in *Proceedings of the Second Conference on Twentieth Century Design History*, 1976, Design Council Publications, London, pp. 38–43

STARSMORE I., *English Fairs*, Thames & Hudson, London, 1975

VENTURI R., SCOTT-BROWN D., IZENOUR S., *Learning from Las Vegas*, MIT/Harvard Press, 1972

WASSERMAN L., *Merchandising Architecture. The Architectural Implications and Applications of Amusement Parks*, National Endowment for the Arts, Washington D.C., 1978

WILLIAMS M. (ed.), SCOTT-STEWART (photographer), *Fairground Snaps*, Gordon Fraser Books, 1974


**Periodicals and Articles:**

*Architectural Design*, Special Issue 52 No. 9/10 September/October 1982, 'Animated Architecture'

PASTIER J., 'The Architecture of Escapism', *American Institute of Architects Journal*, December 1978, pp. 26–37


### FUTURE DIRECTIONS

**Books:**

AICHER/KRAMPEN, *Zeichensysteme der Visuellen Kommunikation*, Verlagsanstalt Koch, Stuttgart, 1978

ALEXANDER C., *The Oregon Experiment*, Oxford University Press, 1979

ANDERSON S., *On Streets*, MIT Press, Cambridge, Mass., 1978

BOHIGAS O., GLUSBERG J. (eds.), and ROCA M.A., *Miguel Angel Roca*, Academy Editions, London, 1981

COLQUHOUN A., *Essays in Architectural Criticism*, Oppositions Books, MIT Press, 1981

COOK, P., *Melting Architecture*, Catalogue to exhibition at Art Net, London, December 1975

DAVIS I., *Disaster and the Small Dwelling*, Pergamon Press, New York, 1981

GOSLING D., CULLEN G., DONOHUE D., *Maryculter: A new community*, Kincardine County Council & Christian Salvesen Ltd. (Edinburgh) 1974

GREEN C., *Gambit* (Gaming Simulation for Architecture Methods for Building with Integrated Technology), Sheffield University, England, 1977

JENCKS C., *The Language of Post-Modern Architecture*, Academy Editions, London, 1977, revised edition 1981

JENCKS C. AND CHAITKIN W., *Current Architecture*, Academy Editions, London, 1982

KNOWLES R.L., *Energy and Form: An Ecological Approach to Urban Growth*, MIT Press, Cambridge, Mass., 1974

KRIER L., *Leon Krier—Drawings 1967–1980*, Archives d'Architecture Moderne, Brussels, 1982

KRIER R., *Urban Space*, Academy Editions, London, 1979

LAWSON B.R., *How Designers Think*, Architectural Press, London, 1980

LYNCH K., *A Theory of Good City Form*, MIT Press, Cambridge, Mass., 1981

MOSCHINI F. (ed.), *Paolo Portoghesi*, Academy Editions, London, 1979

NEGROPONTE N., *Soft Architecture Machines*, MIT Press, Cambridge, Mass., 1975

PORPHYRIOS D., *Sources of Modern Eclecticism*, Academy Editions, London, 1982

POSOKHIN M.V., *Cities to Live In*, Novosti Press Agency Publishing House, Moscow, 1974

RESTANY P., ZEVI B., (eds.) AND *SITE, Architecture as Art*, Academy Editions, London, 1980

ROWE C. AND KOETTER F., *Collage City*, MIT Press, Cambridge, Mass., 1978

SPIEKER, *Totalitäre Architektur*, Karl Krämer Verlag, Stuttgart, 1981

STERN R., *Let There be Neon*, Academy Editions, London, 1979

TAYLOR J.L. AND WALFORD R., *Simulation in the Classroom*, Penguin Books, Harmondsworth, 1972

VENTURI R., SCOTT-BROWN D., IZENOUR S., *Learning from Las Vegas: The Forgotten Symbolism of Architectural Form*, MIT Press, Cambridge, Mass., 1977

WAISMAN M., *Emilio Ambasz, Alternative Architecture*, translated from the monograph, *La Arquitectura Alternative de Emilio Ambasz* by M. Waisman, Editorial Summa, Buenos Aires, Argentina, 1977

WILLIAMS-ELLIS C., *Portmeirion—the Place and its Meaning*, Portmeirion Ltd., Penrhyndeudraeth, Wales, 1973

**Periodicals and Articles**

BROADBENT G. (ed.), 'Neo-Classicism', *Architectural Design*, Special Issue Vol. 49, August/September 1979

GRAVES M. (ed.), 'Rome Interrotta', *Architectural Design*, Special Issue Vol. 49, March/April 1979

GREEN C., 'Inhabs' (Instructional Housing and Building Simulation), *Architects' Journal*, 3rd March 1971, p. 490

GREEN C., *Scribe* (Space, Cost, Resources and Integrated Building Evaluation: Microcomputer-aided architectural design modelling system), *RIBA Journal*, June 1982, Vol. 89 No. 6, p. 77

KRIER L., 'The Cities within the City', *Architectural Design*, Special Issue Vol. 49, January 1979

LAWSON B.R., 'Gable: An integrated approach to interactive graphical techniques for modelling buildings and urban design', Sheffield University, England (*Computer Arts Society Quarterly*, No. 50, pp. 29–33, 1982 and *Architects' Journal*, Vol. 175 no. 25, pp. 81–84, 1982)

PEREZ DE ARCE R., 'Transformations', *International Architect* (London), No. 4 Issue 4, 1981

TSCHUMI B., 'The Manhattan Transcripts', *Architectural Design*, Special Profile, 1981

## CONCLUSIONS

**Books:**

ALEXANDER C. ET AL, *A Pattern Language*, Oxford University Press, 1977

AL-SEDAIRY S. (ed.), *Urban Design and Community Development in Saudi Arabia*, Ministry of the Interior, Saudi Arabia, 1983

BREWER C., CLARKE J., CUNNINGHAM B., LEWIS D. ET AL, *Urban Design, News from the Front*, American Regional/Urban Design Assistance Team Final Report, American Institute of Architects, Washington D.C., 1983

CASTELLS M., *City, Class and Power*, Macmillan, New York, 1979

COLE J., *The Poor of the Earth*, Macmillan, New York, 1976

GOSLING D., CULLEN G. ET AL, *Isle of Dogs: A Guide to Design and Development Opportunities*, London Docklands Development Corporation, 1982

KRIER L., *Architecture Rationelle*, Archives d'Architecture Moderne, Bruxelles, 1978

MAITLAND B., 'A Minimal Urban Structure', Ph.D. Thesis, Sheffield University, England 1982

TASHKANDI F.K., *Urban Dwellings in Rapidly Growing Cities*, M.I.T. Published Report, 1979

ZEKAVAT K., 'The Urban Street', Ph.D. Thesis, Sheffield University, England, 1981

## ACKNOWLEDGEMENTS

We would like to thank the following individuals and organisations for their invaluable assistance in the preparation of this book.

### GREAT BRITAIN

**Academy Editions** Dr. Andreas Papadakis; Frank Russell; Richard Cheatle; Christine Murdock; Vicky Wilson; Alexandra Artley (formerly Orbis Publishers)

**University of Sheffield** Alison J. Bertie; Jack Bricklebank and Peter Lathey (photographic laboratory); Roy and Jane Darke (Department of Town and Regional Planning); Cedric Green; Denise Harrison (Librarian); Dr. Bryan Lawson (GABLE computer-aided design research unit); Professor Kenneth Murta; Professor H. Ritchie (Department of German)

**Sheffield: Architects** Peter Fauset; John Ferguson; Christopher Liddle; Drawings, Richard Dinsdale

**Architects** Peter Aldington (Aldington & Craig); Brian Anson; Michael Bayer; Peter Cook; Gordon Cullen; Edward Cullinan; Geoffrey Darke (Darbourne & Darke); Ken Davie (Cumbernauld Development Corporation); Irvine Development Corporation: Ian Downs (Chief Architect and Technical Director), Tony Scott (Graphic Designer), Keith Gibson (photographer); Sir Philip Dowson & Marianne Timmer (Librarian) (Arup Associates); Mel Dunbar (Essex County Council); the late Sir Frederic Gibberd; Vernon Gracie; Greville Griffiths (Building Design Partnership); Rod Hackney; Norman Foster, Birkin Haward (Foster Associates); Ron Herron; Patrick Hodgkinson; Geoffrey Holland (GLC); Jim Johnson & Michael Thornley (ASSIST); Leon Krier; Dudley Leaker and Peter Barker (Milton Keynes Development Corporation); Drew Mackie; Richard MacCormac (MacCormac & Jamieson); Alex McCowan (Harlow Development Corporation); Richard Moira (Moira & Moira); Wolf Pearlman; Colin Penn; Cedric Price; Richard Rogers (Richard Rogers & Associates); Keith Smith (Runcorn Development Corporation); Alison & Peter Smithson; Bernard Tschumi; John F. C. Turner; Sam Webb; Michael Wilford (James Stirling and Michael Wilford); the late Sir Clough Williams-Ellis; Derek Walker; Nigel Woolner (Chapman Taylor); John Yarwood (Telford Development Corporation)

**Schools of Architecture** Simon Atkinson and Brian Goodey (Oxford Polytechnic); Alvin Boyarsky (Architectural Association); Professor Geoffrey Broadbent (Portsmouth Polytechnic); Professor John Miller and Christopher Cross (Royal College of Art)

**Other Organisations** Rosemary Bloofield, librarian (United States Information Service, London); Donald McGill (Mobil North Sea Ltd); Alan Paterson (Anglo-Chinese Educational Institute); Geoffrey Thompson, Managing Director, Blackpool Pleasure Beach; Elizabeth Wright (Great Britain China Centre); Michael Wright (Country Life)

**UNITED STATES OF AMERICA** Emilio Ambasz (New York City); the late Professor Donald Appleyard (University of California, Berkeley); Edmund Bacon (Philadelphia); Roger Conover (MIT Press); Thomas Counter (Vineyard Open Land Foundation); Ulrich Franzen (New York City); Professor N. John Habraken (Massachusetts Institute of Technology); Lawrence Halprin (San Francisco); Zvi Hecker (New York); Robert Kennedy (Kennedy/Montgomery, Cambridge, Mass.); Professor Richard Krauss (Harvard University & Arrowstreet Inc., Cambridge); The late Professor Kevin Lynch (Massachutsetts Institute of Technology); Cynthia Mast (MTLW/Turnbull Associates, San Francisco); Professor Michael McKinnell (Harvard University and Kallmann & McKinnell); Professor Charles Moore (Santa Monica); Dee Mullen (Round House, San Francisco); Cesar Pelli (Dean, Yale University School of Architecture); Martin Schwartz (Santa Monica); the late James Skerritt (new Haven, Conn.); Stanley Tigerman (Chicago); the late Professor Christopher Tunnard (Yale University); James Wines and Alison Sky (SITE, New York City)

### BRAZIL

**University of Brasilia** Professor Geraldo Batista; Professor Gunther Kohlsdorf; Professor Maria-Elaine Kohlsdorf; Professor Paulo Zimbres

Officials of CODEPLAN (Brasilia); Officials of EMBRATUR (Brazilian Tourist Board) (Brasilia & Rio de Janeiro); Officials of BNH (Rio de Janeiro); Officials of IBAM (Rio de Janeiro); Officials of Ministério do Interior (Brasilia); Officials of Fundaçao João Pinheiro (Belo Horizonte) **Individuals** Mery Anton (British Embassy, Brasilia); Rogerio Aroeira (Rio de Janeiro); Dr. Lúcio Costa (Brasilia and Rio de Janeiro); Pedro Paulo Abramo Domingues (Rio de Janeiro); M.M.M. Roberto Associados (Rio de Janeiro); Galileu Reis (Belo Horizonte); Carlos Nelson F. dos Santos (Rio de Janeiro); Dr. Antonio de deus Vieira (Rio de Janeiro); Edna Borman Vieira (Brasilia)

### EUROPE

**ITALY** Carlo Aymonino; Giancarlo de Carlo (Milan); Michele Chiuini (Perugia); Vittorio Gregotti (Naples); Aldo Rossi (Milan); L. Savioli (Florence); The Italian Tourist Board

**GERMANY** Karl Schaper (*Der Spiegel*, Hamburg); Max Simon (Associated Press, Frankfurt and New York)

**HOLLAND** J. T. Boekholt (Design Methods Group, University of Technology, Eindhoven)

**FRANCE** François Spoerry and Elfi Vucco (Port Grimaud)

**BELGUIM** Lucien Kroll

**SPAIN** Javier Cenicacelaya Marijuan

**SWEDEN** Ralph Erskine and Lisa Rowe (Ralph Erskine Associates, Stockholm)

**DENMARK** Messrs. Kaiser-Hans and Nils (Tivoli Ltd., Copenhagen); Berit Sandfeld (Farum Midtpunkt, Copenhagen)

**POLAND** Professor Zbigniew Gadek and Ewa Szymanska (Cracow)

**JAPAN** Kiyonori Kikutake (Kikutake Associates, Tokyo); Minoru Takeyama (Tokyo)

**SAUDI ARABIA** Salman Al-Sedairy (Riyadh); Hosni Badawi (Riyadh); Farhat Khourshid Tashkandi (Riyadh); Dr. Mustafa Ahmed al Bagi (Mecca)

**NEW ZEALAND** Ian Athfield; Roger Walker (Wellington)

**SOVIET UNION** Dimitry Fonin (Foreign Relations Department); Pyotr Kirovich (Deputy Chief Architect, State Committee for Civil Construction); Vladimir Renovich Krogius (Head of Coordination, Central Scientific Research Institute); Dr. Illya Moisevich Smoljar (Chief of New Town Planning) **City of Moscow** Serge Kovaltchouk (Public Relations); Sergei N. Kulikov (GLAV-APU Section, Architecture and Town Planning); Mikhail Vassilyevich Posokhin (Chief Architect) **Dubna New Town** Victor Ahrimenko (Mayor); Nikolay Korstashov (Deputy Director of Joint Institute for Nuclear Research); Boris Safonov (Chief Architect) **Puschino New Town** Maryena Mizonova; The Mayor; The Chief Architect; The Director of Works; The Chief Administrative Officer

# INDEX

brise-soleil, *21*
Britain, 9, 39, 68, 74–5
Broadacre City, 33, 37
Broadbent, Geoffrey, 40, 78, 126, 140
Brown, Neave, 75
Browne, Kenneth, 47, 132, *132*
Bruges, 27
Brunswick Centre, 96, 97, *97*
Brussels, *104*, 105
Brutalism (Brutalist), 74–5, 93
Buchanan, Peter, 137
Buckingham, J.S. *34*, 35
Buenos Aires, 87
buffer areas, 29
Building Design Partnership, *101*, 102
building systems, Sitte's three, 26
buses, 66, 67, 97

Cabtrack, 67, *67*
Cairo, 31
Calcutta, 33
Calhoun, J.B., 40, 52
Cambodia, 18
Cambridge Seven Associates, 112
Camergo, Jose Geraldo de Cunha, 24
Campanella, 32
Canada, 68, *68*, 99, *119*
Canter, David, 141
*Capital* (see also Marx), 10, 24
capital, capitalism (investments, valuations), 11, 125, 156
Cap Martin, 30
Caracas, 15
Carcassonne, 64
cars, car ownership, 10, 64, 66, 70
Cassirer, Ernst, 52
Casson, Sir Hugh, 93
CBD (Central Business District) 10, 14
*Ceilandia*, 23
'cells' (household, housing: see also biological analogues), 33, 62, 71, 152
Center for Environmental Studies, 70
central area development projects, 53, 96–8, 165
Centre Point, 11, 129
Chalk, Warren, 63
Chandigarh, 20, 135
Chapman Taylor Partners, 97
checks and balances of social behaviour, 41
Chicago, 15, 37, 42, 54
*Child's Conception of Space, A*, 52
China, 27, 72, 81, *81*
Christiana, 126, *126*
Christianopolis, 33
CIAM, 21
*Cidade Livre*, 23, *23*
*cidades satelites*, 22
circulation (see also streets, traffic) 10, 11, 21, 35, 56, 62, 64, 65, 66, 71, 83, 93, 97, 99, 100, 101
citizen, concept of, 62
city:
— agrarian, 153
— American, 14, 17, 143
— ancient, 24
— and country, 33
— 'archipelago', 137

— as battleground for competing private interests, 129
— as coherent experience, 103–117
— as collage, 138–140
— as cultural invention, 40
— as expression of social order, 72–86
— as federation of quarters, 105
— as financial device, 10
— as form of anxious rent, 37
— as image, 22–4, 61, 159
— as laboratory, 40
— as machine, 19, 35, 37
— as mnemonic and symbolic device, 24
— as model for restitution, 107
— as 'new commune', 34
— as organism, 40
— as process, 54–61
— as resolution of design problems, 87–102
— as sequences, 156
— as single piece of public hardware, 34
— as spectrum of technologies, 123
— as strategic unit, 34
— as technical solution, 62–71
— bi-technic city, 123
— *City is not a Tree, A*, 20, 52
— *City is the Frontier, The*, 24
— *City of Tomorrow, The*, 40, 51
— *City: Problems of Planning, The*, 24
— *Cities To Live In*, 140
— 'Crater City', 63
— *Death and Life of Great American Cities, The*, 24, 52
— *Disappearing City, The*, 52
— European, 12, 18, 23, 104, 135
— Georgian building, 107
— historical, 105, 107–8
— 'Ideal City', 33
— idealized, 25, 35
— *Image of the City, The*, 52
— industrial, 19
— inner, 14–18
— 'Instant City', 33
— Le Corbusier's view, 30; 'Ideal', 33
— linear, 22, *22*, 23, 33
— mono-technic, 123
— 'of efficient consumption', 34
— 'of necessity', 14, 17
— Planning Frameworks, 64–5
— pre-industrial, 19, 34, 153
— problems: social, economic, engineering, ecological, 19; 'organized complexity', 20
— 'unplanned', 19
— utopian forms of, 32–41
— visual phenomena of, 127; see also 42–5, 58
'civilized', 27
'cognitive mapping', 51, 52, 141
COHAB, 16, 83
'Collage City', 24, 95, 117, 139, *139*, 140
Cologne, 31, 88, *89*
Colqhoun, Alan, 106
'comic strips', 44, *44*, 112
'commercial strip', 112, 130
'common building type', 96
commune, 33
communication, 40
*Communitas*, 34, 52

community, 17, 33, 36, 39, 60, 71, 75 (see also squatter settlements)
— appropriate size, 32; scale, 33
— 'bamboo-type', 54
— breakdown of, 14
— Chinese, 81
— 'cylindrical', 54, *54*
— hierarchic structures, 17
— holiday, 76
— ideal, 35
— multi-racial, 144
— 'plant-type', *54*
— retention of, 59
— route as design element, 91–2
— vacation, 72
commuting, 16
competitions, architectural, 8, 54, 141
— Lima, 70–1, *70*, *71*
— Manila, 85–6, *85*, *86*
— Roma Interrotta, 116–17, *116*, *117*
— Telford, 60–1, *60*, *61*
'complexity factor', 47
components, 28, 31, 34, 70, 87
computer (modelling, sequences, terminals), 7, *50*, 122, 128
*Concise Townscape, The*, 8
congestion, 12, 58
*conjuntos*, 8, 15
conservation, 53, 106, 107–8, 109, 135
Considérant, Victor, 33, 52
consumer utopias, 37, 39
context, 38, 117
Cook, Peter, 36, 62, 63, *63*, 119, *120*, 121, 140, 147
cooperative society, 77
Copcutt, Geoffrey, 31, 56, *56*
Copenhagen, 10, 11, 40, 58, 77, 114, 126, *126*
corner shops, 10, 155
— architect's office as, 59
corridor, 29, 33
Cortona, 29
Costa, Lúcio, 13, *21*, 22, *22*, 23
Counter Information Services, 11
courtyards, 74, 76, 81, 91, 110
Covent Garden, 97–8, *97*
'Crater City', 63
'Creative Confession', 43
crescents, 74
crime (see also delinquency, violence), 17
— and poor design, 49
Crompton, Dennis, 63
Cross, Christopher, 145
Cubists, 42
Cullen, Gordon, 6, 7, 8, 40, 48, *49*, *50*, 51, 52, 60, 67, *67*, 78, 113, 132, 141, 147, 150, 153
Cullinan, Edward, 92, *92*, 122
Culot, Maurice, 106
Cultural Revolution, 81
culture, *30*, 112
Cumbernauld Town Centre, 31, 56, *56*
cylindrical communities, 54, *54*

Dallas/Fort Worth Airport, 66
Darbourne and Darke, 123
Darke, Jane and Roy, 74, 75
Davidoff, Paul, 9, 24